MW01675147

# The Windows 95 Textbook

## Standard Edition

**Stewart Venit**

California State University
Los Angeles

**Scott/Jones, Inc., Publishers**

P. O. Box 696, El Granada, CA 94018
scotjones2@aol.com
(415) 726-2436 *or* Fax: (415) 726-4693
http://www.scottjonespub.com

**The Windows 95 Textbook: Standard Edition**
Stewart Venit



ISBN 1-881991-45-8

*Book Production*: The Canfield Bookworks
*Book Manufacturing*: Malloy Lithographing, Inc.
*Composition*: Stewart Venit
*Text Design*: V & J Enterprises

8 7 6 X Y Z

# Contents

# Preface

*The Windows 95 Textbook: Standard Edition* is intended for use in an introductory course on the Windows 95 operating system. It is expected that some readers will have had little or no experience with computers, whereas others will be familiar, to various degrees, with the workings of DOS or Windows 3.1. With this in mind, we have written the text for the novice user, but in such a way that those with more experience can easily skip over or quickly read the material with which they are familiar. For example, almost all the general information about computers has been placed in the Introduction. Other aids to quickly locating and moving through familiar topics are described under *Features of the Text*, later in this preface.

## Organization of the Text

We have organized this text to provide flexibility in choosing topics and the order in which they are presented. A pictorial representation of the text's organization is shown in the Chapter Dependency Flowchart on the next page. Here is a more detailed description:

- An Introduction provides general information about computer hardware and software. It is intended primarily for those students who have little or no experience with computers, but may also be useful reading for others.
- Chapter 1, which covers the basics of using Windows 95, is the normal jumping-off point for students who have some familiarity with computers, but none with Windows 95. Most of the concepts

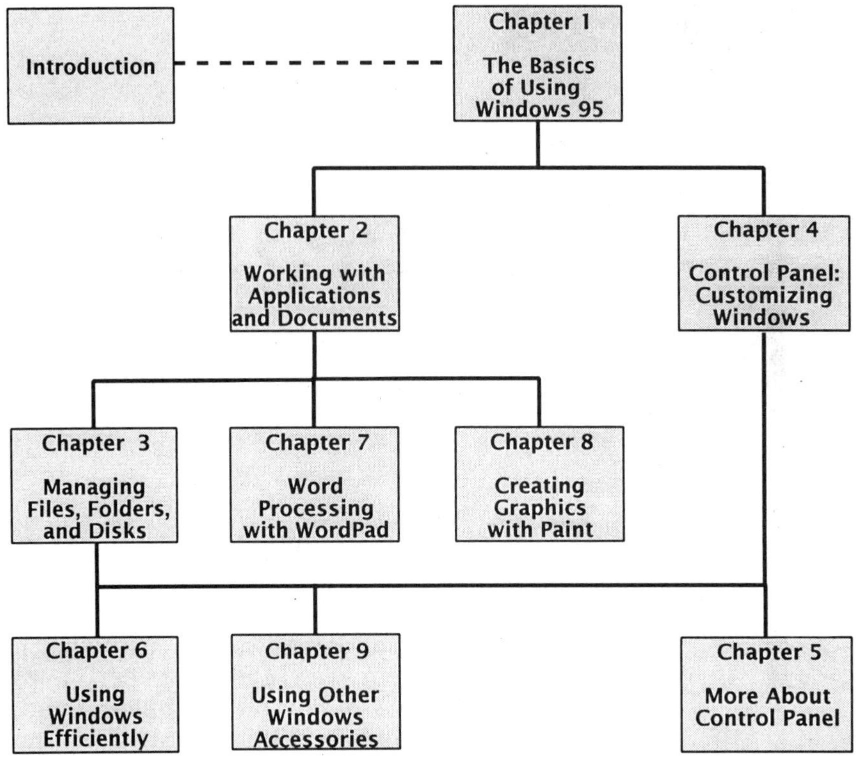


**Chapter Dependency Flowchart**

that are discussed here should seem fairly familiar to those who have used Windows 3.1. Be aware that the terminology and techniques discussed in Chapter 1 are used throughout the text.

- Chapter 2 presents some fundamental material on working with applications and documents, and would typically be covered next. However, those instructors who want to follow a more gentle path can instead jump to Chapter 4, which deals with some of the ways to customize Windows 95.
- After completing Chapter 2, Chapter 3, 4, 7 or 8 could be covered next. Chapter 3 is the most difficult of these, but also contains the most important material.
- After completing Chapter 3, all the remaining chapters are accessible to the reader, although we do suggest covering the first chapter on Control Panel (Chapter 4) before tackling the more advanced aspects of this utility in Chapter 5.

- Chapters 6 and 9 each deal with an assortment of related, but independent topics. In both of these chapters, individual sections may be omitted, if so desired. Moreover, the first two sections in each chapter cover relatively straightforward material that does not require the Chapter 3 prerequisite stated in the flowchart above.

## *Features of the Text*

**End-of-section Tutorials**

1. Certainly, the best way to learn Windows 95 is to use Windows 95. With this in mind, we have written the text in a way that encourages students to follow along at the computer. Moreover, almost all sections end with a brief Tutorial that reviews the material by leading the student through a hands-on exercise.

**No delay in starting up**

2. The text introduces Windows' terminology and techniques immediately; we start up Windows on the first page of the first chapter. On the other hand, for those courses that require it, the Introduction provides general information on using personal computers.

**Objectives**

3. Each chapter (and the Introduction, as well) begins with a brief overview and list of objectives.

**Chapter exercises**

4. The text contains two types of exercises at the end of every chapter:
   - Review Exercises (completion, true/false, and multiple choice) test the students' knowledge of facts presented in the chapter. Answers to the odd-numbered questions are provided in Appendix C.
   - Lab Exercises require the students to perform the kinds of tasks they will encounter in using Windows on an everyday basis.

**TIPs**

5. TIPs appear periodically throughout the text. These short notes provide insight into, or specialized knowledge about, the topic at hand. A fact or technique may be called a TIP because it is especially important or because it is interesting or unusual.

**WARNINGs**

6. Other specialized notes are designated as WARNINGs. They caution the reader against taking certain actions, which in some circumstances could lead to extreme regret.

**Margin notes**

7. Occasional brief phrases in the left margin of the text make it easy for the reader to locate subtopics and important procedures.

**Supplements**

8. The following ancillary material is available for this textbook:
   - A *Lab Exercises* diskette, containing the files referenced in the

Tutorials and Lab Exercises, accompanies the text.

- The answers to the even-numbered Review Exercises are available to instructors directly from the publisher*.
- A test bank of additional short-answer questions (prepared by Wesley Scruggs of Brazosport College), keyed to the material in the text, is also available to instructors directly from the publisher.

## *A Few Words about Homework*

This text, through its end-of-chapter exercises, provides an ample supply of homework problems. The Review Exercises can usually be answered with a single word (or letter, in the case of the multiple choice problems), and the Lab Exercises contain frequent questions that require a brief answer or explanation. (The Lab Exercises also occasionally call for an optional screen capture.)

In a computer course, it is desirable to provide students, as quickly as possible, with the ability to use the computer for printing solutions to their homework problems. For this reason, we introduce, relatively early in the text, the basics of WordPad (Section 2.2) and the techniques for capturing windows and screens (Section 2.3). Once this material has been completed, students will be able to hand in computer-printed homework.

## *Acknowledgments*

I would like to thank the many people who helped bring this project to fruition. A textbook always benefits from varied points of view and I was lucky to have the following experienced instructors offer helpful suggestions for the developing manuscript:

**Faculty reviewers**

Fred Clark
*Peninsula College*

Charles Christensen
*Waubonsee Community College*

Dineen Ebert
*St. Louis CC — Meramec*

Nina Edgmand
*Salt Lake Community College*

Charles Fromme
*Queensborough Community College*

Wade Graves
*Grayson Community College*

*The address and telephone numbers of the publisher appear on the back cover.

Thomas Hodgson
*St. Louis CC — Meramec*

Kathy Jesiolowski
*Milwaukee Area Technical College*

Usha Jindal
*Washtenaw Community College*

Alex Kane
*Western Iowa Tech CC*

Jill Lombardo
*Wenatchee Valley College*

Shirley Orsinelli
*San Diego Mesa College*

Wesley Scruggs
*Brazosport College*

Jin Wang
*Alabama State University*

The text was class-tested in part by Tom Hodgson and in its entirety by Ron Burgher. I would like to thank the following students, who submitted reviews upon completion of their course:

**Student testers**

Thomas Burns

Christy Chassere

Omar Fernandez

Ruth Hille

Joseph Kofron

Diane Lott

Angela Martin

Mark Mindu

Kathleen Nolte

Kathryn Young

A special thanks to Ruth Hille, who went over the entire text with a fine-tooth comb and found many errors that others had missed.

My publisher, Richard Jones, gave enthusiastic and unwavering support for this text, and managed, as usual, to make criticism sound like praise. I am also grateful to Wayne Meyer at Scott/Jones, who provided extensive feedback concerning newly-developing Windows 95 courses.

I would like to thank my wife, Corinne, and my daughter, Tamara, for understanding that a project of this sort requires the author to spend countless hours glued to a computer monitor. Finally, special mention should be made of my dogs, Maggie and Abby, who often kept me company, sleeping peacefully next to the humming computer.

# Introduction

We are living in a world that is becoming increasingly dependent on the electronic computer. Computers help run our businesses and institutions, design and build manufactured products, provide instantaneous worldwide communication, publish our newspapers, magazines, and books, and supply all sorts of educational and recreational activities. Many forms of employment now require some kind of **computer literacy** — an understanding of how to use a computer effectively.

In this introduction, we will describe, in general terms, the computer's *hardware* and *software* — the components and programs that make it work. Although this material is not essential for an understanding of Windows 95, it may help with certain topics and will probably increase your computer literacy. More specifically, you will learn about:

1. Computers in general and personal computers in particular.
2. The components of a computer: its central processing unit, internal memory, mass storage, and input and output devices.
3. Types of computer applications.
4. The function of an operating system.
5. Microsoft Windows — what it is and why it's important.
6. The history of the personal computer.

# Personal Computers

Everyone who uses a computer on a daily basis becomes accustomed to dealing with special computer-related terminology. Yet, to a beginner, many of these terms can be confusing and even intimidating. There are floppy disks and hard disks, kilobytes and megabytes, mice and monitors, and much, much more. In this section, we will try to take some of the mystery out of computer terminology.

## What is a Computer?

As with any evolving technology, precisely defining the term *computer* is not easy. Computers can take many different forms and their capabilities are constantly expanding. Yet, all computers do the same basic things. Every **computer** can input, store, manipulate, and output vast quantities of data at very high speed. Moreover, all computers are *programmable* — they can follow a list of instructions (a **program**) and act upon intermediate results without human intervention.

A **personal computer** (also called a **microcomputer** or a **PC**) is a relatively small type of computer, intended for use by one person at a time. (Larger machines — known as *minicomputers*, *mainframes*, and *supercomputers*, in order of increasing size and power — can be simultaneously shared by many users, connected to the computer by cables or telephone lines.) All personal computers are small enough to fit on a desktop; portable PCs are even smaller — usually no larger than a looseleaf binder. A drawing of a typical PC is shown in Figure 1.

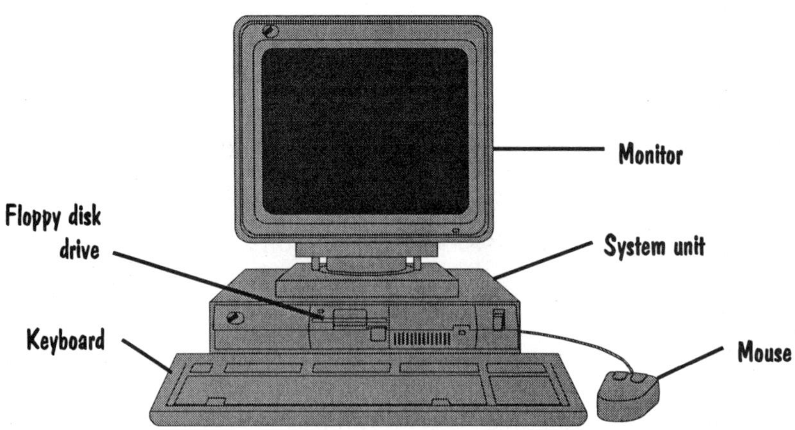


**Figure 1** A Typical Personal Computer

**Components of a computer**

As the definition implies, a computer must have the ability to input, store, manipulate, and output data. These functions are carried out by the five main components of a computer system:

1. The central processing unit
2. Internal memory
3. Mass storage devices
4. Input devices
5. Output devices

In a personal computer, the first two of these components (and usually the third as well) are housed in the **system unit** (see Figure 1). The input devices, such as the keyboard and mouse, and output devices, such as the monitor, are housed in their own enclosures and are connected to the system unit by cables. Devices like these, that are used by a computer but located outside the system unit, are sometimes called **peripherals**. All the physical equipment that makes up the computer system is known as **hardware**.

## *The Central Processing Unit*

The **central processing unit** (also called the **processor** or **CPU**) is the brain of the computer. It receives all program instructions, performs the arithmetic and logical operations necessary to execute them, and controls all the other computer components. In a personal computer, the processor consists of hundreds of thousands of transistors residing on a single *chip* the size of a large postage stamp and plugged into the computer's main circuit board, the *motherboard*.

More than any other component, the CPU distinguishes one computer from another. In the kind of computer you will be using, which is known as **IBM-compatible**, the processor is one of the following types (in order of increasing power): 386 (pronounced "three-86"), 486 ("four-86"), *Pentium*, or *Pentium Pro*.

The power of a processor is determined largely by two factors: its speed, measured in *megahertz* (MHz), and the amount, or number of *bits*, of data it can process at a time. (A **bit** is the smallest piece of information a computer can manipulate; its value is represented by either a 0 or 1.) For example, the Pentium is a 64-bit chip that comes in variations that run at speeds from 60 MHz to (as of this writing) 200 MHz. To use Windows 95, you need a computer with at least a 32-bit chip, and the more speed the better.

## *Internal Memory*

A computer uses its **internal memory** to store the instructions and data to be processed by the CPU. In a personal computer, memory resides on a series of chips either plugged directly into the motherboard or into one or more smaller circuit boards connected to the motherboard.

**ROM and RAM** Internal memory is divided into two types: ROM and RAM. **ROM** stands for *Read-Only Memory*. It contains an unalterable set of instructions that the computer consults during its start-up process and during certain other basic operations. **RAM** (*Random Access Memory*), on the other hand, can be both read from and written to. (Think of ROM as a reference sheet, while RAM is a scratchpad — a very large scratchpad.) RAM is used by the computer to hold program instructions and data. Whereas ROM is a permanent form of memory storage, all the information stored in RAM is lost when the computer is turned off.

Memory is usually measured in *kilobytes* and *megabytes*, where one **byte** consists of eight bits and is the amount of memory used to store one character of information. (Loosely speaking, a *character* is any symbol you can type, such as a letter, a digit, or a punctuation mark.) One **kilobyte**, abbreviated *KB*, is 1,024 (= $2^{10}$) bytes and one **megabyte** (*MB*) is 1,024 kilobytes. Thus, a computer with eight megabytes of RAM, a typical amount nowadays, can store 8,388,606 (= 8 × 1,024 × 1,024) characters of information.

## *Mass Storage Devices*

In addition to ROM and RAM, a computer needs **mass storage**, another form of memory, which stores programs and data semi-permanently. (They remain in mass storage until you decide to erase them.) However, to make use of any information stored on a mass storage device, that information must first be *loaded* (copied) into RAM.

**Disk drives** On personal computers, the primary type of mass storage device is the **disk drive**. Most PCs contain a **hard disk drive** housed within the system unit and one or two **floppy disk drives**, also housed within the system unit but accessible from the outside (see Figure 1). To store information, the hard disk drive makes use of a constantly spinning magnetic platter — the **hard disk** — which is sealed within the drive. **Floppy disks** (or **diskettes**), on the other hand, are stored away from the computer and, when needed, are inserted into the diskette drive.

**Floppy disks** Floppy disks and their drives come in two sizes: 3½ or 5¼ inches in diameter (Figure 2). Surprisingly, the smaller 3½-inch disk has a greater storage capacity than the larger one. *High density* 3½-inch diskettes hold up to 1.44 MB of data; high density 5¼-inch diskettes hold up to 1.2 MB. *Low density* diskettes, which are used in older machines, store less information. Hard drives hold much more data than floppies. Nowadays, computers come with hard drives that often exceed 1,000 megabytes (or one *gigabyte*) of storage.

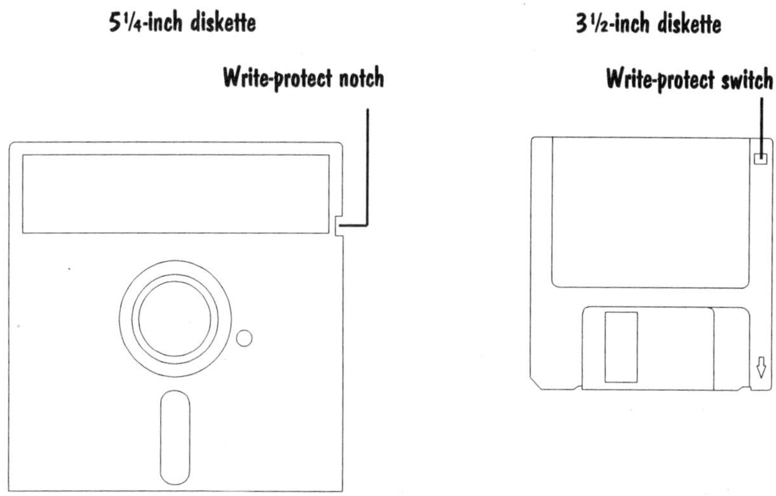


**Figure 2** Floppy Disks

**Write-protecting a diskette** If you want to prevent the accidental erasure of data on a floppy disk, you can *write-protect* it. A write protected diskette can be read from, but not written to or erased. To write-protect a 5¼-inch floppy, cover its write-protect notch with a small piece of tape; to write-protect a 3½-inch diskette, throw its write-protect switch (see Figure 2).

You may be wondering why computers contain both hard and floppy drives. Typically, the hard drive is used to store most of the programs and data to be used by a PC. Floppy drives, which are much slower in operation, are typically used in the following ways:

- To transfer newly purchased programs from the distribution disks to the computer's hard disk.
- For *backup* purposes — to make copies of valuable hard disk data in the event that the hard disk becomes damaged.
- To help transfer information from one computer to another.

- For *archival* purposes — to move information from the hard disk to floppies when it is unlikely to be needed in the foreseeable future.

**Other mass storage devices**

Some personal computers are equipped with additional types of mass storage devices. A **tape drive**, which uses media that resemble audio cassettes, can be used to copy (back up) the entire contents of a hard disk. Should the hard disk become inoperable — should it *crash* — its data could then be retrieved from the backup tape. A tape drive works slowly, but this isn't too important considering its intended role.

A **CD-ROM drive** uses disks that are similar to audio compact discs (hence the "CD" in its name). These disks, like floppies, are removable and portable, but, unlike floppies, hold huge amounts of information — about 500 MB each. Because CD-ROM drives are read-only devices (hence the "ROM" in the name), they are used primarily:

- To distribute large applications to the computer user (instead of using dozens of floppies).
- To hold reference material such as encyclopedias, dictionaries, photographs, and the like.

## *Input Devices*

The computer uses its **input devices** to receive data from the outside world. For this purpose, every computer includes a typewriter-like **keyboard** (see Figure 3). To enter information into the computer, you simply type it at the keyboard in the same way you would using an ordinary typewriter. The characters you type will simultaneously appear on the computer's display screen.

**Special keys**

Computer keyboards contain quite a few keys not found on a typewriter. (Figure 3 shows the most common keyboard layout for IBM-compatible machines.) These "extra" keys include:

- Twelve *function keys* labeled F1 through F12 are arrayed across the top of the keyboard. They perform special tasks that vary depending on the program you are using.
- Just to the right of the large block of typewriter-like keys are ten *cursor control keys*: the four *Arrow keys* (↑, ↓, ←, and →) plus Insert, Home, and so on. These keys allow you to move the *cursor*, which indicates the current typing position, around the screen.
- A *numeric keypad*, at the far right of the keyboard, allows you to enter numbers quickly. If the *Num Lock* light (above the keypad) is off, pressing one of these keys doesn't input a number; it per-

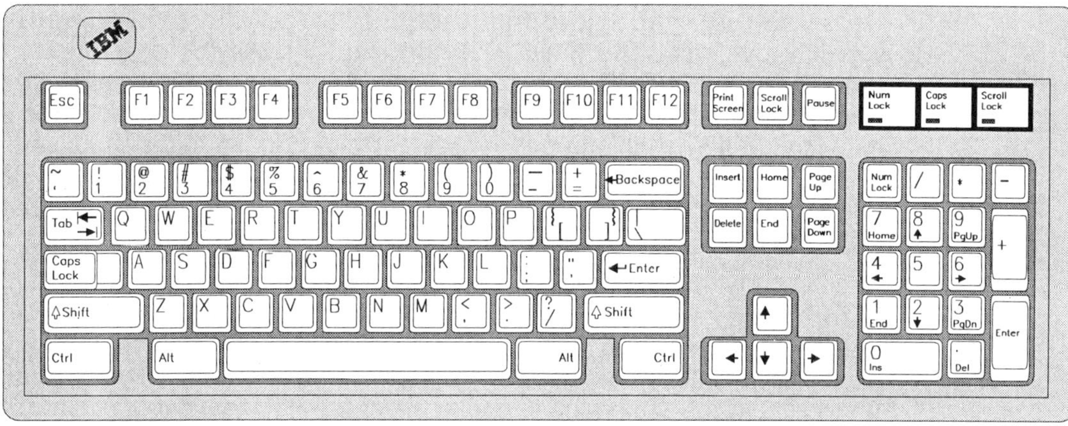


**Figure 3** A Typical Keyboard Layout

forms the secondary function indicated on the key (for example, Home or ↑). To turn the Num Lock light on or off, press the Num Lock key.

You may notice a few other special keys (such as Esc and Print Screen) here and there on the keyboard. We will explain their function when appropriate, later in the text.

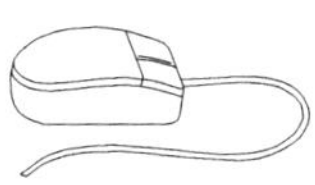

Another standard input device is the **mouse**, a hand-held object containing two or three buttons, which (together with the cable that connects it to the computer) vaguely resembles a long-tailed rodent. When you roll the mouse around on the desk top, a pointer moves correspondingly on the screen. For example, if you roll the mouse to the left, the pointer moves left. Once the pointer is positioned appropriately on the screen, pressing a mouse button (*clicking the mouse*) performs a program function. The mouse can speed up many Windows operations, but it lacks the versatility of the keyboard.

## *Output Devices*

Whereas input devices allow us to communicate with the computer, **output devices** make it possible for the computer to "talk" to us. The most common output devices are *monitors* and *printers.*

A **monitor** is a high resolution television-like screen enclosed in a case and controlled by circuitry — the *video adapter* — within the computer. (The screens on portable computers use an entirely different technology; they are usually *LCD* — liquid crystal display — *panels.*)

As is the case with televisions, monitor size is measured along the screen's diagonal. The most common screen sizes for desktop computers are 14 and 15 inches, but larger screens are also available. Another characteristic that affects the quality and cost of a monitor is its *resolution* — the number of *pixels* (tiny dots of light) it uses to create images. Nowadays, screen resolutions of 1024 × 768 — 768 horizontal rows, each containing 1,024 pixels — are becoming increasingly common. This kind of resolution puts even the finest of televisions to shame.

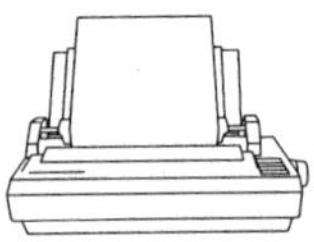

Unfortunately, output to the screen is both impermanent (it disappears when the power is turned off) and not terribly portable (you'd need a pretty long extension cord to take your screen output home from school). If you want to make a permanent copy of a program's output on paper, you need to use a **printer**.

The text and pictures produced by virtually all printers are composed of tiny dots of ink or an ink-like substance. The size of these dots and how closely they are packed together determines the quality of the output. Here are the most common types of printers in use today, in order of increasing price and quality of output:

- *Dot matrix printers* produce the "tiny dots" by rapidly striking an inked ribbon against the paper with a row of small pins. This kind of printer is relatively inexpensive and very reliable, but the quality of its output cannot match that produced by the other types. Its primary use nowadays is to print on multipart forms.
- *Ink jet printers* spray incredibly tiny drops of ink on the paper producing finer images than their dot matrix counterparts at a slightly higher speed and cost. Moreover, many ink jet printers can produce relatively good *color* output at a reasonable price. The main disadvantage of ink jets is their relatively high cost of operation.
- *Laser printers* produce the best output at the highest rate of speed, and are remarkably reliable. Although they are more expensive than other types of printers, lasers have become the standard for business use and are becoming increasingly common in the home, as well.

# *Software, Operating Systems, and Windows*

The most powerful hardware cannot accomplish anything by itself. It needs **software** — computer programs — to bring it to life. Software provides instructions for the central processing unit and, in so doing, allows the computer user to write letters, calculate loan balances, draw pictures, play games, and perform countless other tasks.

## Applications Software

Software is divided into two general categories: applications and system software. **Applications software** (or more simply, *applications*) are programs you use to enhance your productivity, solve problems, supply information, or provide recreation. To be able to run programs like these is the reason one learns to use a computer.

The most commonly used applications include:

**Types of applications**

- *Word processors* help you create, edit, and print documents such as letters, reports, memos, and so on.
- *Database managers* allow you to enter, access, and modify large quantities of data. You might use a database program to create a personal phone directory. A business can use this kind of application to maintain customer lists and employee records.
- *Spreadsheet programs* simplify the manipulation and calculation of large amounts of tabular data (spreadsheets). These programs are often used by businesses to try to foresee the effect of different strategies on their bottom line.
- *Drawing and painting programs* allow one to use the computer to (as you may have guessed) draw or paint pictures — *graphics* — on the screen and print them on paper.
- *Multimedia applications* make extensive use of graphics, sound, and sometimes video images to provide information or entertainment.

Applications are developed and published by many different companies and are sold by retail stores and mail order firms. Each software package consists of a *user's guide* together with one or more diskettes or CDs that contain the application *files* — the programs, data, and documents needed by the application. Before you can use a software package, it must be *installed* — some of its files must be copied (by the computer) from the floppies or CDs to the hard disk.

## The Operating System

The second general software type is **system software**, the programs used by the computer to control its hardware. The most important piece of system software is the **operating system** — the computer's master control program. The operating system has two general functions:

1. It helps the application you are using to communicate with the computer hardware. Applications are written to run under a specific operating system, which supplies easy ways for the programmers to access the computer's disk drives, memory, and so on.
2. It provides an *interface* — a link — between you and the computer that allows you to install and start up applications, manipulate disk files, and perform other very basic tasks.

**DOS** The central processing unit may be the brain of the computer, but the operating system gives the machine its personality. Most IBM-compatible computers use an operating system known as **DOS** (for *disk operating system*), which was developed by Microsoft Corporation for the original IBM Personal Computer introduced in 1981. Although major changes have been made to it over the years, DOS still retains much of the awkwardness of its distant past.

An immediate clue to an operating system's personality is its *start-up screen*, the one you see after you turn on the computer and it has gone through its preliminary functions. With pure, unadorned DOS, you are presented with a few lines of mysterious-looking text ending with the **DOS prompt** (most likely, `C:\>` ) followed by a blinking underline (the *cursor*). This is DOS' way of asking you to enter a command. For example, if you want to start up your word processor, you might type the following two lines (pressing the Enter key at the end of each):

```
CD \WP51\DATA
\WP51\WP
```

This kind of **command line interface** is classic DOS. In order to direct DOS to perform a function, the computer user must memorize (or have a handy list of) a large number of arcane commands. This is certainly not a *user-friendly* system.

**GUIs** A vast improvement in user-friendliness is the **graphical user interface** (**GUI**, pronounced "gooey") popularized by the Apple Macintosh line of computers. In a GUI, the start-up screen contains a collection of small stylized pictures called **icons** (see Figure 4) together with a set of **menus** that supplies available options. (The menus in Figure 4 are entitled *File*, *Options*, *Window*, and *Help*.) With a graphical user interface, you can start up applications and perform other operating system functions as easily as moving the mouse pointer to the corresponding icon or menu item and pressing a mouse button. The keyboard can also be employed to carry out functions, but using a GUI is much easier with a mouse.

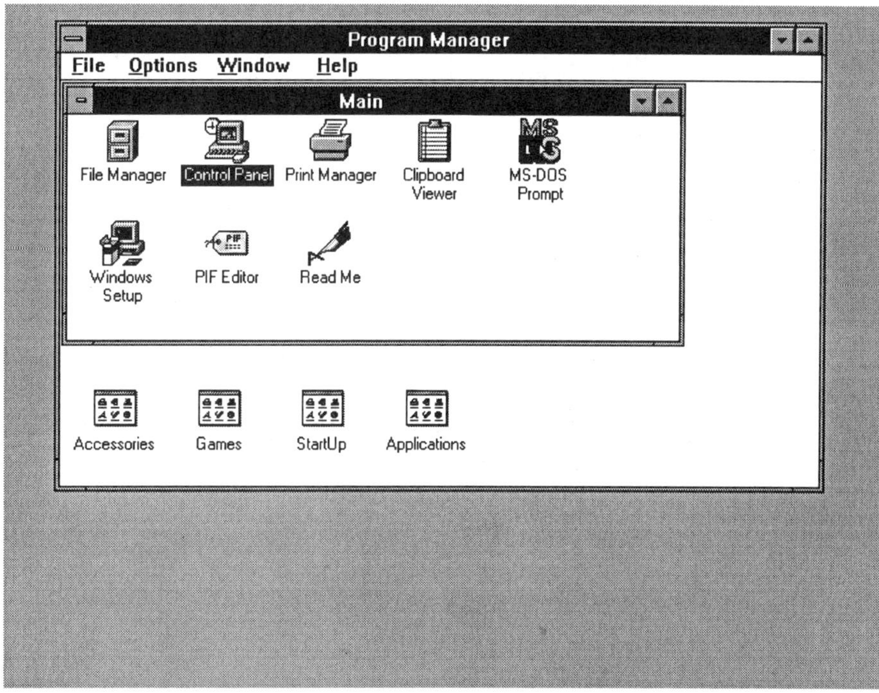


**Figure 4** A Typical Windows 3.1 Start-up Screen

## *Microsoft Windows*

**Windows** is a very sophisticated piece of software, originally developed in 1985 by Microsoft Corporation, that employs a graphical user interface to help make IBM-compatible computers easier to use. Although Windows sold slowly at first, version 3.0 (introduced in 1990) and especially version 3.1 (1992) were wildly popular. The latter version established Windows as the standard operating environment for IBM-compatible computers. (Figure 4 shows its start-up screen.)

**Windows 95**

However, Windows 3.1 is not an operating system in the true sense of the term; it will not run unless DOS is present in RAM. This limitation, in turn, leads to certain problems and inefficiencies in its use. In August 1995, Microsoft brought the long-awaited Windows 4.0 to market. Officially known as **Windows 95**, this new version no longer requires DOS in order to run. Windows 95 is a true operating system.

**Advantages of Windows**

Using Windows provides many advantages over plain old DOS:

- Its graphical user interface is much easier to use than DOS' command line interface.

- Windows has **multitasking** capabilities — you can run more than one application at a time, each occupying its own area on the screen. For example, you can start up a paint program to draw a picture without closing down the word processor that is already running.
- You can easily transfer data from one application to another. For example, the picture you've just completed in the paint program can be inserted by Windows into your word processing document.
- Windows provides uniform standards for the look and feel of applications developed to run under it. (Such programs are called *Windows applications*; those not designed specifically for Windows are called *DOS applications*.) This is of great benefit to the computer user, making it easier to learn and use new applications.
- The Windows user interface is highly customizable; you are given a great amount of control over the way that it looks and acts. For example, you can design your own start-up screen, choose your own screen colors, position and size the areas on the screen in which your applications are running, and much, much more.
- Windows supplies a large number of useful small and medium-sized applications. These include an on-screen calculator, a word processor, a paint program, an easy-to-use file manager, and even a couple of games.
- Windows provides modules that control a wide assortment of different monitors, printers, mice, and other peripherals. As a result, applications programmers don't have to worry about writing their own software to communicate with the huge variety of available input and output devices.

**New features of Windows 95**

Windows 95 generally improves on the advantages mentioned above and adds some new features as well:

1. The most noticeable change in Windows 95 is in the user interface. It is still a GUI, but with a much different look than Windows 3.1. Until you customize it, the start-up screen has the somewhat spartan look shown in Figure 5, but in many respects, the new interface is easier to use than that of Windows 3.1.
2. Windows 95 has added features that allow you to get work done faster and more easily. These include the Start button for easy startup of your programs, the Taskbar for quickly switching between applications, Desktop shortcuts for frequently used items, and the ability to give files more reasonable names than previously allowed.

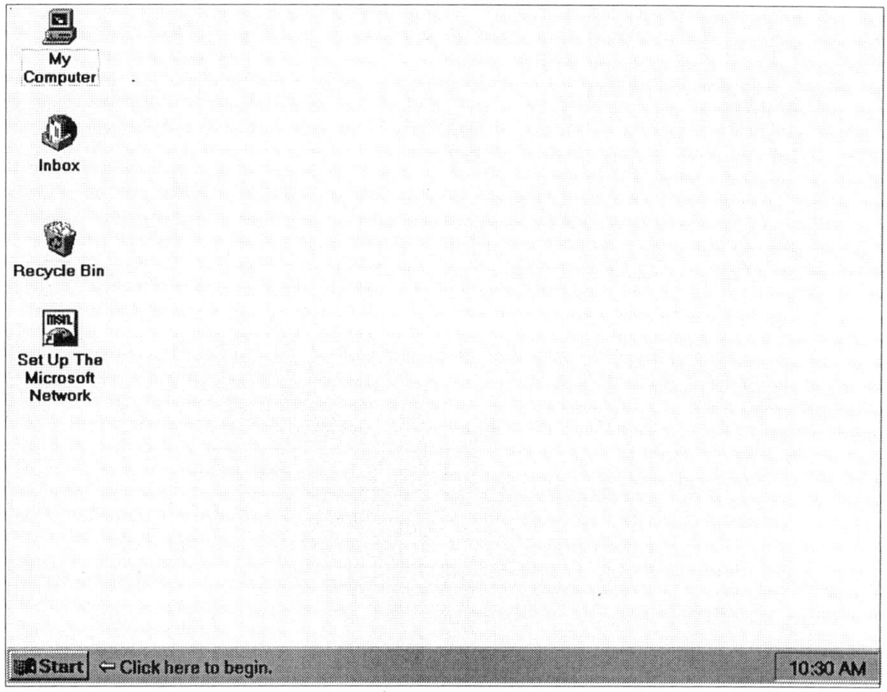


**Figure 5** A Windows 95 Start-up Screen

3. Adding new hardware is easier under Windows 95; it provides a hardware "wizard" to guide the process and *Plug and Play* technology to prevent conflicts with other devices.
4. Windows 95 has new built-in programs, including improved communications, more sophisticated multimedia tools, and a few utilities for maintaining and better utilizing the hard disk.
5. Recognizing the growing importance of both networks and portable computers, Windows 95 has
   - Improved networking capabilities, including easier network setup and browsing; and
   - Provided better support for portable computers, including power management and file transfer between laptop and desktop.

Many of these features may make little sense to you now, but you will surely come to understand most of them as you progress through the text.

# *A Brief History of Personal Computers*

**Early computers**

The electronic computer is a relatively modern invention; the first fully-operable computer was developed about 50 years ago, at the end of World War II, by a team at the University of Pennsylvania's Moore School of Engineering. This team was headed by John Mauchly and J. Presper Eckert, who named the new machine *ENIAC*, for Electronic Numerical Integrator and Calculator. ENIAC was hardly a *personal* computer, occupying a large room and weighing about 33 tons. By today's standards, ENIAC was also extremely slow, unreliable, and expensive to operate. In 1945, on the other hand, it was considered a marvel.

Over the next 30 years, computers became smaller, faster, and less expensive. However, most of these machines were kept isolated in their own air-conditioned rooms, tended by specially trained personnel. By 1975, computers were in great demand at universities, government agencies, and large businesses, but relatively few people had ever come face-to-face with an actual computer. This all began to change in the late 1970s.

To understand why, let's take a closer look at the early computers. ENIAC and its immediate successors were large, slow, and unreliable primarily because they used thousands of large, slow, and unreliable *vacuum tubes* in their electronic circuits. Vacuum tubes were glass cylinders, typically about four inches high and an inch in diameter, which generated a lot of heat and thus couldn't be placed very close together. Then, in 1947, a momentous event occurred at Bell Labs — William Shockley, John Bardeen, and Walter Brattain announced the invention of the *transistor.* Only about an inch long and a quarter inch across, a transistor did the same job as a vacuum tube but produced very little heat.

The downsizing of computers began in the 1950s as transistors replaced vacuum tubes, and continued into the 1960s with the introduction of the *integrated circuit* (IC) — an ice cube-sized package containing hundreds of transistors. By the late 1960s, *microchips*, consisting of thousands of electronic components residing on a piece of silicon the size of a postage stamp, had begun to replace ICs. At this time, a new breed of *minicomputers* appeared, costing less than $25,000 and occupying a space no larger than a small filing cabinet. Then, in 1970, Ted Hoff, Jr., working at Intel Corporation, invented the **microprocessor**, a central processing unit on a chip. The technological world was now ready for the personal computer.

**The personal computer**

The first personal computer to be successfully marketed to the public was built in 1974. It was designed by Micro Instrumentation and Telemetry Systems (MITS), a small electronics firm located in New

Mexico, which named it the Altair 8800. The Altair was a very primitive machine, about the size of a bread box; it contained 256 bytes (not kilobytes) of RAM, had no ROM, and its input and output devices consisted of rows of toggle switches and lights, respectively. It was also quite inexpensive — $395 in kit form. Sales of the Altair took off after an article about it appeared in the January, 1975 issue of *Popular Electronics* magazine.

Although add-on products for the Altair 8800 (such as memory boards and paper tape readers) gradually appeared over the next couple of years, it's questionable whether anyone ever did any useful work on this machine. Nevertheless, the Altair is of major historical significance because it inspired thousands of computer hobbyists and professionals to become interested in personal computers.

Two of the hobbyists inspired by the Altair were Paul Allen and Bill Gates, both about twenty years old and living in the Boston area at the time. They joined together to write and sell a version of the BASIC programming language for the new computer. With the easy-to-use BASIC available, Altair owners no longer had to write programs in low-level, mind-numbing machine language. Soon thereafter, Gates and Allen formed Microsoft Corporation, which is now the world's largest software company (and the publisher of Windows).

Another Altair aficionado was Stephen Wozniak, who joined forces with his friend and fellow Californian, Steven Jobs, to form Apple Computer, Inc. In 1977, they brought the now legendary Apple II personal computer to market. The Apple II was an instant hit and for the next few years, Apple was the fastest growing company in the United States.

### The IBM PC

By 1980, there were dozens of companies manufacturing personal computers, but the major producers of the larger minicomputers and mainframes had not yet entered the fray. This changed dramatically in 1981, when IBM brought out its first personal computer (which was not so imaginatively named the *IBM Personal Computer*). Although it wasn't much more powerful than most other personal computers of the time, the IBM PC (Figure 6) was a milestone in the history of personal computers for two basic reasons:

1. For many businesses, especially the larger ones, it "legitimized" personal computers. If IBM was selling them, the reasoning went, then maybe PCs really could be useful business tools. As a result, the IBM PC became wildly popular; IBM could not produce them fast enough to keep up with the demand.
2. It was built with generic parts and used the PC-DOS operating system, which was developed by Microsoft and was virtually identical to MS-DOS, a Microsoft product. The IBM PC also used

*open architecture* — IBM published detailed specifications so that anyone could build circuit boards for it to expand its capabilities. These features enabled enterprising companies to "clone" the PC — to build their own "IBM-compatible" personal computers.

**Figure 6** Two Historic Computers

### The Apple Macintosh

For the next few years, the personal computer industry slowly evolved as a few IBM clones and dozens of non-IBM-compatible PCs were brought to market. Then, in 1984, Apple introduced the Macintosh (Figure 6), which it advertised, with a decidedly anti-IBM slant, as "the computer for the rest of us". With its small size and integral screen, the "Mac" certainly *looked* different, but what really made it stand out was its easy-to-use, mouse-driven, graphical user interface. (This GUI is similar, broadly speaking, to the Windows interface developed later by Microsoft. Both interfaces, and the mouse as well, trace their roots back to work done about 1980 at Xerox Corporation's Palo Alto Research Center.) The Apple Macintosh was not at all compatible with the IBM PC. Nevertheless, after a slow start, it became increasingly popular. Today, the Macintosh and its descendants are the only remaining popular alternative to IBM-compatible personal computers.

### Recent developments

From this point on, the increased competition for the PC buyer's dollar brought forth new and more powerful computers at an ever-accelerating rate. This boom was fueled by Intel Corporation, which introduced a new generation of microprocessor every few years. Whenever they did, microcomputer manufacturers quickly brought out machines designed around the new chip and software developers used the greater speed to create more sophisticated applications.

**Windows** Microsoft Windows was one of the major beneficiaries of the more powerful computers. When it was first introduced in 1985, Windows ran sluggishly on the existing hardware (graphics-intensive programs require relatively fast computers), and it did not have much success. However, by the time the much improved version 3.0 was brought to market in 1990, hardware had caught up with the demands of the software and this version of Windows was an immediate hit. Then, when an even better version 3.1 was introduced in 1992 in the midst of a computer price war that made top-of-the-line machines affordable, Windows became the standard operating environment for IBM-compatible microcomputers. The current version of Windows, Windows 95, was rolled out in August, 1995 with the most publicized (and most costly) introduction for any computer product ever.

## *Review Exercises*

**Personal Computers**

1. The physical components of a computer system are referred to as its ____________.
2. A computer's main circuit board is called its ____________.
3. One byte of memory consists of ____________ bits.
4. One kilobyte is equal to ____________ bytes.
5. Some examples of mass storage devices are floppy disk drives, hard disk drives, and ____________ drives.
6. Of the various types of printers, the highest quality output is produced by a ____________ printer.
7. True or false: Computer components housed outside the system unit are called peripherals.
8. True or false: A bit can be represented by a 0 or a 1.
9. True or false: The contents of a computer's ROM are lost when the power is turned off.
10. True or false: Floppy disk drives access data more slowly than hard disk drives.
11. True or false: A CD-ROM drive can be used for backup purposes.
12. True or false: Computer keyboards contain fewer keys than a standard typewriter.
13. True or false: Laser printers are especially good at printing on multipart forms.

14. Which of the following components is *not* contained within the system unit of a typical PC?
    a. The motherboard
    b. A floppy disk drive
    c. Random access memory (RAM)
    d. None of the above answers is correct.

15. The computer's central processing unit
    a. Processes program instructions.
    b. Performs arithmetic and logical operations.
    c. Controls the other components of the computer.
    d. Performs all the above functions.

16. Which of the following is an input device?
    a. A monitor
    b. A keyboard
    c. A printer
    d. Read-only memory (ROM)

17. One advantage of a floppy disk over a hard disk is that
    a. It can be used to transfer data between computers.
    b. It holds more data.
    c. Data can be retrieved from it more quickly.
    d. None of the above answers is correct.

**Software and Operating Systems**

18. Software is divided into two broad categories: ____________ software and system software.

19. The master control program that oversees the computer's operations is called its ____________.

20. The generic name for the operating system used by virtually all IBM-compatible computers until the advent of Windows 95 is ____________.

21. Windows makes use of a GUI, which stands for ____________.

22. True or false: Computer programs are also known as software.

23. True or false: Most computer users find it easier to use a command line interface than a graphical user interface.

24. True or false: One of the advantages of Windows over DOS is the speed with which it runs applications.

25. True or false: Unlike Windows 3.1, Windows 95 is a true operating system.

26. Which of the following is an example of system software?
    a. The computer's RAM

b. The computer's operating system
c. A computer game
d. A word processor

27. One advantage of DOS over Windows is that

    a. It can run several programs at once.
    b. It is easier to learn to use.
    c. It requires less powerful hardware.
    d. All of the above are correct.

28. Windows 95

    a. Requires DOS to be running before it can be started up.
    b. Can run most programs that were written for DOS and Windows 3.1.
    c. Runs on both IBM-compatibles and the Apple Macintosh.
    d. Was the first operating system to use a graphical user interface.

**History**

29. The first fully-operable electronic computer was known by the acronym ____________.

30. The ____________, a CPU residing on a single computer chip, was invented in 1970.

31. The first personal computer received national attention in the year ____________.

32. The first microcomputer built by International Business Machines Corporation was called the ____________.

33. The first widely-used computer to make use of a graphical user interface was the ____________.

34. True or false: The invention of the transistor led to smaller, cheaper, more reliable computers.

35. True or false: The first personal computer was manufactured by Apple Computer, Inc.

36. True or false: The Apple Macintosh makes use of the Windows 95 operating system.

37. True or false: Computers have not increased appreciably in speed and power in the last ten years.

38. The first *personal* computer was

    a. ENIAC.
    b. The Altair 8800.
    c. The Apple II.
    d. The IBM Personal Computer.

39. Microsoft Corporation was founded by

    a. Stephen Wozniak and Steven Jobs.
    b. Richard Rodgers and Oscar Hammerstein.
    c. J. Presper Eckert and John Mauchly.
    d. Paul Allen and William Gates.

40. In the 1990s

    a. Intel Corporation introduced its first computer chip.
    b. Microsoft Corporation brought out Windows.
    c. Apple Computer, Inc. introduced the Macintosh computer.
    d. None of the above is correct.

CHAPTER 1

# The Basics of Using Windows 95

In the introduction to this text, we discussed the *what* and *why* of Windows 95. Recall that the primary goal of this powerful operating system is to make computers easier to use. In this chapter, you will begin to see some of the things that Windows can do and how easily they are done. More specifically, you will learn to:

1. Recognize the elements of the Windows 95 Desktop.
2. Use the mouse to perform basic Windows operations.
3. Choose items from menus.
4. Move, resize, minimize, maximize, and close windows.
5. Scroll through the contents of a window.
6. Use dialog boxes to indicate preferences.
7. Shut down Windows 95.

# 1.1 *The Windows 95 Desktop*

If Windows 95 is installed on your computer, when you turn on the machine, you will soon see the words *Starting Windows 95 ...* and then the Windows logo will appear. After a while, the Windows 95 opening screen will be displayed. A simple opening screen is shown in Figure 1. Depending on how your computer has been set up, its opening screen might look quite different from the one pictured here.

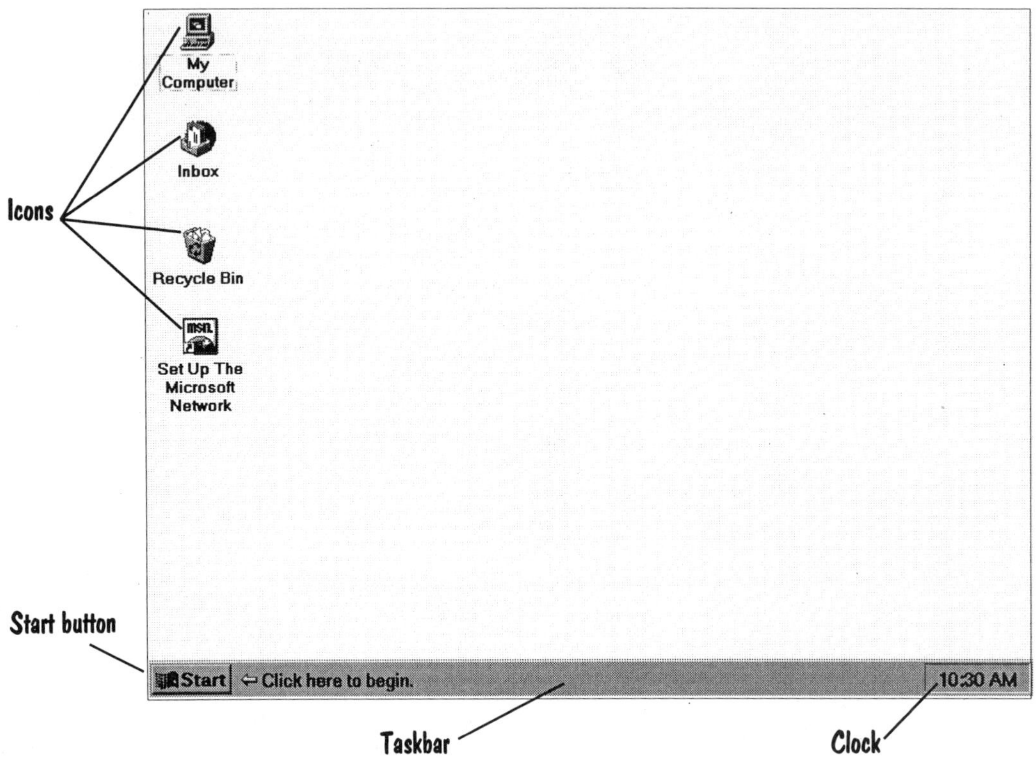


**Figure 1** The Windows 95 Desktop

The entire screen area is referred to as the Windows **Desktop**. Just like a regular desk top, it's the place on which you will do your work. Currently (in Figure 1), there are only a few objects on the Desktop. After we begin working with a program or two, however, most of the Desktop will be covered by *windows* of various sorts and the objects you see here (except the Taskbar) will usually become obscured.

The **Start button**, located in the lower left corner of the screen in Figure 1, is, as the text "Click here to begin" suggests, the jumping off point for a typical Windows session. It provides access to all the applications (programs) installed on your computer. We will discuss the use of the Start button at the beginning of Chapter 2.

The labeled pictures along the left side of the screen are called **icons.** These icons (and others like them throughout the Windows environment) provide easy access to various aspects of Windows 95. For example, as you will see in Chapter 3, the icon labeled "My Computer" allows you to work with virtually every piece of hardware and software that is part of your computer system.

The **Taskbar** displays the applications and documents that you are currently using. The only item on the Taskbar in Figure 1 is the Clock utility, which not only provides the time of day but, as you will see later, can also be used to display the date and a month-by-month calendar.

# 1.2 Of Mice and Menus

As you know, one of the primary advantages of working with Windows 95 is that it is easy to use. It accomplishes this, in part, by the extensive use of the mouse and menus.

## Using the Mouse

When a mouse is moved around on a flat surface, its pointer moves in a corresponding way on the screen. The shape of the mouse pointer depends on the application that is running and the use to which it is being put. The pointer may look like an arrow, a double-headed arrow, an I-beam, or a hand, among other things.

In Windows and its applications, the mouse can be used to select items displayed on the screen, initiate actions, and move and resize certain objects. Before we illustrate these uses, let's discuss some important mouse terminology.

**Mouse terminology**

- To *point at* an object means to move the mouse so that its on-screen pointer is positioned over the specified object and held in place for a few moments.
- To *click* the mouse means to press and release the left mouse button. To *right-click* is to press and release the right mouse button. To click (or right-click) *on* an object means to point at the

object and then click (or right-click).*

- To *double-click* on an object means to point at the object and click the left mouse button twice in rapid succession.
- To *drag* an object with the mouse means to point at the object, press (but not release) the left mouse button, move the mouse pointer to a new location, and then release the button. To *right-drag* an object is to perform the same actions using the right mouse button instead of the left.

To illustrate these operations, let's return to the computer screen shown in Figure 1. If we double-click on the My Computer icon, the **window** — boxed-in area on the screen — shown in Figure 2 appears. (Your My Computer window may look quite different from the one pictured here. Don't worry; for the purposes of the current discussion, it does not matter.)

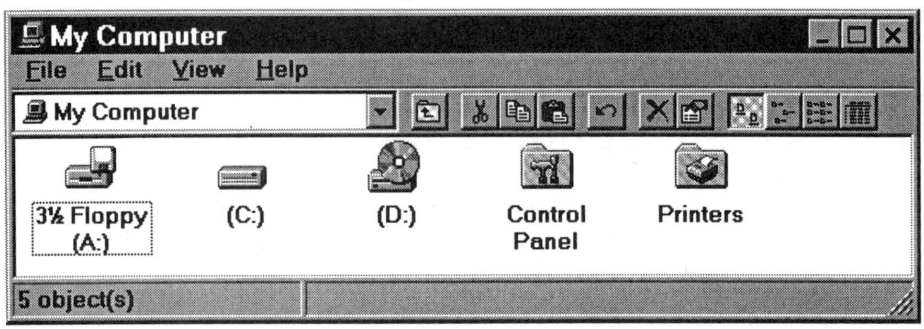


**Figure 2** The My Computer Window

If you double-click on an object and it doesn't initiate an action, you may have moved the mouse slightly between clicks or perhaps you didn't follow the first click by the second quickly enough. Try double-clicking again.

## *Using Menus*

The first line of the My Computer window (Figure 2) is called its **title bar**; it contains the name of the window together with some symbols

*If the functions of your left and right mouse buttons seem to be reversed, they can easily be restored to their "normal" settings. Either ask your lab coordinator to do this for you or see Section 4.4. (If you want to try it yourself, first finish reading Chapter 1.)

that we'll discuss in Section 1.3. Below the title bar is the My Computer **menu bar**:

**Opening a menu**

These words are the names of **menus** —lists of commands — that can be used to manipulate the contents of the My Computer window. To *open* (display) a menu, simply click on its name. For example, if you click on the word *View*, the menu pictured in Figure 3 appears. (Because this kind of menu looks as if it were pulled down, like a window shade unrolling from the word View, it is called a **pull-down menu**.)

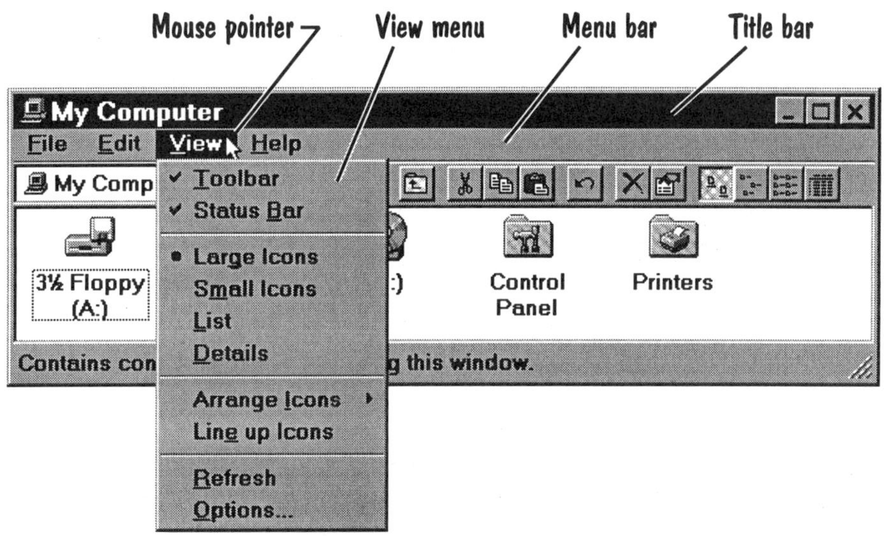


**Figure 3** A Typical Pull-down Menu

**Selecting a menu option**

Once a menu has been opened, you can choose one of the options listed by clicking on that item. (Doing so will also close the menu.) For example, to choose the "Line up Icons" option from the View menu in Figure 3, move the mouse pointer straight down until it is positioned over this item (it will become highlighted) and click the left button.

**NOTE**

If you prefer, the options listed on a pull-down menu can be accessed using the keyboard. Notice that each name on the menu bar has one letter underlined; for example, the *V* in View. To display a pull-down menu, hold down either Alt key, press the key corresponding to the underlined letter, and then release the Alt key. (We will write this sequence of actions as — if the underlined letter is V — "press Alt+V".) Then, to select an option on that menu, either:

- Press the key corresponding to the underlined letter in the desired option.

*or*

- Press the Down Arrow key (↓) until the desired option is highlighted and then press the Enter key.

For example, to display the View menu as in Figure 3, hold down the Alt key, press the key labeled V, and release Alt. Then, to select the Line up Icons option, *either* press the E key *or* press the Down Arrow key several times until the option is highlighted and then press the Enter key.

**Canceling a menu** If you want to close a menu without selecting any of the options, just click on any other part of the screen. As an alternative, press the Escape key.

## *Types of Menu Items*

Let's take a closer look at the View menu that is displayed in Figure 3. Notice that some options on this menu are preceded or followed by a special symbol, such as a check mark or bullet (see Figure 4).

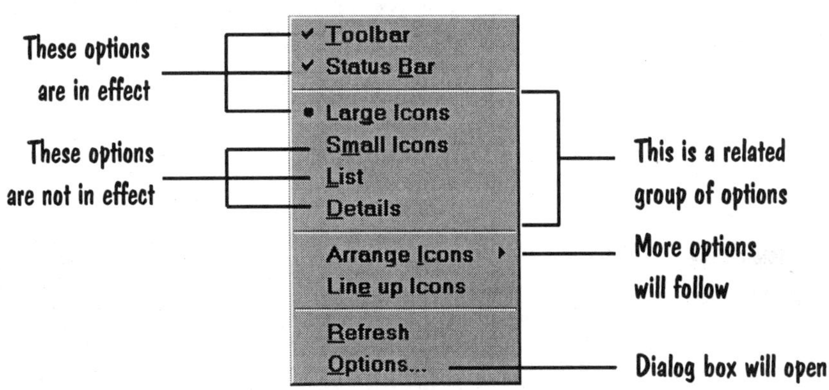


**Figure 4** Special Symbols for Menu Options

These symbols have a consistent meaning in Windows and its applications:

**Menu symbols**

- If a *check mark* (✔) appears next to a menu option, it indicates that this item or characteristic is currently in effect. For example, in Figure 4, the check marks next to Toolbar and Status Bar indicate that both these objects are displayed in the My Computer window. If you click on Toolbar, the menu will close and the Toolbar will disappear from the window. (Try it!) Then, the next time you pull down the My Computer View menu, you'll notice that the check mark next to Toolbar has disappeared as well — this option is no longer in effect. To get it back, choose Toolbar again. We call this kind of option a *toggle*: if the Toolbar *is* currently displayed, choosing the menu option turns it off; if it is *not* displayed, choosing the option turns it on.
- A *bullet* (•) next to a menu option not only means that this option is in effect, but also indicates that the rest of a group of related items are *not* in effect. (The horizontal lines within a menu — see Figure 4 — divide it into these groups.) For example, the bullet on the Large Icons option in Figure 4 describes the contents of the My Computer window (see Figure 3). This window does *not* contain Small Icons, a List, or Details. Only one bulleted item within its group can be in effect at any given time.
- A *triangle symbol* (▸) next to a menu item indicates that a *submenu* of additional options will appear if you "point at" this item. For example, if you move the mouse pointer over the Arrange Icons option in Figure 4 and hold it steady for a few moments, the following submenu is displayed at its right:

- If you choose a menu name that is followed by an *ellipsis* (three consecutive periods), a *dialog box* will appear requesting additional information. (Dialog boxes are discussed in Section 1.4.) For example, choosing the Options item from the View menu of Figure 4 displays a dialog box presenting the available options. (If you open this dialog box, you can close it, removing it from the screen, by clicking on the button labeled Cancel or by pressing the Escape key.)

Before we close this section, let's pull down My Computer's Edit menu (by clicking on the word Edit on the menu bar) to illustrate a couple of additional points. This menu is shown in Figure 5.

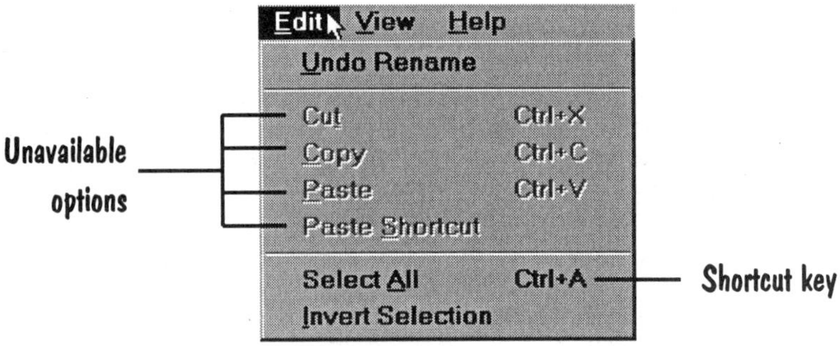


**Figure 5** The My Computer Edit Menu

In Figure 5, notice that:

- The second group of options is *dimmed* — it appears to be "faded out". This indicates that these options are temporarily not available. If you click on one of these items, nothing will happen!
- Keystrokes (such as Ctrl+A) appear next to several menu items. These keystrokes are called **shortcut keys**. They provide a quick way of choosing the corresponding menu option *without displaying the menu itself*. For example, to select all the objects in the My Computer window without displaying the Edit menu, just press Ctrl+A; that is, hold down the Ctrl (Control) key, type A, and then release Ctrl.

NOTE

If you have been following along at the computer and you now want to close the My Computer window, click on the little box marked with an **X** in the upper-right corner of this window. To shut down Windows 95, which is wise to do before turning off your computer, follow the instructions in Section 1.5.

1-2 TUTORIAL

Try the following exercises on your own.

1. Turn on your computer (if it's not already on) to start Windows 95. If the My Computer window is open, close it by clicking (tapping the left mouse button) on the little box marked with an **X** in the upper-right corner of this window.
2. *Click* on the My Computer icon (by moving the mouse pointer — an arrow shape — over this icon, then tapping the left mouse button). The words *My Computer* should now be highlighted.
3. *Drag* the My Computer icon to another location on the Desktop. (Position the mouse pointer over the icon; press, but do not

release, the left mouse button; move the pointer to a new location on the screen, and release the mouse button.)

4. Drag the My Computer icon back to its original location.
5. *Double-click* on the My Computer icon (by clicking twice in rapid succession on this icon). The My Computer window should open. If not, try double-clicking again, being sure not to move the mouse as you do so.
6. Click on the word *View* on the menu bar. The View menu should open.
7. On the View menu, there will be a *bullet* next to one of the options in the second group (beginning with "Large Icons"). Click on one of the other three items in this group. The View menu should close. Notice the change in the My Computer window.
8. Open the View menu and *point at* Arrange Icons by moving the mouse pointer over these words and holding it still for a few moments. A submenu should appear. Note whether or not the option Auto Arrange is checked on this submenu.
9. Now click on the Auto Arrange option. The two menus will close. Reopen the View menu and the Arrange Icons submenu. If Auto Arrange had originally been "checked", it should now be "unchecked", and vice-versa.
10. Reopen the View menu and click on the "Options..." item. A new window — a dialog box — will open. Close it by pressing the Escape key or by clicking on the box marked with an **X** in the upper-right corner of this window.
11. If you want to quit, to shut down Windows 95 see the NOTE that precedes this tutorial.

## 1.3 Windows within Windows

While working at your desk (say, doing homework), you might have several documents open at once — perhaps a textbook, a reference book, and your notebook. This is often the case on the Windows Desktop as well. Here, the documents and other related objects are contained in *windows*. Depending on what you're doing at the moment, you might want to move some of these windows around, make one of them bigger, or perhaps take some of them off the Desktop. In this section, we will describe how to perform these actions —how to move, resize, and close windows.

## Operations on Windows

Before we explain *how* to move or resize a window, let's look at a few reasons *why* you might want to perform these operations. For one thing, it's usually much easier to use the contents of a window when it occupies the entire screen; you can view more information and, in some cases, see more detail as well. Often, however, when a window opens, it just occupies part of the Desktop. (This was the case with our My Computer window in Section 1.2.) In such a case, you might want to increase the size of the window, perhaps **maximizing** it so that it uses as much screen real estate as possible.

The disadvantage of maximizing a window is that it then might obscure everything else on the Desktop. Even when not maximized, it might cover vital information in another window or on the Desktop itself. Thus, at times you will want to reduce the size of a window or even **close** it, which takes it off the Desktop. Instead of closing a window, it is sometimes possible to **minimize** it, which also removes it from the screen. The difference between closing and minimizing a window is a subtle one:

- *Closing a window* removes its contents from the computer's internal memory, RAM (see the Introduction).
- *Minimizing a window* keeps its contents in RAM and reduces the window to a button on the Taskbar, allowing us to restore the window quickly and easily.

## Manipulating Windows

To illustrate the different ways in which we can manipulate a typical window, let's open the My Computer window by double-clicking on the My Computer icon, as we did in Section 1.2. Figure 6 shows the parts of the title bar that are involved in moving, minimizing, maximizing, and closing a window.

**Moving a Window** To *move* a window, drag its title bar to the new location. More specifically, position the mouse pointer over the title bar, press (but don't release) the left mouse button, and move the mouse in the direction you want the window to move.

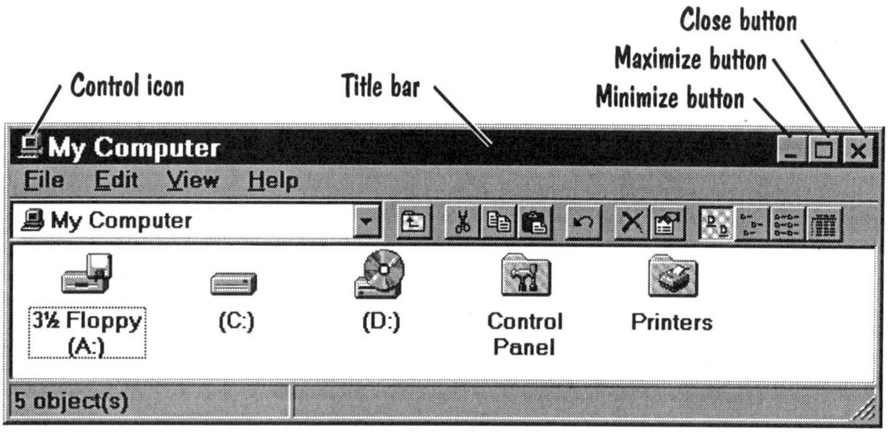


**Figure 6** Parts of the Title Bar

As you do so, an outline of the moving window appears on the screen. When this outline is positioned to your liking, release the mouse button.

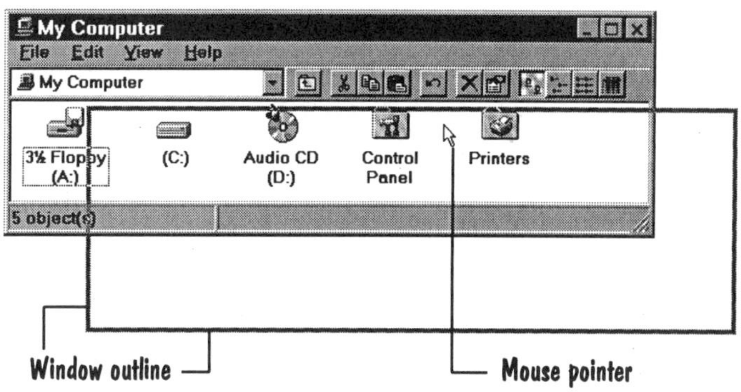

**Resizing a Window** To *resize* a window, drag its border or corner to a new position. For example, to increase the height of a window, position the mouse pointer on the bottom border (it becomes a two-headed arrow, as pictured above) and drag the border down. When the window outline indicates that you've achieved the desired height, release the mouse button; the window will redraw to its new size. (If you drag a window *corner*, both sides attached to that corner move at once.)

TIP

If you change your mind during the process of moving or resizing a window and want to cancel the operation, press the Escape key before releasing the mouse button.

**Minimizing, Maximizing, or Closing a Window** To *minimize*, *maximize*, or *close* a window, click on the **minimize button**, **maximize button**, or **close button**, respectively (on the right end of the title bar).

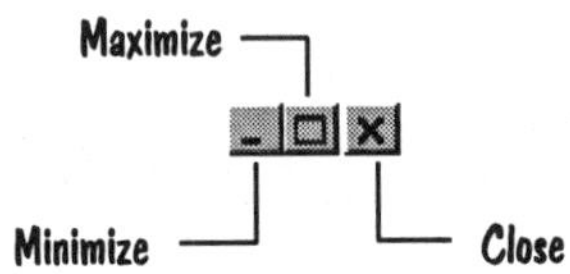


Note that:

- When a window is minimized, it is removed from the screen but its name and icon continue to appear on a button on the Taskbar. To reopen a minimized window, click on its Taskbar button.
- When a window is maximized, it expands to its largest possible size and the maximize button is replaced by a **restore button.** Clicking on the latter, *restores* the window, returning it to its former position and size. 
- When a window is closed, it disappears from the screen.

TIP

You can also *maximize* a window by double-clicking on its title bar. Once a window is maximized, the same operation —double-clicking on the title bar — restores it. A window can also be *closed* by double-clicking on its Control icon (see Figure 6), but since every Windows 95 window has a close button, this fact is useful for little more than impressing your friends, and it's not likely to do even that.

NOTE

Although using the mouse is easier, Windows 95 does allow you to use the keyboard to perform the move, resize, maximize, minimize, and close operations on a window. These operations (when available) are listed on the window's **Control menu**. To open the Control menu using the keyboard, press Alt+Spacebar or Alt+Hyphen, whichever works. (Remember: The notation "Alt+*keystroke*" means "hold down the Alt key, type the keystroke, and then release the Alt key.) The Control menu will appear in the upper left corner of the window, as shown in the following figure:

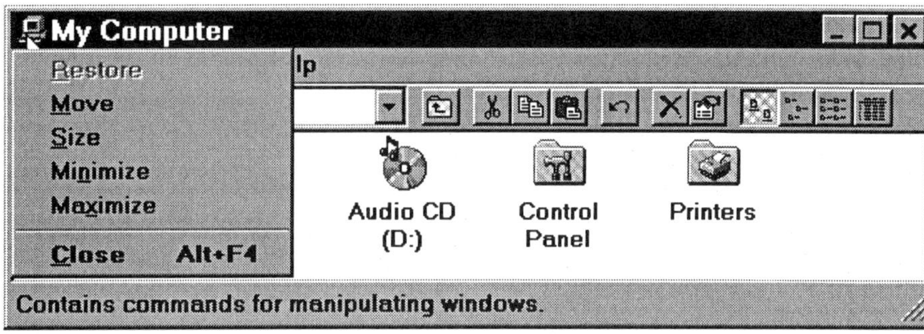


(You can also open its Control menu by right-clicking on the window's title bar or by clicking on its Control icon — see Figure 6 — if the window has one.) Choosing the Minimize, Maximize, Close, or Restore option performs the indicated task. Choosing Move or Size requires some maneuvering with the Arrow keys to complete the task; for these two operations, it's *a lot* easier to use the mouse!

## *Scroll Bars*

When a window is not large enough to view all its contents at once, one or two **scroll bars** will be displayed to allow you to move through the contents without increasing the size of the window. For example, if we decrease the size of the My Computer window shown in Figure 6 so that the icons are partially or completely covered, the resulting window will look similar to the one in Figure 7.

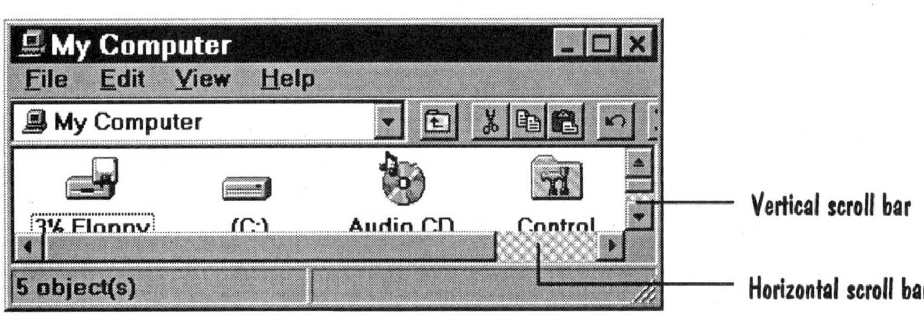


**Figure 7** Scroll Bars Visible in a Window

**Scrolling in a window**

If the contents of a window — let's call it a *document*, even if it's just a collection of icons — is only partly visible, you have to **scroll** to see the rest of it. To understand how this works, imagine that the entire document is lying on the Desktop, but the window acts like a "cutout", allowing us to see only part of it. To see more (without increasing the window's size), we have to move the cutout around. For example, when you *scroll down*, imagine the cutout moving in a downward direction so that a lower part of the document comes into view. (In actuality, the window stays fixed on the screen and, figuratively speaking, the document itself moves around.)

You can use the mouse to scroll through the contents of a window by clicking on various parts of a scroll bar (see Figure 7): the *horizontal* scroll bar scrolls the window left or right; the *vertical* scroll bar scrolls it up or down. Let's take a closer look at a vertical scroll bar:

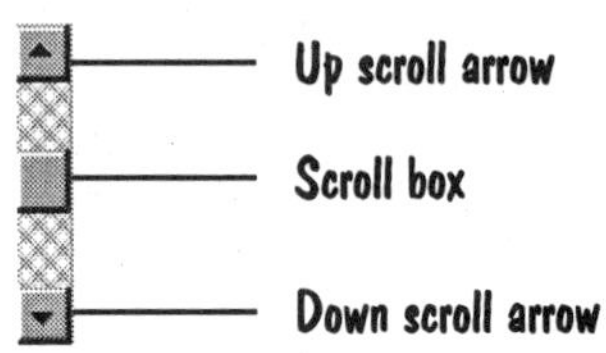


Here's how this scroll bar is used. (A horizontal scroll bar works in an analogous way.)

- Clicking the up or down scroll arrow scrolls the window up or down one "step". Holding down the mouse button while pointing at the up or down scroll arrow scrolls the window continuously in that direction until you release the button.
- Clicking on the scroll bar above or below the scroll box scrolls up or down one window's worth of information.
- Dragging the scroll box up or down scrolls the window proportionally within the document. For example, if you drag the scroll box to the middle of the scroll bar, the window will scroll about halfway through the document.

NOTE

The horizontal and vertical scroll bars also give visual clues to the size of the document in the window and your current location within it:

- The *length* of a scroll box is proportional to the amount of the document you are viewing. For example, the horizontal scroll box in Figure 7 is roughly 80% of the length of the corresponding scroll bar; we can deduce from this that we are seeing about 80% of the width of the underlying "document". The vertical scroll box in Figure 7 is about half the length of its scroll bar; we are viewing about half the height of the document.
- The *position* of a scroll box along its scroll bar gives your relative

location in the document. For example, in Figure 7, the horizontal scroll box is positioned at the left of its bar and the vertical scroll box is positioned at the top of its bar; we conclude that we are viewing the upper-left part of the underlying "document".

1-3 TUTORIAL

Try the following exercise on your own.

1. Start up your computer (if necessary) and open the My Computer window by double-clicking on its icon.
2. If the My Computer window is maximized (occupies the entire screen above the Taskbar), restore it by double-clicking on the title bar.
3. Minimize this window by clicking on its minimize button, toward the right end of the title bar. The title *My Computer* and its icon continue to appear on a button on the Taskbar. 
4. Reopen the My Computer window by clicking on its Taskbar button.
5. Move the My Computer window to the upper-left corner of the screen by positioning the mouse pointer on the title bar and dragging the window outline to the appropriate place.
6. Make the window as small as possible in the horizontal direction. To do so, position the mouse pointer over the right window border (the pointer is placed properly when it turns into a "double arrow") and drag the outline of the border to the left as far as it will go. The horizontal scroll bar (and possibly the vertical one, as well) should appear.
7. Scroll across the window by positioning the mouse pointer over the right scroll arrow and holding down the left mouse button until the scroll box reaches the right end of the scroll bar. Now scroll back the other way by dragging the scroll box to the left end of the scroll bar. Increase the window to its former size.
8. Maximize the My Computer window by clicking on the maximize button, toward the right end of the title bar. 
9. Pull down the Control menu by clicking on the Control icon (which looks like a computer) on the left end of the title bar (or by pressing Alt+Spacebar). Notice that the Maximize option is dimmed.
10. Restore the My Computer window by clicking on the Restore option on the Control menu.
11. Close the My Computer window by clicking on the close button on the right end of the title bar. (Should you now want to shut down your computer, see Section 1.5.) 

# 1.4 Conversing with Dialog Boxes

As you may recall, choosing a menu item followed by an ellipsis (...) displays a dialog box. A **dialog box** is a special type of window that presents groups of related options from which you can make selections. As you work with Windows 95 and its applications, you will encounter a seemingly infinite variety of dialog boxes. Yet, all dialog boxes have certain things in common. In this section, we will discuss these common features.

## A Typical Dialog Box

To illustrate the features of a dialog box, let's take a look at a very interesting one. (Although we will discuss the types of objects in this dialog box here, a description of its capabilities will come later, in Chapter 4.) If you right-click (click the right mouse button) on an empty area of the Desktop, the following menu appears:

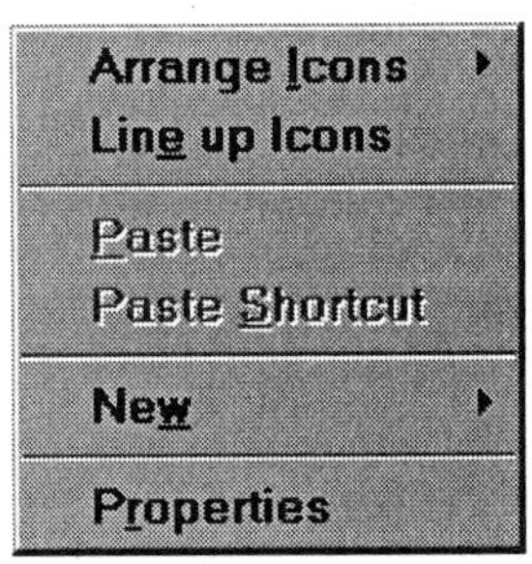


Choosing the Properties option from this menu opens the Display Properties dialog box shown in Figure 8. (Notice that there isn't any ellipsis next to the Properties option on the menu!)

At the top of this dialog box is the familiar title bar, which supplies the name of the window. It also contains a close button (marked with an X) and a help button (marked with a ?), but not a minimize or maximize button. In general, dialog boxes cannot be resized in any way; in particular, they cannot be minimized or maximized. Dialog boxes *can* be moved about the screen; as with any window, just drag its title bar to the desired location.

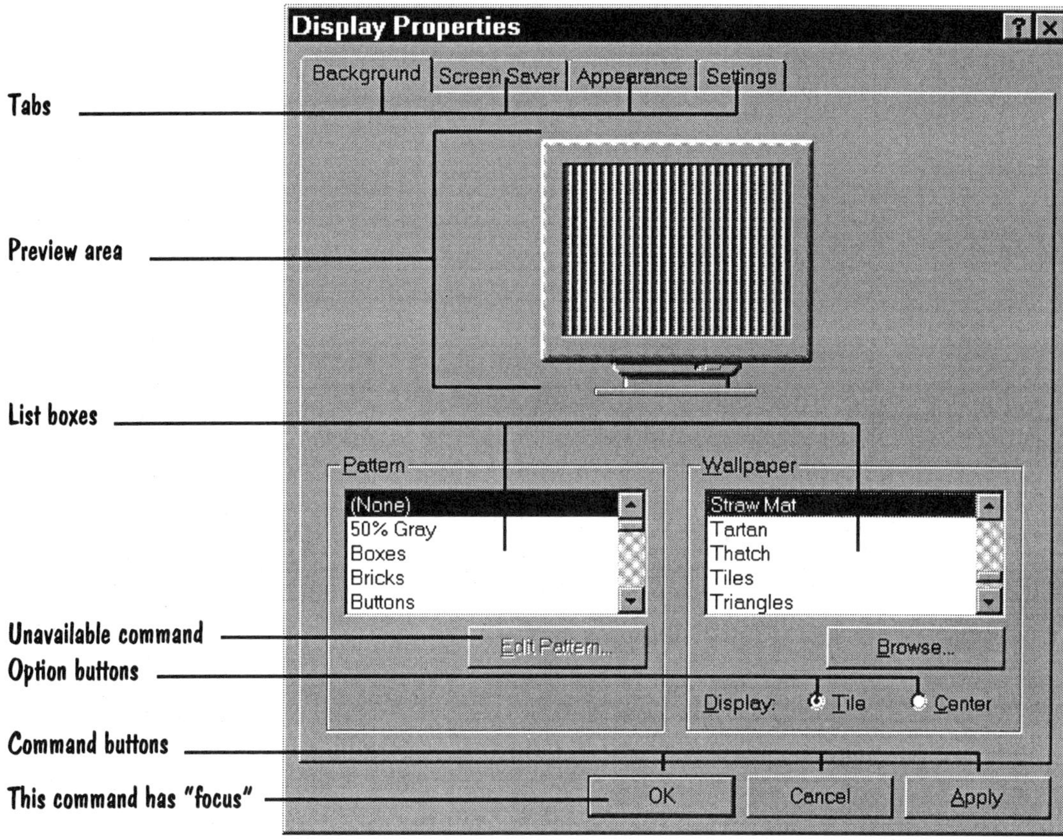


**Figure 8** A Typical Dialog Box

Most objects in a dialog box allow the user (that's you!) to specify preferences or execute commands. These objects (for example, the tabs, command buttons, option buttons, and list boxes of Figure 8) are arranged in related groups and associated with easily recognized symbols. Each symbol indicates a different function, as described below.

**Command buttons** are represented by large labeled rectangles. When you click on a command button, it initiates an action. For example, clicking on the Browse button in Figure 8 opens another dialog box. (Notice the ellipsis following the word *Browse*.) Here are a few special features of command buttons:

- Exactly one command button in a dialog box is enclosed in a heavy outline. (In Figure 8, it's the OK button.) We say that this is "the default button" or that it "has the focus". As you select options in a dialog box, the focus sometimes moves to another button. Nevertheless, the button that currently has the focus can always be activated by pressing the Enter key (or by clicking on the button).

- Almost all dialog boxes have a button labeled "OK" or "Close". When this button is activated, the dialog box closes and the options you have selected go into effect.
- The Cancel button allows you to close a dialog box without putting any of your new selections into effect. (Pressing the Escape key has the same effect as clicking on the Cancel button.)
- If the label on a command button is dimmed (for example, the Edit Pattern button in Figure 8), this option is not available at this time. (In this particular case, there is no pattern to edit!)

**Option buttons** are represented by small circles. These buttons are sometimes called *radio buttons* because they work like the station selection push buttons on a radio — when you click on one of them, it is *selected* (turned on) and the others are automatically *deselected* (turned off). For this reason, in a group of these buttons, exactly one of the corresponding options is selected at any given time. The currently selected option button is indicated by a "bullet". For example, in Figure 8, the Tile option is currently selected. If you click on the Center button, it will acquire the bullet (indicating that this option has been selected), and the Tile option will be deselected.

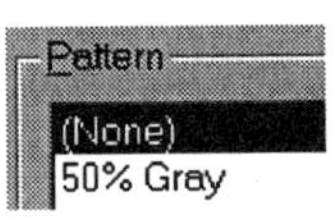


A **list box** is a rectangular box that contains a list of items from which you can choose. To select an item, click on its name. If the list is too long to fit in the box, a scroll bar will be displayed so that you can scroll through the entire list. The currently selected item in the list is highlighted. For example, in Figure 8, the selected item in the Pattern list box is "(None)" and the selected Wallpaper is "Straw Mat".

**Tabs**, which resemble file folder tabs, always appear at the top of a dialog box (if they appear at all). The currently selected tab (which is "Background" in Figure 8) appears to be in front of the others. The name on the tab provides a short description of the group of options currently visible in the dialog box. To select another tab, click on it; a new "page" of options will become available. Figure 9 shows the result of clicking on the Screen Saver tab in the dialog box of Figure 8.

NOTE

Some dialog boxes also display written or pictorial information for the user. For example, the dialog box in Figure 8 contains a *preview window* that shows the effect your selections will have on the Windows Desktop should you choose the OK (or Apply) command button.

## *Additional Dialog Box Features*

If you click on the Screen Saver tab in the Display Properties dialog box of Figure 8, most of the contents of this window change, providing a new set (*page*) of options from which to choose. The result is shown in Figure 9, which illustrates additional features of a dialog box.

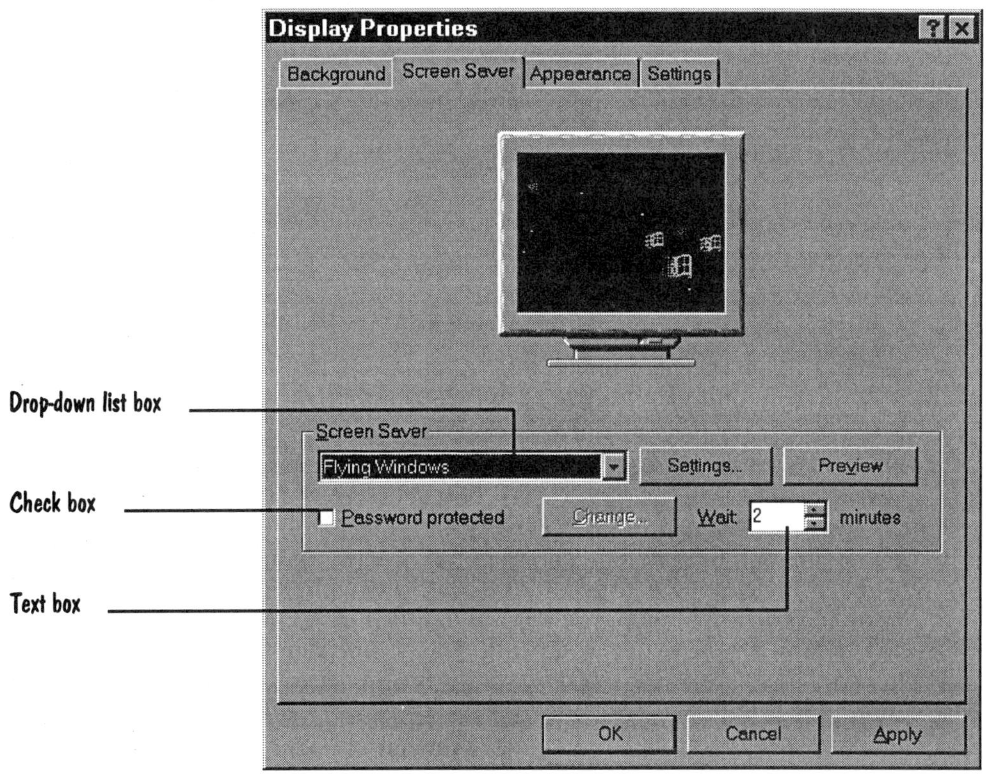


**Figure 9** Additional Features of a Dialog Box

A **check box** is represented by a small square, which may or may not contain a check mark. When the check box is selected, the check mark is present; when it is deselected, the check mark does not appear. For example, the deselected check box in Figure 9 indicates that this screen saver is not "password protected". A check box is a toggle:

- If you click on it when it's deselected, then it becomes selected (and a check mark appears).
- If you click on it when it's selected, then it becomes deselected (and the check mark disappears).

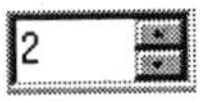


A **text box** allows you to input a number or name into a dialog box. It is symbolized by a rectangle that contains the *current value* for that option — the number or name that is used if you don't change it. For example, in Figure 9, 2 is the current value for the Wait text box. To change it, click on the text box, press the Backspace key to erase the current value, and then type a new one. (Do not press the Enter key after typing unless you want to activate the command button that has the focus!) Some text boxes, like the one in Figure 9, contain up and down arrows which provide an alternate way to change the current value. Here, each click on the appropriate arrow moves the time up or down one minute.

A **drop-down list box** is a special type of list box. Here, only one of the listed items (the current value) is initially visible. To see the rest of the list, click on the downward-facing triangle at the right end of the box. Then, to select an item from the list, click on that item. The list will close and the new item will be the one displayed.

TUTORIAL

Try the following exercise on your own.

1. Start up your computer (if necessary) and/or close any open windows by clicking on their close buttons.
2. Open the Display Properties dialog box by right-clicking on (an empty area of) the Desktop and then selecting Properties from the resulting menu.
3. If the Tile option button is not selected (if it doesn't have a darkened center), select it by clicking on it.
4. From the Wallpaper text box, select the Straw Mat wallpaper. To do so, scroll down the list until Straw Mat appears and then click on this item. The "screen" in the preview window should look like the one shown in Figure 8.
5. Select the Center option button. You should see a dramatic difference in the preview window.
6. Click on the Screen Saver tab to view a new page in the dialog box. It should look similar to the one in Figure 9.
7. Open the Screen Saver drop-down list by clicking on the down triangle in this box.

8. Select Mystify from this list (by clicking on it) and then choose the Preview button (by clicking on it) to view the Mystify screen saver. To return to the Display Properties dialog box, click the mouse.
9. Change the time in the Wait text box to 5 minutes by clicking on this box and then on its up or down arrow until "5" appears in the text box.
10. Choose Cancel by clicking on the Cancel command button or by pressing the Escape key. If you now want to shut down your computer, follow the instructions in Section 1.5.

# *1.5 Shutting Down Windows 95*

All good things (in fact, all things in general) must come to an end. At some point, you're going to want to quit working with Windows 95 and turn off your computer. To do so, you should:

1. Close all applications that are currently running. If an application's window is open on the Desktop, click on its close button (see Section 1.3); if the application has been minimized, right-click on its Taskbar button and then choose Close from the resulting menu. If you have used an application to modify a document and have not saved these changes to disk, Windows will display a message warning you of this fact. (We will discuss closing applications and saving documents in Section 2.2.)

2. Click on the Start button, which can normally be found in the lower-left corner of the Desktop. This action opens the Start menu:

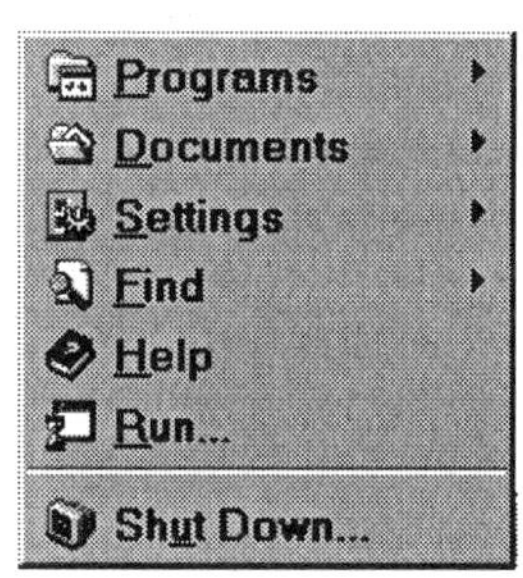


**NOTE** If the Start button is not visible anywhere on the Desktop, you can open the Start menu by pressing Ctrl+Esc; that is, hold down the Ctrl (Control) key, press the Esc (Escape) key, and then release Ctrl.

3. Click on the Shut Down option on the Start menu. The dialog box shown in Figure 10 will open.

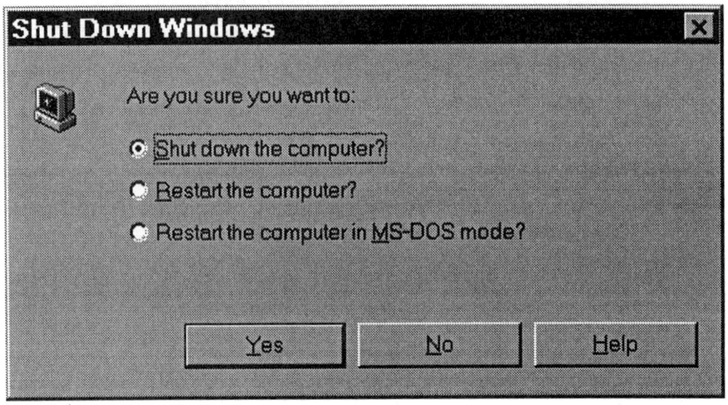


**Figure 10** The Shut Down Windows Dialog Box

4. Now select an option* by clicking, if necessary, on the appropriate option button and choosing the Yes command button. Or, close this dialog box and return to Windows 95 by choosing No (or by pressing the Escape key).
   - The first option, "Shut down the computer?", should be selected when you want to turn off your computer. Activating this option eventually brings up the message: "It's now safe to turn off your computer."

**WARNING** If you want to turn off your computer, you should first shut down Windows 95. Doing so ensures that all open files will be properly closed. As a result, you are much less likely to inadvertently lose data or your preferred Windows settings.

   - Activating the second option, "Restart the computer?", restarts Windows 95, reinitializing all its settings. This option is usually used after a program *crashes* (terminates abruptly) and/or Windows itself does not seem to be responding properly to your commands.
   - The third option, "Restart the computer in MS-DOS mode?",

*If your computer is connected to a network, there may be a fourth available option listed in this dialog box.

shuts down Windows 95 and starts **DOS**, Microsoft's plain vanilla operating system (see the Introduction). Once in DOS, you can safely turn off the computer when you see the DOS prompt (probably, `C:\WINDOWS>`). You can also start Windows 95 at the DOS prompt by typing `WIN` and pressing the Enter key.

TIP

Here are a couple of shortcuts for shutting down Windows:

- You can display the Shut Down Windows dialog box after closing down all applications by pressing the Alt+F4 keystroke combination.
- You can activate the "Shut down the computer?" option in the Shut Down Windows dialog box even if there are applications running. In this case, Windows will attempt to close these applications and, if successful, shut down your computer. (If you try this approach, you may see a message prompting you to save changes in a document or requesting that you close certain applications yourself.)

1.5

TUTORIAL

Try the following exercise on your own.

1. Turn on your computer, if necessary, to start Windows 95. If Windows is already running, close all windows by clicking on their close buttons.
2. Restart Windows 95: Open the Start menu by clicking on the Start button (if you can't find this button, press Ctrl+Esc to open the Start menu); choose Shut Down from the menu; select the "Restart the computer?" option button in the resulting dialog box; and choose the Yes command button.
3. When Windows 95 starts again, press Alt+F4 to open the Shut Down Windows dialog box. This time, select the "Restart the computer in MS-DOS mode?" option button and choose Yes. After a few seconds, you should see a mostly blank screen displaying the DOS prompt, probably `C:\WINDOWS>`.
4. Type `WIN` and press the Enter key to start Windows 95.
5. This time, open the Shut Down Windows dialog box, select the "Shut down the computer?" option button, and choose Yes. When the message "It's now safe to turn off your computer." appears, do just that.

# Review Exercises

**Section 1.1**

1. A(n) ___________ is a small stylized picture used to represent a Windows 95 object.
2. The ___________ button is positioned to the left of the Taskbar.
3. True or false: To start Windows 95, you must type the proper command after turning on your computer.
4. The Windows *Desktop* refers to:

   a. The area occupied by your computer, keyboard, and mouse.
   b. The windows that are currently open.
   c. The application that is currently running, including its menus, toolbars, and so on.
   d. None of the above is the Windows Desktop.

**Section 1.2**

5. To click on an object on the screen, move the mouse pointer over that object and press the ___________.
6. To open an application's View menu, you can click on the word ___________ on the menu bar.
7. If the name of a menu item is followed by an ellipsis (...), then choosing that menu item opens a(n) ___________.
8. True or false: When double-clicking the mouse, you should pause for a second or two between clicks.
9. True or false: To use a shortcut key to perform a task, open the menu that lists that task, and then press the shortcut key.
10. True or false: To right-drag an object, move the mouse pointer over it and click the right button.
11. When you position the mouse pointer over an object, hold down the left button, and move the pointer to a new location, it is called

    a. Clicking on the object.
    b. Double-clicking on the object.
    c. Dragging the object.
    d. Pointing at the object.

12. If an item on a menu is dimmed, clicking on that item

    a. Opens a dialog box.
    b. Opens a submenu.
    c. Closes the menu.
    d. Does nothing at all.

**Section 1.3**

13. To move a window, drag its ___________ to the desired location on the screen.

14. Clicking on a window's ___________ increases the window's size as much as possible.
15. To increase the width of a window without increasing its height, drag its ____________ to the right or its ____________ to the left.
16. True or false: You can close a window by clicking on its title bar.
17. True or false: When a window is minimized, the window disappears from the screen.
18. True or false: When a window opens, horizontal and vertical scroll bars are always displayed.
19. Which part of a window contains its maximize, minimize, and close buttons?
    a. Its title bar.
    b. Its menu bar.
    c. Its toolbar.
    d. Its status bar.
20. If an application is maximized, from its Control menu, you *cannot*
    a. Open the application's window.
    b. Close the application's window.
    c. Minimize the application's window.
    d. Restore the application's window.

In Exercises 21 and 22, identify the indicated parts of the window shown in Figure 11. Your answers should come from the following list:

| | |
|---|---|
| Close button | Control icon |
| Horizontal scroll bar | Maximize button |
| Menu bar | Minimize button |
| Title bar | Vertical scroll bar |

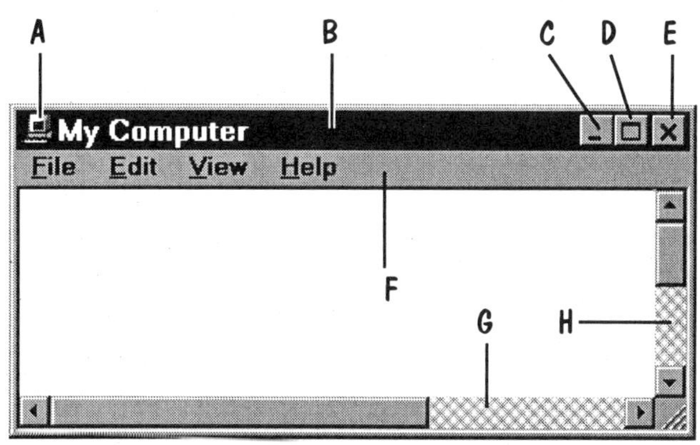


**Figure 11** Window for Exercises 21 and 22

21. Identify the components of the window in Figure 11 that are marked A, B, C, and D.

22. Identify the components of the window in Figure 11 that are marked E, F, G, and H.

**Section 1.4**

23. When you click on the command button labeled ____________ in a dialog box, the box closes and the selected options go into effect.

24. In a dialog box, instead of clicking on the Cancel button, you can press the ____________ key.

25. In a dialog box, a ____________ allows the user to turn an option on or off without affecting other options.

26. True or false: Dialog boxes can be moved around the screen.

27. True or false: A drop-down list box only displays a single item until you click on the appropriate symbol to "open" it.

28. True or false: In a group of related option buttons, only one button can be selected at any given time.

29. Which of the following objects appears on the title bar of a dialog box?

    a. A minimize button.
    b. A maximize button.
    c. A close button.
    d. A Control icon.

30. Dialog boxes never contain:

    a. Command buttons.
    b. Restore buttons.
    c. Option buttons.
    d. Tabs.

**Section 1.5**

31. The Shut Down option, which allows us to shut down Windows 95, appears on the ____________ menu.

32. The Shut Down Windows dialog box gives us the option of shutting down or ____________ Windows 95.

33. True or false: It is a good idea to shut down Windows 95 before turning off your computer.

34. True or false: To display the Start menu, even if the Start button is not visible on the screen, press Ctrl+Esc.

35. You can display the Shut Down Windows dialog box after closing all applications by pressing the keystroke combination:

    a. Alt+Spacebar
    b. Alt+Hyphen

c. Alt+F4.
d. None of these keystrokes works.

# *Lab Exercises*

Work each of the following exercises at your computer. Begin by turning the machine on (if necessary) to start Windows 95. Then, close all open windows by clicking on the button labeled with an X in the upper-right corner of each window. If you want to shut down the computer after completing an exercise, follow the instructions in Section 1.5.

**Lab Exercise 1 (Section 1.2)**

a. *Right*-click (click with the right mouse button) on an empty part of the Desktop. On the resulting menu:

   Which options (if any) are dimmed?
   Which options (if any) will open a dialog box when selected?
   Does a bullet appear next to any option?

b. Point at the Arrange Icons option to open its submenu. Notice that there is an Auto Arrange item on the submenu. (Don't click on it!) The Auto Arrange item is a toggle. Is it selected? How do you know?

c. Point at the New option on the original menu. In the submenu that appears, click on Folder. What is the name of the new icon that has appeared on the Desktop?

d. Click on an empty part of the Desktop. Then *right*-drag the new icon to another empty part of the Desktop. How many items are listed on the menu that appears when you release the mouse button?

e. Select the Copy Here option. How many copies of the new icon now appear on the Desktop?

f. Drag each copy of the new icon on top of the Recycle Bin icon. What happens each time?

**Lab Exercise 2 (Section 1.2)**

a. Double-click on the Recycle Bin icon to open its window. List the names of the menus that appear on the menu bar.

b. Open the Edit menu. What is the shortcut key for the Cut option? Is this option dimmed?

c. Press Ctrl+A, the shortcut key for the Select All option. Why didn't anything happen?

d. Cancel the Edit menu (close it without choosing any item). What mouse action or keystroke did you use?

e. Open the View menu. How many items have bullets next to them? How many items have submenus?

f. The Toolbar menu item is a toggle; is there a check mark next to it? Choose the Toolbar item. The View menu will close. What else happened?

g. Reopen the View menu. Is the Toolbar menu item "checked" now?

h. *Right*-click (click with the right button) on the Status Bar item. What, if anything, happened?

i. Click on the word *View* to close this menu. Then, click on the button labeled with an X in the upper-right corner of the Recycle Bin window to close it.

**Lab Exercise 3 (Section 1.3)**

a. Click on an empty part of the Desktop, then press the F3 function key to open the Find window. Does this window have a Control icon on its title bar?

b. If the Find window is maximized, restore it. Then, decrease its width as much as possible. Is the entire window title visible now? Did any scroll bars appear?

c. Try to increase or decrease the height of this window. Was it possible to do either?

d. Maximize the Find window. Does it occupy the entire screen?

e. Right-click the title bar to display the Control menu. List the items that appear on this menu. Cancel the Control menu by clicking elsewhere in the window.

f. Move the window in a *horizontal* direction. Has the restore button been replaced by a maximize button? If not, click on the restore button.

g. Minimize the window to a button on the Taskbar; then restore it to a window. Is it the same size as it was before being minimized?

h. Resize the Find window to the approximate size it had when you began this exercise and close this window.

**Lab Exercise 4 (Section 1.3)**

a. Right-click on an empty part of the Desktop; then select Properties from the resulting menu to open the Display Properties window.

b. Notice that this window (a *dialog box*) does not contain a minimize or maximize, button or a Control icon. Try to maximize the window by double-clicking on its title bar. Did this work?

c. Can this dialog box be: Moved? Resized? Minimized?

d. Open the window's Control menu. What mouse action or keystroke combination did you use? What items are listed on the Control menu? Cancel this menu.

e. In the small window entitled *Pattern*, use the vertical scroll bar to scroll to the bottom of the list. What name appears there? Why isn't a *horizontal* scroll bar displayed?

f. Try closing the Display Properties window by pressing Alt+F4. Did it work? If not, close it by clicking the close button.

**Lab Exercise 5 (Section 1.4)**

a. Double-click on the Clock on the Taskbar to open the Date/Time Properties dialog box. (If you can't find the Taskbar, press Ctrl+Esc to display it.)

b. Try to change the year displayed in the Date text box to 1800. Were you able to do this?

c. Using the up and down arrows in the Date text box, determine the allowable range of years. What is it?

d. Click on the Time Zone tab to change to this set of options.

e. Open the drop-down list and scroll to the bottom. What place is given for the "GMT+12:00" entry? Close the drop-down list.

f. Click on the ? button on the title bar; then click on the text to the right of the check box. What happened?

g. Close this dialog box by clicking on Cancel or by pressing the Escape key.

**Lab Exercise 6 (Section 1.4)**

a. Click on an empty part of the Desktop; then press the F3 function key to open the Find window.

b. Deselect the *Include subfolders* check box. Did the text in the *Look in* drop-down list box change?

c. Click on the Date Modified tab. Notice that the *All files* option button is selected.

d. Select the *between* option button. What happened to the *All files* button?

e. Select one of the *previous* option buttons. Try to enter the number 0 in the corresponding text box. Could you do this?

f. Click on the Advanced tab and open the drop-down list. Why is a vertical scroll bar necessary here? What name is at the bottom of the list?

g. Close the Find window by clicking on its close button.

**Lab Exercise 7 (Section 1.5)**

a. Open the Shut Down Windows dialog box; then close it without shutting down or restarting the computer. How did you do this?

b. Reopen the Shut Down Windows dialog box and activate the "Restart the computer in MS-DOS mode?" option. What text eventually appears on the screen?

c. Insert the Lab Exercises disk that accompanies this text into its drive; then type `dosprog` and press the Enter key. Does the application you just started appear in a *window*?

d. Follow the on-screen instructions to exit this application. What did you do to exit?

e. Restart Windows 95 by typing `win` and pressing the Enter key. Was the Windows 95 logo displayed before Windows started?

f. Open the Shut Down Windows dialog box and activate the "Shut down the computer?" option. What message is displayed prior to "It's now safe to turn off your computer"?

g. Turn off your computer.

CHAPTER 2

# *Working with Applications and Documents*

In Chapter 1 we discussed the structure and general use of some basic Windows 95 objects — the Desktop, menus, windows, and dialog boxes. In this chapter, we will concentrate on how to use Windows 95 to run your **applications** (programs) and manipulate your **documents** (the work created by an application). To be more specific, you will learn:

1. Various ways to start and close applications.
2. How to use the WordPad application to create simple word processing documents.
3. How to open, save, print, and close documents.
4. How to switch among the applications that are running.
5. How to transfer information from one document to another.
6. How to "capture" windows and screens.
7. How to use the online Windows 95 Help system to locate information about a desired topic.
8. How to obtain online context-sensitive help.

After completing this chapter, you should be able to use Windows 95 to print a copy of your homework!

# 2.1 Starting and Closing Applications

Windows 95 supplies a myriad of ways to start (or *open*) and exit (or *close*) applications. In this section we will describe most of these techniques.

## Using the Start Menu

Recall that if you click on the Start button to the left of the Taskbar or press the Ctrl+Esc keystroke combination, the Windows 95 Start menu opens (Figure 1). In Section 1.5, we discussed how to use the last item on this menu to shut down or restart Windows 95. Here, we will describe how to use the Start menu to open the applications available on your computer.

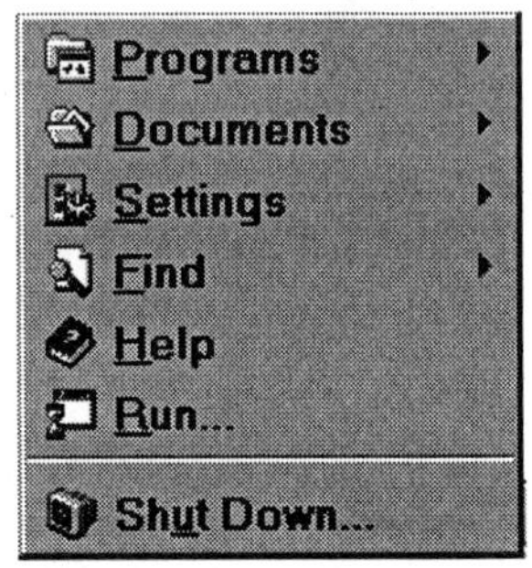


**Figure 1**
The Start Menu

**The Programs option**

Usually, the most straightforward way to open a program is to select the **Programs option** from the Start menu. When you point at this item (holding the arrow-shaped mouse pointer steady for a moment or two), a submenu listing specific applications and groups of applications will be displayed, as shown in Figure 2. (Your list of programs will undoubtedly be different from the one that appears here.)

On the submenu, the items followed by a right-facing triangle (such as Accessories, at the top in Figure 2) represent *groups* of applications; if you point at one of these items, another submenu will open, presenting further applications and possibly groups of applications. A submenu item that is not followed by a right triangle (such as Windows Explorer at the bottom of the list) represents a program. To start a program, just click on it! The Start menu will close and the program will begin running.

For example, suppose you want to open WordPad, a word processor that is included with the Windows 95 software package. To do so, click on the Start button to open the Start menu and point at the Programs option to open its submenu (Figure 2). Then, point at the Accessories option, which opens another submenu, and finally click on the WordPad item at the bottom of the latter. After a few moments, the WordPad opening screen will be displayed.

**Figure 2**
Pointing at the Programs Option on the Start Menu

**The Documents option**

Using the **Documents option** on the Start menu can sometimes be a real time-saver. Pointing at this item (see Figure 3) displays a submenu containing a list of the last 15 documents you saved to disk while running programs designed for Windows 95. (We will discuss saving documents in Section 2.2.) Clicking on one of the listed documents starts the application that created it and also displays (*opens*) the designated document within it.

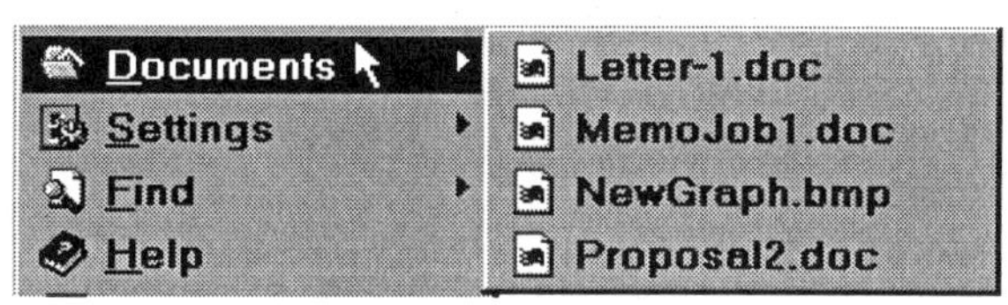


**Figure 3** Pointing at the Documents Option

**The Run option**

The techniques we have just described for starting an application are quick and easy, but require that the program, or a document created by it, appear on one of the Start submenus. The **Run option**, which appears near the bottom of the Start menu, can be used to open *any* application on your hard or floppy disks.

When you click on the Run command, the following dialog box is displayed:

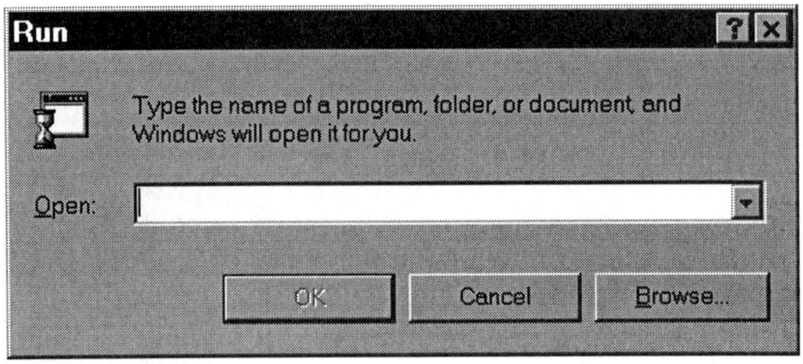


To start a program from this dialog box, you must know its file name, and possibly the folder in which that file is located — this is the major drawback of using the Run option. (We will discuss files and folders in Section 3.1.) If you have this required information, you can open the desired application by performing any of the following actions:

- Type the appropriate folder and file names (the program's *path name*) in the Open text box. (If a highlighted name already appears there, just type over it!) Then, click on the OK button or press the Enter key.
- If you have previously started the desired application from the Run dialog box, its name may appear on the Open drop-down list. Display this list (by clicking on the down-triangle), select the program's file name, and activate the OK button.
- Click on the Browse command button to open the Browse dialog box and use it to help you locate the program's file name; then activate the OK button. (This technique requires some familiarity with the Windows 95 folder system, which we will discuss in Chapter 3.)

In any case, the Run dialog box will close and the program will start.

As you can see, using the Run option is usually not the easiest way to start a program. However, there is one case in which Run is especially useful: when the program you want to start is on a floppy disk (diskette). To start a program from a floppy:

1. Insert the diskette in its drive.
2. Select the Run option from the Start menu.
3. Type the characters a: (assuming that the diskette is in this drive) followed by the program's file name in the text box; for example, a:big-game.

4. Press the Enter key or click on the OK button. The Run dialog box will close and the program will start.

## *Other Ways to Start Applications*

Typically, Windows 95 provides a variety of ways of performing just about any task, and opening applications is no exception. You have already seen several ways in which the Start menu can be used for this purpose. Here are a few additional important techniques for starting programs:

**The easiest way**

If an icon representing an application or document appears on the Desktop, just *double*-click on it to open that application or document. (In Chapter 1, we used this technique to open the My Computer application.) If you use a particular application frequently, it makes a lot of sense to place an icon (*shortcut*) for it on the Desktop. We will discuss how to do this in Section 3.4.

**Using Windows Explorer or My Computer**

Just about every aspect of your computer system can be accessed using either Windows Explorer (on the Programs submenu) or My Computer (which is represented by an icon on the Desktop). Both of these applications can locate and start any program on your hard or floppy disks. We will discuss Windows Explorer and My Computer in Chapter 3.

## *Closing an Application*

If you read Chapter 1 carefully (or worked its tutorials), you already know how to close a Windows-based application — just close its window. As usual, this task can be done in several ways. The following techniques are listed (more or less) in order of likely use; take your pick:

**Ways to close Windows-based applications**

- Click on the application window's close button (on the right end of the title bar). 
- Choose Exit from the application's File menu.
- Right-click on the application's Taskbar button and choose Close from the resulting menu.
- Press Alt+F4 (hold down the Alt key, tap the F4 key, and release Alt).
- Double-click on the application's Control icon (on the left end of the title bar).
- Open the application's Control menu by clicking on its Control

icon (right-clicking the title bar may also work) and choose the Close option.

**NOTE**

If you have used the application to make changes to a document and did not subsequently save the document to disk, Windows will display a warning message before closing the application. We will discuss this further in Section 2.2.

**Closing DOS applications**

As we mentioned in the Introduction, Windows 95 not only runs applications specifically designed for itself and Windows 3.1, but it also runs *DOS applications.* Although some DOS applications can be closed by selecting Exit from their File menus (if they have one!), none of the other techniques listed above is likely to work. If you try one of them, you'll probably just get a message that "Windows cannot shut down this program automatically."

Unfortunately, DOS applications, especially older ones, are notorious for performing common tasks in their own peculiar ways. So, you'll just have to learn the keystrokes or mouse clicks necessary to exit each DOS application you use. After exiting the program, its window may still remain on the screen, with the word *Finished* displayed at the left end of the title bar. To close the window, use any of the usual techniques (such as clicking on the close button).

**TIP**

There is another way to exit *any* application, but it should only be used in an emergency; for example, if the application has "locked up", and no longer responds to the keyboard or mouse. In this case, hold down the Ctrl and Alt keys, tap the Del key, and then release Ctrl and Alt. A dialog box will open, listing all programs that are currently running. The offending application should be highlighted in this list. (If it isn't, click on it.) Now activate the End Task command button and follow the on-screen instructions. Using this procedure, you will probably lose all unsaved work in the application that has locked up, but other open programs should survive unscathed.

**2-1 TUTORIAL**

Try the following exercises on your own.

1. Turn on your computer, if necessary, to start up Windows 95.
2. Open the WordPad application from the Start menu:
   - Click on the Start button to open the Start menu.
   - Point at the Programs option (and keep the mouse pointer stationary for a few moments) to open this submenu.

- Now, point at the Accessories item at the top, to display another submenu.
- Finally, click on the WordPad item to start this application.

3. Close the WordPad application by clicking on its close button.
4. Open the Start menu and point at the Documents option to open this submenu.
5. If any documents are listed, click on one of them, which should open that document within the application that created it. Close this application by choosing Exit from its File menu.
6. Place the Lab Exercises diskette in its drive.
7. Start the DOSPROG application on this diskette:
   - Open the Start menu and click on the Run option to open the Run dialog box.
   - Type `a:dosprog` in the Open text box and press the Enter key. The Run dialog box will close and the program will start.
8. Exit the DOSPROG application by following the on-screen instructions. If the application window remains on the screen, close it by pressing Alt+F4.

## 2.2 Working with Documents

In Windows, the word *document* is used to refer to any collection of data that is created by an application. Thus, a document could be a letter written using a word processor, a picture created by a painting program, or a collection of numbers produced by a spreadsheet program. Nevertheless, there are certain operations that are common to almost all documents: they must be created, saved, opened, printed, and closed. The way in which a document is created *does* vary considerably from application to application. However, all Windows documents are opened, saved, printed, and closed in a uniform way. (This is one of the beauties of using Windows!) In this section, we will use the WordPad application to illustrate these operations.

### An Introduction to WordPad

**WordPad** is one of the small applications (sometimes called *applets* or *accessories*) that is included as part of the Windows 95 package. WordPad is a *word processor* — an application used to create text-based documents such as memos, letters, reports, and so on. In this section, we will be viewing WordPad as an example of a typical Windows 95 application, but in the process you will learn enough to use it to produce very simple documents. WordPad's features will be discussed in more detail in Chapter 7.

To start WordPad, select Programs from the Start menu and Accessories from the resulting submenu. Then, click on the WordPad item on the Accessories submenu. This action starts WordPad and opens a window similar to the one in Figure 4. (The Toolbar, Format Bar, Ruler, and Status Bar may or may not be displayed.)

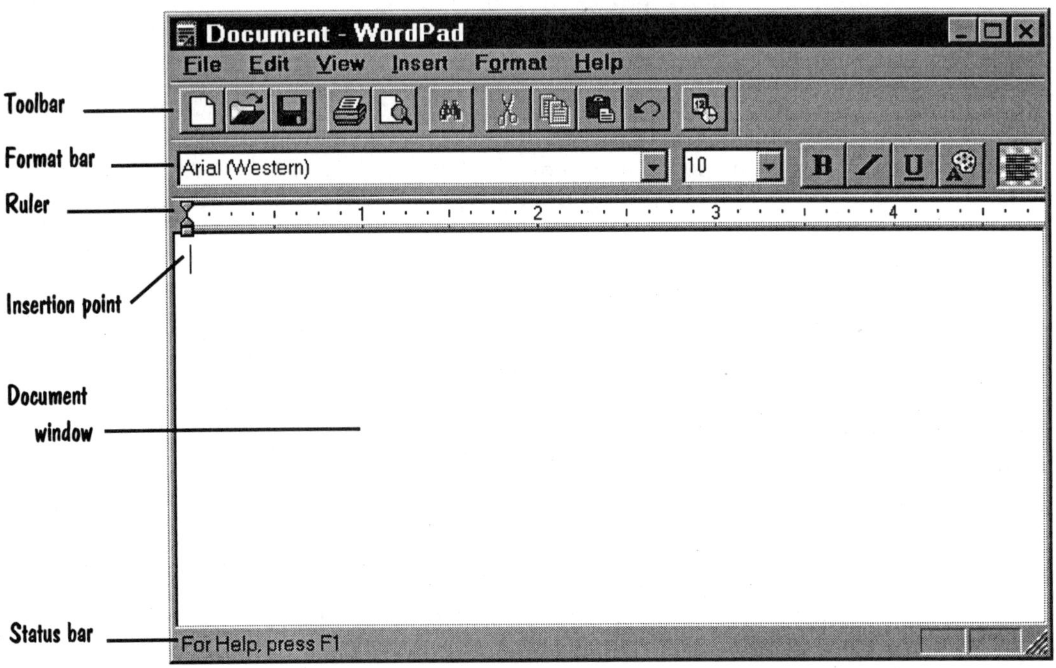


**Figure 4** The WordPad Window

**Entering text** Once you have started WordPad, type whatever you want at the keyboard; the corresponding text will appear in the *document window* and be stored in the computer's internal memory, RAM. The *insertion point*, the blinking vertical bar, indicates where the next character you type will appear on the screen.

When you reach the end of a line, just keep typing; WordPad's *word wrap* feature will automatically continue the text at the beginning of the next line. To start a new line manually, press the Enter key and the insertion point will also move to the beginning of the next line. To skip a line, press Enter again. (When you reach the bottom of the window, moving to the next line will scroll the window down.)

For example, if you type your name, your class, and the date, pressing the Enter key after your name and class, the three entries will appear on separate lines. Moreover, if you press Enter *twice* after the date and then type Homework 1, the screen will look like the one shown in Figure 5.

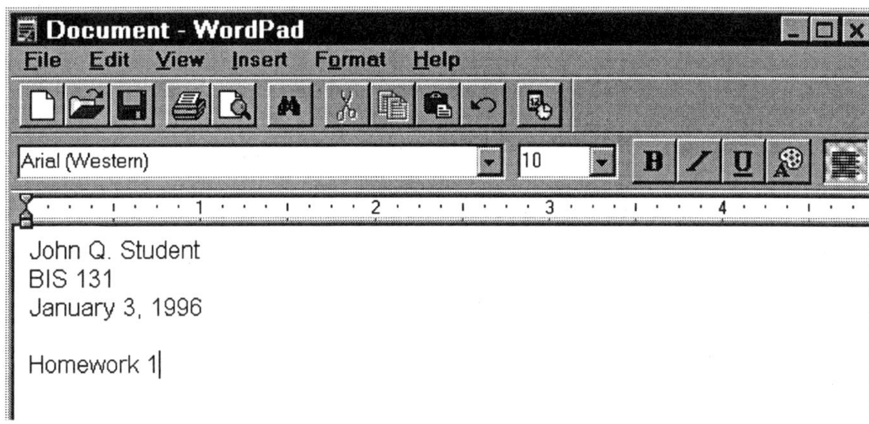


**Figure 5** Entering Text into the WordPad Window

**Correcting mistakes** It is very easy to correct typing errors. To erase the character just to the *left* of the insertion point, press the Backspace key (which may be labeled ←); to delete the character just to the *right* of the insertion point, press the Delete (Del) key. Holding down either key erases a succession of characters. You can use the mouse or the keyboard to move the insertion point to a mistake anywhere in the document:

- To use the mouse, scroll the document window (Section 1.3), if necessary, until the desired location is visible on the screen. Then, click on this location to move the insertion point there.
- You can also use the Arrow keys (←, →. ↑, ↓) to move the insertion point left, right, up, or down and to scroll the window.

For example, suppose your screen looks like the one in Figure 5, and you realize you've made a mistake: your middle initial is "X", not "Q". To correct the error:

1. Move the insertion point just before the Q by either mouse-clicking on this location or pressing the Up Arrow key four times and the Left Arrow key six times.

2. Press the Delete key to erase the Q.
3. Type an X.

## *Saving a Document*

The short document we just created (Figure 5) is not only displayed on the screen, but also stored in RAM. If we start a new document, close WordPad, or shut down Windows, the document will be removed from both the screen and RAM. Thus, if we want to retrieve this document in the future, we must store a copy of it on a more permanent medium — we must **save** the document to disk! The save operation, with your help, also provides a name for the document. In this section, we will only discuss how to save a document to a floppy disk (diskette), but once you learn to navigate the Windows 95 folder system (Chapter 3), you will see how to save it to a specified location on a hard disk.

**The Save command**

To save the document that is currently displayed to a floppy disk:

1. Insert the diskette into its drive.
2. Choose Save from the File menu.
   - If this document has been saved before, the current version will be saved under the same name, *replacing the former version on disk.* The File menu will close and you will be returned to the document window.
   - If this document has *not* been saved before, the Save As dialog box (Figure 6) opens and you must carry out all the remaining steps of this procedure.
3. If the *Save in* box does not contain "3½ Floppy" or "5¼ Floppy", then display its drop-down list (like the one at the right) by clicking on the down-triangle. Now select the appropriate floppy drive by clicking on it.

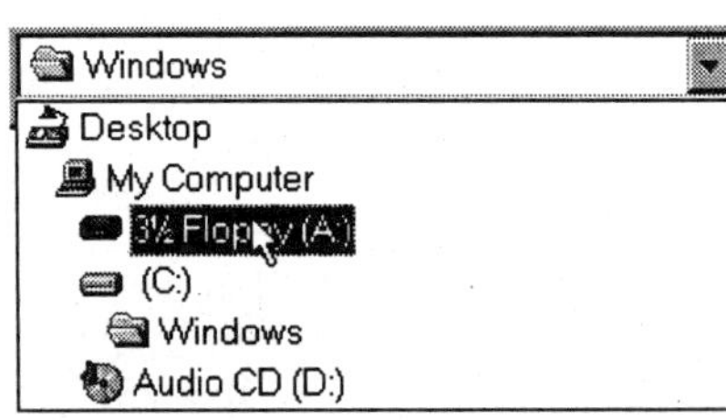


4. Erase the name in the File name text box (click in the box and then use the Delete or Backspace key) and type a name* for the

*If you're using WordPad or another application designed to run under Windows 95, you may choose almost any name up to 255 characters in length. If you're using any other application, the name should be no longer than 8 characters and there are restrictions on the characters you can use. (See Section 3.1 for more information.)

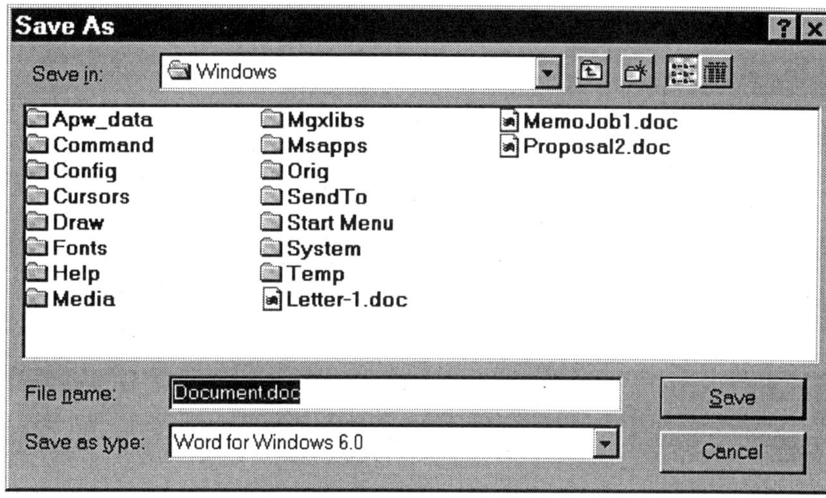


**Figure 6** The Save As Dialog Box

document. For example, in saving the document displayed in Figure 5, we might use the name Homework 1.

5. To complete the save operation (and close the dialog box), press the Enter key or click on the Save command button.

**NOTE**

A simpler way to save a document in WordPad and many other Windows 95 applications is to use its **Toolbar**, which sits just under the title bar, as shown in Figure 4. (If the Toolbar is not visible on the screen, choose the Toolbar item from the View menu to display it.) The icons on the Toolbar provide quick access to certain menu commands. When you mouse-point at one of the icons, a **tool tip** appears, indicating the icon's function:

To activate a Toolbar function, just click on it. For example, clicking on the floppy disk icon has the same effect as choosing Save from the File menu!

TIP

The Save As command

On occasion, you may make changes to a document, but want to keep both the old and new versions. In this case, you cannot use the Save command; it will automatically erase the old version while saving the new one. Instead, you should choose the Save As item from the File menu, which displays the Save As dialog box even though the current document has been previously saved. Now, just save the new (current) version under a name different from the old one, and both versions are safely stored on disk.

## Closing a Document

To **close** a document means to remove it from both the screen and RAM. When you exit a Windows application, any open documents are closed automatically. You may, however, wish to close a document before exiting your application, perhaps to begin working on another document. To accomplish this in WordPad:

The New command

1. Choose New from the File menu or click on the New icon on the Toolbar. The New dialog box will be displayed.

2. Activate the OK command button to accept the default document type. If you have not saved the latest changes to this document, a message similar to the following one will appear:

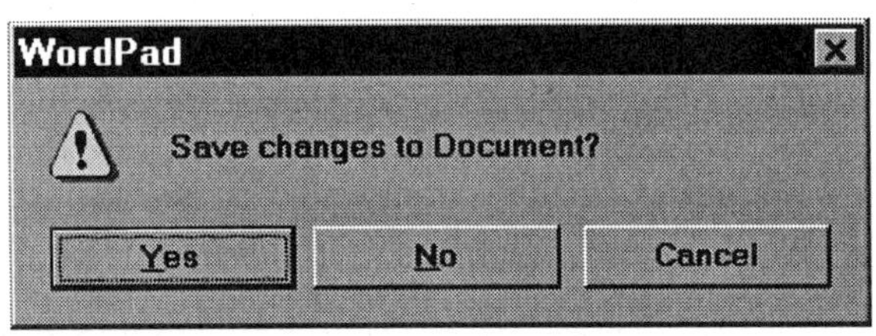


3. Choose the Yes command button and Windows will give you the opportunity to save your changes; choose No and the document will close, but your changes will not be saved to disk. Clicking on the Cancel button (or pressing the Escape key) returns you to the document; it will not close.

NOTE

WordPad only allows one document window to be open at any time. Certain other Windows applications allow multiple open document windows. Choosing New in such a case does not close the current document; it just clears it from the screen. To close a document when multiple open windows are allowed, choose Close from the File menu.

## *Opening a Document*

When you save a document, it is stored on disk under the name you have chosen for it. Saving it does not remove it from the screen or the computer's RAM, so you *can* continue to work on it. However, after the document has been closed, to work on it again you must have Windows copy it from disk into RAM and display it on the screen. In other words, you must **open** the document. Just as there are many ways to open an application, Windows 95 provides many ways to open a document.

**The Open command**

To open a document within an application that is already running, one normally uses the Open command. We will demonstrate here how to use this command to open a document that is stored on a floppy disk, but once you learn to navigate the Windows 95 folder system, it will be just as easy to open any document. To open a document stored on a diskette:

1. Start (if necessary) the application that created the document.
2. Insert the diskette containing the document into its drive.
3. Choose Open from the File menu or click on the Open icon on the Toolbar. The Open dialog box, like the one in Figure 7, will be displayed. If the floppy drive does not appear in the *Look in* text box, click on the down-triangle and select the floppy drive from the drop-down list.

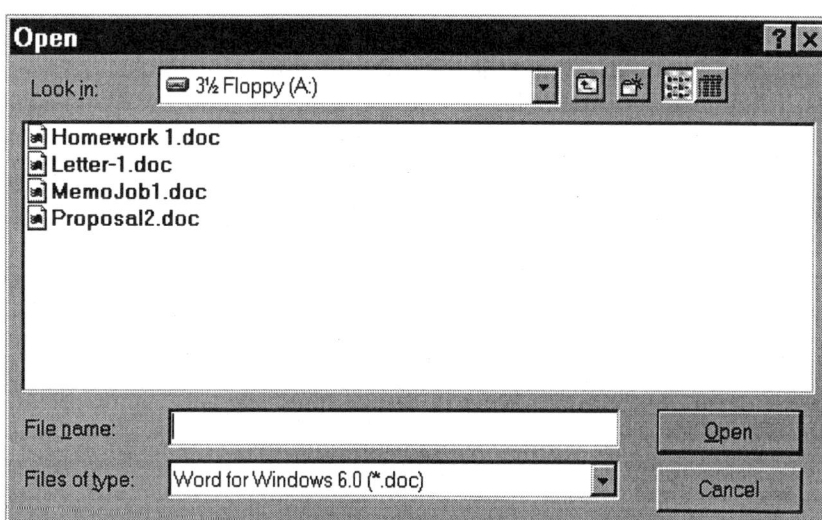


**Figure 7** The Open Dialog Box

4. If the name of the document you want to open isn't listed, display the *Files of type* drop-down list and select the entry labeled "All Documents (*.*)". A new, probably longer, list of names will be displayed and the document you are seeking may be one of them.
5. Select the document you want to open from the list. It will become highlighted.
6. Activate the Open command button. The dialog box will close and the specified document will open.

**Open programs and documents simultaneously**

The Open command works well if the relevant application is already running. If it isn't, you may be able to open a document and the application that created it at the same time using one of the following simple techniques:

- If the document to be opened is represented by an icon (a *shortcut*) on the Desktop, just double-click on this icon. The application associated with the document will start running and the document will open within it. (We will discuss how to create shortcuts in Section 3.4.)

**The Documents option**

- If the document was created by a Windows 95-based application and was saved recently, then to open it:
  1. Select the Documents option from the Start menu (by clicking on the Start button and pointing at *Documents*). A submenu of the last 15 documents that were saved will be displayed.
  2. Click on the desired document. The application associated with it will start and open the document, as well.

**NOTE**

These simple techniques may not always work as planned. When you double-click on a document's icon or select an item from the Documents submenu, Windows 95 sometimes starts an application other than the one that created the specified document.

For example, on our Documents submenu, there is a file named "Homework 1.doc". This document was created by WordPad and saved earlier in this section. (The ".doc" *extension* in the name was added automatically by Windows when the document was saved.) But, when we click on Homework 1.doc in the list of documents, Windows interprets the extension as that of a document created by the Microsoft Word word processor, and starts this application instead of WordPad.

## *Printing a Document*

When you **print** a document, you send a copy of it to a printer. Here is the most straightforward way to print a document:

1. Open the document if it is not already on screen.
2. Choose the Print command from the File menu. The Print dialog box will open, as shown in Figure 8.

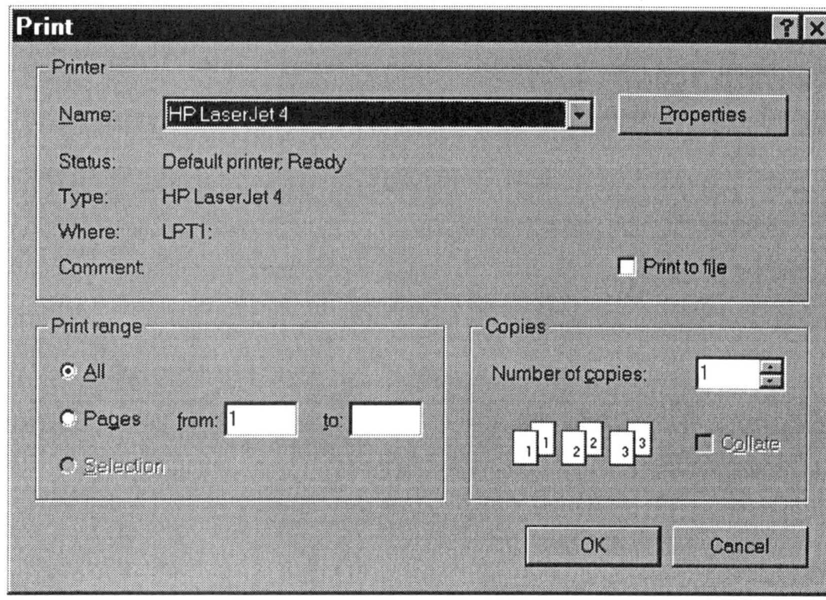


**Figure 8** The Print Dialog Box

3. Make the desired selections from this dialog box:
   - If your computer is connected to more than one printer, you can select the one you want to use from the Printer Name drop-down list.
   - If you don't want to print the entire document (indicated by the *All* option button), you can print a range of pages by clicking on the *Pages* option button and then filling in the *from* and *to* text boxes. You can also *select* a portion of your document (as described in Section 2.3) prior to opening the Print dialog box and then print just the selected text by clicking on the Selection option button.
   - If you want to print more than one copy, change the number that appears in the *Number of copies* text box. To collate (sort) the copies, select this check box.
4. Make sure that the selected printer is ready to receive information.

5. Activate the OK command button. The document (or the selected portion of the document) will be printed.

TIP

If you want to print a document using the default information in the Print dialog box (for example, all pages and one copy), you need not open this dialog box. Just click on the Print icon on the Toolbar. The dialog box will not be displayed and the print process will begin immediately.

2.2 TUTORIAL

Try the following exercises on your own.

1. Turn on your computer (if it's not already on) to start up Windows 95.
2. Start the WordPad word processor: Click on the Start button, point at Programs to open this submenu, point at Accessories to open a second submenu, and then click on WordPad on the latter.
3. Insert the Lab Exercises diskette in its drive and open the `Homework 1` document that is stored on it: Choose Open from the File menu, select the floppy drive from the *Look in* drop-down list, click on the name "Homework 1", and activate the Open command button.
4. Edit the Homework 1 document so that it gives *your* name and class and the current date. To do so:
   - Repeatedly press the Delete key until the current name is erased.
   - Type in your name.
   - Click the mouse pointer (an "I-beam" symbol) at the beginning of the next line (or press the Right Arrow key once) to move the insertion point to this location.
   - Repeat these steps to correct the class and date.
5. Save the new document under the new name `My Homework 1`: Choose the Save As (*not* Save) command from the File menu, select the floppy drive from the *Save in* drop-down list, type the new name in the *File name* text box, and activate the Save command button.
6. Print the current document: Either
   - Choose Print from the File menu and activate the OK button.

   *or*
   - Click on the printer icon on the Toolbar. (If it is currently not visible, choose Toolbar from the View menu to display it.)
7. Clear the current document from the screen: Select New from the

File menu (or click on the "page" icon on the Toolbar) and then activate the OK command button in the dialog box.

8. Exit WordPad: Choose Exit from its File menu or click on the close button on the title bar.

## 2.3 Running Several Applications at Once

As you know, Windows allows you to run several applications at the same time, each of which is instantly available. To see how this can be useful, suppose that you are using the WordPad word processor to write a report and you realize that a picture will illustrate your point better than the proverbial thousand words. To create the picture, you start Paint, the painting program supplied with Windows 95 and which (like WordPad) is found on the Accessories submenu of the Start menu's Programs option.

Starting Paint does not close WordPad, so these two applications are now both running at the same time (see Figure 9). After completing

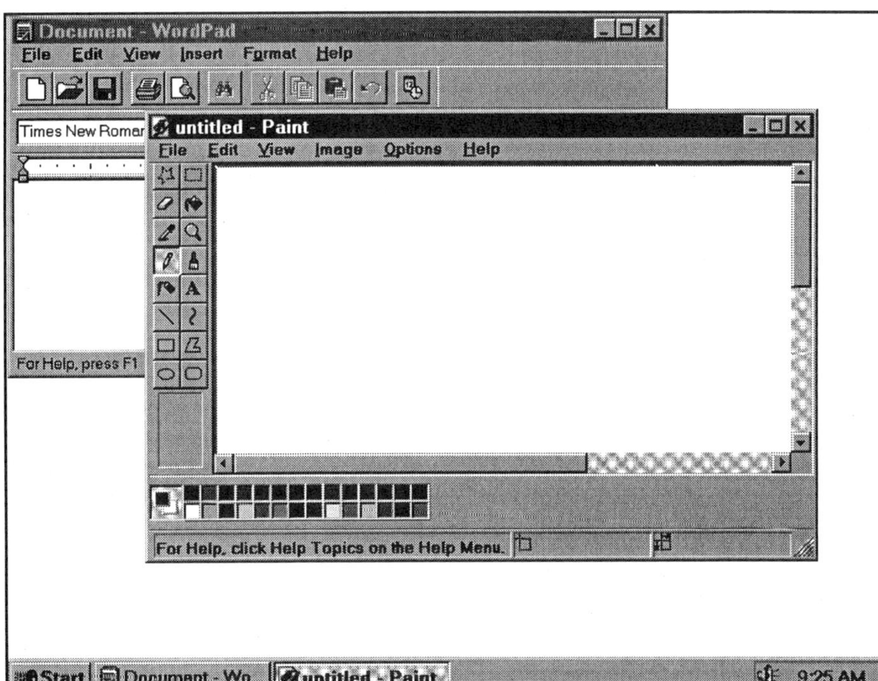


**Figure 9** WordPad and Paint Open on the Desktop

your picture, you switch back to WordPad, copy the picture into the word processing document, and continue writing. Before you finish this Windows session, you might use other applications as well, perhaps to make a backup copy of your documents or just to take a break with a computer game.

To make use of the kind of flexibility illustrated in this scenario, you have to be able to quickly and easily switch among several running applications and to transfer information between them. We will discuss these techniques in the remainder of this section.

## *Switching Among Applications*

Each application that is currently running is represented by a button on the Taskbar. The program in which you are currently working is called the **active application.** Its Taskbar button appears to be "brighter" than the others and its title bar is highlighted (see the Paint button and title bar in Figure 9).

**Ways to switch applications**

To switch from the active application to an inactive one, perform any of the following actions:

- If any portion of the inactive program's window is visible, just click within that window. It becomes the active one and moves to the front.
- Click on the inactive program's Taskbar button. (Remember: If the Taskbar is not visible on the screen, it can be displayed by pressing the Ctrl+Esc keystroke combination.) This application becomes the active one and its window is displayed on the screen.
- Hold down the Alt key and press the Tab key. A window similar to the following one will appear on the screen:

In this window, each icon represents a currently running program. The application corresponding to the "boxed in" icon has its name displayed on the line below. To cycle through your running applications, continue to hold down the Alt key, and repeatedly press the Tab key; the "box" will move from icon to icon. When the name of the desired application appears in the window, release the Alt key. Windows makes this application the active one and displays it on the screen.

## *Transferring Information between Documents*

The process of transferring information — for example, a block of text or a picture — from one document (the *source*) to another (the *target*) usually involves the following steps:

1. In the source document, *select the information* to be transferred. Here's how to select a *block of text* while running any Windows application. Either

   - Position the mouse pointer in front of the first character in the desired block of text and drag the insertion point to the end of the block.

   *or*

   - Position the insertion point in front of the first character in the desired block of text, hold down the Shift key, move the insertion point to the end of the block (for example, using the Arrow keys), and then release Shift.

   In either case, the selected text will be highlighted. (If you want to *deselect* the text, just click the mouse anywhere else in the document or press an Arrow key.)

2. *Cut* or *copy* the selected information to the Windows **Clipboard**, a temporary storage location in RAM set aside for this purpose. When information is **cut**, it is deleted from the source document and moved to the Clipboard; when information is **copied**, it is also transferred to the Clipboard, but the source document remains unchanged. To perform the cut or copy operation, choose the Cut or Copy command from the source application's Edit menu.

**WARNING**

The Clipboard can only hold one block of information at a time. Thus, when you cut or copy something to the Clipboard, Windows automatically erases the previous contents (if any). No warning message will be issued!

You can examine the current contents of the Clipboard by opening the **Clipboard Viewer** utility. (Some configurations of Windows 95 contain **Clip*book* Viewer** instead.) To start Clipboard Viewer, choose this item from the Accessories submenu of the Start button. The current Clipboard contents will be displayed in the Clipboard Viewer window. (Clipbook is also started from the Accessories submenu, but the contents of the Clipboard are not displayed automatically; you have to choose the Clipboard command from the Window menu.)

3. Start, or switch to, the target application (unless the source and target are the same) and open the target document, if necessary.
4. In the target document, position the cursor where you want to insert the information.
5. **Paste** (insert) the information on the Clipboard into the target document at the cursor position by choosing the Paste command from the target application's Edit menu.

   Pictorially, the process looks like this:

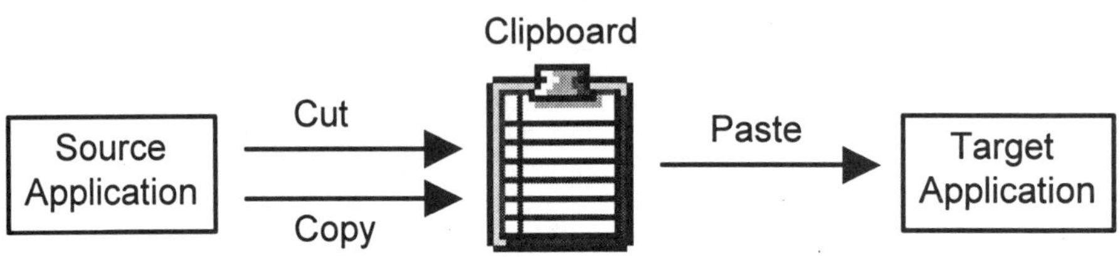


TIP

Here are a couple of other ways to issue the cut/copy or paste commands that work with many Windows applications. After selecting the text to be transferred to the Clipboard, you can *cut or copy* it by either

- Pressing Ctrl+X for cut or Ctrl+C for copy.

*or*

- Positioning the mouse pointer over the selected text, right-clicking, and choosing Cut or Copy from the resulting menu.

To *paste* text from the Clipboard, position the cursor where you want to insert the text and then, either press Ctrl+V or right-click the mouse and choose Paste from the resulting menu.

NOTE

If you want to copy the *entire current screen* to the Clipboard, press the Print Screen key. To copy the *active window* to the Clipboard, press Alt+Print Screen. In both cases, you can paste these graphics into the target document in the usual way, as described in steps 4 and 5 of the procedure given above.

## An Example

Now let's take a look at a specific example of the cut/copy and paste process. We will copy some text from a WordPad document into a Notepad document. (Notepad is a very simple word processor, a *text editor*, supplied with Windows 95.) First we start WordPad and open the Homework 1 document, which can be found on the Lab Exercises disk. The resulting WordPad window is shown in Figure 10.

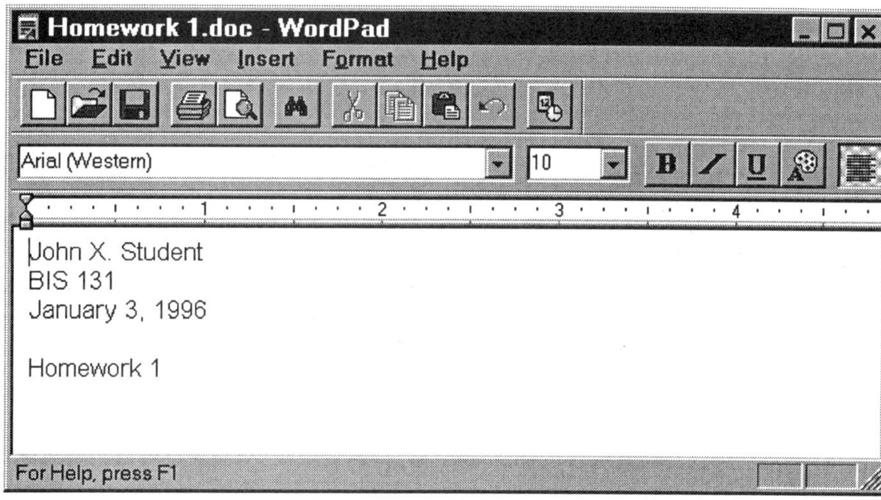


**Figure 10** The Text to be Copied

Suppose we want to copy the first three lines (the student's name, his class, and the date). To do so, we must first select the text. Notice that the insertion point in Figure 10 is already positioned at the beginning of this block of text. So, all we need do to select it is

- Hold down the Shift key, tap the Down Arrow key three times, and release Shift.

*or*

- Position the mouse pointer at the insertion point and drag it down until the first three lines are highlighted.

in either case, the text in the window will look like this:

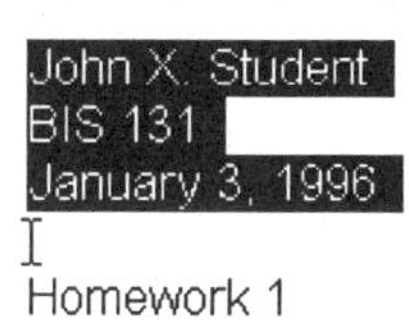


Now, we copy the selected text to the Clipboard by choosing the Copy command from WordPad's Edit menu.

To paste the contents of the Clipboard into Notepad, we start this application by clicking on its name on the Accessories submenu of the

Start menu's Programs option. (Or, if Notepad is already running, we switch to it by clicking on its Taskbar button.) Then, we choose the Paste command from Notepad's Edit menu. The selected text will be transferred to the beginning of the Notepad document, as pictured in Figure 11. (Notice that the pasted text has a somewhat different appearance from the original. This occurs because Notepad only displays text in the font — typeface — shown in the figure.)

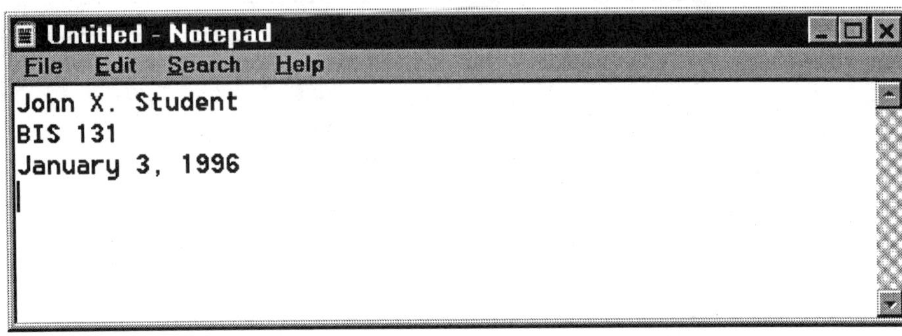


**Figure 11** The Original Text Pasted into Notepad

**2-3 TUTORIAL**

Try the following exercises on your own.

1. Turn on your computer (if it's not already on) to start up Windows 95. Close any open windows.
2. Start the WordPad word processor (from the Accessories submenu of the Start menu's Programs option).
3. Type the text: `This is a test.`
4. Select this block of text by either:
   - Dragging the insertion point to the beginning of the sentence.

   *or*
   - Holding down the Shift key, tapping the Left Arrow key until the insertion point is at the beginning of the sentence, and releasing Shift.

   In either case, the sentence should now be highlighted.
5. *Cut* the selected text to the Clipboard by choosing Cut from WordPad's Edit menu or by pressing Ctrl+X.
6. Start the Notepad application by clicking on its name on the Accessories submenu of the Start menu's Programs option.

7. *Paste* the text from the Clipboard into Notepad by choosing Paste from its Edit menu or by pressing Ctrl+V.
8. Switch to WordPad by clicking on its Taskbar button. (If the Taskbar isn't visible, press Ctrl+Esc to display it.)
9. Paste the sentence into the WordPad document by right-clicking the mouse and selecting Paste from the resulting menu.
10. Close WordPad and then close Notepad, answering No to the "Save changes?" warning message in both cases.

# 2.4 Getting On-screen Help

No matter how experienced you become at using Windows and its applications, there will be times when you'll need some help in performing a particular task. At such a time, you might find the answer to your questions in this book, but it may be more convenient to use the Windows 95 **online help** system. This powerful feature provides immediate on-screen information about Windows itself or the Windows application that is currently active on your Desktop.

## Accessing Online Help

**Types of help available**

The Windows 95 Help system provides access to several kinds of online help:

1. Extensive help is available for Windows itself and can be accessed at any time. This kind of help includes general information about using Windows, procedures for performing specific tasks, and troubleshooting advice when things go wrong.
2. Application-specific help is provided by the publisher of each program you use. This help can be accessed while that application is running.
3. *Context-sensitive* help provides help with the task at hand. It is available for Windows 95 itself and for most Windows-based applications.

**Starting the Help system**

How you enter the Windows Help system depends on the kind of help you need:

- To access help with Windows 95, click on the Start button and then click on the Help option on the Start menu. The dialog box shown in Figure 12 will open.

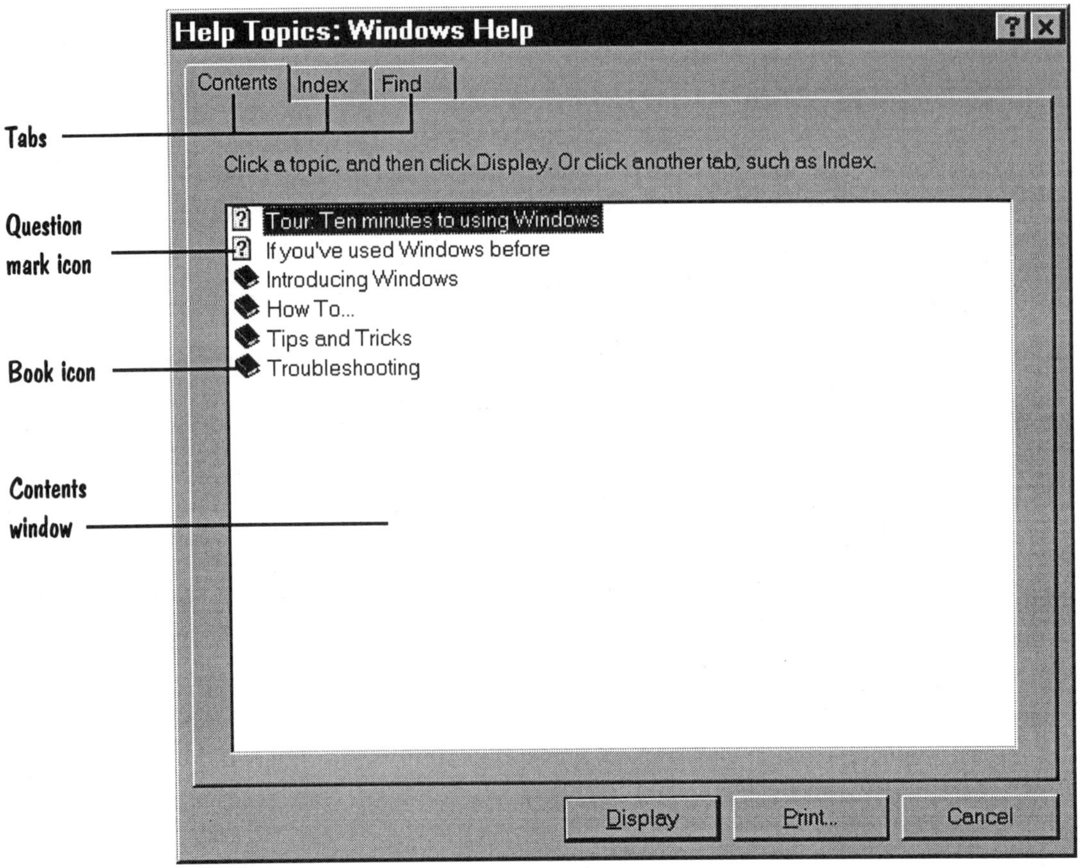


**Figure 12** The Windows Help Topics Dialog Box

- Help for the active Windows application can be accessed by displaying that program's Help menu and choosing the option entitled Help Topics or Help Contents. If this application was designed to run under Windows 95, a dialog box similar to the one in Figure 12 will open; if not, a Help dialog box will open, but it may look considerably different from the one in Figure 12.
- There are a couple of ways to access context-sensitive help. We will discuss them at the end of this section.

## *Locating the Information You Need*

Notice that the Help Topics dialog box in Figure 12 has three tabs: Contents, Index, and Find. The corresponding pages of this dialog box provide different ways to locate the information you need.

**The Contents Page** Clicking on the Contents tab (if this page is not already displayed) provides access to information of a general nature. For example, as you can see in Figure 12, the Windows Help Contents topics include a brief "tour" of Windows, procedures for performing some common tasks, and help with troubleshooting.

If a topic in the Contents window is preceded by a book icon (such as "Introducing Windows" in Figure 12), double-clicking on this topic will "open the book" and display a list of subtopics. For example, Figure 13 shows the Contents window after double-clicking on Introducing Windows and then double-clicking on Welcome.

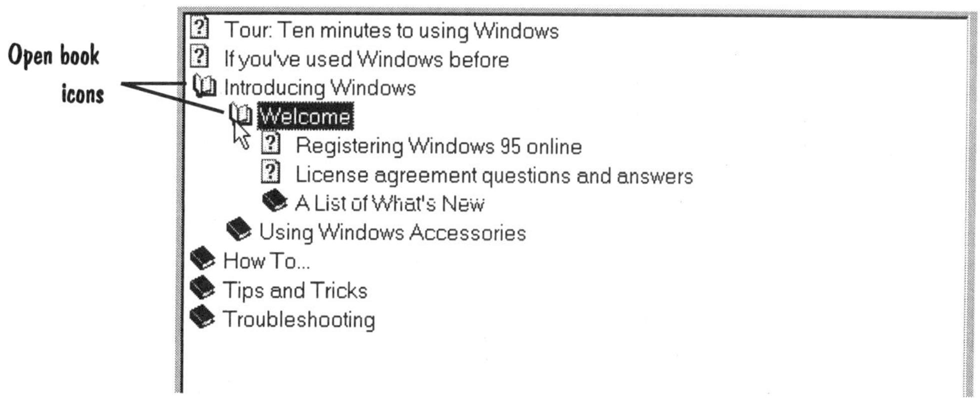


**Figure 13** Displaying Subtopics in the Contents Window

If a topic on the Contents list is preceded by a question-mark icon (such as "If you've used Windows before" in Figure 13), double-clicking on that topic will open a Help window supplying information about it. (You can also open the topic's Help window by clicking on the topic, which highlights it, and then activating the Display command button.) We will discuss these Help windows later in this section.

Instead of viewing information about a topic on-screen, you can print this material by clicking on the desired topic and activating the Print command button. The Print dialog box, like the one shown in Figure 8 of Section 2.2, will appear on the screen. To begin printing, activate the OK command button.

**The Index Page** Clicking on the Index tab of the Help Topics dialog box displays a much more detailed list of items than Contents (see Figure 14).

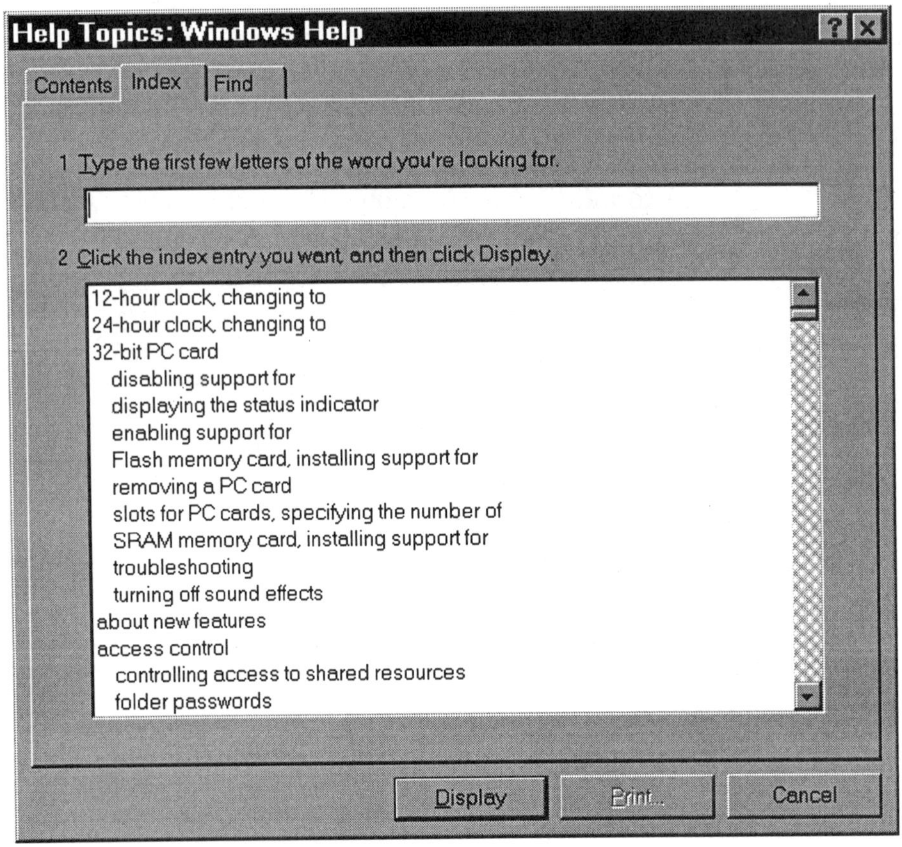


**Figure 14** The Index Page of the Help Topics Dialog Box

To use Index to open a Help window for a particular topic:

1. Double-click on the desired item, or click on it and then click on the Display button. (To move quickly through the list of items, type the first few letters of the topic you're seeking in the text box; the first topic beginning with these letters is highlighted.)
2. If there is more than one topic associated with the item you have chosen in step 1, a Topics Found dialog box will open, displaying a list of subtopics. Double-click on the desired topic (or click on it and then on Display).

**The Find Page** Windows 95 and applications designed for it contain a *Find utility* that enables you to search Help for a specific word or phrase. When the Find utility is first accessed for Windows or an application, it searches the relevant Help files and creates a database of the words it finds. Once the database is set up, you can use Find by clicking on its tab in the Help Topics dialog box (the result is shown in Figure 15) and carrying out these three steps:

1. Type a key word in the text box at the top of the Find page. For example, if you are trying to determine how to use your modem with Windows to place a phone call, you might type *phone.* Now click on the Find Now command button, and a list of words in the Find database that match your key word will appear in the middle window. (If Find Now is dimmed, the list of words will appear as you type.)
2. From the list in the middle window, select the words in which you are interested. To select words, click on the first, then hold down the Ctrl key as you click on the others. For example, if you're interested in phone calls, select *phone*, *Phone*, and *telephone* in

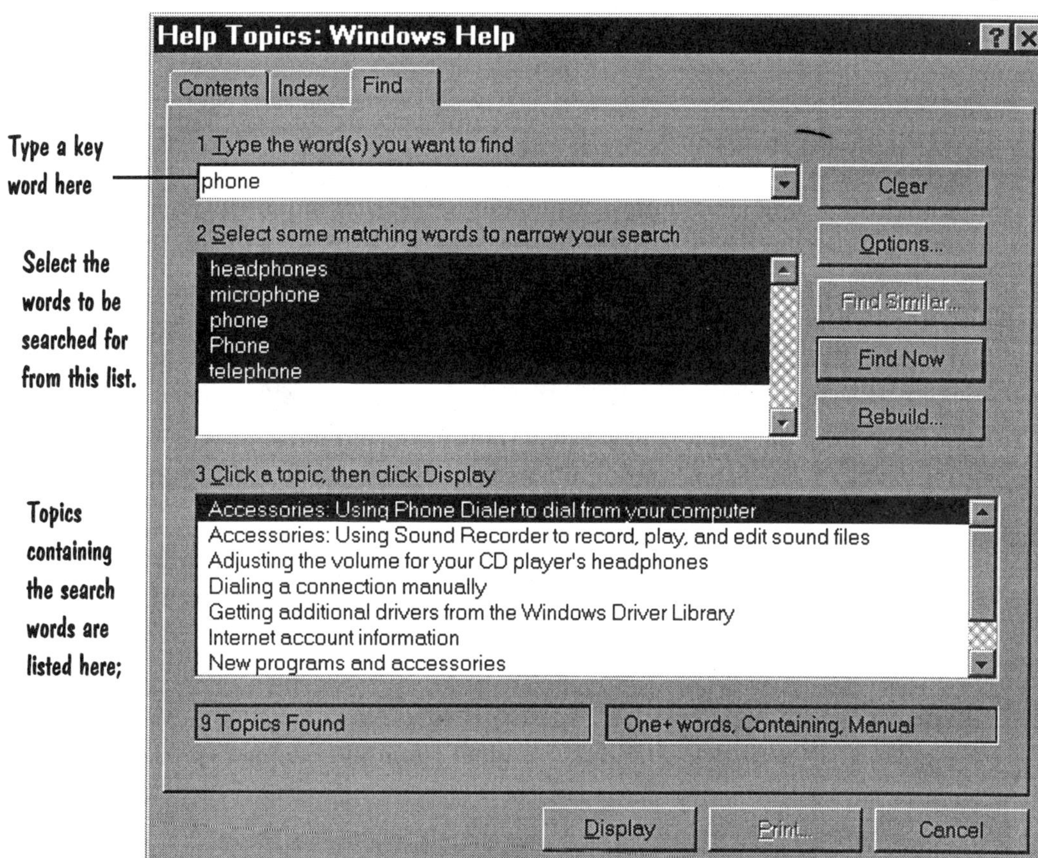


**Figure 15** The Find Page of the Help Topics Dialog Box

this manner. The topics that contain these words then appear in the bottom window.

3. Select a topic from the bottom window by clicking on it and then activating the Display button (or just double-clicking on the topic). The Help window for this topic will open.

TIP You can use any of the three Help Topics pages — Contents, Index, or Find — to display the Help window for a specific topic. The Contents option (like the table of contents for a book) usually contains just a few relatively broad topics. This option is useful if you want to browse through general information. The Index option (like the index of a book) contains a much more detailed list of topics. This is usually the first place you would go for help with a specific task. The Find utility is a little less convenient to use than the Contents or Index, but it will locate information that the other two cannot.

## *Using a Help Window*

Activating the Display command button in the Help Topics dialog box opens a **Help window** displaying information about the selected topic. For example, Figure 16 shows the Help window containing information about using the Windows 95 Phone Dialer accessory.

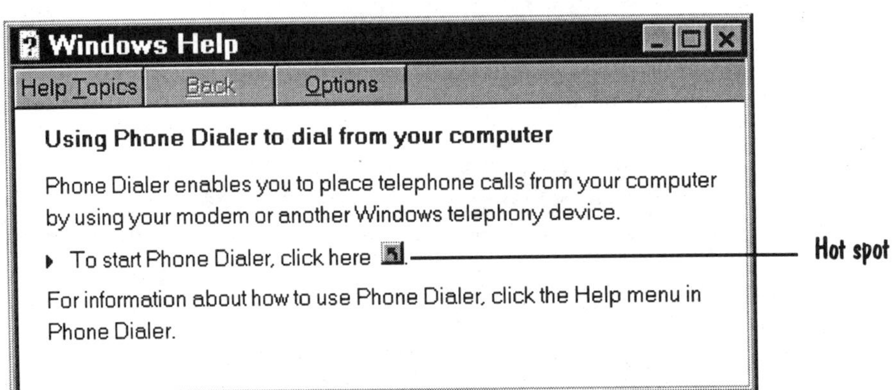


**Figure 16** A Typical Help Window

**Features of a Help window**

Here are some features of the Help window:

- You can return to the Help Topics dialog box by clicking on the

Help Topics command button.

- You can return to a previous Help window by clicking on the Back command button.
- If you click on the Options command button (or right-click in the window) a menu is displayed that allows you to

    *Annotate* the topic; that is, associate additional information with it. Once the topic is annotated, a paper clip icon appears next to its title; clicking on this icon opens a dialog box that displays your annotation.

    *Copy* the contents of the Help window to the Clipboard.

    *Print* the contents of the Help window on a printer.

    Choose from three *font* sizes for the Help window's text.

    Choose to keep the Help window *on top* so that it doesn't disappear from view when you switch to an application.

- Some windows contain **hot spots**, represented by small square buttons. If you mouse point at one of these, the pointer becomes a hand icon. Clicking on a hot spot, opens a new window with related information, or, if the hot spot contains an arrow, clicking on it opens an application.

## *Context-Sensitive Help*

**Context-sensitive help** provides information about some aspect of the task at hand. For example, suppose you've opened the Run dialog box (see Section 2.1) but have forgotten the purpose of the Browse command button. You can use Windows 95 online context-sensitive help to explain its function without bringing up the entire Help system. Context-sensitive help, when it's available, can be accessed in several ways:

- If the active window contains a question-mark button on the title bar, click on this button. The cursor will become an arrow with the question-mark attached, as shown at the right. Now click on the item for which you want help, and a small window will pop up, displaying information about this object. For example, if you click on the question-mark icon in the Run dialog box and then click on the Browse command button, the pop-up window shown at the top of the next page will appear.

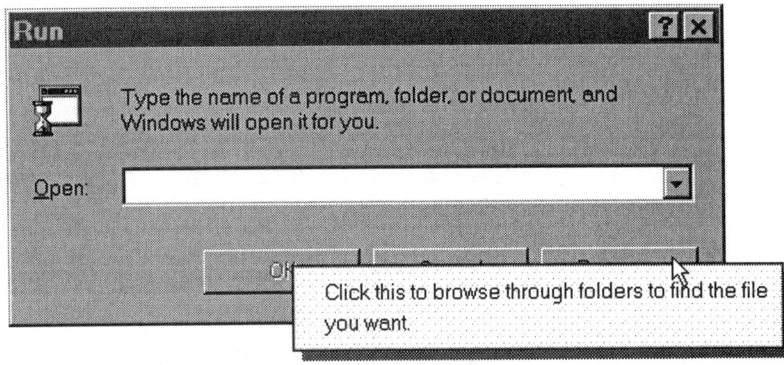


To close the pop up window, click anywhere on the screen.

- With Windows 95 and most applications designed for it, you can right-click on an object to access context-sensitive help. Right-clicking displays a one-item *What's This?* menu:

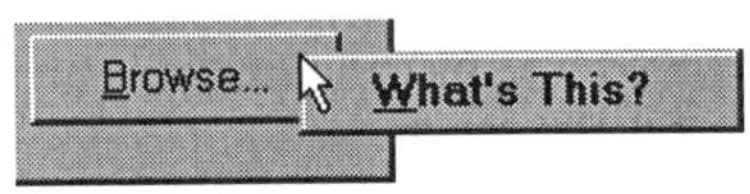


Click on this command to open an explanatory pop-up window.

- When using an older Windows application, you probably won't see a question-mark button and right-clicking on an object probably won't work either. However, the application's dialog boxes may contain a Help command that gives information about using that dialog box. If not, try pressing the Shift+F1 keystroke combination or just the F1 function key to get help with the dialog box.

**2-4 TUTORIAL**

Try the following exercises on your own.

1. Turn on your computer (if necessary) to start Windows 95.
2. Start Windows 95 Help by clicking on the Start button and then clicking on the Start menu's Help option. The Windows Help Topics dialog box will open.
3. Let's locate information about the Calculator accessory that is supplied with Windows 95:
   - Click on the Index tab to display the Index page.
   - Type the word *calculator* in the text box.
   - In the topics window, double-click on the word *starting* a couple of lines below the "Calculator" entry.

A Help window entitled "Using Calculator to make calculations" will open.

4. Click on the *hot spot* — the small gray button with a curved arrow on it — to start Calculator. Its window will appear on the screen.
5. Now let's get some general information about Calculator:
   - Choose Help Topics from the Help menu. The Calculator Help Topics window will open.
   - Click on the Contents tab (if necessary) to display this page.
   - Display the list of subtopics under *Performing Calculations* by double-clicking on its "book" icon. Then, click on *Performing a simple calculation* and click on the Display command button. A Help window with information about this topic will open.
6. Click on the Options command button to display the Options menu and successively choose each option to see what it does.
7. Click on the Help Topics command button to return to the Calculator Help Topics dialog box.
8. Click on the Find tab to display the Find page. (If the Find Setup Wizard dialog box appears, click on the Next command button, then on the Finish button.)
9. Let's search for information on clearing the calculator's memory:
   - Type *clear* in the text box. One or two words will appear in the middle window and one or two topics in the bottom window.
   - Select (click on) the topic "Working with numbers stored in memory" and activate the Display command button. A Help window with information on this topic will open.
10. Click on the Back command button to return to the first Calculator Help window. Close this window. Calculator will become active.
11. Notice that one of the calculator keys is labeled *Back*. To determine the function of this key:
    - Right-click on it. The one-item *What's This?* menu will be displayed.
    - Click on the *What's This?* command. A window will pop up explaining the function of the Back key. Click anywhere in the Calculator window to close the pop-up window.
12. Close the Calculator application.

# Review Exercises

**Section 2.1**

1. You can open the Start menu by clicking on the Start button or by pressing the ___________ keystroke combination.
2. Positioning the mouse pointer over the ___________ item on the Start menu displays a menu of applications and groups of applications.
3. To close an application, you can choose ___________ from the File menu.
4. True or false: You can start an application that is represented by an icon on the Desktop by double-clicking on that icon.
5. True or false: To start a program named MyProg on the floppy disk in the A: drive, choose Run from the Start menu, type A:MyProg in the dialog box, and press the Enter key.
6. True or false: All DOS applications are exited in the same way as a Windows application.
7. Which of the following items on the Start menu cannot be used to open an application?
   a. Programs
   b. Documents
   c. Settings
   d. Run
8. Which of the following actions will not close a Windows application?
   a. Clicking on its close button.
   b. Clicking on its minimize button.
   c. Right-clicking on its Taskbar button and choosing Close from the resulting menu.
   d. Pressing the Alt+F4 keystroke combination.

**Section 2.2**

9. WordPad is listed on the ___________ submenu, which contains a group of small applications built into Windows 95.
10. To ___________ a document means to copy it from the computer's RAM onto disk.
11. To ___________ a document means to copy it from disk into RAM and simultaneously display it on the screen.
12. The ___________ option on the Start menu displays a list of the last 15 documents that were saved by Windows 95-based applications.

13. True or false: Choosing New from WordPad's File menu closes the current document and clears the document window.
14. True or false: If you create but never save a document, you will not be able to open it once it has been closed.
15. True or false: You can open, close, save, and print a WordPad document by using its Toolbar.
16. True or false: If you click on the print icon on the WordPad Toolbar, one copy of the entire on-screen document will be printed.
17. WordPad's File menu contains two different commands for
    a. Saving a document.
    b. Opening a document.
    c. Printing a document.
    d. Exiting the application.
18. To save a document that is not yet named:
    a. You can use the Open command.
    b. You can use the Save command.
    c. You can use the New command.
    d. None of the above commands can do the job.

**Section 2.3**

19. To switch to an inactive application, you can click on its button located on the ___________.
20. You can select a block of text by positioning the insertion point at the beginning of the block and holding down the ___________ key as you move the insertion point to the end of the block.
21. When information is cut or copied from a document, it is transferred to the Windows ___________.
22. True or false: Windows 95 allows you to have more than one application window open on the screen.
23. True or false: When information is transferred to the Clipboard, its previous contents (if any) are erased.
24. True or false: Pressing the Print Screen key copies the entire screen to the Clipboard.
25. Which of the following techniques cannot be used to switch to an inactive application?
    a. Click on the inactive application's window.
    b. Click on the inactive application's Taskbar button.
    c. Press the Ctrl+Esc keystroke combination.
    d. Press the Alt+Tab keystroke combination.

26. To transfer selected information to the Clipboard and simultaneously delete it from a document:
    a. Choose Cut from the application's Edit menu.
    b. Choose Copy from the application's Edit menu.
    c. Choose Paste from the application's Edit menu.
    d. Choose Delete from the application's Edit menu.

**Section 2.4**

27. To obtain online help for Windows itself, click on the Help item on the ___________ menu.
28. To obtain online help for the active application, click on Help Topics on the ___________ menu.
29. If a topic on the Contents page of the Help Topics dialog box is preceded by a ___________ icon, it contains a list of subtopics.
30. If you would like to change the font size of the text in a Help window, begin by clicking on the ___________ command button.
31. True or false: If a window has a question-mark button on the title bar, you can click on this button to access context-sensitive help.
32. True or false: Clicking on a hot spot in a Help window displays a new window or starts an application.
33. True or false: If you can't locate the topic you're seeking in the Help Topics Index, you should try the Help Topics Find utility.
34. Which of the following is not a tab in a Help Topics dialog box:
    a. Contents
    b. Glossary
    c. Index
    d. Find
35. The Options menu in a Help window allows you to
    a. Return to the Help Topics dialog box.
    b. Return to a previous Help window.
    c. Print the contents of the window.
    d. Change the size of the Help window.
36. To obtain context-sensitive help in a Windows 95 dialog box:
    a. Click on an object in the box.
    b Double-click on an object in the box.
    c. Right-click on an object in the box.
    d. Drag the *What's This?* button onto an object.

# Lab Exercises

Work each of the following exercises at your computer. Begin by turning the machine on (if necessary) to start Windows 95. Then, close all open windows.

**Lab Exercise 1 (Section 2.1)**

a. Start MS-DOS Prompt, which is a DOS application that appears on the Programs submenu of the Start menu. If, once MS-DOS Prompt is open, you don't see a title bar, press Alt+Enter to run MS-DOS Prompt in a window.

b. Try to close MS-DOS Prompt by pressing Alt+F4. Does this work? If not, try to close its window by clicking on the close button. If this doesn't work, type Exit and press the Enter key.

c. Insert the Lab Exercises disk in its drive and start the Dosprog program on this disk by using the Start menu's Run command. What did you type in the text box to get Dosprog to open?

d. If Dosprog is not running in a window, press Alt+Enter. Try to close this application by clicking on its close button. What does the resulting dialog box tell you? (Click on the No button.)

e. Exit Dosprog by pressing the Enter key. Notice that its window remains on the screen, but the title bar has changed. What word now appears on it?

f. Click on the close button again to close the Dosprog window, and remove the Lab Exercises disk from its drive.

g. Repeatedly open and close the Windows Explorer application, which can be found on the Programs submenu of the Start menu. Try the following methods for closing it:

Click on its close button.
Right-click on its Taskbar button and choose Close from the resulting menu, if one appears.
Press Alt+F4.
Right-click the title bar and choose Close from the resulting menu, if one appears.

Which techniques worked?

**Lab Exercise 2 (Section 2.2)**

a. Start the WordPad word processor.

b. Type your name, your class, and the date on separate lines. Then, skip a line and type: Chapter 2, Lab Exercise 2

c. Insert the Lab Exercises disk in its drive.

d. Save your document to this diskette; use the name Ch 2, LabEx 1. What name appears on the title bar?

e. Print the document.

f. Type the current time on the same line as the date.

g. Save the revised document using the Save command on the File menu. Did the name on the title bar change?

h. Print the revised document.

i. Exit WordPad and remove the diskette from its drive.

**Lab Exercise 3 (Section 2.2)**

a. Start the WordPad word processor and insert the Lab Exercises disk in its drive.

b. Open the document named Memo on this diskette.

c. Change the date to the current date, the *From* entry to your name, and the *Re* entry to Windows 95.

d. Move the insertion point to the end of the document (two lines below *Re*) and type a short description of Windows 95.

e. Save the document to the floppy disk under the new name Win95 Memo (using the Save *As* command).

f. Print the revised document.

g. Exit WordPad and remove the diskette from its drive.

**Lab Exercise 4 (Section 2.3)**

a. Start the WordPad word processor and insert the Lab Exercises disk in its drive.

b. Open the document named Preamble on this diskette.

c. Select all the text in this document except for the title.

d. Copy the selected text to the Clipboard.

e. Move the insertion point to the end of the document (deselecting the block of text in the process) and then move the insertion point down two lines by pressing the Enter key twice.

f. Paste the contents of the Clipboard into the document.

g. Repeat steps *e* and *f*. (The Preamble should now appear three times.)

h. Print the current document.

i. Exit WordPad, answering No to the "Save changes" message, and remove the diskette from its drive.

**Lab Exercise 5 (Section 2.3)**

a. Start the WordPad word processor and then start the Calculator application by clicking on Calculator on the Accessories submenu of the Start menu's Programs option.

b. Open Calculator's View menu. If Standard is not checked, choose this item; otherwise, press the Escape key to close the View menu.

c. Click successively on the 1, 2, and 3 calculator keys (which enters the number 123 into the calculator's "display").

d. Copy the contents of the display to the Clipboard by choosing Copy from the Edit menu. (Notice that in the Calculator application, you need not select the number before copying it.)

e. Switch to WordPad and paste the Clipboard contents into the document.

f. Switch back to Calculator and copy its window to the Clipboard (using *Alt*+Print Screen, not Print Screen).

g. Exit Calculator, which makes WordPad active.

h. Skip a couple of lines and paste the contents of the Clipboard (the captured window) into the WordPad document.

i. Print the document and exit WordPad (saving the document to a floppy disk if you want).

**Lab Exercise 6 (Section 2.4)**

a. Start Windows 95 Help by choosing Help from the Start menu (which opens the Windows Help Topics dialog box).

b. If the Contents page is not displayed, click on its tab.

c. Right-click within the Contents topics window and click on the *What's This?* command. What is the subject of this context-sensitive help? Close the pop-up window.

d. Click on the question-mark button on the title bar; then on the Contents tab. What message is displayed? Close the pop-up window.

e. Display the topic entitled "If you've used Windows before". What is the title of the resulting Help window?

f. In the Help window, click on the "How to start programs" hot spot. Which technique for starting programs is described?

g. Open the Options menu for this Help window and point at the Font item. What choices do you have for font size?

h. Close the Help window to exit Help.

**Lab Exercise 7 (Section 2.4)**

a. Start WordPad and choose Help Topics from the Help menu to open the WordPad Help Topics dialog box.

b. Let's try to determine the function of the WordPad Ruler. Click on the Index tab (if this page is currently not displayed).

c. Type *ruler* in the text box. What is the name of the topic that is highlighted?

d. Activate the Display command button to open the Help window corresponding to the highlighted topic. According to the "Tip", what is the apparent function of the Ruler?

e. Return to the Help Topics dialog box and click on the Find tab. (If the Find Setup Wizard dialog box appears, click on Next, then on Finish.)

f. Type *ruler* in the text box. How many topics are listed in the bottom window?

g. Display the topic entitled "Setting tabs". On which WordPad menu is the Tabs command located?

h. Choose the Tabs command from the appropriate WordPad menu. The Tabs dialog box will open. Now, using either the *Setting tabs* Help window or context-sensitive help in the Tabs dialog box, answer the following questions:

   - What is the difference between the Clear and Clear All commands?
   - What is the purpose of the Set command button in the Tabs dialog box?
   - How does one delete a tab using the Ruler?

i. Close the Help window and exit WordPad.

CHAPTER 3

# Managing Files, Folders, and Disks

In Chapter 2 we discussed, in a general way, how to use applications (programs) and documents. Both applications and documents are stored in files, which in turn are located in folders on a disk. This chapter describes how to use Windows Explorer and My Computer to perform basic operations on files, folders, and disks. To be more specific, you will learn:

1. How the Windows 95 file system is organized.
2. The rules for creating valid file and folder names.
3. How to select files and folders in Explorer.
4. How to use Explorer to
   - Move or copy files and folders.
   - Create, rename, and delete files and folders.
   - Create shortcuts.
5. How to use My Computer to locate and manipulate files and folders.
6. How to use Explorer or My Computer to format and copy floppy disks.

# 3.1 The Windows 95 File System

Computer disks are capable of storing a lot of information — both data and programs. In order to facilitate access to this information, Windows 95, with your help, organizes it into files and folders. In this section, we will provide some useful information about these concepts.

## What are Files and Folders?

**Files** A **file** is a collection of information that has been generated by the computer and stored (saved) on disk. A file may contain an application, in which case it's called a *program file*, or data created by an application, which is a *data file*. For example, recall that when you save a document for the first time in the WordPad word processor (itself a collection of files stored on your hard disk), you choose a name for that document. When you issue the Save (or Save As) command, Windows creates a file by copying the document from internal memory (RAM) to disk and assigning the name you chose to it.

**Folders** Since a hard disk can contain thousands of files, it is necessary to organize them into **folders** (or **directories***). Each folder is a collection of related files that you (or a program) have grouped together and given a name. For example, you might place all the letters you've written in one folder called Letters and all your reports in another folder (uncreatively) called Reports.

Sometimes it makes sense to place a related group of folders within a larger folder. In this case, the bigger folder is called the **parent folder** and each of the folders within it is a **subfolder** (or *child folder*) of the parent. For example, your disk might have several folders that contain word processing data files: Letters, Reports, and so on. To better organize the disk, you could place all of these in a (parent) folder called, say, Word Processing. (A parent folder can contain files as well as subfolders. For example, on a hard disk, the Word Processing folder might hold the *program* files for your word processing application.)

The folders on a disk form a tree-like structure with subfolders branching out from their parents, which in turn may be subfolders themselves. On each disk there is one folder, called the **root folder**, that contains all the others. Figure 1 shows a *folder tree* — a graphical

*The Windows 95 documentation uses the term *folder* instead of *directory*. If you are familiar with DOS or Windows 3.1, just think *directory* whenever you see *folder*. Don't worry; you'll soon get used to the new terminology.

way of representing the folder structure of a disk. It may take a little imagination to see this structure as a tree; in particular, notice that the root is at the top!

In Figure 1, the root folder is designated by "3½ Floppy (A:)" and its three subfolders (Drawing Files, Word Processing, and Zingers) are shown connected to it by dotted lines. Notice that the Drawing Files and Word Processing folders have subfolders of their own (each connected to its parent by dotted lines), and one of these subfolders (Letters) also has subfolders. Each folder, including the root, may contain files as well.

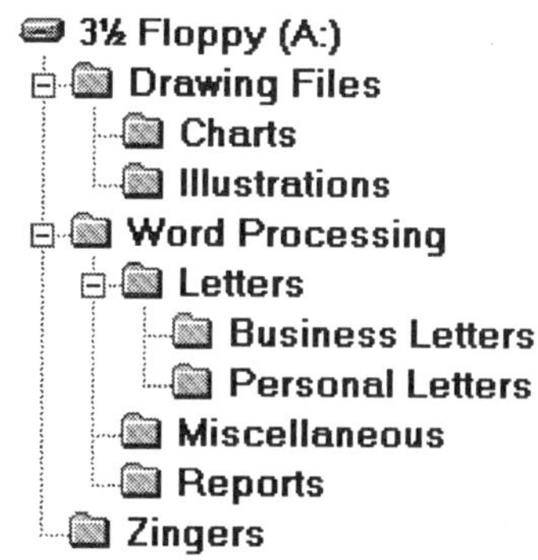


**Figure 1** A Folder Tree

## *Naming Files and Folders*

**Disk drive designations**

Every drive, folder, and file used by your computer must have a name. Drive designations (for hard and floppy disk drives, CD-ROM drives, network drives, and the like) are assigned by the operating system. They consist of a single letter followed by a colon; for example, A: and B: are reserved for the computer's floppy drives and its primary hard disk is designated C:, even if there is only one floppy drive. Other drives (D:, E:, etc.) may be present as well.

**DOS file names**

Naming files can get complicated. There are different rules for what constitutes a valid file name depending on whether the program that created the file was designed to run under DOS or Windows 3.1 on the one hand, or under Windows 95 on the other. If the program that created the file is a DOS or Windows 3.1 application, the resulting name is known as a **DOS file name**, and must follow these rules:

- The name may consist of two parts: A required *filename* containing from one to eight characters, possibly followed by an *extension* consisting of up to three characters. If the extension is present, it must be separated from the filename by a period (.). For example, for the file Joe.Ltr, Joe is the filename and Ltr is the extension.
- The filename and extension may contain any characters *except*

| | | |
|---|---|---|
| period (.) | comma (,) | colon (:) |
| semicolon (;) | quotation mark (") | brackets ([ ]) |
| slash (/) | backslash (\) | equals sign (=) |
| vertical bar (\|) | question mark (?) | asterisk (*) |

Moreover, *no spaces* are permitted in a DOS file name.

- Lowercase letters are not distinguished from uppercase letters. So, the names MyFile, myfile, and MYFILE are considered identical.

For example, the following names are all valid:

Ch1  Ch1.Txt  Ch-1.{  history.rpt  X  1(#$%).n1

However, the following names are *invalid* DOS file names:

| | |
|---|---|
| inventory.dat | (Filename is too long.) |
| Top Gun | (Spaces are not allowed.) |
| File:1 | (The colon is an illegal character.) |

**Windows 95 file and folder names**

Windows 95 frees us from many of the restrictions imposed by DOS file names. Most importantly, in naming a file created by a Windows 95-based application or *any* Windows 95 folder, you may use up to 255 characters, including spaces. (For this reason, these names are called **long file names.**) Moreover, all punctuation marks *except* for the following ones are permitted in long file names:

| | | |
|---|---|---|
| colon (:) | vertical bar (\|) | quotation mark (") |
| slash (/) | backslash (\) | question mark (?) |
| asterisk (*) | | |

As a result, the following names are valid for a folder or for a file created by an application designed to run under Windows 95:

| | |
|---|---|
| J. Gomez - Letter 1 | (but *not* J. Gomez: Letter 1) |
| BIS HW #7 1-5-96 | (but *not* BIS HW #7 1/5/96) |
| Annual Report - 1995 | (but *not* "Annual Report - 1995") |

Long file names may have extensions, but they are usually assigned by Windows, not the user.

**NOTE**

Long file names can only be created and used by Windows 95 itself and Windows 95-based applications. So, when you are running a DOS or Windows 3.1 program, you have to follow the stricter rules for DOS file names.

This situation raises an interesting question: What happens if you try to open a document with a long file name in an application that doesn't support long file names? In this case, Windows 95 supplies a "DOS alias", a related DOS file name, for use in this application. To form the alias, Windows truncates the original file name to six characters and inserts two special symbols followed by the file's extension. In addition, any blank spaces are deleted and illegal characters are replaced by underscores. For example, suppose you create documents named `Assignment #5`, `Assignment #6`, and `Asg [7]` in WordPad and then open each of these documents in a Windows 3.1-based word processor. Here, the document file names become assign~1.doc, assign~2.doc, and asg_7_~1.doc.

### *Path Names*

When you start an application, Windows automatically specifies a certain folder as the current (or default) folder for that application. (To see which folder is the current one, just open the Save As or Open dialog box; it will be displayed in the *Save in* or *Look in* text box.) If you want to refer to any file in the current folder, you need only give its file name. For example, if you save a file, naming it Sam.doc, it is automatically placed in the current folder.

To refer to a file that is not in the current folder, you must change folders or give the file's **path name**, a kind of road map that tells Windows how to find the file. The path name for a file begins with the drive designation (for example, C:), followed by the names of the root folder (which is \, a backslash) and all subfolders (from largest to smallest) that contain the file, and ends with the name of the file itself. All subfolder names must be followed by backslashes. Thus, the complete path name for a file called Sam.doc in the Personal Letters folder in the folder tree shown in Figure 1 is:

A:\Word Processing\Letters\Personal Letters\Sam.doc

## *3.2 An Introduction to Windows Explorer*

When you use Windows on a regular basis, you will frequently find it convenient to delete, move, copy, or rename files and folders. Windows' primary tool for performing these kinds of operations is the **Explorer** application. In this section, we will provide some basic information about Explorer; its capabilities will be discussed in more detail in Sections 3.3 and 3.4.

### *The Explorer Window*

To start Explorer, click on the Start button (or press Ctrl+Esc) to open the Start menu. Then, point at the Programs option and click on Windows Explorer on the resulting submenu. When you do, a window similar to the one in Figure 2 will open.

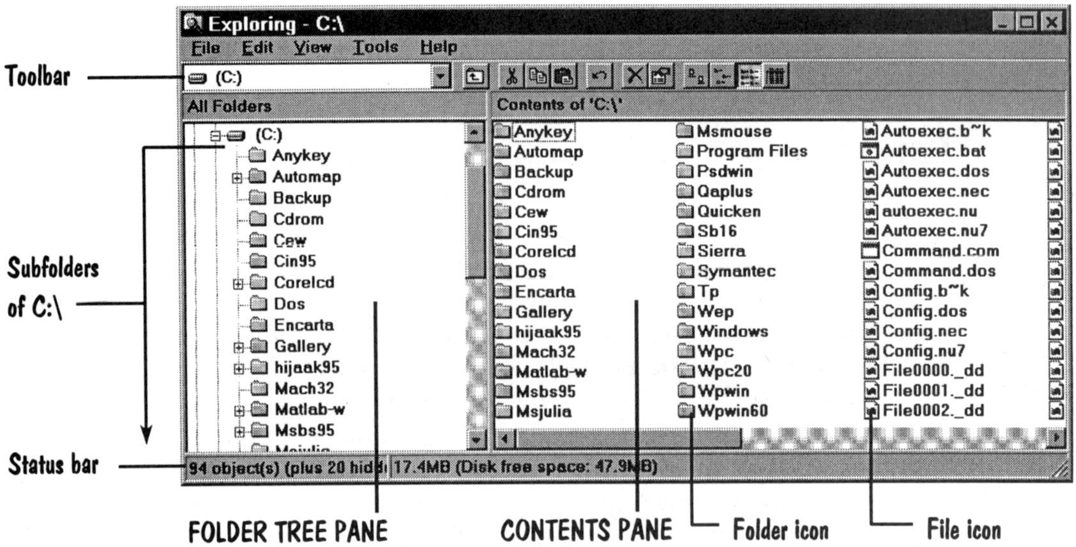


**Figure 2** The Explorer Window

The Explorer window has a title bar, menu bar, and Toolbar at the top and a status bar at the bottom. The Toolbar and status bar can be hidden. To hide either bar (or display it if it's currently hidden), choose the item bearing its name from the View menu. Most of the Explorer window is divided into two large subwindows or *panes*: the *folder tree* pane on the left and the *contents* pane on the right.

## *The Folder Tree Pane*

The **folder tree pane** lists all folders on all drives connected to your computer and also provides access to other objects on the Desktop, such as My Computer and the Recycle Bin. In fact, if you scroll up the folder tree pane, you'll see that all objects listed in this window, including drives, are considered subfolders of the Desktop folder!

When you start Explorer, the drive containing the Windows folder is displayed at the top of the folder tree pane and all immediate (*child*) subfolders are listed in alphabetical order beneath it. The files and folders contained within the current (or *open*) folder are shown in the contents pane. For example, in Figure 2, the contents pane displays the subfolders and some of the files in the C:\ folder. If you want to view the contents of another object in the folder tree pane, just scroll the folder tree up or down until that object is visible and click on it. Its name will become highlighted and, if it is represented by a folder icon, that icon will "open", as shown at the right.

**NOTE**

Opening a folder displays an up-to-the-moment list of its contents, even if they have changed in the current session. You should be aware, however, that there are situations in which the contents pane does not accurately reflect the contents of the open folder. The most common of these occurs if you change the disk in a floppy drive when its folder is open; in this case, Windows will continue to display the contents of the previous disk. To view the contents of the new disk, either click again on the floppy drive icon in the folder tree pane or choose the Refresh command from the View menu.

**Expanding the folder tree**

To see subfolders that are hidden from view (even after scrolling), you have to *expand* a branch of the folder tree. When a folder contains hidden subfolders, its name and icon are preceded by a plus (+) symbol (see, for example, the Automap folder in Figure 2). To view these subfolders, expanding this branch of the folder tree, either

- Click on the plus symbol.

*or*

- Double-click on the folder name or icon.

In either case, the subfolders will be displayed and the plus symbol will become a minus (-) symbol. (If you double-click on the folder's name, that folder also becomes the current folder and its contents are displayed in the contents pane.) Clicking on the minus symbol *collapses* the branch, hiding the subfolders.

For example, if we click on the plus symbol next to the Automap folder icon, a list of subfolders will be displayed, as shown at the right. Notice that there is a plus symbol attached to the Userdata subfolder, indicating that this folder has subfolders of its own. Now, if we click on the minus sign preceding Automap, this branch collapses, returning the folder tree to its original look, as in Figure 2.

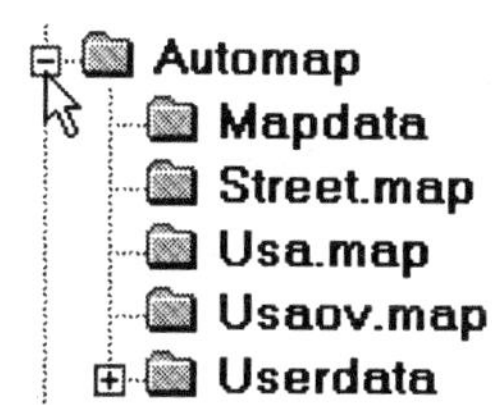


## *The Contents Pane*

As you know, the **contents pane** of the Explorer window lists all folders and files contained in the current folder. The word *folder* in this context refers to any folder, drive, or other object (such as My

Computer) that can be accessed through Explorer.

Just as in the folder tree pane, clicking on an object in the contents pane selects that object, highlighting its name and icon. (We will have more to say about selecting objects in Section 3.3.) If you *double*-click on an object, what happens next depends on the nature of the object:

**Double-clicking an object in the contents pane**

- Double-clicking on a folder icon opens that folder, displaying its contents in the contents pane. (In other words, double-clicking on a folder icon in the contents pane has the same effect as clicking on the corresponding icon in the folder tree pane.)
- Double-clicking on a program file icon opens the corresponding application. This technique provides an effective way to start any application on your hard or floppy disks.
- Double-clicking on a document file that is associated with an application starts that application and opens the given document within it. (We will discuss the process of associating documents with a particular application in Section 6.4.)
- Double-clicking on any other kind of file icon displays the Open With dialog box. This dialog box allows you to select an application to be used with the given file. Choosing the OK command button starts that application and opens the file within it.

**TIP**

**The Tools menu**

On a well-used hard disk, there may be hundreds of folders, with a correspondingly intricate folder tree. It's not surprising that finding a particular folder may be difficult. To help you in this regard, Explorer provides easy access to the Windows Find utility. You can open this utility by pointing at the Find item on the Tools menu and then choosing Files and Folders from the submenu. (We will discuss Find in Section 6.3.)

The other Tools menu item, Go To, is less helpful but easier to use. If you know the path name of the desired folder, choose the Go To command; the following dialog box will be displayed:

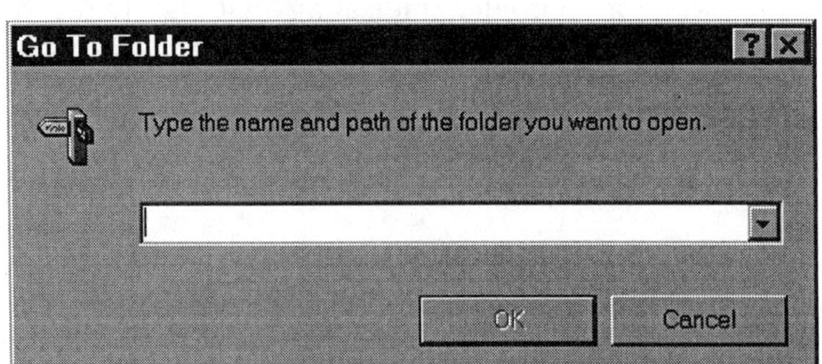

As the instructions suggest, type the path name of the desired folder in the text box; then choose the OK command button. The dialog box will close, returning you to Explorer. The selected folder will be highlighted in the folder tree pane and its contents will be displayed in the contents pane.

## *Contents Pane View Options*

Explorer displays the contents pane in one of four ways, depending on your preference. These options are described below; to select one of them, choose the corresponding item from the View menu. The selected view option will remain in effect, even in future Windows sessions, until you change it again.

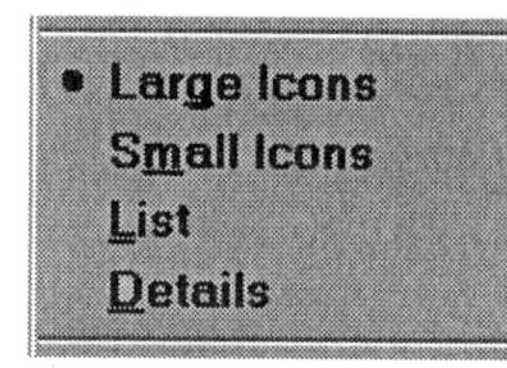


**The Large Icons and Small Icons View Options** Here, each object in the contents pane is represented by an icon (either large or small) labeled with the name of the object (Figures 3 and 4). You can move these icons one by one to a prominent position in the window (say, the upper left corner) by dragging them with the mouse. To be more specific:

**Moving icons**

1. Select the icon that you want to move by clicking on it.
2. Position the mouse pointer over this icon, hold down the left mouse button, and move the pointer to the icon's new location. An outline of the icon (and its label) will move with the pointer, as shown at the right.
3. When the icon is positioned where you want it, release the mouse button.

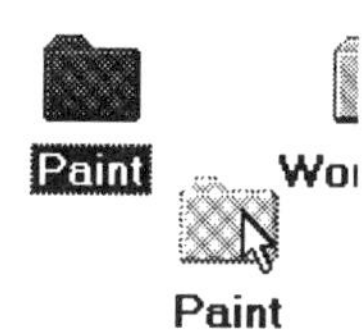


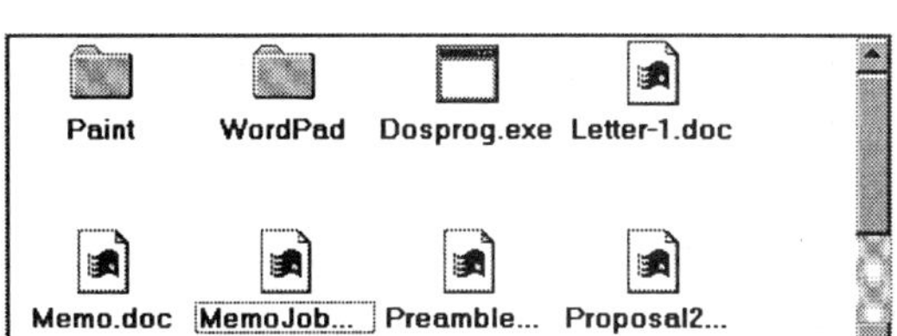


**Figure 3** Contents Pane — Large Icons

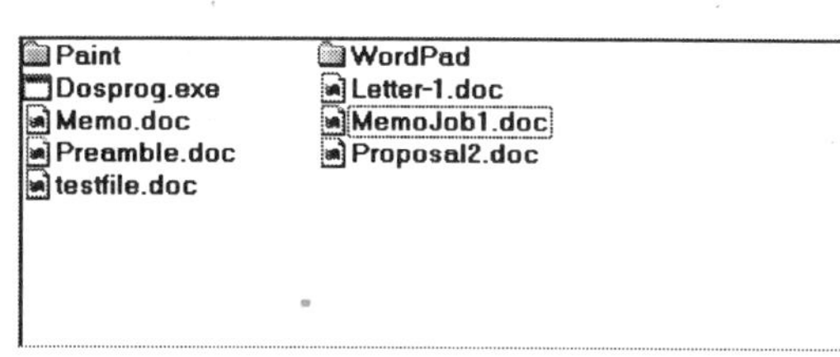


**Figure 4** Contents Pane — Small Icons

**Lining up the icons**

To display the new arrangement of icons in neatly ordered rows and columns (as illustrated in Figures 3 and 4), choose Line Up Icons from the View menu. Or, to have Windows automatically line up the icons whenever they are moved, turn on the Auto Arrange option from the Arrange Icons submenu of the View menu. (Turning *off* this option before rearranging icons may make it easier to carry out the process.)

**The List and Details View Options** Choosing the List option (Figure 5) from the View menu displays the icons and names in the contents pane in a similar way to that of the Small Icons option. (With the List option, the icons are displayed in columns instead of rows and cannot be individually moved about.) The Details option (Figure 6) lists the objects in the contents pane, one per line, together with the information specified on the buttons at the top if this pane:

- *Size* refers to the size of a file in kilobytes (KB) or megabytes (MB).
- *Type* refers to the kind of object; for a file, Windows determines its type (for example, *application*) from the file name extension.
- *Modified* provides the most recent date and time that a file was saved; for folders, it is the time it was created.

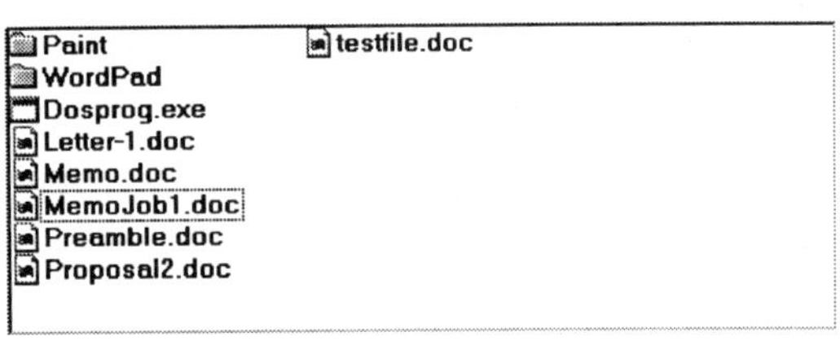


**Figure 5** Contents Pane — List Option

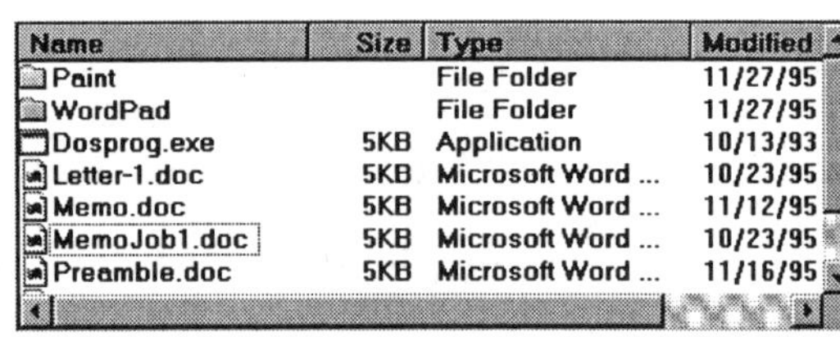


**Figure 6** Contents Pane — Details

**Ordering files in the Details view**

By default, the Details view displays the files in the contents pane in the alphabetical order of their names. (Folders in the contents pane are always displayed at the top of the list.) You can list files in other orders, as well. To do so, click on the appropriate button at the top of the contents pane; that is:

- Click on the Size button to list files in order of increasing size; click again on this button to list them in decreasing size order.
- Click on the Type button to list files in alphabetical order by type; click again on this button to list them in reverse alphabetical order by type.
- Click on the Modified button to list files in order of their last modification date; most recently modified files are listed first.

Clicking again on this button lists recently modified files last.

- Click on the Name button to restore alphabetical order by name; clicking again on this button lists files in reverse alphabetical order.

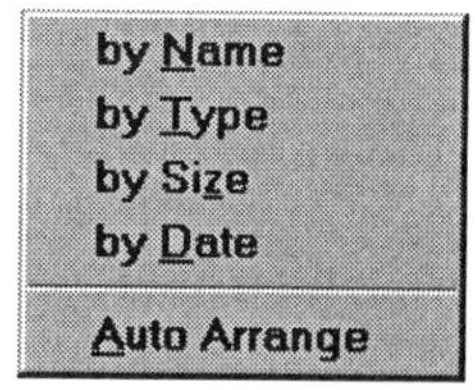


The icons in *all* the view options (Large Icons, Small Icons, List, and Details) can be ordered by either name, file size, type, or modification date. Just choose the appropriate item from the Arrange Icons submenu of the View menu. However, "reverse orders" are not possible using the Arrange Icons submenu. For example, selecting *by Size* from this menu lists the icons in order of increasing file size; icons cannot be listed in order of *decreasing* size using the Arrange Icons menu.

TIP

You can use Explorer's Toolbar to quickly select a different contents pane view option. Just click on the appropriate button, as indicated below. (The "List" button is shown selected.)

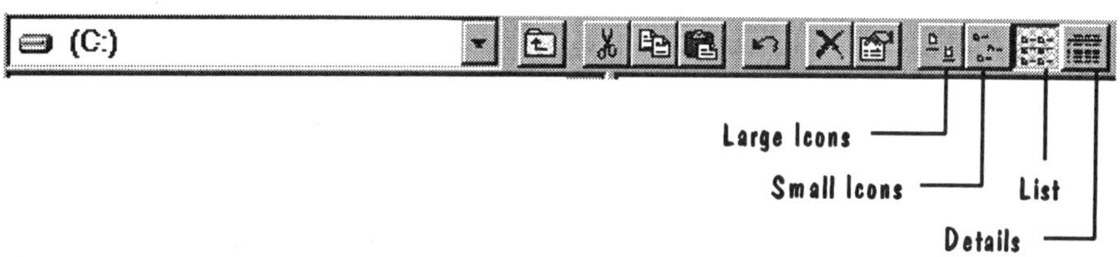


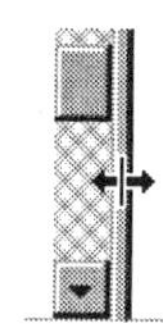

In any view, you may want to make the contents pane as large as possible. To do so, first maximize the Explorer window. Then, move the mouse pointer over the vertical bar separating the folder tree and contents panes (the pointer becomes a double-headed arrow, as pictured at the right). Now, drag the bar to the left, and the contents pane will expand accordingly.

NOTE

As you can see, the Toolbar contains several other buttons and a drop-down list, as well. The drop-down list and the Up One Level button next to it provide alternate ways to navigate the Windows folder system. They are of more benefit in My Computer than in Explorer, and will be described when we discuss the former in Section 3.5. Some of the other buttons on the Toolbar are helpful in performing operations on files and folders; they will be discussed in Sections 3.3 and 3.4.

**3-2 TUTORIAL**

Try the following exercises on your own.

1. Turn on your computer, if necessary, to start up Windows 95 and close any open windows.
2. Start Explorer: Click on the Start button, then point at the Programs option on the Start menu, and finally click on Windows Explorer on the resulting submenu. The Explorer window will open. Maximize this window.
3. Insert the Lab Exercises disk in its drive and select this drive in the folder tree (left) pane of the Explorer window. For example, if the Lab Exercises disk is in the A: drive, scroll the folder tree pane up until the "3½ Floppy (A:)" folder appears; then, click on this item. The files and folders in the root folder of the disk will be displayed in the contents (right) pane of the window.
4. Expand the "3½ Floppy (A:)" branch of the folder tree by clicking on the plus symbol to the left of this item. (You can also do this by double-clicking on the name "3½ Floppy (A:)".)
5. Choose the Large Icons option from the View menu. Now, drag the Paint folder icon to a new position in the contents pane: Position the mouse pointer over it, then hold down the left mouse button while moving the pointer (and icon) to a new location in the contents pane, and finally release the mouse button.
6. Arrange the icons in the contents pane neatly by choosing Line Up Icons from the View menu.
7. Point at the Arrange Icons item on the View menu and then choose *by Size* from the submenu to sort the files in order of increasing size. Take note of the other sorting options available on the submenu!
8. If the Toolbar is not visible in the Explorer window, choose Toolbar from the View menu to display it.
9. Successively click on the Small Icons, List, and Details Toolbar buttons. (To determine which ones they are, hold the mouse over each Toolbar button until the identifying *Tool Tip* appears.) Notice the effect of each view option.
10. With the Details view in effect, sort the files in order of the last date they were saved by clicking on the button labeled *Modified* at the top of the contents pane. Click on this button again to reverse the order. Also try the other buttons (Name, Size, and Type) to see their effect.
11. Exit Explorer (as you would any application) and remove the Lab Exercises disk from its drive.

# 3.3 *Moving and Copying Files and Folders*

An application like WordPad allows you to modify the content of *files*; Explorer, on the other hand, allows you to manipulate the contents of *folders*. Using Explorer, you can move, copy, rename, delete, and create files and subfolders. In Sections 3.3 and 3.4, we will describe how to accomplish each of these tasks.

## *Selecting Files and Folders*

The first step in using Explorer to manipulate a file, a folder, or a group of files or folders is to identify or *select* the objects* in which you are interested. A selected object is displayed with a highlighted name and icon, as illustrated below.

Selected object　　　Object not selected

**How to select an object**

To select an object from the *folder tree pane*:

1. If necessary, scroll the pane or expand the tree (see Section 3.2) until the name of the object appears.
2. Click on the object to select it. (The selected folder will open, displaying its contents in the contents pane.)

To select an object from the *contents pane*.

1. Scroll the pane, if necessary, until the name of the object appears.
2. Click on the object to select it. (If the selected object is a folder, it will *not* open; the current folder remains unchanged. However, *double*-clicking on a folder in the contents pane *does* open it, making it the current folder.)

**Selecting multiple objects**

To save time in performing operations on files and folders, it is often useful to manipulate several of them at once. For example, if you want to delete ten files from disk, it is faster to select all ten and then perform the delete operation, rather than selecting and deleting them one at a time. Selecting *multiple* (more than one) objects can only be done in the contents pane, but it can be done in several ways:

---

*Recall that, in this context, an *object* is any item listed in Explorer's folder tree or contents pane. Any Explorer object (including My Computer, a floppy drive, and the Desktop itself!) that is not a file is considered to be a *folder*.

- Click on one of the objects to be selected; then, hold down the Ctrl key and click on the others; finally, release Ctrl.
- If the objects to be selected are *in consecutive order*: click on the first object; then, hold down the Shift key and click on the last object in the group; finally, release Shift.
- If the objects to be selected are *adjacent to one another*, drag a box around them, as illustrated at the right. To be more specific, position the mouse pointer to the upper left of the objects to be selected, hold down the left mouse button, move the pointer to the lower right of the desired objects, and release the button.

- To select *all* objects in the contents pane, choose Select All from Explorer's Edit menu. To select *almost all* the objects in the contents pane, select those objects you do *not* want and choose Invert Selection from the Edit menu.

As an example of the selection process, here's one way to select the objects shown highlighted in Figure 7:

1. The files Memo.doc, MemoJob1.doc, and Preamble.doc are in consecutive order, so we click on the first, hold down the Shift key, click on the last, and release Shift.
2. To select the remaining files, Dosprog.exe and testfile.doc, we hold down the Ctrl key, click on each file, and release Ctrl.

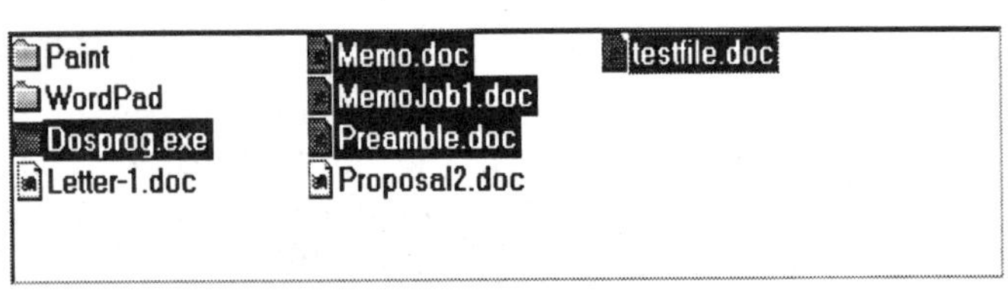


**Figure 7** Selection Process Example

TIP

To select additional objects after at least one has been selected, be sure to hold down the Ctrl key while clicking. If you forget to press this key, all previously selected objects will be deselected!

If you want to deselect an object after some have been selected, hold down the Ctrl key while clicking on the object. Here, too, don't forget to hold down Ctrl. Otherwise, all objects *except* the one you click on will be deselected!

## *Moving and Copying Objects*

When you *move* an object, it is deleted from its original location and placed in a new location. When you *copy* an object, a duplicate of that object is placed in the new location, but it is not deleted from the original. If the object being moved or copied is a folder, then it and all its contents (files and subfolders alike) are moved or copied to the new location. With one exception (which we will mention later), the move and copy operations are performed in analogous ways, so we will discuss them together.

You can move or copy an object from one folder (the *source*) to another (the *destination*) in two fundamental ways:

1. Drag the object from the source and drop it onto the destination.
2. Cut or copy the object from the source and paste it into the destination.

**Drag-and-Drop Move or Copy** To move or copy objects using the **drag-and-drop** method sometimes takes a little preparation, but the actual operation is very simple. It involves the following steps:

1. Select the objects to be moved or copied.
2. Arrange the Explorer window so that at least one of the selected objects as well as the destination folder are both visible. To do this, you may have to scroll or expand the folder tree to display the destination folder.
3. Position the mouse pointer over any selected object and:
   - If you want to *move* the object, hold down the Shift key and drag the pointer to the destination.
   - If you want to *copy* the object, hold down the Ctrl key and drag the pointer to the destination.

   As you drag the mouse pointer, it seems to pull the objects' icons and names with it (see Figure 8, on the next page). The plus symbol below the pointer arrow in Figure 8 indicates that this is a copy operation. When *moving* objects, the plus symbol will not appear.
4. As the mouse pointer approaches the destination folder, the latter will become highlighted (see the Windows folder in Figure 8) to let you know that you're on target. Now, release the mouse button (and the Ctrl or Shift key) and the *Moving...* or *Copying...* animated dialog box will appear, confirming that the operation is taking place. (If you change your mind and want to abort the process, press the Escape key before releasing the mouse button.)

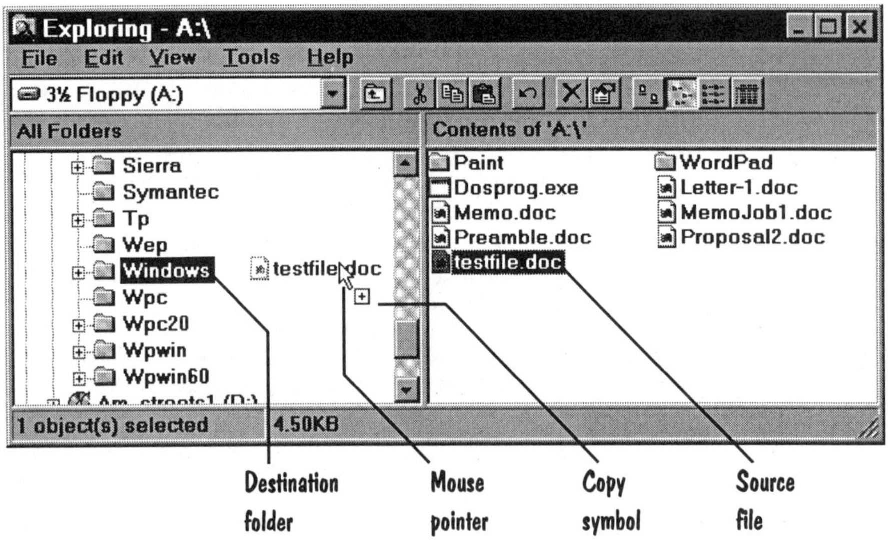


**Figure 8** Drag-and-Drop Copying

If you try to move or copy an object into a folder that already contains an object with the same name, the Confirm File Replace (or Confirm Folder Replace) dialog box (Figure 9) will appear. Choose the Yes command button if you want the source file to replace the destination file in this folder, *deleting the destination file* in the process. Otherwise, click on the No button. (If you are moving or copying multiple

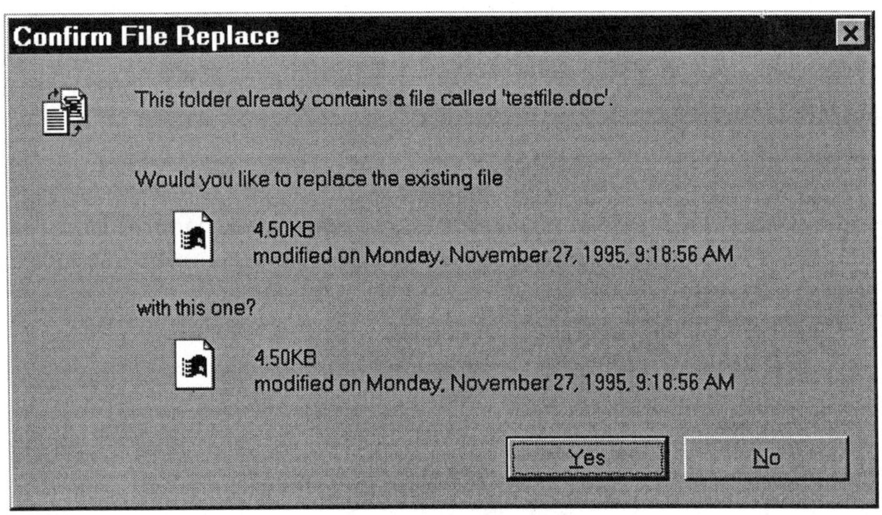


**Figure 9** The Confirm File Replace Dialog Box

objects, this dialog box will also contain Yes to All and Cancel buttons. Choosing Yes to All indicates that you want to replace all destination files that have the same name as a source file; choosing Cancel aborts the Move or Copy operation.)

TIP

When *moving* objects between folders on the *same drive*, you do not have to hold down the Shift key while performing the drag-and-drop. When *copying* objects between folders on *different drives*, you do not have to hold down the Ctrl key.

If you don't want to memorize the Shift/Ctrl rules, Windows 95 provides an alternative: just *right-drag* a selected object from the source to the destination. In this case, when you release the mouse button, the menu shown here will appear. To *move* the file to the destination, choose the Move Here command; to *copy* the file, choose the Copy Here command.

Both the left-drag and right-drag techniques work when the destination is an icon on the Desktop or the Desktop itself. For example, to copy a file to the My Computer folder, select the file in Explorer and either

- Drag it onto the My Computer icon on the Desktop (you need not hold down the Ctrl key).

*or*

- Right-drag it onto the My Computer icon and choose Copy Here from the menu that pops up when you release the mouse button.

**Cut/Copy and Paste Move or Copy** The second basic method for moving or copying objects resembles the process for transferring information from one document to another (see Section 2.3). It involves the following steps:

1. Select the objects to be moved or copied.
2. Choose Cut (if you're moving the objects) or Copy (if you're copying the objects) from any of the following:
    - Explorer's Edit menu.
    - Explorer's Toolbar.

- The menu (pictured at the right) that pops up when you right-click on one of the selected files.

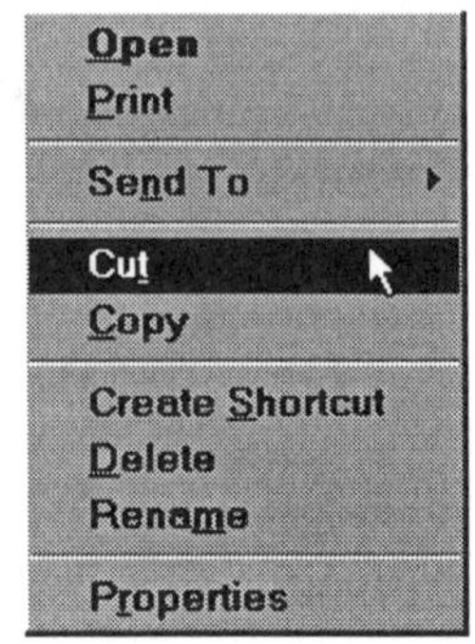


3. Select the destination folder in the folder tree pane.
4. Choose Paste from Explorer's Edit menu, Toolbar, or the menu that pops up when you right-click the destination folder.

If there is an object in the destination folder with the same name as one of the objects being moved or copied, a Confirm File Replace or Confirm Folder Replace dialog box will be displayed (see Figure 9). Choose the Yes or No command buttons, as you wish.

Suppose you move or copy an object (using any method) and then decide that this wasn't such a good idea. You could move the object back to the source folder or delete it from the destination, but there is an easier way. Windows supplies an Undo command that cancels the last move or copy. This command is located on Explorer's Edit menu. It can also be executed by clicking on the Undo Toolbar button (shown at the right).

## *The Send To Command*

Perhaps the most common use of the copy operation in Windows is to copy a file or group of files to a floppy disk. This action is usually taken for one of two reasons:

- To *back up* files on the hard disk (to make copies in case the hard disk becomes damaged or its files cannot be accessed for some other reason).
- To transfer files to another computer.

Windows 95 makes it very easy to copy files or entire folders to a floppy disk. To do so:

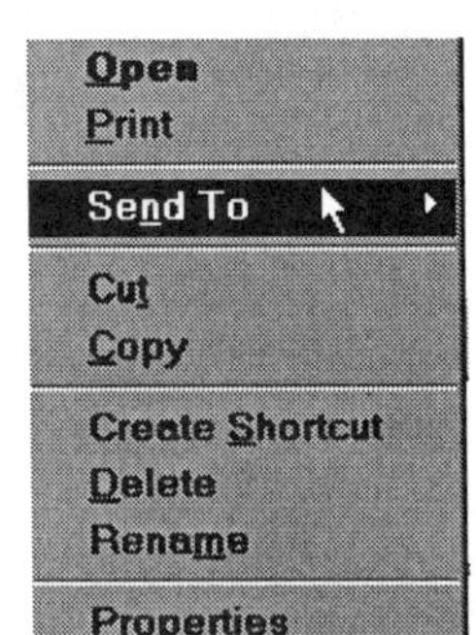


1. Select the objects you want to copy.
2. Right-click on one of them, which opens the menu shown at the right.
3. Point at the Send To command on this menu.

4. Choose the appropriate floppy disk drive from the resulting submenu.

3.3 TUTORIAL

Try the following exercises on your own.

1. Turn on your computer, if necessary, to start up Windows 95, and close any open windows.
2. Start Explorer, maximize its window, and select the List view option from the View menu or Toolbar.
3. Insert the Lab Exercises disk in its drive and select this drive (for example, "3½ Floppy (A:)") in the folder tree pane.
4. Select the last five (consecutive) files listed by clicking on the first of them, then holding down the Shift key while clicking on the last.
5. Deselect the selected files by clicking on an empty part of the contents pane.
6. Select the files Fonts, Preamble, and Testfile by clicking on the first of these, then holding down the Ctrl key as you click on the other two.
7. Deselect the Fonts file by holding down the Ctrl key while clicking on it.
8. Move the two remaining selected files to the Paint subfolder using the (right-) drag-and-drop method:
   - Move the mouse pointer over either file name and press, but do not release, the *right* mouse button.
   - Reposition the pointer so that the Paint folder name and icon become highlighted and release the mouse button.
   - Choose Move Here from the resulting pop up menu.
9. Move the Testfile and Preamble files back to the root folder of the Lab Exercises disk using the cut and paste method:
   - Open the Paint folder by double-clicking on its icon in the contents pane.
   - Select Testfile and Preamble.
   - Choose Cut from Explorer's Edit menu or click on the Cut Toolbar button.
   - Open the diskette's root folder by clicking on its drive icon (for example, "3½ Floppy (A:)") in the folder tree pane.
   - Choose Paste from Explorer's Edit menu or click on the Paste Toolbar button.
10. Copy the Fonts file from the root folder to the Paint subfolder

using (left-) drag-and-drop:

- Select the Fonts file.
- Position the mouse pointer over the selected file name, hold down the left mouse button and the Ctrl key (Ctrl is for *copy*, Shift is for *move*).
- Reposition the pointer so that the Paint folder name and icon become highlighted, and release the mouse button and Ctrl key.

11. Undo the last copy operation by choosing Undo Copy from the Edit menu or clicking on the Undo Toolbar button.

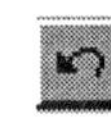

12. Exit Explorer and remove the Lab Exercises disk from its drive.

# 3.4 *Other Operations on Files and Folders*

In Section 3.3, we described how to select, move, and copy objects (files and folders). In this section we will continue this discussion, describing how to use Explorer to delete, rename, and create files and folders. We will also introduce the concept of a *shortcut*.

## *Deleting Files and Folders*

Deleting objects from disk is a common operation, often used to create additional free disk space or just to reduce clutter. In the usual sense of the word, to **delete** a file or folder means to remove it and all its contents from disk. When you use Explorer to delete an object, however, that object is normally (but not necessarily always) just copied to a special folder called the **Recycle Bin**. To remove the object from disk, you then have to delete it from the Recycle Bin.

**Ways to delete objects**

To delete files or folders, start Explorer and select the objects to be deleted (see Section 3.3). Then, perform any of the following actions:

- Press the Delete (Del) key.
- Drag any of the selected objects onto the Recycle Bin icon on the Desktop.

- Click on the Delete button (shown at the right) on Explorer's Toolbar.

- Choose the Delete command from Explorer's File menu.
- Right-click on any of the selected objects and choose the Delete command from the resulting pop-up menu.

After performing one of these actions, the Confirm File Delete or Confirm Folder Delete dialog box shown in Figure 10 may appear. Choose the Yes or No command button, as appropriate.

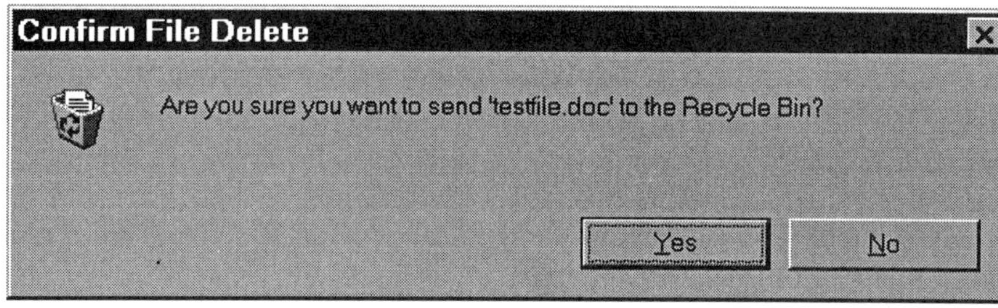


**Figure 10** The Confirm File Delete Dialog Box

**WARNING**

By default, Windows 95 does not send files deleted from floppy disks to the Recycle Bin. In this case, the message in the Confirm Delete dialog box will read "Are you sure you want to delete ..." and, if you activate the Yes button, the selected objects will immediately be removed from disk. If one of these objects is a folder, all its contents — files and subfolders alike — will be removed from disk. So, before you give the command to delete files or folders, think about what you are doing and whether you really want to do it!

**The Recycle Bin** The Recycle Bin is simply a Windows 95 folder. When files or folders are "deleted" by sending them to the Recycle Bin, these objects still take up disk space and can still be retrieved (or *restored*). If you are sure you no longer need an object in the Recycle Bin, you should delete that object to increase your free disk space. The safest way to accomplish this is to:

1. Open the Recycle Bin by double-clicking on its Desktop icon. The Recycle Bin window will be displayed (see Figure 11 on the next page).
2. Select the objects you want to delete.
3. Delete the selected objects: Press the Delete key, or choose Delete from the File menu, or click on the Toolbar's Delete button, or right-click on a selected object and choose Delete from the pop-up menu.
4. If a Confirm Delete dialog box appears, asking whether you're sure you want to delete the objects, choose the Yes button (unless

you've changed your mind). The selected objects are now removed from disk.

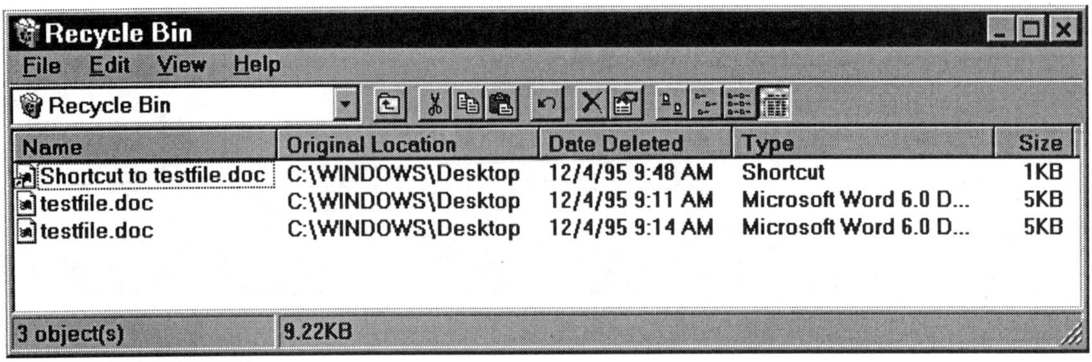


**Figure 11** The Recycle Bin Window

NOTE

As you can see in Figure 11, the Recycle Bin window strongly resembles the Explorer window. In fact, the Recycle Bin window is just Explorer's view of the Recycle Bin folder without the folder tree pane. There are, however, two menu options available for the Recycle Bin that are not available for a typical folder:

1. You can choose Empty Recycle Bin from the File menu to delete *all* objects in the Recycle Bin. (You can also accomplish this task by right-clicking on the Recycle Bin's Desktop icon and then choosing Empty Recycle Bin from the pop-up menu.)
2. You can choose Restore from the File menu to move selected objects back to their original location.

## *Renaming Files and Folders*

To **rename** (change the name of) a file or folder:

1. Start Explorer and select the object to be renamed.
2. Perform any of the following actions:
   - Choose Rename from Explorer's File menu.
   - Right-click on the selected object and choose Rename from the pop-up menu.
   - Click again on the selected object.

In any case, Windows places a box around the selected object's name (as shown at the right) to let you know that this object can now be renamed.

3. Type a new name for the object and press the Enter key.

If an object in the current folder has the same name as the one you are trying to assign to the selected object, the following dialog box will be displayed:

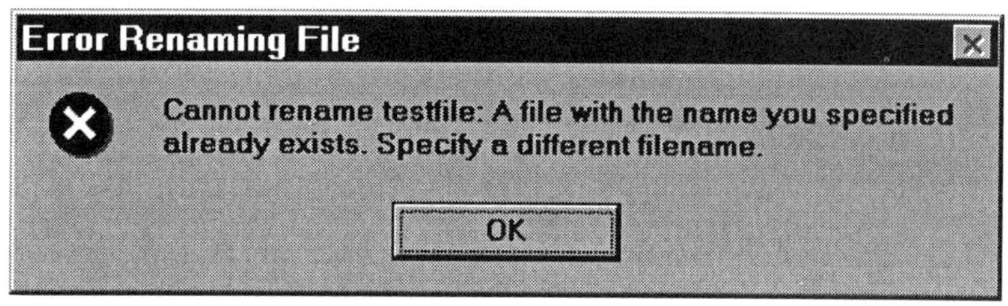


Click on the OK button (or press the Enter key) and this message will be cleared from the screen. If you want to give the selected object the same name as an existing object in that folder, you have to first rename or delete the existing one.

**NOTE**

You can rename objects on the Desktop in a similar way:

1. Select the object to be renamed by clicking on it.
2. Either click on the object again; or right-click on the object and choose Rename from the pop-up menu. Windows will place a box around the object's name.
3. Type a new name and press the Enter key.

## *Creating New Files and Folders*

As you know, data files (documents) are normally created within a specific application. For example, if you start WordPad, type some text, and save the resulting document (assigning it a name in the process), a file with that name is created on disk. Most of the folders on your hard disk were also created "automatically"— usually when Windows 95 or an application was installed.

You can also use Explorer to create both files and folders. (Creating a file this way is not terribly useful, but creating a new folder — say, to hold certain related documents — is an important operation.) To create a file or folder:

1. Start Explorer and select (in the folder tree pane) the folder in which you want the new object to reside.
2. Take either of the following actions:
   - Point at the New item on the File menu.

   *or*
   - Right-click on an empty part of the contents pane and point at the New item on the resulting pop-up menu.

   In either case, a submenu, similar to the one in Figure 12, will be displayed.

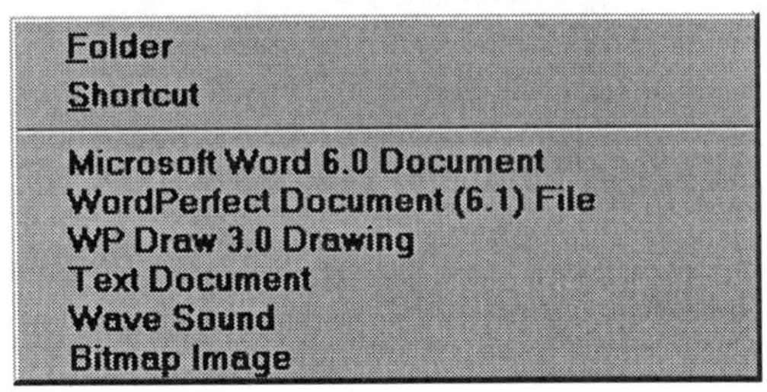


**Figure 12** The New Menu

3. Choose either Folder or one of the file types listed at the bottom of this menu. A new object will appear in the contents pane named, for example, New Folder, New Text Document, or New Bitmap Image. The name of the object will be highlighted and boxed-in, ready for renaming.
4. Rename the object whatever you want by typing a new name and pressing the Enter key.

As an example, we will create a new subfolder of the Windows folder and name it Data Files. To do so, we:

1. Start Explorer.
2. Scroll the Folder tree pane until the Windows folder comes into view.
3. Click on the Windows folder to select it. (The word *Windows* becomes highlighted.)
4. Point at the New command on Explorer's File menu and choose Folder from the resulting submenu. (A highlighted object called *New Folder* appears in the contents pane; the "box" around its name indicates that it's ready to be renamed.)
5. To rename the folder, type Data Files and press the Enter key.

## *Creating Shortcuts*

Recall (from Section 2.1) that one of the easiest ways to start an application is to double-click on its Desktop icon. Consequently, it would certainly be convenient to have an icon on the Desktop for each of your favorite programs. As you will see, Windows makes this easy to do.

**What's a shortcut?**

Some Desktop icons actually represent **shortcuts** to objects (files or folders); when you double-click on such an icon, the shortcut provides Windows 95 with the location and name (the path name) of the corresponding object. Thus, a shortcut is not a copy of an object, just a small file called a *pointer* (or *link*) that tells Windows where to find the relevant file or folder. For this reason, you can create shortcuts to your heart's content with very little adverse effect on your free disk space.

There are several ways to create a shortcut and place it on the Desktop. Here's one way to use Explorer to accomplish this task. (Another technique is given in Section 3.5.)

1. Start Explorer and open the folder that contains the object for which you want to create a shortcut.
2. Right-click on the object, selecting it and also opening a menu similar to the one shown at the right.

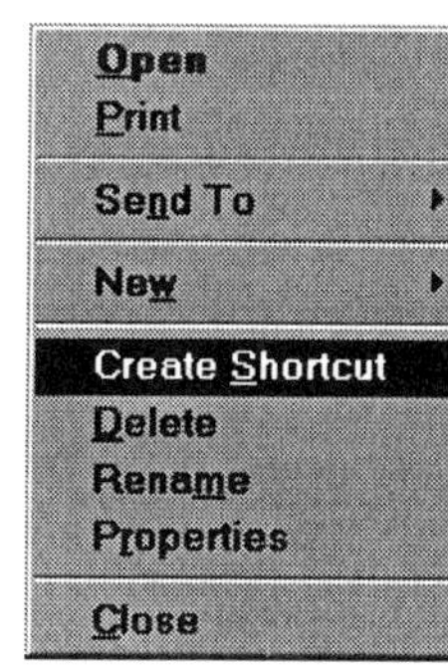


3. Choose Create Shortcut form the pop-up menu. A new object entitled "Shortcut to ..." will appear in the contents pane.
4. To move the shortcut to the Desktop, either
   - Drag it onto the Desktop (you may have to reduce the size of the Explorer window to accomplish this).

   *or*
   - Cut the object to the Clipboard (by clicking on the Cut Edit menu command or Toolbar button) and paste it onto the Desktop (by right-clicking on the Desktop and choosing Paste from the pop-up menu).
5. The shortcut will now appear on the Desktop as an icon. (Icons for shortcuts contain a small arrow in the lower left corner, as shown here for the WordPad shortcut icon.) Once on the Desktop, you can:

**Shortcut "arrow"**

   - Move the shortcut to a new location by dragging it with the mouse.

- Rename the shortcut by clicking on its highlighted icon or right-clicking on it and choosing Rename from the pop-up menu. In either case, a "box" will appear around the shortcut's name. Now, type a new name and press the Enter key.

TIP

You can also create shortcuts directly on the Desktop without starting up Explorer. To do so:

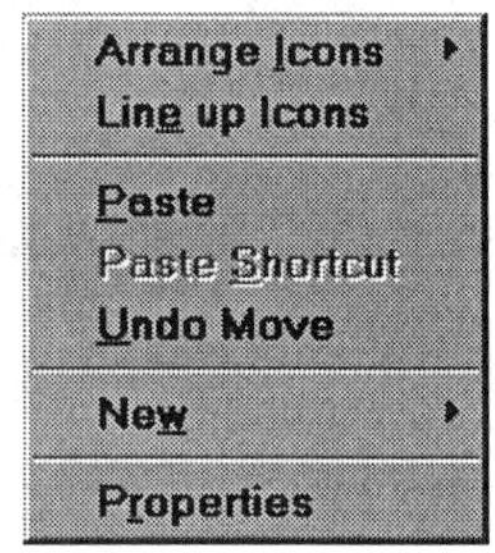


1. Right-click on an empty part of the Desktop. The menu shown at the right will pop up.
2. Point at New on this menu and then choose the Shortcut option on the resulting submenu. This action starts the Create Shortcut "wizard".
3. Either type the path name of the desired file in the *Command line* text box or click on the Browse button to have Windows help you locate this file. (We will discuss *browsing* in Section 3.5.)
4. Choose the Next command button and you will be asked if you want to rename the shortcut.
5. Type a new name, if you want, and then choose the Finish command button. The new shortcut will appear on the Desktop.

This technique works from within Explorer, as well — the New command can be accessed from the File menu or the menu that pops up when you right-click on a selected object (see Figure 12). However, from within Explorer, you'll have to move the new shortcut to the Desktop "manually".

3.4 TUTORIAL

Try the following exercises on your own.

1. Turn on your computer, if necessary, to start up Windows 95, and close any open windows.
2. Start Explorer and select the List view option from the View menu or Toolbar.
3. Insert the Lab Exercises disk in its drive and select this drive (for example, "3½ Floppy (A:)") in the folder tree pane.
4. Select the file named DeleteFile from the contents pane.
5. Size and move the Explorer window so that the selected file, the Recycle Bin Desktop icon, and an empty part of the Desktop are all visible.

6. Create a shortcut for the selected file and place it on the Desktop:
   - Right-drag the file onto an empty part of the Desktop.
   - Choose Create Shortcut(s) Here from the menu that pops up when you release the mouse button.
   - Rename the shortcut icon "DelFile" by clicking on it, typing the new name, and pressing the Enter key.
7. Delete the new DelFile icon by dragging it (using the left mouse button) onto the Recycle Bin icon.
8. Restore the DelFile shortcut: Open the Recycle Bin (by double-clicking on its icon), select the DelFile shortcut, and choose the Restore command from the File menu. Now, close the Recycle Bin.
9. Delete the DelFile shortcut again, this time by selecting it and pressing the Del key. Answer Yes to the Confirm Delete query.
10. Rename the DeleteFile object in the root folder of the floppy disk by selecting this file in Explorer's contents pane, right-clicking on it, choosing Rename from the pop-up menu, typing a new name of your choosing, and pressing the Enter key.
11. Delete this newly-renamed file by choosing Delete from Explorer's File menu. Answer Yes to the Confirm Delete query.
12. Exit Explorer and remove the Lab Exercises disk from its drive.

# 3.5 My Computer

As you saw in Chapter 1, the Desktop contains an icon called *My Computer* that provides access to virtually all aspects of your computer system. In particular, from the My Computer window you can carry out all the operations on files and folders that we have discussed in this chapter. This is not surprising once you realize that the My Computer icon is simply a built-in shortcut to Explorer's My Computer folder! If you keep this fact in mind, it will be easier to understand the workings of My Computer.

## Starting My Computer

My Computer

As you know, you can open the My Computer window, which is shown in Figure 13 on the next page, by double-clicking on its Desktop icon. Notice that this window is similar in appearance to the Explorer window, but My Computer lacks a folder tree pane; it uses a single subwindow, a contents pane, to display information.

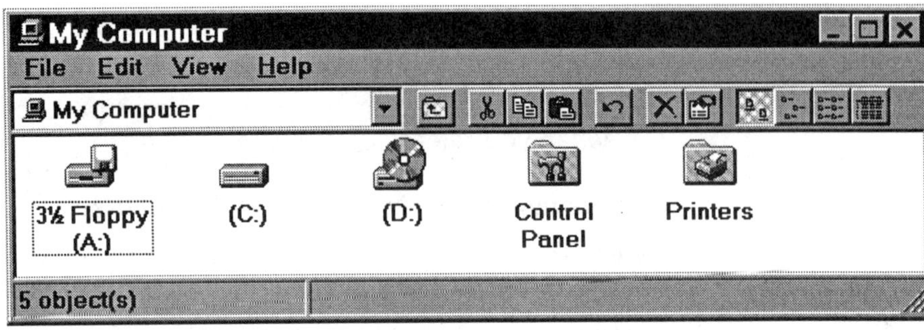


**Figure 13** The My Computer Window — Large Icons View

**NOTE**

You can also start My Computer by right-clicking on its icon and choosing Open from the resulting pop-up menu. Interestingly enough, if you choose Explore instead of Open from this menu, Explorer will start and display a two-paned view of the My Computer folder.

The fact that the My Computer window lacks a tree pane results in two basic differences between the way My Computer and Explorer are used to locate and manipulate objects:

1. My Computer provides less flexibility than Explorer in navigating (or **browsing**) the Windows file system. For example, it is often more difficult to locate a particular folder in My Computer.
2. Certain drag-and-drop operations are not carried out as easily in My Computer as in Explorer. For example, it is usually more difficult to drag a given file onto a certain folder in My Computer.*

We will now examine the consequences of each of these differences.

## *Using My Computer to Browse Folders*

**Opening a subfolder**

Once you have started My Computer, you can easily access its subfolders: your computer's drives, the Printers folder, and so on (see Figure 13). Just double-click on an icon to open one of these folders, and its contents will be displayed in a new window. For example, if you double-click on the "(C:)" icon, a window will open displaying all the

*In light of these deficiencies, you might be wondering why Microsoft chose to give My Computer such prominence in the Windows 95 interface. One reason for this approach is to provide easy access, especially for the novice user, to all aspects of the computer system — its drives, files, printers, settings, and so on.

files and subfolders in the root folder of the C: drive. A subfolder of *any* folder is opened in the same way — by double-clicking on its icon.

**NOTE**

The previous My Computer window may or may not close when a new one opens. You can control whether or not a separate window opens whenever you change folders by choosing the Options command from the View menu, selecting the appropriate option button in the resulting dialog box, and choosing the OK command button. We will further discuss this feature later in this section.

**Opening a parent folder**

If you want to open the parent folder of the current folder (going up one level in the folder tree), take any of the following actions:

- Press the Backspace key.
- Click on the Up One Level button on the current window's Toolbar (Figure 14). Remember: If the Toolbar is not displayed, choose Toolbar from the View menu to display it.
- If the parent window is visible on the screen, click on it; or, if the parent window's button appears on the Taskbar, click on that.

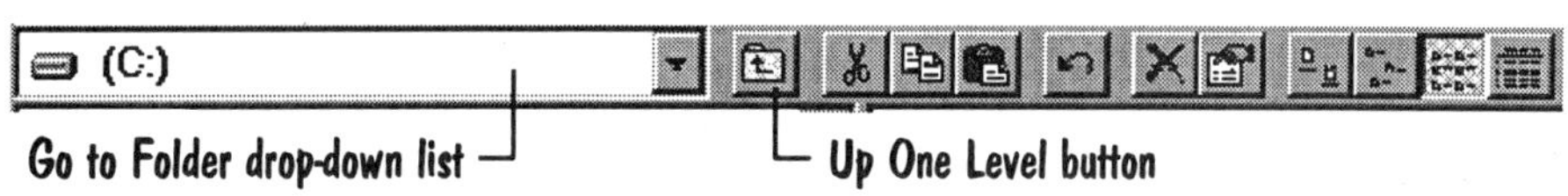


**Figure 14** The My Computer Toolbar

**Using the Go to Folder drop-down list**

The Go to Folder drop-down list on the Toolbar (see Figure 14) provides a way to change folders more quickly in certain situations. When you open this drop-down list (by clicking on the down-triangle), a "mini-tree" is displayed, showing the immediate (child) subfolders of the Desktop and My Computer, as well as the chain of subfolders forming the path to the current folder (Figure 15). The current folder is shown in the text box at the top of the list.

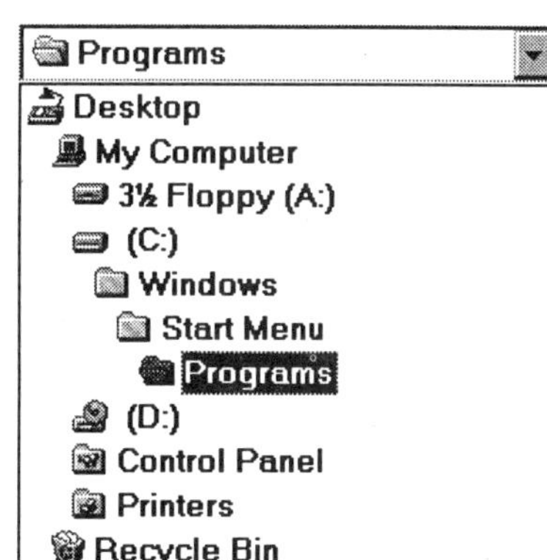


**Figure 15** A Typical Go to Folder Drop-down List

To display the contents of one of the listed folders, just click on it.

The Go to Folder drop-down list can be a great time-saving convenience. For example, suppose the current folder is Programs, as in Figure 15. To display the contents of the disk in the 3½" floppy drive, just open the drop-down list and click on the "3½ Floppy (A:)" object.

TIP

The following tips make it easier to use My Computer to browse folders:

- The default view option for My Computer is Large Icons. It's much easier to see what's in the current folder if you use the View menu or the Toolbar buttons to switch to the Small Icons or List view option (see Section 3.2).
- Display the *path* of the current folder on its window's title bar (if it is not already displayed there) by choosing the Options command from the View menu, clicking on the View tab in the resulting dialog box, selecting the *Display the full MS-DOS path in the title bar* check box, and choosing the OK command button.
- If each change of folder has opened a separate window, you can close all these windows at the same time by holding down the Shift key while clicking on the last window's close button.

NOTE

Some Windows dialog boxes (such as Run, Save As, and Open) allow you to browse folders as you do in My Computer. For example, if you activate the Browse command button in the Run dialog box (see Section 2.1), a dialog box like the one in Figure 16 will open. Using the Toolbar buttons, you can select a List or Details view option or go Up One Level. You can also Go to Folder via the Toolbar drop-down list. In addition, if you're looking for a file of a particular type, you can restrict the kinds of files that are displayed by using the *Files of type* drop-down list.

## *Using My Computer to Operate on Files and Folders*

Objects — files, folders and shortcuts — are manipulated from within a My Computer window in essentially the same way as in Explorer (see Sections 3.3 and 3.4). For example, you can copy a file from one folder to another using the Copy and Paste commands, as follows:

1. Open the folder containing the file to be copied.
2. Right-click on the desired file, which selects it and displays a pop-up menu.

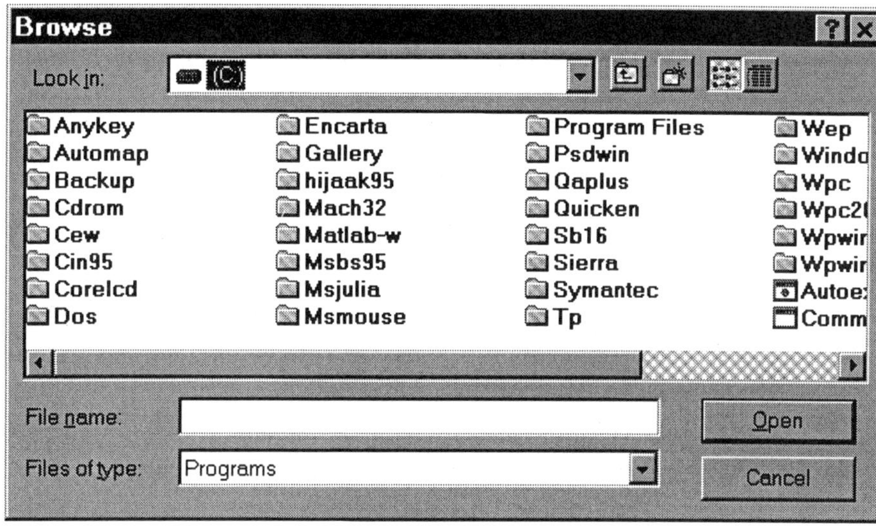


**Figure 16** A Browse Dialog Box

3. Choose the Copy command from the pop-up menu.
4. Right-click on the destination folder's name, which displays a pop-up menu.
5. Choose the Paste command from this pop-up menu and the process is complete.

Notice that this procedure could be used without change in Explorer, but there is one subtle difference in its execution here. To carry out steps 1 and 4 in Explorer, you would most likely just scroll and expand the folder tree pane (if necessary) until the name of the desired folder appeared; then click on it. In My Computer, on the other hand, you might have to open several windows in each of steps 1 and 4 before the desired folder became visible!

**Drag-and-drop in My Computer**

The difference just described causes the greatest trouble if you want to perform a drag-and-drop move or copy (see Section 3.3). The problem here is that the object to be moved or copied *and* the destination folder must be visible at the same time. This is not much of a problem in Explorer, but requires some preparation in My Computer.

The trick to drag-and-drop moving or copying in My Computer is to open both the source and destination folders and arrange them so that both are visible on the screen. For example, suppose we want to copy a file named Testfile.doc from a floppy disk to the Windows folder on the C: drive. To do this using drag-and-drop in My Computer:

1. Insert the floppy disk into its drive and start My Computer.
2. Ensure that a separate window will open for each new folder by choosing the Options command from the View menu and (if necessary) selecting the *Browse folders using a separate window for each folder* option button in the resulting dialog box before activating the OK command button.
3. Back in My Computer, double-click on the (C:) icon to open the root folder of the C: drive, C:\.
4. Scroll the C:\ window until the Windows folder's name appears.
5. Switch back to the My Computer window by clicking on it or its Taskbar button.
6. Double-click on the appropriate floppy drive icon to open its window.
7. Scroll this window (if necessary) until Testfile.doc appears and click on it to select this file. The current arrangement of windows is shown in Figure 17.

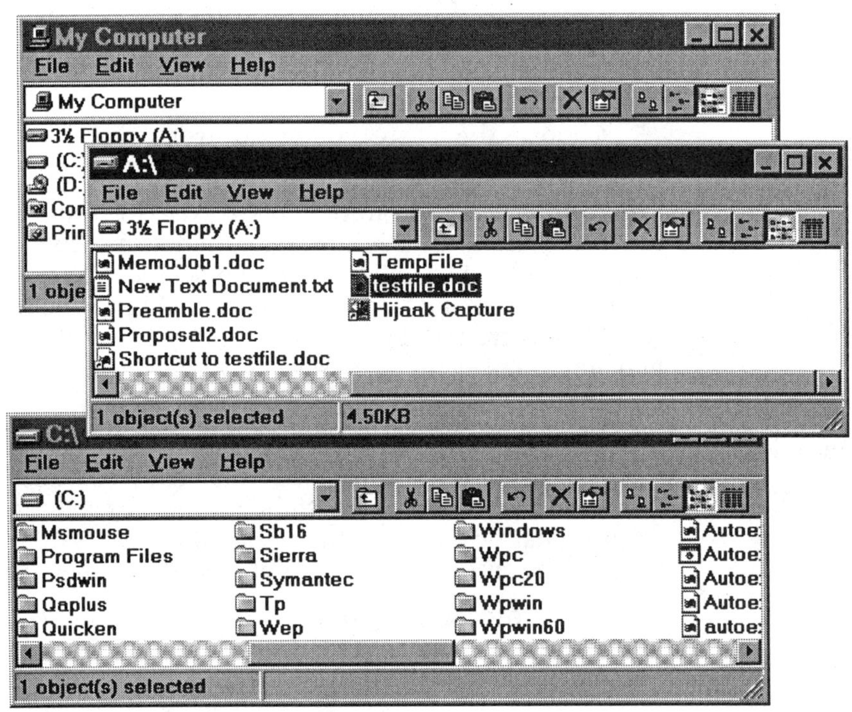


**Figure 17** Preparing to Copy with My Computer

8. If necessary, resize or move the floppy drive window and the C:\ window so that the names Testfile.doc and Windows are both visible.
9. Drag the Testfile.doc file onto the Windows folder. The Copying animated dialog box will confirm that the copy operation is taking place.

3-5 TUTORIAL

Try the following exercises on your own.

1. Turn on your computer, if necessary, to start up Windows 95, and close any open windows.
2. Start My Computer by double-clicking on its Desktop icon.
3. Elect to use a single My Computer window to display all folders:
   - Choose Options from the View menu to open the Options dialog box.
   - Select the "Browse folders by using a single window that changes as you open each folder." option button.
   - Choose the OK command button.
4. Insert the Lab Exercises disk in its drive and then select this drive by double-clicking on the appropriate icon (for example, "3½ Floppy (A:)").
5. Open the WordPad subfolder by double-clicking on it.
6. Right-click on the Fonts file in the WordPad subfolder and copy it to the Clipboard by choosing the Copy command from the pop-up menu.
7. Open the root folder on the A: drive (A:\), the parent of the WordPad folder, by either clicking on the Up One Level Toolbar button or pressing the Backspace key.
8. Paste the Fonts file into the A:\ folder by choosing the Paste command from the Edit menu. If the Confirm File Replace dialog box appears, choose the No command button.
9. If the Toolbar is not visible in the My Computer window, display it by choosing Toolbar from the View menu. Open the root folder on the C: drive:
   - Open the Toolbar's Go to Folder drop-down list (see Figure 14 on page 97).
   - Click on the "(C:)" item in the drop-down list.
10. Close the My Computer window and remove the Lab Exercises disk from its drive.

# 3.6 *Formatting and Copying Floppy Disks*

All the procedures we have discussed in this chapter apply to files and folders on floppy disks (diskettes) as well as hard disks. Two additional operations are useful with floppies: formatting and copying disks. In this section, we will discuss these procedures.

## *Formatting a Floppy Disk*

Before information can be stored on a disk, the disk must be **formatted**. This process prepares the disk to store information, dividing it into sectors and creating a file allocation table on it, and also erases any data that had been stored on the disk prior to formatting. Hard disks are usually formatted by the manufacturer or dealer, and most floppies are also sold already formatted. (In the latter case, the word "formatted" will appear on the box and on each individual disk.) Nevertheless, from time to time, you will have to format a diskette for one of the following reasons:

- To prepare an unformatted diskette for use.
- To reformat a Macintosh disk for use on your IBM-compatible computer.
- To quickly erase all files on a disk.

**WARNING**

Keep in mind that the format procedure erases all information on the disk being formatted! So, never format a disk unless you are sure there is nothing stored on it or (if there is data on the disk) that you no longer need its contents. Unless the disk is fresh out of the box, it's wise to check its contents before formatting it. To do so, insert the diskette in its drive, start Explorer, and select the appropriate floppy drive (3½ or 5¼) in the folder tree pane. If a message is displayed informing you that the disk is not formatted, fine. Otherwise, check each file listed in the contents pane. If you see a file that you're not sure you want erased, open it to view its contents before proceeding.

If you format a disk and then realize you made a mistake — it did contain some information you need — immediately inform your instructor or lab coordinator. It *might* be possible to recover the desired files if you have not yet used the newly-formatted diskette.

To format a floppy disk:

1. Insert the diskette to be formatted in its drive.

2. Start My Computer or Explorer and select this drive.
3. Right-click on the selected drive and choose Format from the resulting pop-up menu (Figure 18). Or, in My Computer, choose Format from the File menu. A Format dialog box, like the one in Figure 19, will be displayed.
4. Select the proper Capacity for the diskette from the drop-down list:
   - For 3.5" disks, select *1.44 Mb* if the disk is a high density one (with an "HD" on its label); select *720 Kb*, otherwise.
   - For 5.25" disks, select *1.2 Mb* if the disk is a high density one (with an "HD" on its label); select *360 Kb*, otherwise.

**Figure 18**
Floppy Disk Menu

5. Select a "Format type" option from the option buttons:

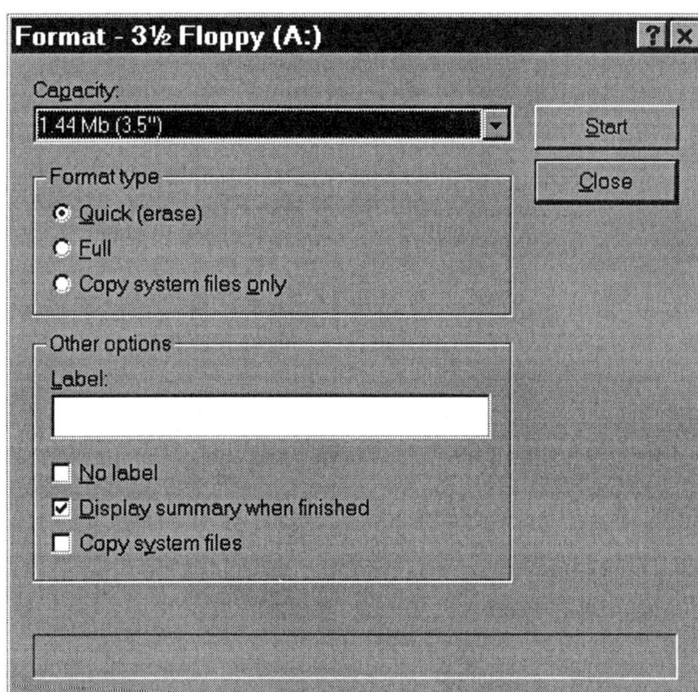


**Figure 19** The Format Dialog Box

- *Quick (erase)* can only be used with diskettes that have already been formatted. It "erases" all information on the disk (by removing the file allocation table and other system information). This option provides a convenient way to erase old, unneeded disks so they can be used again. Quick format is much faster than the normal (or *full*) format process.
- *Full* is the option used to format a diskette which has not yet been formatted for an IBM-compatible computer.
- *Copy system files only* is used with formatted diskettes. It creates a *bootable* diskette — if placed in the computer's A: drive at startup, the computer will access the information on this disk, instead of the hard disk, and start DOS. A bootable diskette is useful if your hard disk has become damaged.

6. Type a name for the diskette in the Label text box if you want to associate a name with this diskette. The label (or *volume label*) for a diskette is displayed by certain programs. Select the *No label* check box if you want to delete a previous label for the diskette.
7. Select the *Display summary when finished* check box to display information about the free space on the disk when the formatting process is complete.
8. Select the *Copy system files* check box to create a bootable diskette during the formatting process.
9. Choose the Start command button to begin the formatting process. The message "Formatting" and a bar graph showing the percentage of the process completed will appear at the bottom of the Format dialog box.

## *Copying an Entire Diskette*

If your computer has two floppy disk drives, you can use the copy procedure, described in Section 3.3, to copy all files from one diskette to another. Windows provides a simpler way to copy all the contents of one diskette to another, even if your machine only has one floppy disk drive, as long as the diskettes have the *same size and capacity*. Here's how it works:

1. Insert the diskette to be copied (the *source disk*) in its drive. If you have two drives of the same capacity, insert the disk to be copied to (the *destination disk*) in the other drive.
2. Start My Computer or Explorer and select the source drive.
3. Right-click on this drive and choose Copy Disk from the pop-up menu (see Figure 18). Or, in My Computer, choose Copy Disk from

the File menu. A Copy Disk dialog box, similar to the one in Figure 20, will be be displayed.

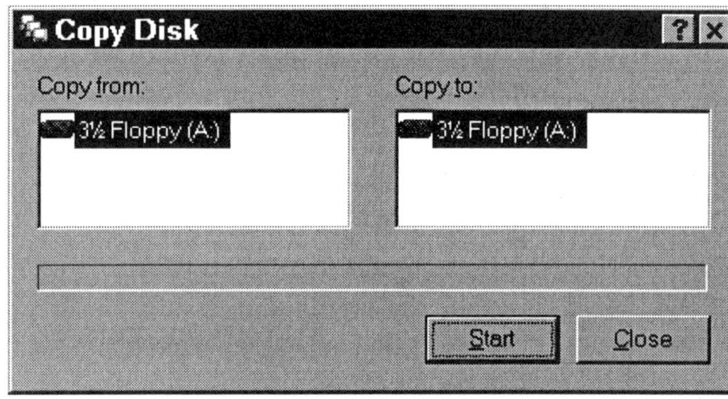


**Figure 20** The Copy Disk Dialog Box

4. Choose the Start command button to begin the copying process. Messages and a bar graph at the bottom of the Copy Disk dialog box will indicate the progress of the operation.
5. If you have only one floppy drive, the following dialog box will appear halfway through the copy process:

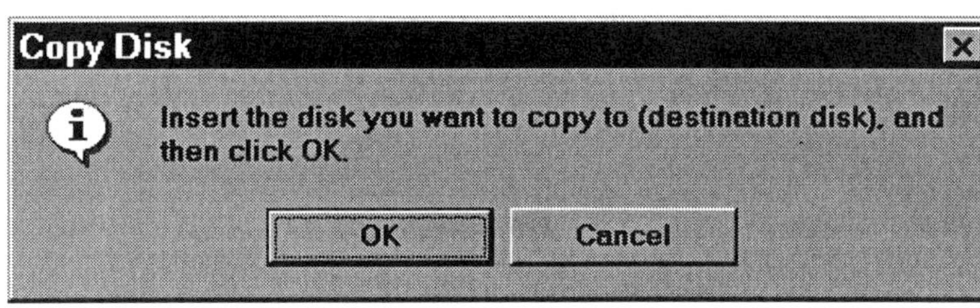


Insert the destination disk in its drive. Be aware that the copy process will *erase all information* on this disk!

6. When the copy process is complete, a message to this effect will appear at the bottom of the Copy Disk dialog box. When it does, choose the Close command button.

**WARNING** When you carry out the copy disk process, all existing information on the destination disk is erased and replaced with a copy of the source disk. Consequently, before beginning the process, be sure that there are no files of any value on the destination disk.

# Review Exercises

**Section 3.1**

1. A ___________ is a collection of information generated by a program and saved on disk.
2. A ___________ is a collection of files that have been grouped together and given a name.
3. True or false: A folder may contain files and/or subfolders.
4. True or false: If the path name for a file is `A:\Paint\Truck.bmp`, then it is located in the Paint folder on the disk in the A: drive.
5. Which of the following is a valid DOS file name?
   a. `Homework 1`
   b. `Homework.1`
   c. `HomeworkOne`
   d. All of these names are valid DOS file names.
6. Which of the following is a valid long file name?
   a. `Homework 1`
   b. `Homework.1`
   c. `HomeworkOne`
   d. All of these names are valid long file names.

**Section 3.2**

7. In the Explorer window, the ___________ pane can contain both files and folders.
8. To see the subfolders of a given folder in Explorer's left pane (if they are not currently displayed), click on the ___________ symbol that precedes the name of the folder.
9. If you want to display the size of a file shown in Explorer's contents pane, click on the ___________ item on the View menu.
10. True or false: Explorer's left pane only shows the folders present on the C: drive.
11. True or false: In Explorer, you can use the Toolbar to select one of four view options (Large Icons, Small Icons, List, or Details).
12. True or false: In Small Icons view in Explorer, it is possible to order the icons in alphabetical order by file type.
13. The only Explorer view option in which you can display files in decreasing size order is:
    a. Large Icons
    b. Small Icons
    c. List
    d. Details

14. In which of the following view options can file and folder names and their icons be moved, one by one, around Explorer's contents pane?

    a. Large Icons only
    b. Small icons only
    c. Both Large Icons and Small Icons
    d. Neither Large Icons nor Small Icons

**Section 3.3**

15. To select two nonconsecutive files in Explorer, click on the first and hold down the ____________ key while clicking on the second.

16. To copy a file from one folder to another on the C: drive, hold down the ____________ key while dragging the file to its destination.

17. A simple way to copy a selected file to the disk in the A: drive is to right-click on the file, point at the ____________ command on the pop-up menu, and choose 3½ Floppy (A) from the submenu.

18. True or false: To select a group of objects that are in consecutive order in Explorer's contents pane, click on the first and then hold down the Shift key while clicking on the last.

19. True or false: When you right-drag an object in Explorer and release the mouse button, the pop-up menu allows you to move *or* copy it to the new location.

20. True or false: The Cut and Copy buttons on Explorer's Toolbar can be used to move text, but not files.

21. If one object in Explorer's contents pane is selected and you click on another (without holding down any key), then

    a. The first object is deselected and the second is selected.
    b. The first object remains selected, but the second is not selected.
    c. Both objects are selected.
    d. Neither object is selected.

22. To *move* a file from the Windows folder to the disk in the A: drive, you can

    a. Use the Cut and Paste commands on Explorer's Edit menu.
    b. Drag the file from the Windows folder and drop it on the A: drive icon.
    c. Use the Send To command.
    d. None of these techniques can be used to move the file.

**Section 3.4**

23. If you select an object in Explorer and press the Delete key, that object is normally moved to a folder called the ____________.

24. To create a subfolder of the Windows folder using Explorer, right-

click in the contents pane and point at the ___________ command on the resulting pop-up menu.

25. Windows places a ___________ around an object's name to let you know that this object can now be renamed.
26. True or false: If you choose the Empty Recycle Bin command from its File menu, all objects in the Recycle Bin are removed from disk.
27. True or false: Shortcuts placed on the Desktop cannot be renamed.
28. True or false: A shortcut to a file is actually a copy of that file.
29. To delete an object that has been selected in Explorer's contents pane, you can
    a. Press the Delete key.
    b. Choose the Delete command from the File menu.
    c. Click on the Toolbar's Delete button.
    d. Perform any of the above actions.
30. Suppose you have just created a shortcut in Explorer. To place this shortcut on the Desktop, you can
    a. Drag it onto the Desktop.
    b. Cut it to the Clipboard and Paste in onto the Desktop.
    c. Copy it onto the Clipboard and Paste it onto the Desktop.
    d. Perform any of the above actions.

**Section 3.5**

31. To start My Computer, ___________ on its Desktop icon.
32. In My Computer, to open the parent folder of the one currently open, press the ___________ key on the keyboard.
33. True or false: A command on My Computer's View menu allows you to control whether or not a separate window is displayed when you open a new folder.
34. True or false: You can use My Computer to move, copy, delete, rename, and create files, but not folders.
35. Suppose My Computer is displaying the contents of the Windows folder, which is a subfolder of the root folder on the C: drive. Opening the Go to Folder drop-down list, you will see
    a. Every subfolder of the Windows folder.
    b. Every subfolder of the root folder on the A: drive.
    c. Every subfolder of the My Computer folder.
    d. None of the above folders.
36. In My Computer, which view options are available?
    a. Large Icons and Small Icons, but not List or Details.

b. List and Details, but not Large Icons or Small Icons.
c. Large Icons, Small Icons, List, and Details.
d. Only the default view is available.

**Section 3.6**

37. To format a floppy disk using Explorer, begin by ____________ on the appropriate drive icon in the folder tree pane.
38. The Copy Disk command can only be used with floppy disks of the same ____________ and ____________.
39. True or false: After formatting a disk, you will not be able to access the information that had previously been stored on it.
40. True or false: When you use the Copy Disk command, all information on the source disk is erased.
41. Which option button should you select in the Format dialog box to format an unformatted diskette?
    a. Quick
    b. Full
    c. Copy system files only
    d. None of these options will format an unformatted diskette.
42. To create a bootable diskette without erasing the data on it, in the Format dialog box
    a. Select the *Quick* option button.
    b. Select the *Full* option button.
    c. Select the *Copy system files only* option button.
    d. Select the *Copy system files* check box.

# *Lab Exercises*

Work each of the following exercises at your computer. Begin by turning the machine on (if necessary) to start Windows 95. If you want to produce a written record of your answers, review the material on WordPad and capturing screens in Sections 2.2 and 2.3.

**Lab Exercise 1 (Section 3.2)**

a. Start Windows Explorer and maximize its window.
b. Insert the Lab Exercises diskette in its drive and select this drive in the folder tree pane.
c. Display, *in the folder tree pane*, the subfolders of the floppy disk drive's (root) folder. How did you do this?
d. Select the Details view option. In what year was the Dosprog

application created?

e. Sort the files by modification date. Which *object* is at the top of the list? Which *file* is highest on the list?

f. Select the Large Icons view.

g. Interchange the positions of the Paint and Memo icons. Use the View menu to line up the icons. Did the icons return to their original positions?

h. Restore the Explorer window and resize it so that the Paint and Memo icons are visible but the window is as small as possible. Which scroll bars appeared? *Optional*: Capture this Explorer window.

i. Close Explorer and remove the diskette from its drive.

**Lab Exercise 2 (Section 3.3)**

a. Start Windows Explorer and maximize its window.

b. Insert the Lab Exercises diskette in its drive and select this drive in the folder tree pane.

c. Select Small Icons view. How are the files in the contents pane ordered?

d. Select all files (but no folders). How did you do this?

e. *Copy* the selected files to the Paint folder on the floppy disk by dragging them onto the Paint icon. Is it *necessary* to hold down the Ctrl key while dragging the files?

f. Open the Paint folder and select the Details option. How many of the listed files are *not* of the "Bitmap Image" type?

g. *Move* (by drag-and-drop) the copied files back to the root folder of the floppy disk. (Answer "Yes to All" to the Confirm Replace message.) Is it *necessary* to hold down the Shift key while dragging the files?

h. Close Explorer and remove the diskette from its drive.

**Lab Exercise 3 (Section 3.3)**

a. Start Windows Explorer, maximize its window, and select the Small Icons view option.

b. Insert the Lab Exercises diskette in its drive and select this drive in the folder tree pane.

c. Select the file MemoJob1 and *cut* it to the Clipboard. Then, select the file Memo and *copy* it to the Clipboard. Was either file deleted from the contents pane?

d. Minimize Explorer and any other open windows.

e. Right-click on the Desktop and choose Paste from the pop-up menu. Which file has appeared on the Desktop?

f. Restore the Explorer window and resize and move it so that the copied file is visible on the Desktop. Now, using the right-drag technique, *move* the file back to the contents pane. (Answer "Yes" to the Confirm File Replace message.) Where in the contents pane were the file name and icon placed?

g. Close Explorer and remove the diskette from its drive.

**Lab Exercise 4 (Section 3.4)**

a. Start Windows Explorer, maximize its window, and select the Small Icons view option.

b. Insert the Lab Exercises diskette in its drive and select this drive in the folder tree pane.

c. Create a new subfolder of the (root) floppy drive folder. It appears highlighted in the contents pane. What is it called?

d. Rename the new folder My Folder. How did you accomplish the Rename operation?

e. Size the Explorer window so that an empty part of the Desktop is visible. Then, right-drag My Folder to the Desktop, release the mouse button, and choose Create Shortcut(s) Here from the pop-up menu. How would one know, just by looking at the *icon*, that it represents a shortcut?

f. Open My Folder by double-clicking on its Desktop shortcut. Does its window have both a left and right pane? *Optional*: Reduce the window to a small size and capture it.

g. Delete the My Folder *folder* from the floppy drive. Did the My Folder *window* close when the folder was deleted?

h. Close the My Folder window, if necessary, and delete its shortcut.

i. Open the Recycle Bin and delete any references to My Folder. Was a Confirm Delete message displayed?

j. Close Explorer and remove the diskette from its drive.

**Lab Exercise 5 (Section 3.5)**

a. Start My Computer, maximize its window, and select the List view option.

b. Choose the Options command from the View menu. In the resulting dialog box, select the lower of the two option buttons and choose OK. What is the selected option called?

c. Select the drive that contains the Windows folder by double-clicking on it. Try C: first, then others. On which drive is the Windows folder located?

d. Open the Windows folder. How many subfolders does it have?

e. Successively open the following subfolders: Start Menu, Programs, and Accessories. What are the subfolders of Accessories?

f. Display the Go to Folder drop-down list. Are all the folders you've opened in this exercise listed there? *Optional*: Close the drop-down list and size the current window so that it's not much larger than this list. Then, capture the active window and reopen the drop-down list.

g. Select Recycle Bin from the Go to Folder list. In the new window, open the Go to Folder list again. Is the Accessories folder still listed?

h. Close the Recycle Bin window.

**Lab Exercise 6 (Section 3.5)**

Repeat Exercise 2, replacing every occurrence of *Explorer* by *My Computer* and *folder tree pane* or *contents pane* by *My Computer window.*

**Lab Exercise 7 (Section 3.6)**

[This exercise requires a blank floppy disk.]

a. Start Windows Explorer and insert a blank diskette in the appropriate drive.

b. Check the contents of the diskette by selecting its drive from the folder tree. What is displayed in the contents pane?

c. If the diskette contains any files or folders, do *not* continue this exercise! Otherwise, format the diskette, selecting the *Full* option and deselecting all check boxes in the Format dialog box. When you choose the Start command button, what message appears at the bottom of the dialog box?

d. Again use Explorer to check the contents of the diskette. Are any files or folders listed now?

e. Open the Format dialog box again. This time, select the *Copy system files only* option button (*not* the check box), and choose Start. What message is displayed in the dialog box?

f. One more time, check the diskette's contents. What are they?

g. Close Explorer and remove the diskette from its drive.

CHAPTER 4

# *Control Panel: Customizing Windows*

People use computers in different ways and for different reasons. With this in mind, the designers of Windows 95 provided many ways to customize its user interface. When this capability is used properly, the result is a more pleasant and productive environment. In Section 3.4, we described one way that Windows can be customized — by placing shortcuts for frequently used applications, documents, or folders right on the Desktop. In this chapter, we will discuss how to use the Control Panel utility to further customize windows. To be more specific, you will learn:

1. How to start, use, and close Control Panel.
2. How to choose a repeating pattern or wallpaper to decorate the Desktop.
3. How to select a screen saver.
4. How to change the color and size of various objects in the Windows 95 interface.
5. How to adjust the keyboard repeat rate and delay.
6. How to modify the operation of the mouse.
7. About setting the computer's clock, installing new software, and viewing fonts.

# 4.1 An Introduction to Control Panel

**Control Panel** is a collection of small programs (*utilities*) that help you customize the Windows user interface — its colors, sounds, mouse operation, etc. — so that it looks and acts the way you want. In this section, we will provide an overview of the workings of Control Panel.

## The Control Panel Window

To open the Control Panel window:

**Starting Control Panel**

1. Click on the Start button (or press Ctrl+Esc) to open the Start menu.
2. Point at the Settings option and hold the mouse steady for a second or two; the Settings submenu will open.

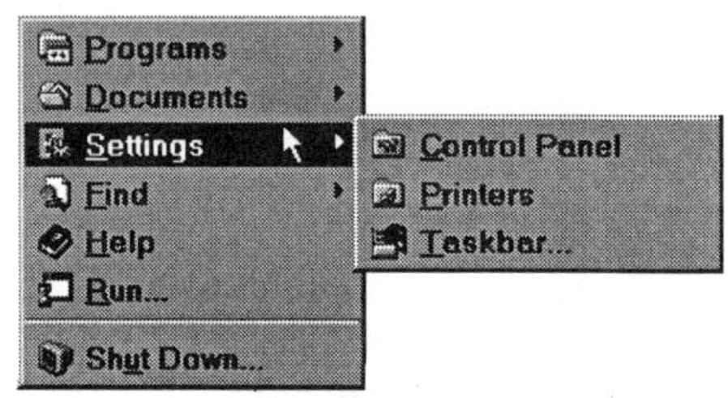


3. Click on the Control Panel item on this submenu. A window, similar to the one shown in Figure 1, will open.

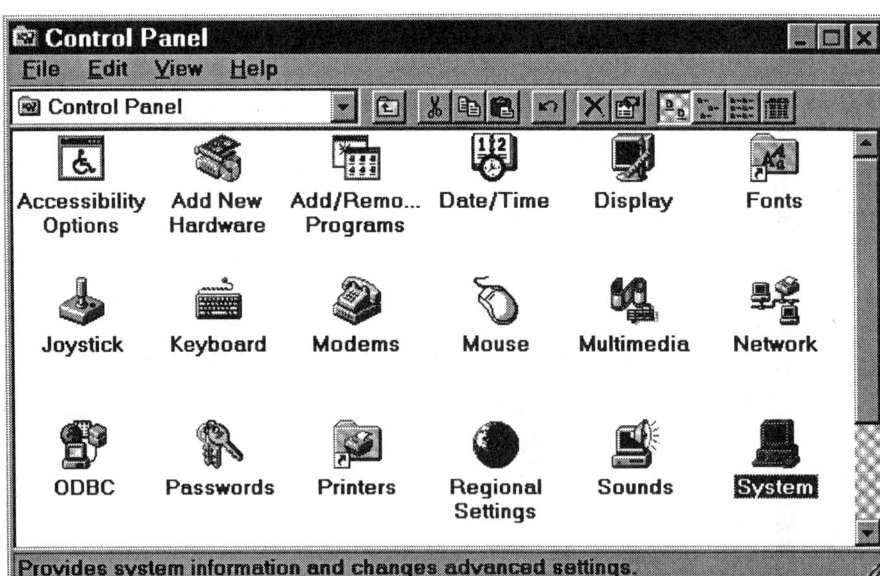


**Figure 1** The Control Panel Window

At the top of the window are the usual title and menu bars. Directly below the menu bar is a Toolbar, which, as you will see, allows us to quickly access some Control Panel features. (If the Toolbar does not appear in your Control Panel window, choose the Toolbar command from the View menu; this command toggles the Toolbar on or off.) At the bottom of the window is a Status Bar (which can also be turned on or off from the View menu). The Status Bar provides a brief description of the currently selected icon (which, in Figure 1, is *System*).

**Control Panel display options**

The window shown in Figure 1 represents each of the Control Panel functions as a "large icon". If you want, you can display the various functions in several other ways. For example, if we choose the List option from the View menu, the window will look like this:

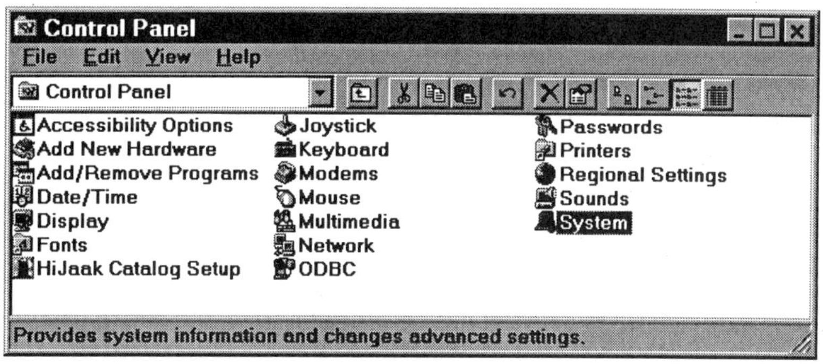


Two other display options are available on the View menu:

- Small Icons view looks similar to List view, but the icons are arranged in a different order.
- Details view lists each function on a separate line, which also contains a brief description of that function.

**NOTE**

The four display options (Large Icons, Small Icons, List, and Details) can also be accessed from the Toolbar. Just click on the appropriate button, as illustrated below:

If you forget the function of a Toolbar button, point at it with the mouse; a *tool tip* will appear, as shown at the left, identifying it!

## *Control Panel Functions*

Each of the icons displayed in the Control Panel window represents a utility that allows you to customize one aspect of Windows. The number, the type, and sometimes even the names of the available Control Panel functions depend on your system's configuration. The following table describes the most common functions.

| Name | Description |
|---|---|
| Accessibility Options | Changes the way the keyboard, sounds, display, or mouse behave to make Windows more accessible to people with disabilities. |
| Add New Hardware | Aids you in installing new hardware such as modems, sound boards, and CD-ROM drives on your system. |
| Add/Remove Programs | Aids you in installing and removing software on your system. |
| Date/Time | Changes the date and time on your computer's clock. |
| Display | Changes screen colors, type appearance, the Desktop background, the size of objects, and screen resolution; installs screen savers. |
| Fonts | Adds, removes, and allows you to view the fonts on your system. |
| Joystick | Selects, calibrates, and tests joystick devices. |
| Keyboard | Changes the keyboard type, layout, and repeat rate and delay; changes the cursor blink rate. |
| Modems | Installs a new modem and changes a modem's properties. |
| Mouse | Changes the mouse type and allows you to modify aspects of its operation such as double-click speed and pointer shape and speed. |
| Multimedia | Changes properties for audio, video, and MIDI (Musical Instrument Digital Interface) devices, and the playing of audio compact discs. |
| Network | Adds, removes, and configures network connections; aids you in accessing an installed network. |
| Passwords | Sets up user passwords and preferences (profiles). |
| Printers | Adds, removes, and changes settings (such as resolution and paper type) for printers. |

**Regional Settings** Changes international settings such as the format of numbers, currencies, dates, and times.

**Sounds** Changes Windows and system sounds, such as the sounds heard when Windows is started and exited.

**System** Provides system information and allows you to change settings that affect system performance.

**Choosing a function**

To choose one of the available Control Panel utilities, perform any of the following actions:

- Double-click on the appropriate icon.
- Click on the appropriate icon to select it and choose the Open command from the File menu.
- Right-click on the appropriate icon, which selects it and pops up a menu, and choose Open from this menu.

When you use a Control Panel utility to modify a setting, the new setting remains in effect every time you use Windows until that setting is changed again.

## *Closing Control Panel*

You can close (or exit) Control Panel in any of the following ways:

- Click on the close button on the right end of the title bar.
- Choose Close from the File menu.
- Press the Alt+F4 keystroke combination.

4-1 TUTORIAL

Try the following exercises on your own.

1. Turn on your computer, if necessary, to start up Windows 95 and close any open windows.
2. Start Control Panel:
   - Click on the Start button (or press Ctrl+Esc) to display the Start menu.
   - Point at the Settings option to open its submenu.
   - Click on the Control Panel item.
3. Maximize the Control Panel window.

4. If the Status Bar is not visible at the bottom of the Control Panel window, choose Status Bar from the View menu. Then, successively select (click on) each item in the window and take note of its function, which is displayed on the Status Bar.
5. If the Toolbar is not visible in the Control Panel window, choose Toolbar from the View menu. Click on each of the four view option buttons on the Toolbar and note its effect on the window.

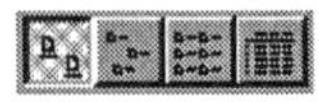

6. Close the Control Panel window by clicking on its close button or choosing the Close command on the File menu.

## 4.2 *Changing the Desktop Background*

The default Windows 95 Desktop has a solid, dark-colored background. In Section 4.3, we will describe how you can change the background color. This section discusses how to change the look of the Desktop in another way: by decorating it with a picture (graphic) and/or a repeating pattern. We will also describe how to have Windows display an animated image — a *screen saver* — when your system has been idle for a specified period of time.

Display

All the changes just described are accomplished using Control Panel's Display function. To start the Display utility, open Control Panel and choose the Display icon from its window (as described in Section 4.1). The Display Properties dialog box, shown in Figure 2, will then open.

You can also open the Display Properties dialog box without starting Control Panel. First, right-click on an empty part of the Desktop, which pops up the menu shown at the right. Then, choose the Properties item from this menu. The Display Properties dialog box will now appear on the screen.

### *Choosing a Desktop Pattern*

As you can see in Figure 2, the Display Properties dialog box contains four tabs. The first of these, *Background*, allows you to decorate the Desktop with a repeating pattern or a graphic image (*wallpaper*). To use one of the supplied Desktop patterns:

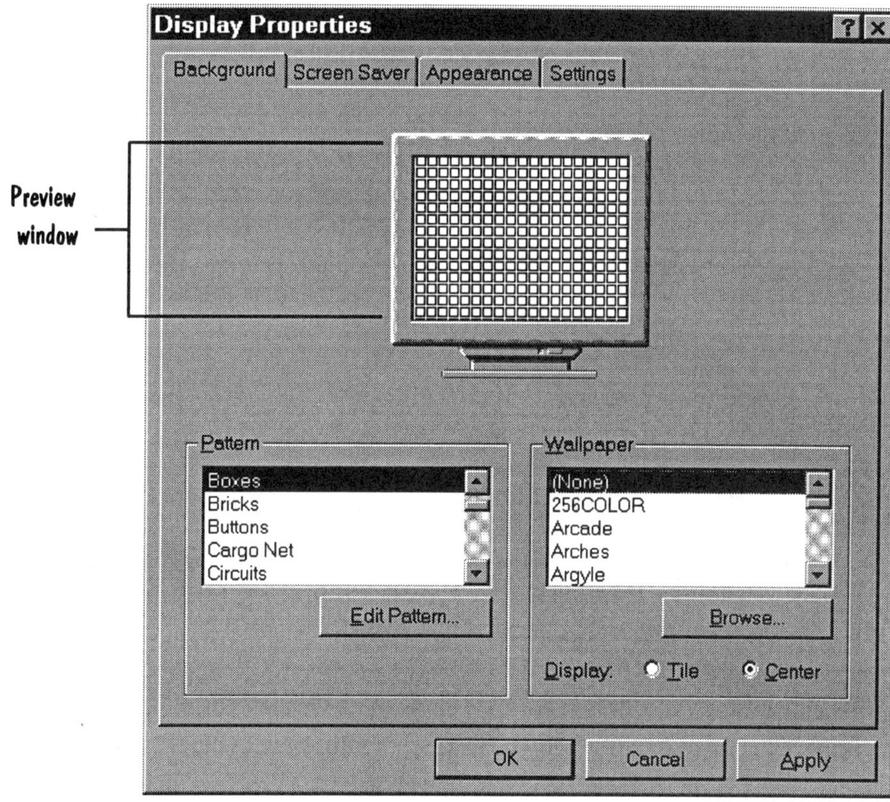


**Figure 2** The Display Properties Dialog Box — Background Page

1. Open the Display Properties dialog box (Figure 2) as described above.

2. Select a pattern by clicking on its name in the Pattern list box. If you don't want to use a Desktop pattern, select "(None)" from the top of the list. The preview window will display a sample of that pattern. (The Boxes pattern is shown in the preview window of Figure 2.)

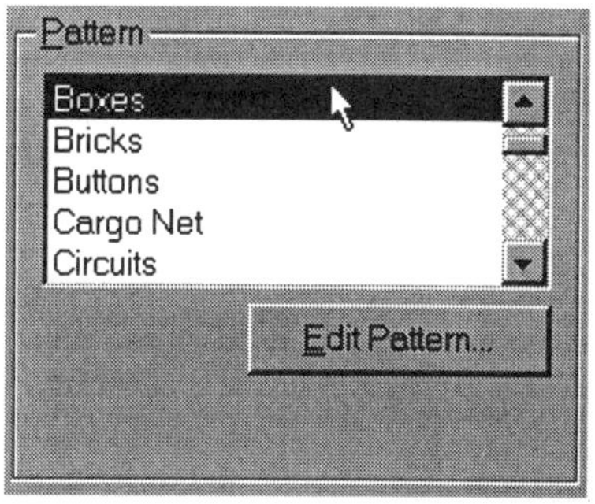


3. Choose the OK command button to put the pattern into effect and close the dialog box, or choose the Apply button to put the pattern into effect without closing the dialog box.

To see the selected pattern in all its glory, minimize all applications, including Control Panel, and close the Display Properties dialog box, if you haven't done so already.

**NOTE**

You can create Desktop patterns of your own design by selecting an existing pattern as described above and then choosing the Edit Pattern command button. The Pattern Editor dialog box will open, allowing you to change the current pattern or create a new one. The Pattern Editor is fun to play with; if you try it out, click on the close button to close its window when you're done.

## *Choosing Wallpaper*

Instead of using a solid color or patterned Desktop, you can decorate it with a graphic image, commonly known as **wallpaper**. (Yes, using wallpaper to decorate a desktop does sound a little strange!) Choosing wallpaper is easy:

1. Open the Display Properties dialog box (Figure 2).
2. Select a particular wallpaper by clicking on its name in the Wallpaper list box. If you don't want to use wallpaper, select "(None)" from the top of the list. The preview window shows how the wallpaper will look on your Desktop.

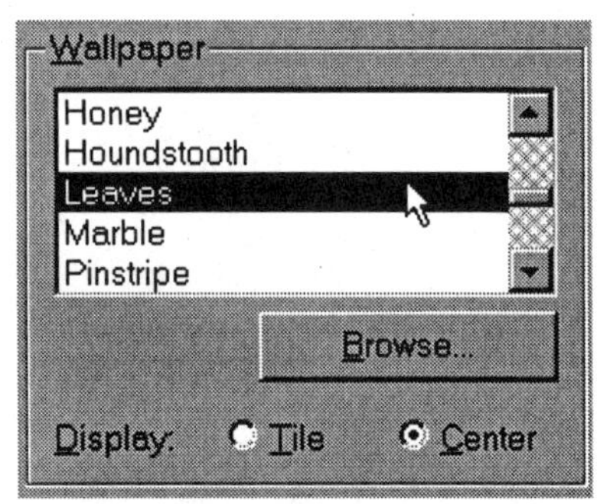


3. Select either the Center or Tile option button.
   - Selecting Center positions the graphic in the center of the screen. If it does not cover the entire screen, the solid or patterned Desktop will be visible around it (see Figure 3a).
   - Selecting Tile repeats the graphic as many times as necessary to cover the entire screen (as in Figure 3b). With small graphics, including most of those supplied with Windows, you will probably want to choose the Tile option.
4. Choose the OK command button to put the selected wallpaper into effect and close the dialog box, or choose the Apply button to put the wallpaper into effect without closing the dialog box.

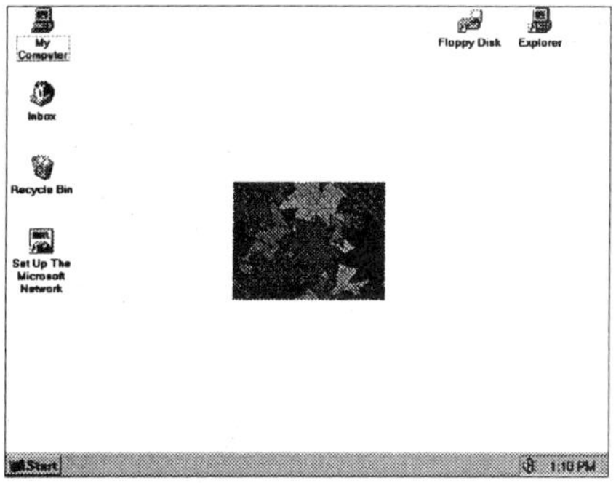

**Figure 3a** Centered Wallpaper

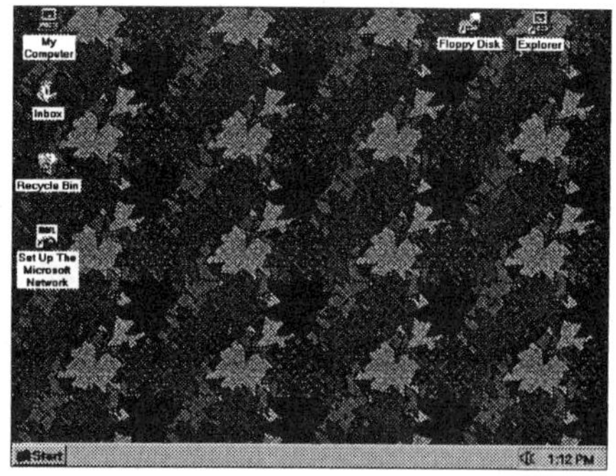

**Figure 3b** Tiled Wallpaper

## *Choosing a Screen Saver*

When a **screen saver** is in effect and neither the mouse nor the keyboard is used for a specified period of time, the screen will go blank or an animated graphic will be displayed. Screen savers are used just for fun or to deter others from viewing your work while you are away from the computer. They may also prevent damage to the screen from an unchanging image being "burned" into it over time.

Using the Display Properties dialog box, you can choose from among several Windows-supplied screen savers, or choose not to use a screen saver. You can also customize existing screen savers and set the *delay time* — how long the system must be inactive before the screen saver appears.

To select a screen saver:

1. Open the Display Properties dialog box (Figure 2).
2. Click on the Screen Saver tab to display the corresponding page of the dialog box, shown in Figure 4 on the next page.
3. Select a screen saver by clicking on its name in the Screen Saver drop-down list. Select "(None)" if you don't want to use a screen saver. With some screen savers, you will then see a simulation of their action in the preview window.

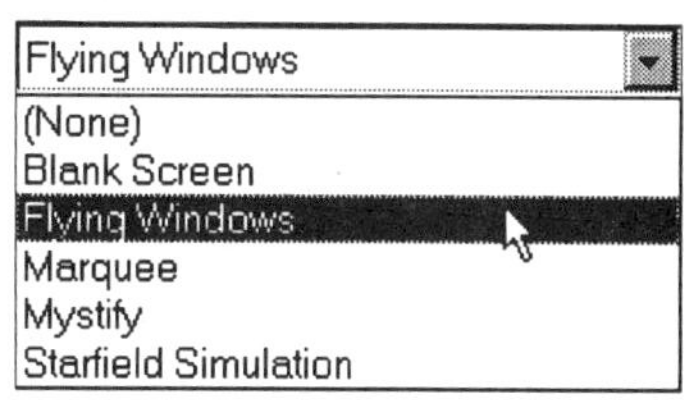


4. To customize the selected screen saver, click on the Settings command button. A dialog box will open allowing you to make certain changes in the way that screen saver works.

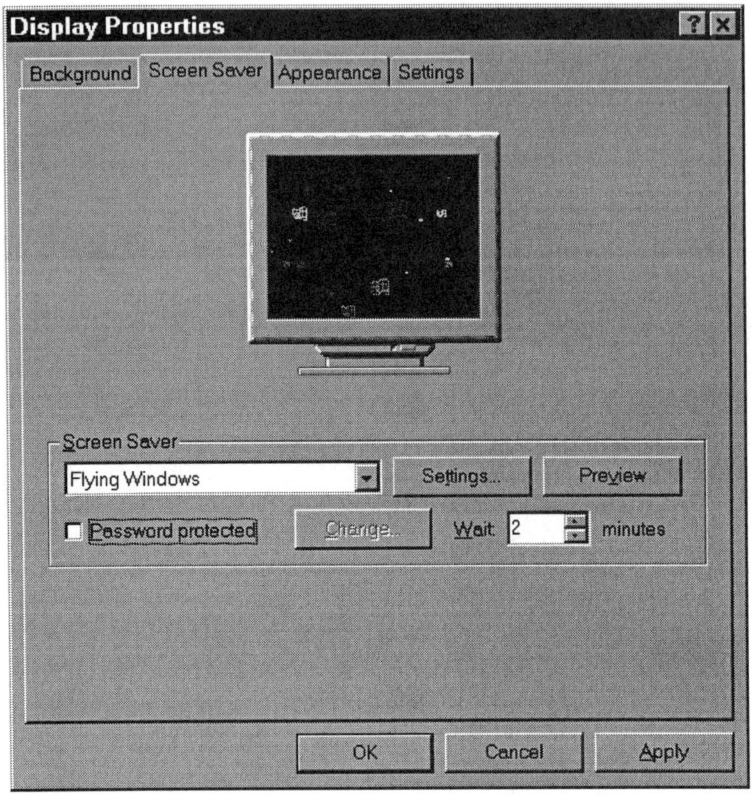


**Figure 4** Display Properties — Screen Saver Page

5. To see what the screen saver looks like full-screen, click on the Preview command button. The selected screen saver will be activated for a few seconds. (You may have to click the mouse to deactivate it.)
6. To set the delay time, type a number in the Wait text box (or make use of the up and down arrows in this box to set the time).
7. Choose the OK command button to complete the process and close the dialog box, or choose the Apply button to record your changes without closing the dialog box.

If a screen saver has been selected, it will be activated after the specified delay time. To have the active application reappear on the screen, press any key or move or click the mouse.

**NOTE**

You can set up certain screen savers so that a password of your choice must be entered to remove the screen saver's image from the screen once it has been activated. To enable password protection, select the *Password protected* check box (see Figure 4), then choose the Change command button and enter your password in the resulting dialog box. (If password protection is not available for the selected screen saver, its check box will be "grayed out".)

**4-2 TUTORIAL**

Try the following exercises on your own.

1. Turn on your computer, if necessary, to start up Windows 95 and close any open windows.
2. Start Control Panel and open the Display utility by double-clicking on its icon.
3. Select several successive Desktop patterns from the Pattern drop-down list and notice their effect in the preview window of the Display Properties dialog box.
4. Select a wallpaper (your choice) from the Wallpaper drop-down list and select the Tile option button. Notice the effect in the preview window. Now, select the Center option button and notice the change in the preview window.
5. Choose the OK command button to close the Display Properties dialog box and put the pattern and wallpaper into effect.
6. Close the Control Panel window to see the full effect of the changes you have made.
7. Right-click on the Desktop and choose Properties from the pop-up menu to reopen the Display Properties dialog box.
8. Return the Pattern and Wallpaper to its original settings.
9. Click on the Screen Saver tab to open a new page of the Display Properties dialog box.
10. Select Flying Windows from the Screen Saver drop-down list and notice the effect on the preview window.
11. Choose the Preview command button to activate the screen saver (full-screen). Click the mouse to deactivate it.
12. Click on the Wait text box, erase the current number, type `1`, and choose the Apply button. This puts the screen saver into effect without closing the Display Properties dialog box.
13. Do not use the mouse or keyboard for one minute. The screen saver will then be activated. Deactivate it by clicking the mouse or pressing a key.

14. Return the Screen Saver drop-down list and Wait time to their original settings and choose the OK command button to close the Display Properties dialog box.

## 4.3 Changing the Appearance of a Window

In Windows 95, a typical window contains a number of different elements: a title and menu bar, buttons of various sorts, text, icons, scroll bars, and so on. Through Control Panel's Display utility, Windows allows you to choose the color and size of such elements. This feature is not only fun to play with, but can also make for a more pleasant working environment.

Windows supplies you with two basic levels of control in customizing the appearance of a window:

1. You can choose a *predefined* (built-in) window scheme.
2. You can create a *custom* window scheme (one of your own design) by:
   - Choosing a color for each of the window elements.
   - Choosing a size for certain elements, such as title, menu, and scroll bars.
   - Choosing a **font** (a type style and size) for identifying text within the window, such as titles and button captions.

All these operations are carried out from the Appearance Page of the Display Properties dialog box. To open this dialog box, either

- Start Control Panel (if it's not already open) and choose the Display icon from its window, as described in Section 4.1.

*or*

- Right-click on an empty part of the Desktop and choose the Properties option from the resulting pop-up menu.

Then, to display the Appearance page of this dialog box, click on the Appearance tab. The resulting window is shown in Figure 5.

### Choosing a Predefined Window Scheme

Windows comes with a wide variety of built-in schemes that consist of a combination of colors, sizes, and/or fonts for the various window elements. To select one of these predefined schemes:

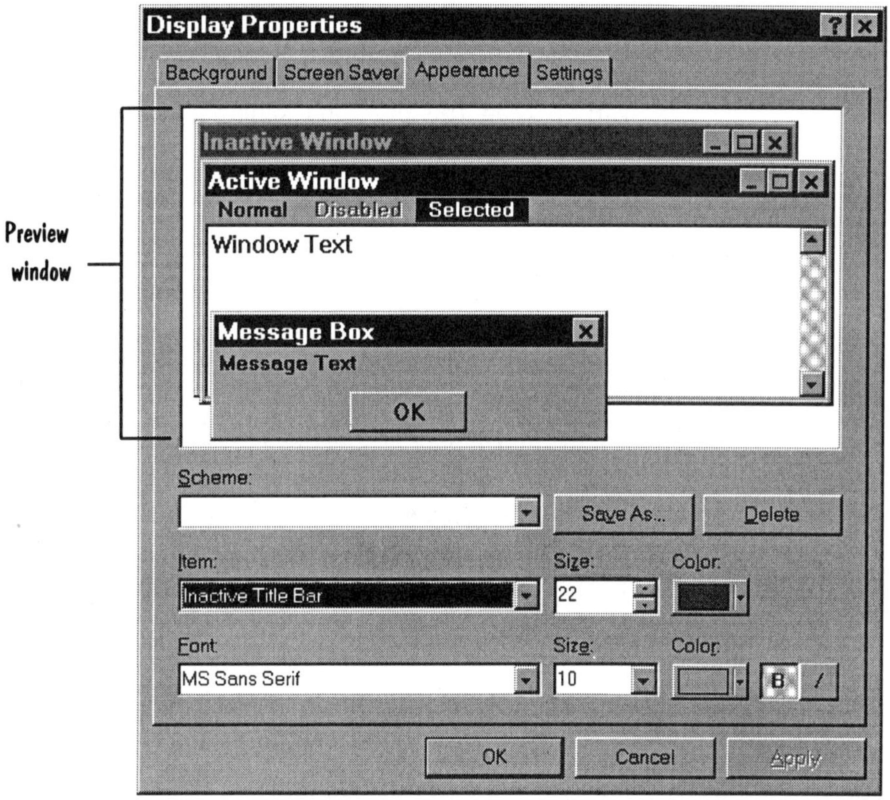


**Figure 5** Display Properties Dialog Box — Appearance Page

1. Open the Display Properties dialog box and select the Appearance page as described above.

2. Open the Scheme drop-down list (by clicking on its down triangle). A list of the available schemes will be displayed.

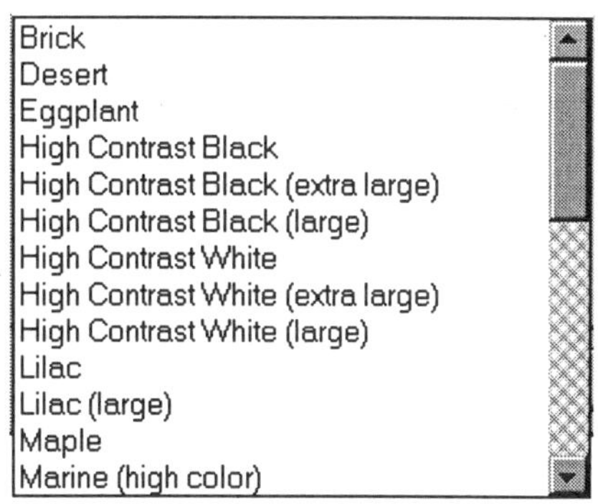


3. Select a scheme from the list. The preview window in the dialog box (see Figure 5) will show the way various screen elements (active and inactive title bars, command buttons, text, and so on) will look under this scheme.

4. Choose the OK command button to put the new scheme into effect and close the dialog box, or choose the Apply button to put the scheme into effect without closing the dialog box. (If you'd rather keep the previous scheme, choose the Cancel command button.)

## *Creating a Custom Window Scheme*

It is likely that you will want to change certain aspects of your favorite predefined window scheme or even create one that is completely different from any built-in scheme. Windows provides you with the tools to fine-tune a scheme as much as you like. Here's how to do it:

1. Open the Display Properties dialog box and select the Appearance page as described at the beginning of this section.
2. Select the predefined scheme that is closest to what you want from the Scheme drop-down list.
3. Select a screen element to be modified by either

   ■ Clicking on that element on the Item drop-down list (see Figure 6).

   *or*

   ■ Clicking on that element in the preview window area.

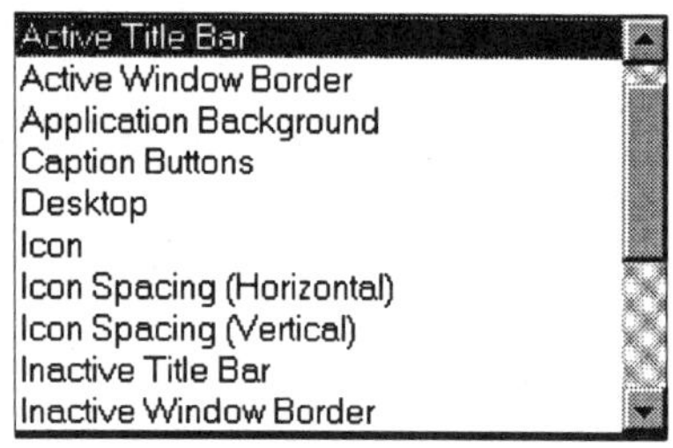


   For example, if you want to change the look of the active title bar or the text that appears on it, either select Active Title Bar from the Item drop-down list or click on "Active Window" in the preview window.

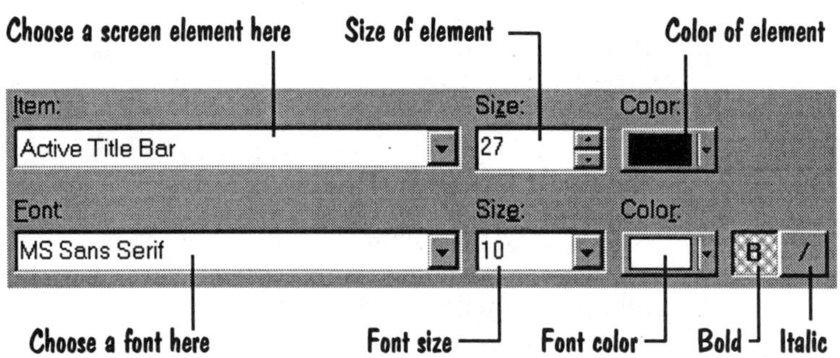


**Figure 6** Selecting a Screen Element and its Size, Color, and Font

4. To choose a size for the selected screen element (if this option is available), click on the Size box next to the Item text box, as shown in Figure 6. The number in the Size box gives the height (or sometimes, width) of the object in *points.* There are 72 points per inch, so the height of the Active Title Bar of Figure 6 is 27/72 of an inch, or 3/8".

5. To choose a color for the selected screen element, click on the Color box to the right of the Item text box (Figure 6). A palette of 20 colors will be displayed, as shown at the right. Now, just click on the desired color or, if you want to view additional colors, click on the Other command button, which opens a dialog box with more color choices. (This dialog box also allows you to create your own colors.)

6. If the selected screen element contains text, you can choose the *typeface, font size, font color,* and elect to use *bold* or *italic* attributes for this text. As you make your selections, the text for the given screen element will change accordingly in the preview window.

   - To select a typeface (the font style), open the Font drop-down list (Figure 6) and select from the available choices.
   - To select a font size, enter a new number in the Size box to the right of the Font text box. The number displayed here represents the height of the font in *points.* (Remember: There are 72 points to the inch.)
   - To select a font color, click on the Color box to the right of the Font text box and select a color from the resulting palette. (See step 5 for more information on selecting a color.)
   - If you want, you can select boldface (thicker) or italic (slanted) type for the text by clicking on the appropriate button (see Figure 6).

7. Save your new window scheme, if so desired, by choosing the Save As command button (see Figure 5) and typing a name for the scheme in the resulting dialog box. This scheme will then be added to the list of available schemes on the Scheme drop-down list.

   If you don't save your scheme, but choose OK or Apply in step 8, the scheme will still be put into effect and used in all Windows sessions until another scheme is selected. After that, however, the only way to retrieve the scheme is to recreate it step-by-step.

8. After you have made all the changes you want, choose the OK

command button to put them into effect and close the dialog box, or choose the Apply button to put the changes into effect without closing the dialog box. (To leave the previous settings in effect, choose the Cancel command button.)

**TIP**

Modifying certain screen elements also affects other aspects of the Windows interface. For example:

- The settings for the Menu screen element are used for all Windows menus, including the Start menu.
- The font specified for the Icon screen element is also used in the Explorer folder tree and contents panes (see Section 3.2).
- The font specified for the Active Title Bar screen element is also used for the Taskbar.

**NOTE**

The Settings page of the Display Properties dialog box provides ways to *globally* change the size of objects on the screen; these settings change the size of *everything* by the same scale factor. We will not discuss these features of the Display Properties dialog box in this text.

**TUTORIAL 4-3**

Try the following exercises on your own.

1. Turn on your computer, if necessary, to start up Windows 95 and close any open windows.
2. Open the Display Properties dialog box: Right-click on an empty part of the Desktop and choose Properties from the pop-up menu.
3. Click on the Appearance tab to open this page of the dialog box.
4. Successively select several window schemes from the Scheme drop-down list and notice their effect on the preview window.
5. Select the Windows Standard scheme.
6. Change the Desktop color to white: Select the Desktop entry in the Item drop-down list, then click on the Color box, and finally, click on the white box in the pop-up palette.
7. Alter the size, color, and text of the active window's title bar:
   - Click on the Active Window title bar *in the preview window.* "Active Title Bar" will appear in the Item text box.
   - Change the height of the title bar to 25 points by clicking on the up-arrow in the Size text box (next to the Item box) until

the entry reads "25".

- Change the color of the active window's title bar to red by clicking on the Color box (to the right of the Item box) and then clicking on the red-colored square in the pop-up palette.
- Change the active window's title bar font by opening the Font drop-down list and selecting Arial from it.
- Increase the size of the active window's title bar font to 10 points by clicking on the Size text box (next to the Font box), deleting the current number, and typing `10`.
- Add italics to the active window's title bar text by clicking on the Italic button. 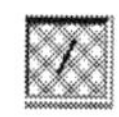

8. Choose the Apply command button to put the new scheme into effect without closing the Display Properties dialog box. (Notice that the font used for the Taskbar buttons has changed.)
9. Select the original window scheme from the Scheme drop-down list (or select Windows Standard, if you're not sure what that scheme was).
10. Choose the OK command button to close the Display Properties dialog box and put the scheme just selected into effect.

# 4.4 Adjusting the Feel of Keyboard and Mouse

In terms of your physical comfort while using a computer, some of the most important factors are the look of the screen display, and the operation of the keyboard and mouse. (Another important factor, the chair you sit on, is beyond our control.) In this section, we will discuss how to alter the operation of the keyboard and mouse so they are easier and more pleasant to use.

## Changing the Speed of the Keyboard

Most keys on the keyboard have a *repeat feature*; when you press such a key and hold it down, the character or action corresponding to it is repeated until the key is released. For example, if you press the B key and hold it down for a few seconds, a sequence of Bs will appear on the screen.

The number of times a key repeats in a given period of time depends on two factors:

- The *repeat delay* — how long it takes for a key to start repeating once it is pressed.
- The *repeat rate* —how fast the key repeats after the delay time has elapsed.

To change these parameters:

Keyboard

1. Start Control Panel (if it's not already open) and choose the Keyboard icon, as described in Section 4.1. The Keyboard Properties dialog box, shown in Figure 7, will be displayed.

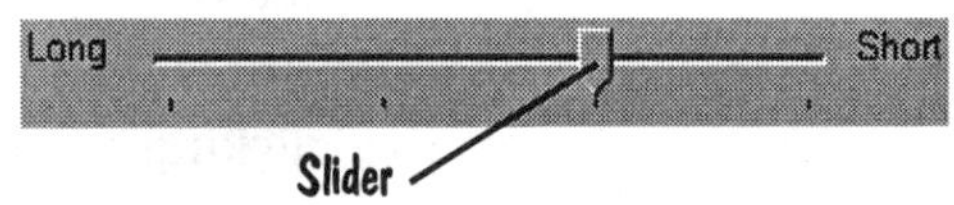


2. To decrease the repeat delay, drag the *Repeat delay* slider toward the word *Short* or click to the

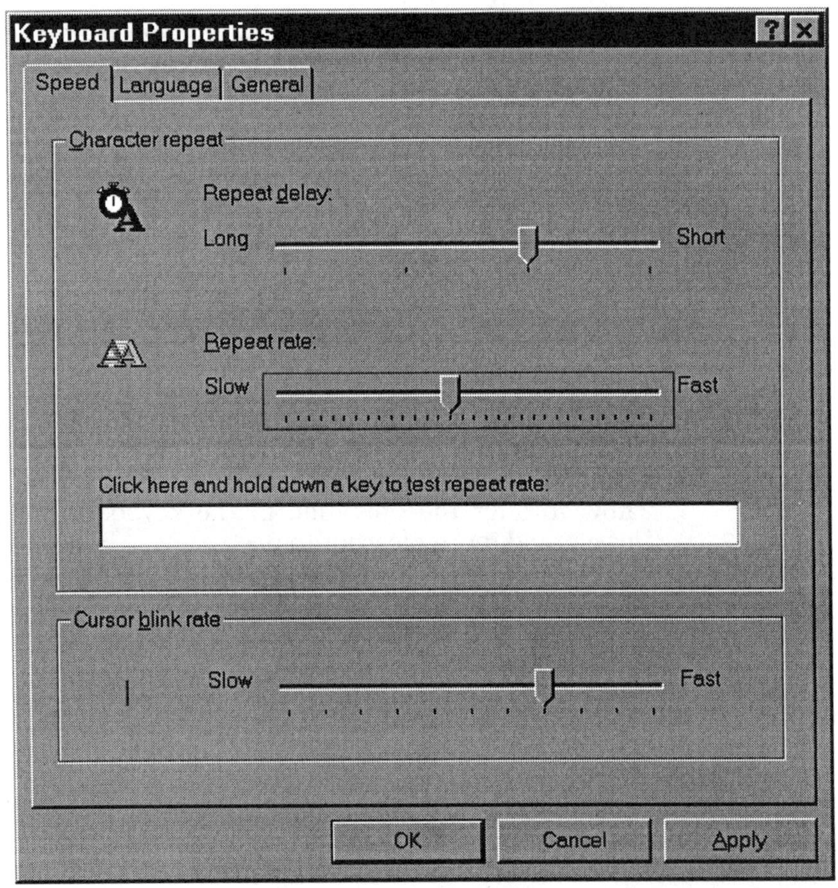


**Figure 7** The Keyboard Properties Dialog Box

right of the slider; to increase the delay, drag the slider toward the word *Long* or click to the left of the slider.

3. To decrease or increase the repeat rate, drag the *repeat rate* slider toward *Slow* or *Fast*, respectively, or click to the left or right of the slider.
4. To see the effect of your changes without closing the Keyboard Properties dialog box, click in the text box; then, observe what happens when you hold down a character key such as B.
5. Choose the OK command button to put your changes into effect, or choose the Cancel button to leave things as they formerly were.

NOTE

As you can see in Figure 7, the Keyboard Properties dialog box can also be used to adjust the cursor blink rate. To do so, just drag the slider toward the left (*Slow*) or right (*Fast*), or click to the left or right of the slider.

## *Changing the Action of the Mouse*

Different people have different preferences for the way the mouse "feels" when you move or click it. The feel of the mouse affects the ease with which you can choose menu items, double-click icons, move windows, and perform many other tasks.

To change the mouse settings:

Mouse

1. Start Control Panel (if it's not already open) and choose the Mouse icon, as described in Section 4.1. The Mouse Properties dialog box, shown in Figure 8 on the next page, will be displayed.
2. On the Buttons page of this dialog box (which is shown in Figure 8), you can:
   - Swap the functions of the left and right mouse buttons. By default, the left mouse button is the *primary button* — it is used to choose menu items, select icons, and so on; the right button performs the functions we have referred to as right-clicking and right-dragging. If you want to make the right mouse button the primary one, select the *Left-handed* option button (so-named because it usually makes the mouse easier to use for left-handed people). To return to the default configuration, select the *Right-handed* option button.

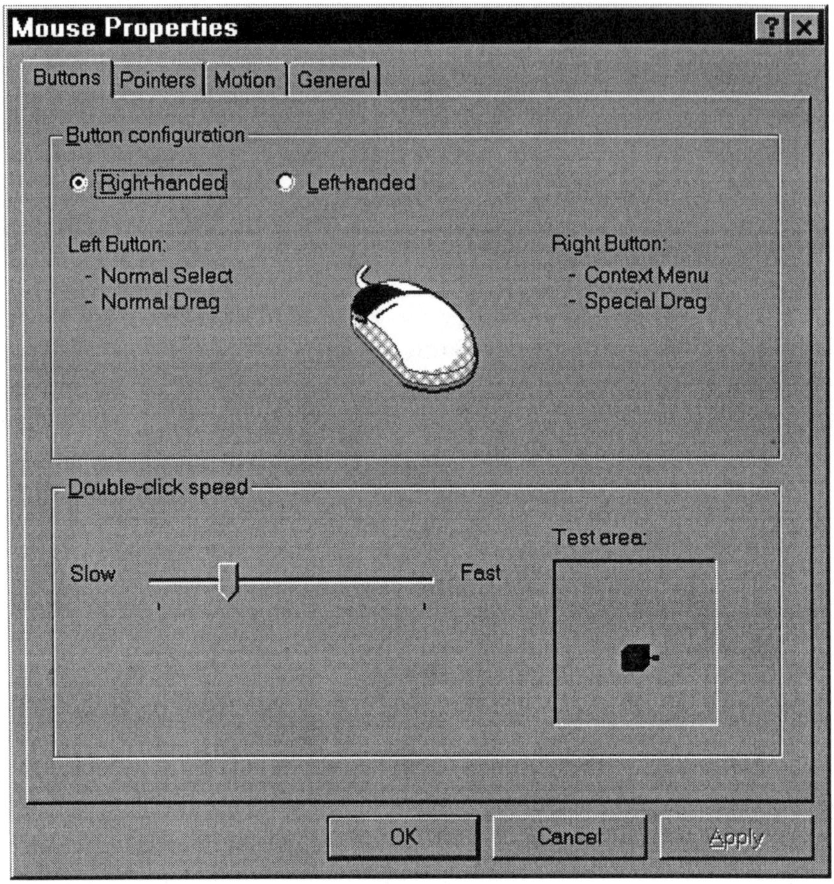


**Figure 8** The Mouse Properties Dialog Box

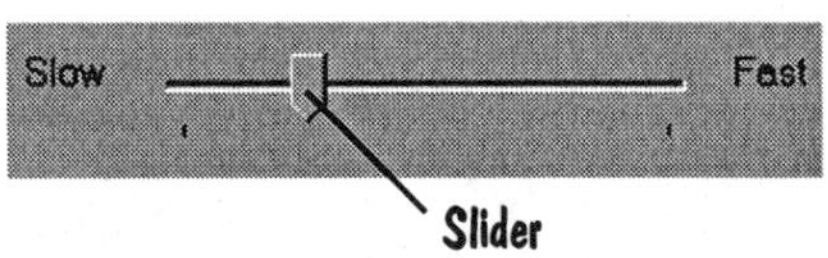


- Change the double-click speed — the amount of time that elapses before Windows 95 interprets a double-click as two separate clicks. Drag the *slider* to the left (toward *Slow*) or click to the left of the slider to allow yourself more time between clicks. You can test the results by double-clicking on the box in the *Test area*; if Windows interprets your two clicks as a double-click, a "jack-in-the-box" pops out.

3. Click on the Pointers tab to provide options that allow you to change the shapes of the various Windows pointers.

4. Click on the Motion tab to provide options that:
   - Change the *pointer speed* — the speed with which the pointer moves across the screen when you move the mouse on the desk top. To increase or decrease the speed, drag the slider in the appropriate direction:

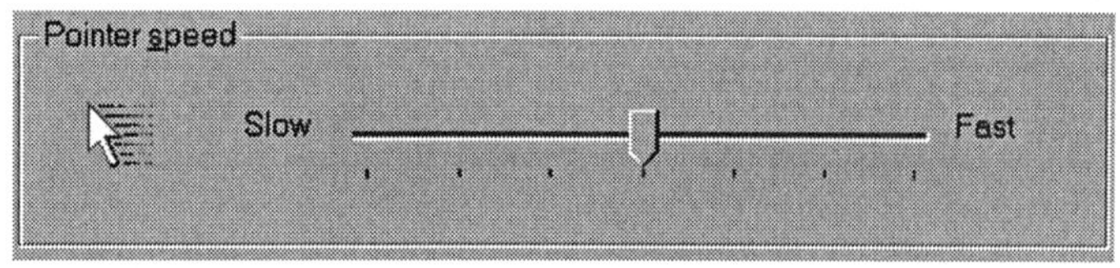


   - Show *mouse trails* — a sequence of pointer icons that follows the path of the mouse across the screen. To turn mouse trails on or off, select or deselect the check box on the Motion page. To increase or decrease the length of the trails, move the slider in the appropriate direction:

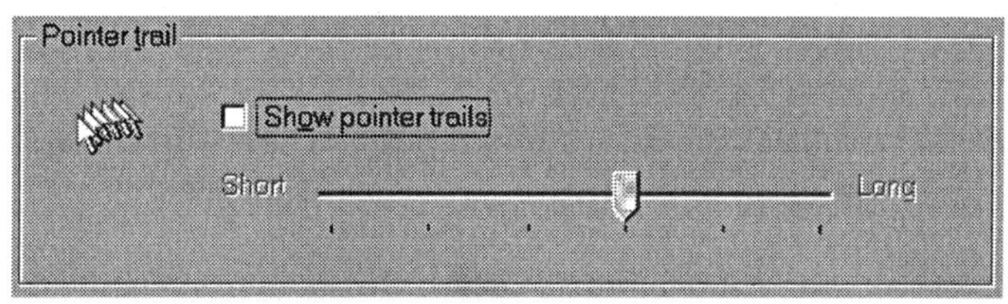


   If the *Show pointer trails* check box is selected, moving the mouse pointer in the dialog box demonstrates the effect. (Most people find pointer trails annoying on a regular monitor, but useful on some portable PC's LCD screens.)

5. Click on the General tab to specify the type of mouse you are using and to see options that are specific to that kind of mouse.
6. Choose the OK command button to put your changes into effect and close the Mouse Properties dialog box, or choose the Apply button to put the changes into effect without closing the dialog box.

4.4 TUTORIAL

Try the following exercises on your own.

1. Turn on your computer, if necessary, to start up Windows 95 and close any open windows.
2. Start Control Panel from the Settings option on the Start menu.

3. Open the Keyboard Properties dialog box by double-clicking on the Keyboard icon in the Control Panel window.
4. Set the *Repeat delay* to Long and the *Repeat rate* to Fast by dragging the sliders to the far left and far right, respectively. With these settings, a key must be held down "a long time" before it starts to repeat, but then repeats rapidly. Click on the test box and hold down a character key (such as A) to see the effect.
5. Set the *Repeat delay* to Short and the *Repeat rate* to Slow by dragging the sliders to the appropriate positions. Click on the test box and hold down a character key (such as A) to see the effect.
6. Set the *Cursor blink rate* slider to Slow; then set it to Fast. Notice the effect of each on the "insertion point" to the left of the slider.
7. Choose the Cancel command button to close the Keyboard Properties dialog box without putting your changes into effect.
8. Open the Mouse Properties dialog box by double-clicking on the Mouse icon in the Control Panel window.
9. Select the *Left-handed* option button and activate the Apply command button. Now, click the left mouse button on the *Right-handed* option button and notice the result. Then, right-click on the *Right-handed* option button and choose Apply again to return the mouse to "right-handed" use.
10. Set the *Double click speed* slider to Fast and then to Slow. In each case, double-click at a few different speeds on the "jack-in-the-box" to see the effect. Jack will pop up or go down if Windows interprets your two clicks as a double-click.
11. Click on the Motion tab to open the corresponding page.
12. Select the *Show pointer trails* check box and drag its slider from Slow to Fast. Notice the effect on the mouse pointer.
13. Click on the General tab and choose the Options command button on the resulting "page". Note the options available for your mouse and then close this dialog box.
14. Choose the Cancel command button in the Mouse Properties dialog box and then close the Control Panel window.

## 4.5 Other Basic Control Panel Options

In this section, we will discuss a few other basic Control Panel functions; they allow you to:

1. Set the computer's internal clock.
2. Install new programs.
3. View the fonts present on your hard disk.

## *Setting the Computer's Clock*

Your computer contains an internal clock powered by a battery that keeps track of the date and time for the computer system. These settings are used by the Taskbar Clock, Explorer, and numerous other applications for various purposes.

The internal clock normally keeps fairly accurate time, but it may need to be adjusted every once in a while. To change the system date and time:

Date/Time

1. Start Control Panel (if it's not already open) and choose the Date/Time icon, as described in Section 4.1. The Date/Time Properties dialog box, shown in Figure 9, will be displayed.

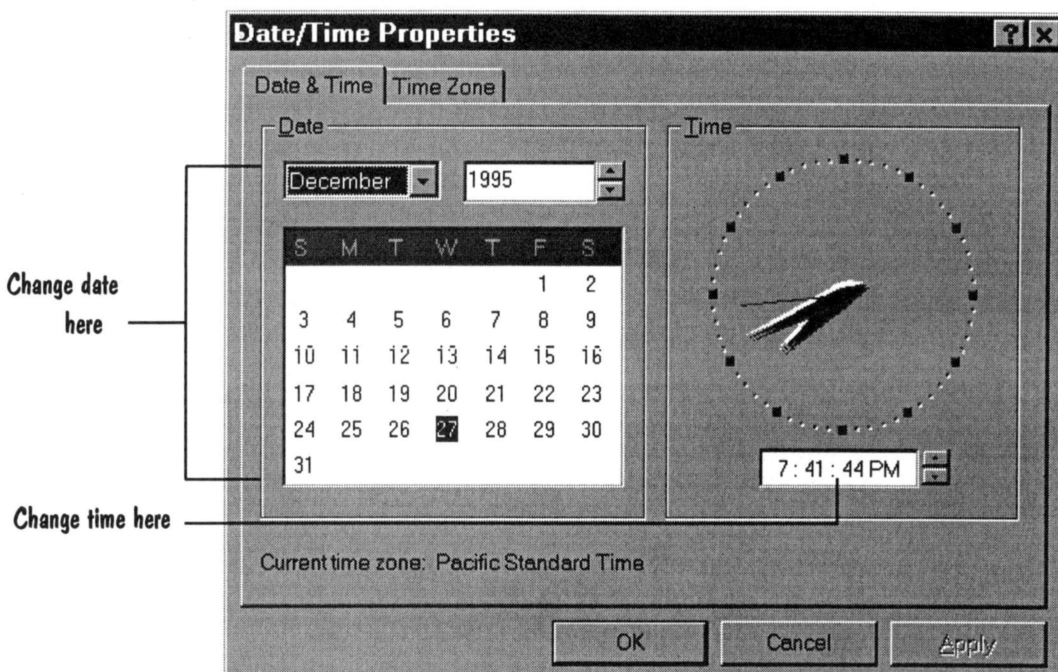


**Figure 9** Date/Time Properties Dialog Box

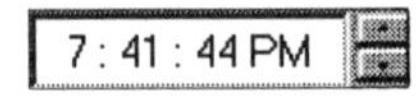


2. Change the time with the aid of the digital clock in the lower right part of this dialog box. The hours, minutes, seconds and AM/PM areas are set separately. To change any of these areas, click on it, use the Backspace or Delete key to delete the current setting, and type in the new one (or click on the up or down arrow button until the correct setting appears).
3. To change the date, use the left side of the dialog box. Select the correct month from the drop-down list and type in the correct year in the text box (or click on the up or down arrow button until the correct year appears). The correct day is set by clicking on the appropriate number on the calendar.
4. Choose the OK command button to put your changes into effect and close the Date/Time Properties dialog box, or choose the Apply button to put the changes into effect without closing the dialog box. (The Cancel button cancels all changes and closes the dialog box.)

TIP

Here are a couple of easier ways to open the Date/Time Properties dialog box shown in Figure 9:

- Double-click on the Clock on the Taskbar.

*or*

- Right-click on the Taskbar Clock and choose the Adjust Date/Time command from the resulting pop-up menu.

## *Installing New Programs*

When you buy application software for use on your computer, it comes on a CD-ROM or a set of floppy disks. Before you can use the application, it must be *installed* on your hard disk. The installation process copies files from the distribution disks to the hard disk and supplies Windows with information about how the program operates. The mechanics of the process differ somewhat from application to application depending on the media (floppy disk or CD-ROM) used and whether or not the software was designed for Windows 95.

**Windows 95 CD-ROMs**

If your new application is designed for Windows 95 and comes on a CD-ROM, the installation process is very simple. Here's all there is to it:

1. Start Windows and insert the CD in its drive. A dialog box, typically entitled "Install New Program Wizard", will appear on the screen.
2. You will then be presented with a sequence of "pages" that pro-

vide information or ask you to state your preferences concerning various aspects of the installation process. To move to the next page, activate the Next command button.

3. When the process is complete, activate the Finish button.

**Installing other applications**

For applications that come on floppy disks or those that are not designed for Windows 95, the installation process is usually almost as easy:

1. Start Windows and insert the floppy disk labeled "Install" or "Setup" or the CD-ROM in its drive.

Add/Remove Programs

2. Start Control Panel (if necessary) and choose the Add/Remove Programs icon, as described in Section 4.1. The Add/Remove Programs Properties dialog box, shown in Figure 10, will appear.

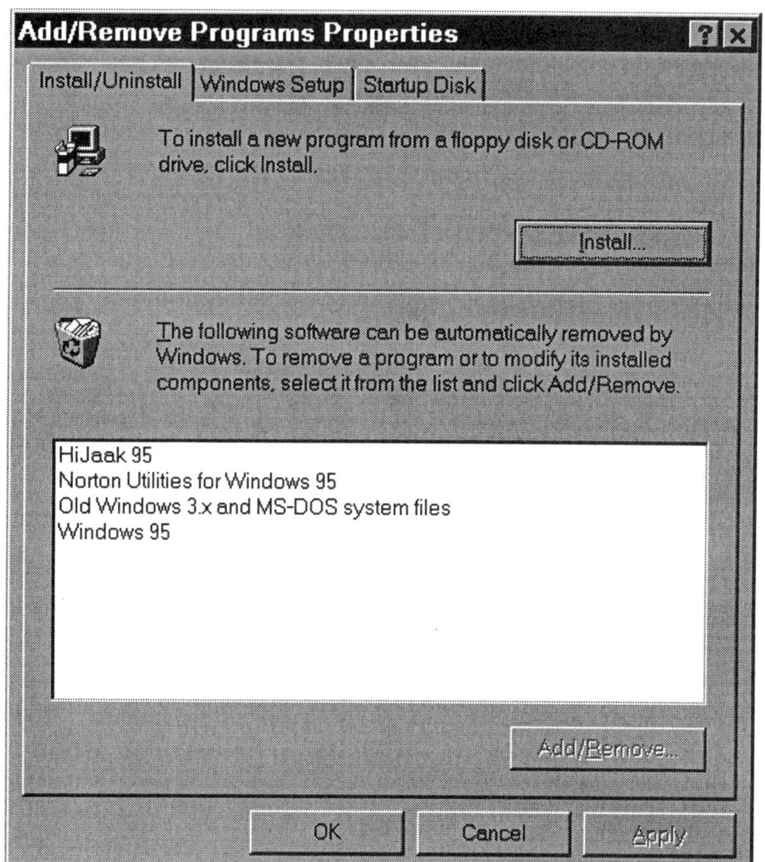


**Figure 10** Add/Remove Programs Properties Dialog Box

3. Choose the Install command button. The Install Program dialog box will appear.
4. Choose the Next command button. Windows will automatically search the floppy disk or CD for an installation program and, if found, display its name.
5. If Windows is unable to locate the installation program (or if you are certain it has not found the right one), type its name in the text box. (You will find this information in the documentation that came with your program or on the installation disk itself.)
6. Choose the Finish command button. The new application's installation program will then begin to run.
7. Respond to any on-screen queries until the installation process is complete. A menu item for the new program is usually placed on one of the Start button's submenus during the process to make it easy to run the newly-installed software.

NOTE

The Add/Remove Programs Properties dialog box also allows you to:

- Remove all remnants of (that is, *uninstall*) an application designed for Windows 95, or Windows 95 itself, from your hard disk. The programs that can be uninstalled are listed on the Install/Uninstall page of the dialog box (see Figure 10).
- Remove old versions of DOS and Windows from your hard disk (which is also done from the Install/Uninstall page).
- Add or remove certain Windows 95 components, such as accessories, disk tools, and the Microsoft Network. (This option appears on the Windows Setup page of the dialog box.)
- Create a *startup disk* (bootable disk) — a floppy disk that can be used to start your system should the hard disk, or key information on it, become inaccessible. (This feature is located on the Startup Disk page of the dialog box.)

## Viewing Your Fonts

A **font** is a collection of characters — letters, numerals, and other symbols — of a given design, size, and style. Examples of fonts are "12-point Times New Roman" and "10-point Arial bold"; these fonts look like this:

12-point Times New Roman **10-point Arial bold**

The design or *typeface* of a font determines the overall look of the characters; the fonts shown above are examples of the Times New Roman and Arial typefaces. The *size* of a font is its height, measured in points; a *point* is 1/72 of an inch. Thus, 12-point type is roughly 1/6-inch high. Fonts are also distinguished by their *attributes*; for example: regular, **bold**, or *italic*.

Some fonts are available in discrete sizes, such as 8-point, 10-point, etc. Others, known as **scalable fonts**, can be used in any size. Times New Roman and Arial are examples of a kind of scalable font called **TrueType**, which is included with the Windows software. TrueType fonts are available from many other sources, as well. (So are scalable fonts of other kinds, notably the widely used *Postscript* typefaces, developed by Adobe Systems, Inc.)

We will show how to make use of fonts in applications in Chapter 7. Here, we describe how to employ Control Panel to view or print samples of the fonts stored on your hard disk. (Control Panel also allows you to add or remove fonts from your disk, but we won't discuss this feature.) To view or print font samples:

Fonts

1. Start Control Panel and choose the Fonts icon, as described in Section 4.1. The Fonts subfolder of the Windows folder, shown in Figure 11, will open. (The "TT" icon indicates a TrueType font.)

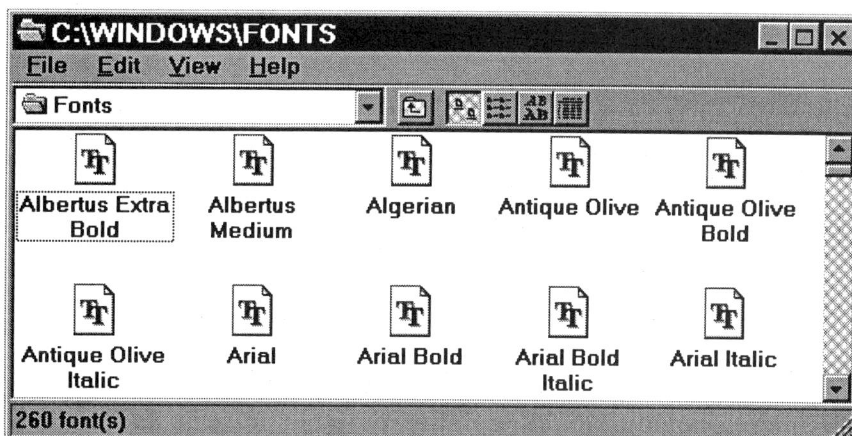


**Figure 11** The Fonts Folder (Large Icons View)

2. Select the font in which you are interested by clicking on its name.
3. To view a sample of the selected font, perform any of the following actions:
   - Choose the Open command from the File menu.

- Double-click on the desired font.
- Right-click on the desired font and choose the Open command from the resulting pop-up menu.

In any case, a dialog box similar to the following one will be displayed:

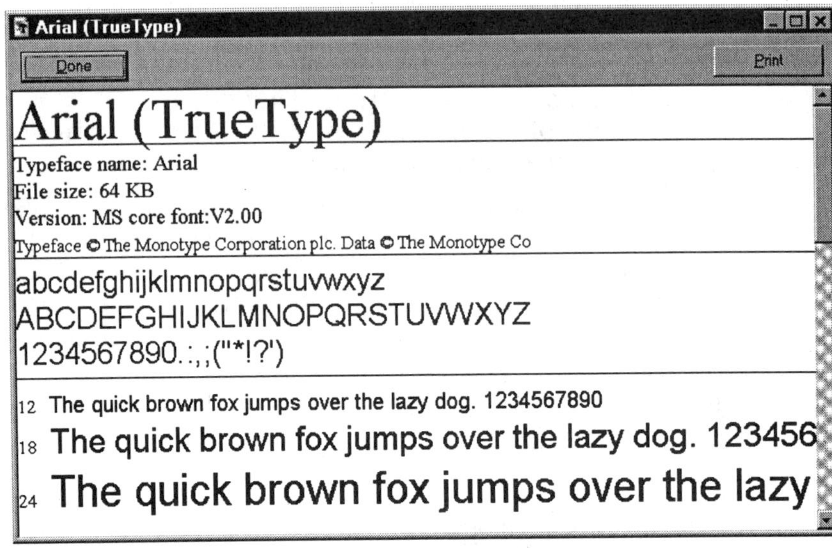


4. To print the displayed font sample, choose the Print command button from this dialog box and then choose OK in the resulting Print dialog box. (A sample of the selected font can also be printed directly from the Fonts folder window — Figure 11 — by choosing the Print command from either the File menu or the right-click pop-up menu.)
5. To close the dialog box and return to the Fonts folder window, click on the close button or choose the Done command button.

TIP

Figure 11 shows the default "Large Icons" view of the Fonts folder. Even when this window is maximized, it will probably only show a small portion of your available fonts without scrolling. To display more font names and icons:

- Choose the *Hide Variations (Bold, Italic, etc.)* command from the View menu if it's not already checked. Then, instead of seeing (for example) "Albertus Extra Bold" and "Albertus Medium", only "Albertus" will be displayed.
- Choose either List, Similarity, or Details from the View menu, or

by clicking a Toolbar button as indicated below. (If the Toolbar is not currently visible in the Fonts folder window, choose the Toolbar command from the View menu.)

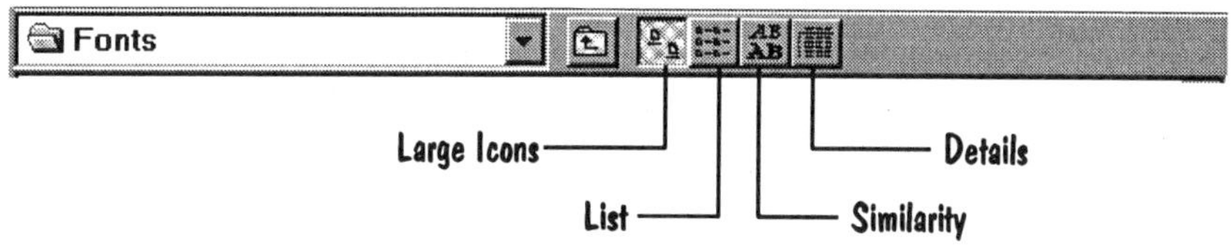


The List option displays the most font names at once; Similarity lists the fonts and describes their degree of similarity to the selected font; Details provides, for each font, the name, size, and creation date of the file that contains it. You will probably find the List view option to be the most useful.

## *Review Exercises*

**Section 4.1**

1. To start Control Panel, point at the ____________ option on the Start menu and then click on the Control Panel item.
2. To start a particular Control Panel utility, select it and choose the ____________ command from the File menu or the right-click pop-up menu.
3. True or false: The type and number of Control Panel functions available for your computer system depend on its configuration.
4. True or false: If you change a Control Panel setting, the original setting will be restored the next time you start Windows.
5. Which of the following Control Panel utilities can be used to change the properties of audio devices connected to your system?

   a. Modems
   b. Multimedia
   c. Sound
   d. Regional Settings

6. Which of the following Control Panel utilities can be used to change settings such as the format of numbers and currencies?

   a. Modems
   b. Multimedia
   c. Regional Settings
   d. System

**Section 4.2**

7. To place a patterned background on your Desktop, begin by opening Control Panel and double-clicking on the ___________ icon.
8. You can use Control Panel to place ___________, a graphic image, either tiled or centered on the Desktop.
9. A ___________ can be used to cause an animated image to appear on the screen after a specified period of inactivity.
10. True or false: To apply a new Desktop pattern or wallpaper to the Desktop, you must first close the Display Properties dialog box.
11. True or false: When wallpaper is centered (instead of tiled), it always completely covers the Desktop.
12. True or false: The delay time for a screen saver is how long the mouse and keyboard must be inactive before the screen saver appears.
13. To open the Display Properties dialog box without first opening Control Panel:
    a. Right-click on the Taskbar and then click on Properties.
    b. Right-click on the Desktop and then click on Properties.
    c. Double-click on the Taskbar and then click on Properties.
    d. Double-click on the Desktop and then click on Properties.
14. If your computer has been inactive for a while and a screen saver has been activated, to return to your work you must:
    a. Click the mouse.
    b. Move the mouse.
    c. Press a key.
    d. Perform any of the above actions.

**Section 4.3**

15. To change the colors of various objects in a window, use the ___________ page of the Display Properties dialog box.
16. To select a predefined window scheme, open the ___________ drop-down list in the Display Properties dialog box.
17. True or false: You can modify certain elements of a predefined window scheme by clicking on an element in the Item drop-down list and then making changes to it.
18. True or false: One-half inch is equivalent to 36 points.
19. From the Appearance page of the Display Properties dialog box, you *cannot* change the size of
    a. Scroll bars
    b. Title bars
    c. Menu entries
    d. The Desktop

20. From the Appearance page of the Display Properties dialog box, you cannot change the color of
    a. Scroll bars
    b. Title bars
    c. Menu entries
    d. The Desktop

**Section 4.4**

21. To change the keyboard repeat rate and delay, begin by double-clicking on the ___________ icon in Control Panel.
22. If it seems as if the functions of the left and right mouse buttons have been interchanged, you can switch them back by using the ___________ utility in Control Panel.
23. True or false: To change the cursor blink rate, use the Cursor utility in Control Panel.
24. True or false: Turning on mouse trails may be useful if you're having trouble following the movement of the mouse pointer.
25. The Mouse Properties dialog box:
    a. Cannot be used to change the double-click speed.
    b. Cannot be used to turn mouse pointer trails on or off.
    c. Cannot be used to change the mouse pointer speed.
    d. Can be used to perform all the above tasks.
26. The Keyboard option in Control Panel cannot be used to
    a. Swap the functions of certain keys on the keyboard.
    b. Change the cursor blink rate.
    c. Extend the time delay for repeating keys on the keyboard.
    d. Increase the repeat rate for repeating keys on the keyboard.

**Section 4.5**

27. If the Taskbar Clock is displaying the wrong time, you can correct it by using Control Panel's ___________ utility.
28. TrueType is a collection of ___________, some of which are included with the Windows software.
29. To add or remove certain Windows components, such as Accessories, use Control Panel's ___________ utility.
30. True or false: The system date and time must be set every time you start Windows.
31. True or false: Some programs that are distributed on CD-ROMs can be installed without starting Control Panel.
32. True or false: Every character in an 18-point font is roughly 1/4-inch wide.

33. The Fonts utility in Control Panel allows you to:

    a. Change the font used for icon titles.
    b. Change the font used in the active application.
    c. Set a default font for your printer.
    d. View the fonts on your hard disk.

34. Using the Add/Remove Programs utility in Control Panel,

    a. You can install programs on your hard disk.
    b. You can remove old versions of DOS from your hard disk.
    c. You can create a "startup disk".
    d. You can perform all of the above tasks.

# *Lab Exercises*

Work each of the following exercises at your computer. Begin by turning the machine on (if necessary) to start Windows 95, closing any open windows, and starting Control Panel. If you want to produce a written record of your answers, review the material on WordPad and capturing screens in Sections 2.2 and 2.3.

**Lab Exercise 1 (Section 4.2)**

a. Start the Display utility from the Control Panel window, which opens the Display Properties dialog box. Which (tab) page of this dialog box is active?

b. Select the "50% Gray" repeating pattern from the Pattern List box. Based on its appearance in the preview window, how would you describe this pattern?

c. Choose the Edit Pattern command button. Based on its appearance in the left side of the Pattern Editor dialog box, what is a better name for the "50% Gray" pattern?

d. Close the Pattern Editor dialog box and return the Desktop pattern to its original setting.

e. Select the Center option button and select the wallpaper images one-by-one. Which, if any, of the wallpapers cover the entire preview window?

f. Select the Tile option button, select a wallpaper from the list box, and then choose the Apply command button. Does the wallpaper cover the entire visible Desktop?

g. Return the wallpaper to its original setting and close the Display Properties dialog box.

**Lab Exercise 2 (Section 4.2)**

a. Start the Display utility from the Control Panel window, which opens the Display Properties dialog box. Now, click on the Screen Saver tab. Which, if any, screen saver is in effect?

b. Select the Flying Windows screen saver from the Screen Saver drop-down list. Is this screen saver displayed in the preview window?

c. Set the delay time for ".5" minutes and choose the Preview command button. What time is displayed in the Wait text box after the preview is complete? What conclusion can you draw about the possible delay times?

d. Choose the Settings command button. Try various warp speeds and densities and observe the effect on the preview window. (You will have to choose OK in the Options for Flying Windows dialog box to see the effect of each change.) Describe the effect of changing warp speed and density.

e. In the Display Properties dialog box, choose the Apply button and wait for a minute or two. Did the screen saver become active? If it did, what action did you take to return to the dialog box?

f. Restore the previous screen saver, if any, and close the Display Properties dialog box.

**Lab Exercise3 (Section 4.3)**

a. Start the Display utility from the Control Panel window, which opens the Display Properties dialog box. Now, click on the Appearance tab. Which, if any, window scheme is named in the Scheme text box?

b. Select the Active Title Bar from the Item list. What font and font size are used for it?

c. Open the Scheme drop-down list. How many schemes are listed?

d. Select, in succession, the "Windows Standard", "Windows Standard (large)", and "Windows Standard (extra large)" schemes. What are the respective font sizes for the Active Title Bar? Is the same font (type style) used for all three schemes?

e. By selecting, one-by-one, all the available schemes, answer the following questions:

- Which schemes use no colors other than black and white (for the items displayed in the preview window)?
- Which schemes use the Times New Roman font for the Active Title Bar?

f. Select the Windows Standard scheme and 3D Objects (from the Item list). Change the font color to bright red. Which objects in the preview window are affected by the 3D Objects color?

g. Choose the Cancel button to close the Display Properties dialog box.

**Lab Exercise 4 (Section 4.3)**

a. Start the Display utility from the Control Panel window, which opens the Display Properties dialog box. Now, click on the Appearance tab. Which, if any, window scheme is named in the Scheme text box?

b. Select the High Contrast White scheme and change 3D Objects to light gray. Which objects in the preview window changed color?

c. Change:

- The Active Title Bar color to dark blue.
- The Desktop color to teal (blue-green).
- The Inactive Title Bar color to dark gray and its font color to light gray.
- Menu items to light gray.

How does the look of the resulting preview window differ from that of the Windows Standard scheme?

d. *Optional*: Capture the Display Properties window, paste it into WordPad, and print the resulting document. (Try this only if you've already read Sections 2.2 and 2.3.)

e. Choose the Cancel button to close the Display Properties dialog box.

**Lab Exercise 5 (Section 4.4)**

a. Start the Keyboard utility from the Control Panel window. Where are the Repeat Delay and Repeat Rate sliders positioned (relative to the "tick marks" that appear just below each slider)?

b. Set the repeat delay as short as possible and the repeat rate as fast as possible. In the test area, hold down a character key for about one second. How many characters were displayed?

c. Now set the repeat delay as long as possible and the repeat rate as slow as possible. In the test area, hold down a different character key, also for about one second. How many characters are displayed this time?

d. Set the cursor blink rate as slow as possible; then set it at the middle of the scale. In each case, with the aid of a watch with a second hand, determine how many "blinks" take place in ten seconds.

e. Click on the Language tab. What language and layout are used by your keyboard?

f. Click on the General tab. What is your keyboard type?

g. Choose the Cancel command button to close the Keyboard Properties dialog box.

**Lab Exercise 6 (Section 4.4)**

a. Start the Mouse utility from the Control Panel window.

b. Switch the button configuration from right-handed to left-handed (or vice-versa). What changes do you see in the dialog box?

c. Set the double-click speed to slow; then to fast. By trying each setting in the Test area, which one requires you to double-click more quickly?

d. Click on the Pointers tab. Make a list of all the available pointer schemes.

e. Click on the Motion tab. What options are available on the Motion page?

f. Set the pointer speed to slow; then, to fast. Do you notice any change in pointer speed?

g. Select the pointer trails check box (or deselect it, if it's currently selected). Do you notice any change in pointer trails?

h. Click on the General tab and choose the Options command button, if it is present. What options, not available elsewhere in the Mouse Properties dialog box, are displayed in the resulting dialog box?

i. Close the Options dialog box and choose the Cancel command button to close the Mouse Properties dialog box.

**Lab Exercise 7 (Section 4.5)**

a. Start the Date/Time utility from the Control Panel window. What is the name of the "current time zone"?

b. By using the up and down arrows, determine the earliest and latest years available for the calendar.

c. Choose the Cancel command button to close this dialog box.

d. Start the Fonts utility from the Control Panel window. How many fonts are available on your system? (Look on the status bar, at the bottom of the Fonts window.)

e. Use the View menu or Toolbar to switch to List view. How many columns are displayed?

f. Select the Times New Roman font; then, view (open) it and choose the Print command button in the dialog box. (Make sure that the printer connected to your computer is ready before issuing the Print command.)

g. Close the Times New Roman dialog box and the Fonts window.

CHAPTER 5

# More About Control Panel

In Chapter 4 we discussed some basic Control Panel options and how you can use them to customize the Windows user interface. In this chapter we will continue this discussion, presenting additional information about Control Panel. The sections in this chapter are independent of one another and, consequently, need not be read in their given order. To be more specific:

- Section 5.1 describes how to change printer settings, manage print jobs, and set up a new printer.
- Section 5.2 discusses how to set up newly-installed hardware, such as a sound card or monitor.
- Section 5.3 describes how to change the sounds associated with certain system "events" (if your computer is equipped with a sound card) and how to change the settings for multimedia devices.
- Section 5.4 deals with the ways that Windows makes the computer more accessible to people with disabilities.
- Section 5.5 presents information about configuring a modem and fine-tuning your hardware, and contains brief descriptions of Control Panel's Network, Passwords, and Regional Settings utilities.

# 5.1 Managing Printers

In Section 2.2, we discussed how to print a document from within a Windows-based application. Recall that choosing Print from the File menu opens a Print dialog box, which allows you to select various print options, such as which pages to print and the number of copies of each. You can exert even more control over the printing process, changing the printer setup, managing the active print jobs, and adding new printers, using the Printers option in Control Panel.

## The Printers Folder

Printers

Recall that to open the Control Panel window, you click on the Start button, point at the Settings option on the Start menu, and choose the Control Panel item from the resulting submenu. Then, double-clicking on the Printers icon opens the **Printers folder** window, which is shown in Figure 1. (Your window may look quite different from the one pictured here.)

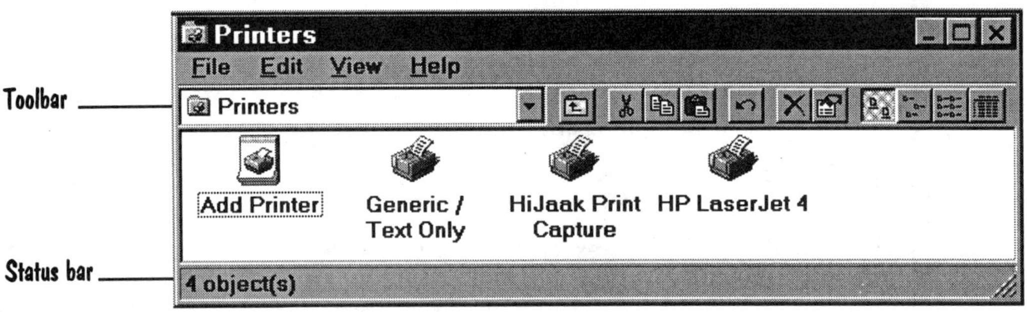


**Figure 1** The Printers Folder Window

NOTE

You can also open the Printers folder window in the following ways:

- Click on the Start button, point at the Settings option on the Start menu, and choose the Printers item from the resulting submenu.
- Start My Computer (by double-clicking on its Desktop icon) and double-click on the Printers icon in the resulting window.
- Start Explorer from the Programs submenu of the Start menu and open the Printers folder — near the bottom of the folder tree pane (see Section 3.2).

If the Toolbar (or Status bar) is not visible in the Printers folder window (see Figure 1), it can be toggled on by choosing its name from the View menu. The last four icons on the Toolbar affect the way the printer names and icons are displayed in the window.

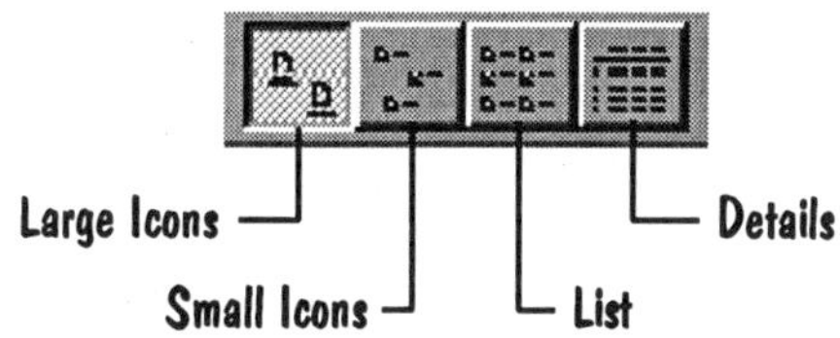


Figure 1 shows the Large Icons view. Clicking on another Toolbar button (or choosing the corresponding item from the View menu) arranges the names and icons differently. For example, Details view, which is shown in Figure 2, gives a little more information about each printer.

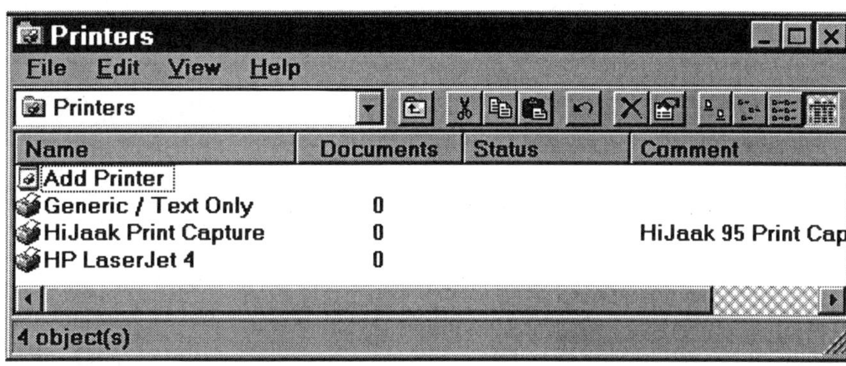


**Figure 2** Details View of the Printers Folder Window

## *Changing the Printer Setup*

From time to time, you may want to change certain printer settings, such as the print quality (resolution) or installed fonts. In Windows 95, printer settings are changed from within the Printer Properties dialog box. To display this dialog box:

1. Open the Printers folder, as described earlier in this section.
2. Right-click on the desired printer icon.
3. Choose the Properties item from the resulting pop-up menu.

The content of the Printer Properties dialog box varies considerably from printer to printer. A typical one is shown in Figure 3.

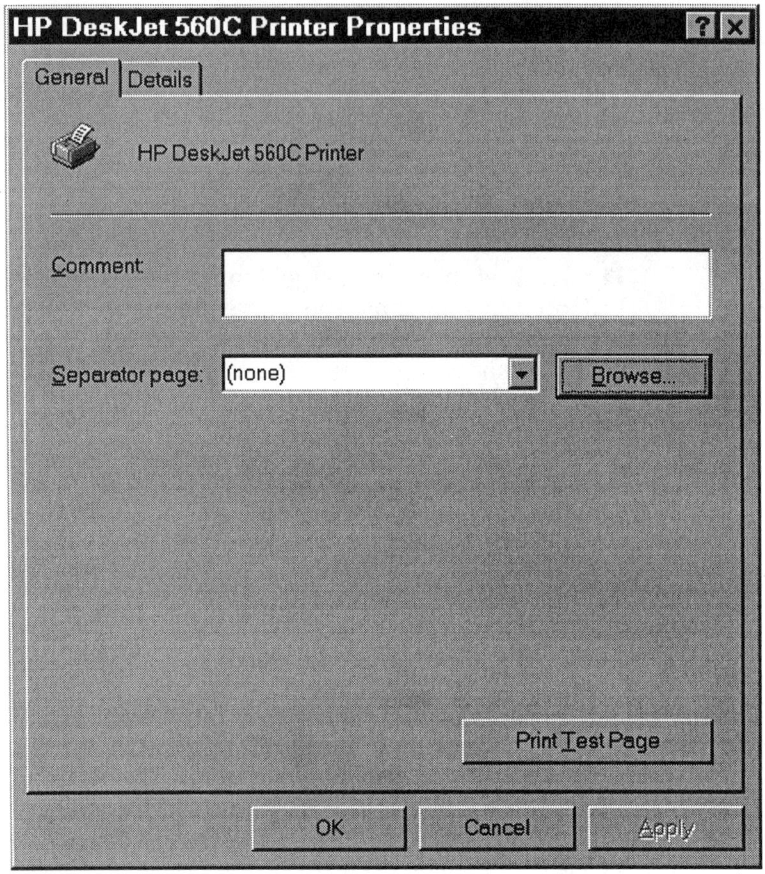


**Figure 3** Printer Properties Dialog Box — *General* Page

The first page (the General page) of this dialog box gives the name of the printer and allows you to:

- Define a "comment" for this printer. The comment will appear in Details view of the Printers folder (see Figure 2).
- Specify a "separator page" — a page that will automatically be inserted between print jobs. It can be blank or be printed from a specified file.
- Print a "Test Page" to check that your printer is working properly.

The Details page (and other pages, if present) allows you to change the way the printer is configured. For example, clicking on the Details tab for the HP DeskJet 560C printer displays the page shown in Figure 4.

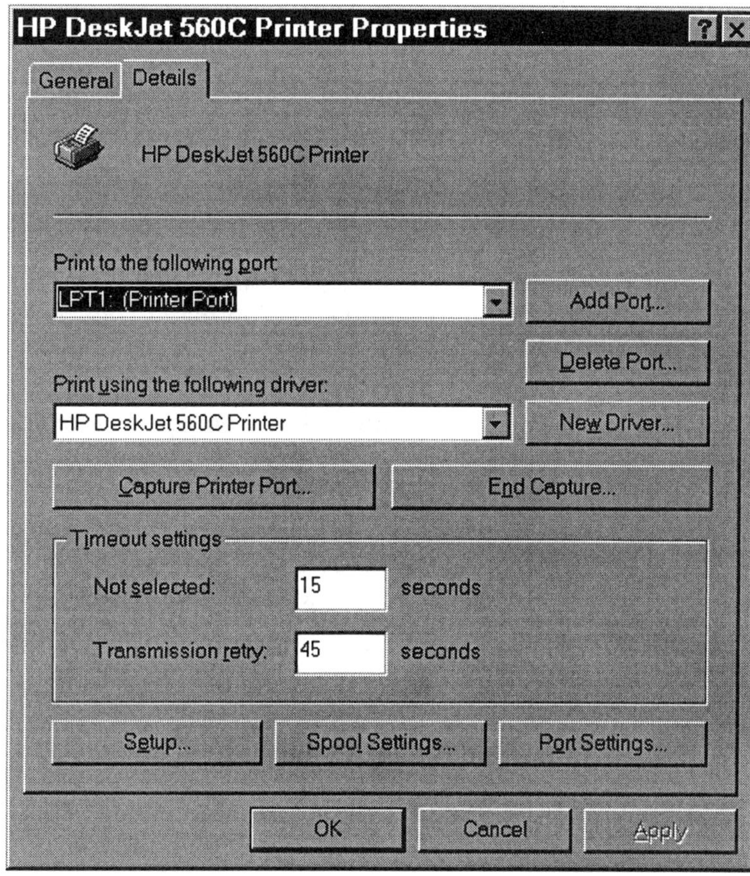


**Figure 4** Printer Properties Dialog Box — *Details* Page

Much of the information on the Details page is fairly technical. Here is a quick run-down of the various options:

- The *Port* drop-down list and command buttons are used to change the settings for how your computer is physically or logically (in the case of a network printer) connected to the printer.
- The *Driver* drop-down-list and command button are used to install a different **printer driver** — a program that translates your document's text, graphics, and special codes into a language that

the printer can understand.

- The *Capture* command buttons are used in *mapping* (or removing the mapping of) a port to a network drive.
- The *Timeout* text boxes determine the amount of time Windows will wait for the printer to come online (*Not selected*) or to be ready to print (*Transmission retry*) before reporting an error.

**Spooling print jobs**

- The *Spool Settings* command button is used to change the manner in which a document is sent from the application to the printer. When a print job is **spooled**, it is temporarily stored on the hard disk (which is a rapid process) and then transferred to the printer at the leisurely pace required by these devices. With spooling in effect, you can use the computer for other tasks once the document has been sent to disk, instead of having to wait until the print job is complete. (You might want to turn spooling *off* if you have little free disk space or if you are encountering certain printing problems.)
- The *Setup* command button opens a dialog box with additional options. (For some printers, additional pages in the Properties dialog box take the place of the Setup button.)

Although the Setup options (or additional dialog box pages) vary from printer to printer, a few are common to virtually all printers. To illustrate these features, consider the Setup options for the HP Deskjet printer, which are shown in Figure 5.

Almost all printers allow you to adjust:

- *Print Quality* In the dialog box of Figure 5, the available print quality choices are labeled *Normal* (medium resolution), *Presentation* (high resolution), and *Fast* (low resolution). The higher the resolution, the nicer text and graphics will look on the page. Some printers refer to these settings using other terms, such as *Draft* for low resolution printing. Other printers (including lasers) use *dots per inch* (dpi) to describe resolution; here, the higher the number, the better-looking the output.
- *Paper Orientation* *Portrait* means that printing takes place parallel to the short side of the paper; the page you are reading is in portrait orientation. *Landscape* means that printing takes place parallel to the long side of the paper; for example, certificates and diplomas are printed in landscape orientation.
- *Media Size* The common 8½" by 11" paper is referred to as *letter size*. If you are about to print on a different size paper or on an envelope, you should let the printer know this by selecting the appropriate paper size.

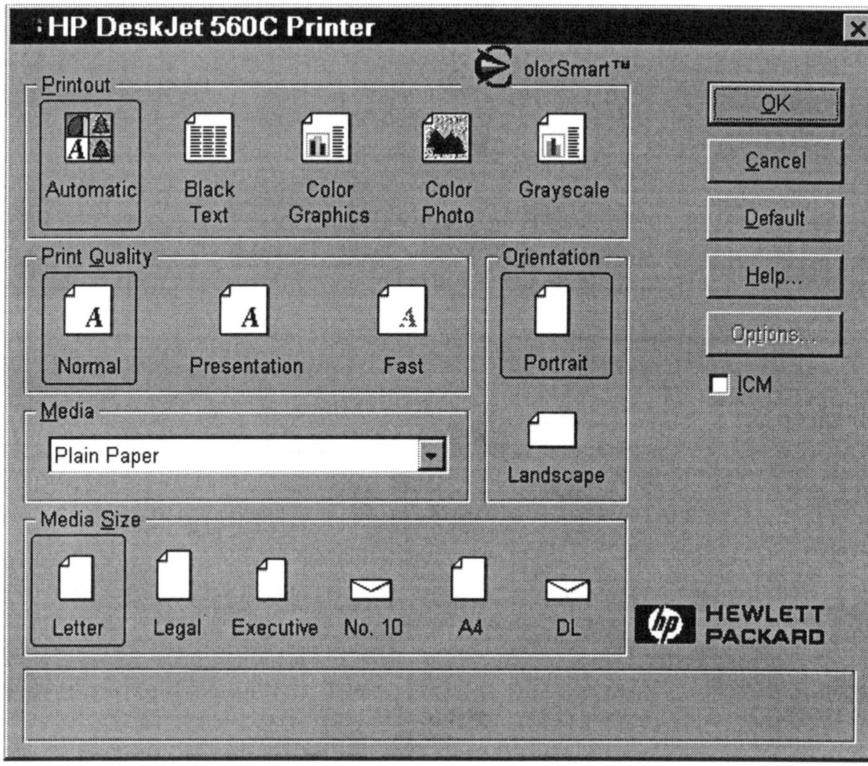


**Figure 5** The Result of Choosing the Setup Command Button

**NOTE** You can usually access some printer properties from within an application. For example, in WordPad, choosing Page Setup from the File menu opens a dialog box that contains options for paper size and orientation. Moreover, choosing the Printer command button and then the Properties button in the resulting dialog box provides access to additional setup options. In many other applications, you access printer properties by choosing Printer Setup from the File menu or by choosing the Properties command button in the Print dialog box.

## *Managing Print Jobs*

If print spooling is in effect (see above), you can control various aspects of your print jobs while they are running or waiting to be printed. To do so, either:

- Open the Printers folder (as described earlier in this section) and double-click on the appropriate printer icon.

*or*

- While a document is printing, double-click on the printer icon to the left of the clock on the Taskbar.

In either case, a print manager window, like the one in Figure 6, will open*. The list of documents displayed in this window is called the *print queue*. The window in Figure 6 was captured during the printing process; it shows two documents in the queue. If you open the print manager window when the printer is idle, the queue will be empty.

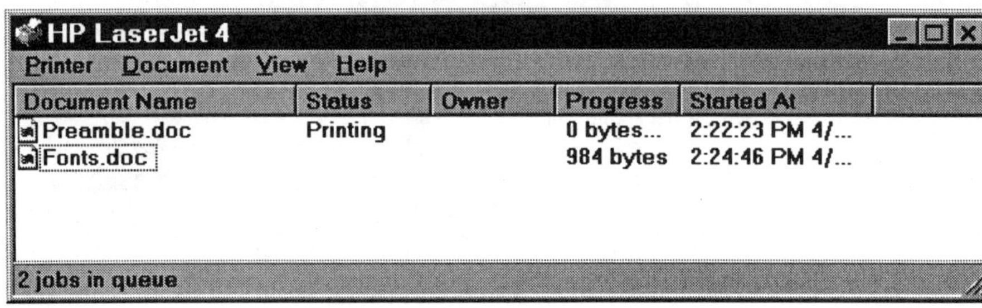


**Figure 6** The "Print Manager" Window

Here's how to use the print manager window:

- To cancel printing of a document, select the desired document in the queue and choose Cancel Printing from the Document menu.
- To cancel all print jobs listed in the queue, choose Purge Print Jobs from the Printer menu. All documents will be removed from the queue.
- To pause the printing of a particular document, select the desired document in the print queue and choose Pause Printing from the Document menu. (A check mark will appear next to this menu item and the word *Paused* will appear next to the document name in the Status column.) To restart a paused print job, select the document and choose Pause Printing from the Document menu.
- To pause all print jobs, choose Pause Printing from the Printer menu. (A check mark will appear next to this menu item and the word *Paused* will appear on the title bar.) To restart a paused printer, choose Pause Printing from the Printer menu.

*This window, which has no official name, takes the place of the Windows 3.1 Print Manager. Most people still refer to it as "the print manager window".

- To change the order of the documents in the print queue, select the document you want to move and drag it to the desired position in the queue.

## *Adding a New Printer*

If you want to use a new printer with your computer, you must first establish a physical connection between the two (say, via a cable) and also provide Windows with some information about the printer. Windows then installs the proper printer driver and sets up the proper pathway between computer and printer. To add a new printer:

1. Open the Printers folder, as described earlier in this section.
2. Double-click on the Add Printer icon (see Figure 1). The Add Printer Wizard will start, displaying an informational page.
3. Click the Next button. If you are connected to a network, you'll then be asked whether you want to install a local or network printer. To install a local printer (one that is directly connected to your computer), select Local and choose the Next button, which displays the dialog box shown in Figure 7.

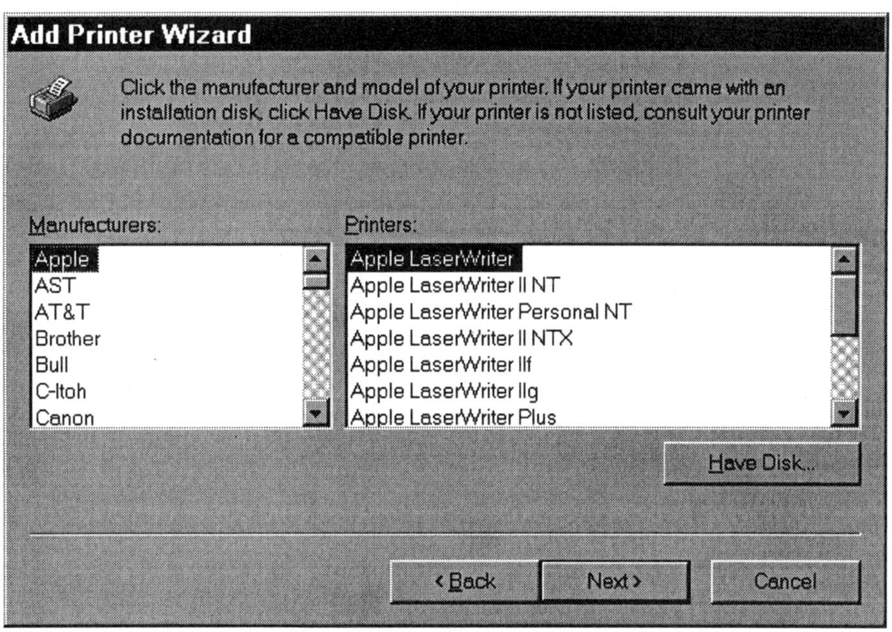


**Figure 7** Choosing the Manufacturer and Model of Printer

4. Select the manufacturer and then the model of the new printer from their respective text boxes. If the manufacturer has supplied a printer driver on disk, insert this disk in its drive, choose the Have Disk command button, enter the appropriate drive in the resulting dialog box, and choose the OK button.
5. Choose the Next button. The Add Printer Wizard page shown in Figure 8 will be displayed.

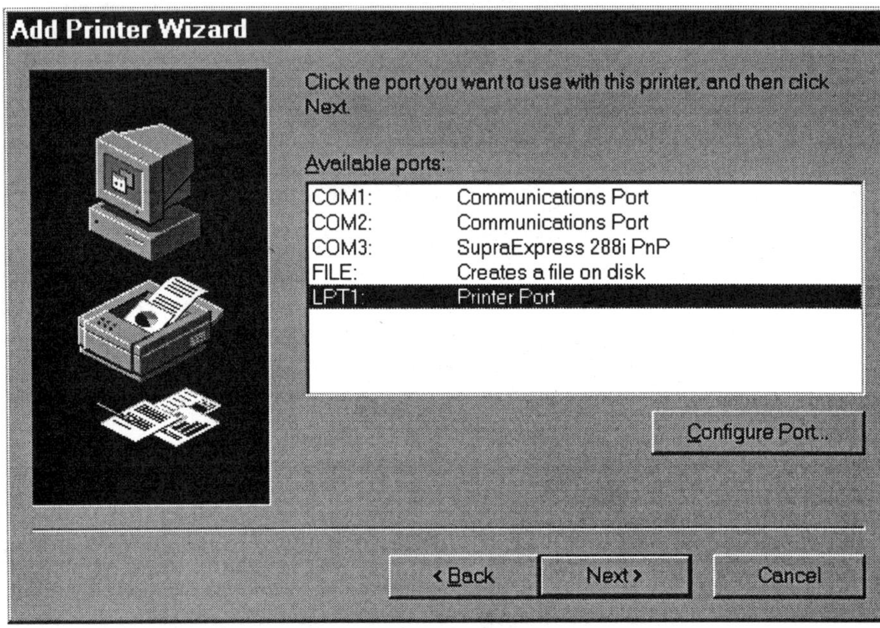


**Figure 8** Choosing a Printer Port for the New Printer

6. Check the printer's documentation to determine if it's a parallel or serial printer. In the former case, select LPT1; in the latter case, select COM1 if no other device is attached to the computer's primary serial port, otherwise select COM2.

   If the printer is of the serial variety, you may have to configure its port. In this case, choose the Configure Port command button, enter the requested information (as specified in the printer manual), and choose the OK button.

   Select the *File* option if the new printer cannot be accessed directly from your computer, but you would occasionally like to print files on it. In this case, when this printer is selected, the print job will be stored on disk and can be copied at a later time to the desired printer (via the computer connected to it).

7. Choose the Next button. The resulting dialog box allows you to select a name for the new printer (which will be listed in the Printers folder window). You can also make this printer the default printer, in which case it will automatically be used to print a document unless you specify otherwise at the time of printing.
8. Choose the Next button one more time. You are now asked if you want to print a test page. This is not necessary, but it is a good idea to see if the new printer is working properly.
9. Choose the Finish button. You may now be prompted to insert a diskette or CD-ROM in its drive. If so, insert it and choose the OK button. The appropriate printer driver files will be copied to the computer's hard disk and, if you requested that a test page be printed, printing will begin.
10. If a test page has been printed, a dialog box will open, asking if the page printed properly. Choose the Yes button, and the process is complete. (If you choose No, you will be led through some troubleshooting procedures.) The new printer will now be listed in the Printers folder window.

5-1

**TUTORIAL**

Try the following exercise on your own.

1. Turn on the computer (if necessary) to start Windows 95, and close any open windows.
2. Open the Printers folder: Click on the Start button, point at the Settings option, and choose Control Panel to start the latter; then, double-click on the Printers icon.
3. Right-click on the icon of one of the available printers and choose Properties from the pop-up menu.
4. In the Properties dialog box, click on the Details tab, choose the Spool Settings command button, then select the *Spool print jobs so that program finishes printing faster* option button (if it's not already selected), and choose the OK button.
5. Check out the function of the various options in the Printer Properties dialog box: Click on the question-mark button on the title bar and then click on the desired item. (To close the resulting window, click anywhere within the dialog box.)
6. Close the Properties dialog box.
7. In the Printers folder window, double-click on the icon of the selected printer. This opens the "print manager" window.

8. Pause the printer by choosing the Pause Printing command on the Printer menu. (Notice that the word *Paused* appears on the title bar.)
9. Insert the Lab Exercises disk in its drive and start WordPad by clicking on the WordPad item on the Accessories submenu of the Start Menu's Programs option.
10. Open (from the File menu) the Fonts document on the Lab Exercises disk and send it to the printer (choose Print from the File menu and then choose OK in the resulting dialog box). Do the same for the Preamble document on the diskette.
11. Switch to the print manager window. The two print jobs will be listed in the "print queue" with the Fonts document first.
12. Change the order of the print jobs (so that Preamble will be printed first) by dragging the Fonts document to the bottom of the queue.
13. Cancel the Preamble print job: Select it and choose Cancel Printing from the Document menu.
14. Cancel the remaining print job by choosing Purge Print Jobs from the Printer menu.
15. "Unpause" the printer by choosing Pause Printing from the Printer menu. (The word *Paused* will disappear from the title bar.)
16. Close the print manager window, the Printers folder, and WordPad, and remove the diskette from its drive.

## 5.2 Installing New Hardware

One of the great things about personal computers is that they are "expandable" — you can install new hardware devices (such as more RAM or a CD-ROM drive) or replace existing components, to adapt the machine to your changing needs.

Installing a piece of hardware involves two fundamental steps:

1. You must physically connect the device to your computer, via either an external *port* (at the back of the system unit) or an internal connector (inside the system unit).
2. You must change certain settings and/or install special software so that the computer recognizes the device and makes full use of its capabilities.

The second step in this process may or may not involve Windows. For example, if you install additional RAM in your computer, the machine will recognize the change when it runs its start-up tests, and either automatically alter the necessary settings or instruct you to do so using a setup program. On the other hand, if you install a modem, Windows will probably detect the new hardware and either accommodate it automatically or guide you through the process.

In this section, we will discuss the way in which Windows deals with a piece of new hardware once the device has been physically connected to the computer. This process is also discussed to some extent in Section 5.1 (for printers), Section 5.3 (for multimedia devices), and Section 5.5 (for modems).

**WARNING**

Before installing a new piece of hardware, you should always read the instruction manual that accompanies it. The manual will include not only instructions for physically connecting the device to your computer system, but also information about configuring it correctly. If it suggests a procedure that is different than the ones described in this section, it is usually best to follow the manufacturer's recommendations.

## *Plug-and-Play*

**Plug-and-play** is an industry-wide standard that makes the configuration of certain hardware devices particularly easy. To make full use of plug-and-play, both the device and your computer must support this standard. Generally speaking, plug-and-play works only with recently manufactured hardware.

**Installing a plug-and-play device**

To add a plug-and-play device to your system, all you have to do is:

1. Physically install the device (with the computer off), following the manufacturer's instructions.
2. Turn on the computer.

When Windows starts up, it will detect the new piece of hardware and inform you of this fact. If special software, such as a **device driver** (a program that translates signals from the device into a language that Windows can understand) is needed, Windows may request that you insert the appropriate disk or CD-ROM in its drive. In any case, Windows will determine the necessary settings and install the relevant software so that the device will run properly. Then, Windows may restart itself to put the changes into effect.

## *The Add New Hardware Utility*

If you want to install a device that has not been designed to meet the plug-and-play standard, or if your computer does not support such devices, the process is more difficult. Once you have physically connected the new hardware to the system, turn on the computer and proceed as follows*:

1. Close all open windows and exit any running applications.
2. Start Control Panel. (Click on the Start button, point at the Settings option, and choose Control Panel from the resulting menu.)
3. Double-click on the Add New Hardware icon, which starts the Add New Hardware Wizard.

Add New Hardware

4. In the resulting dialog box, choose the Next command button, which displays the window shown in Figure 9.
5. You now have to decide whether or not to have Windows try to

**Figure 9** The Add New Hardware Wizard

*These procedures are generic in nature and do not apply to adding RAM, a disk drive, and certain other hardware. The installation of these devices proceeds quite differently; follow the instructions supplied by the manufacturer.

detect the new hardware. If you select the Yes option button and click on Next, a new dialog box will appear providing some information about the process. Then, choose the Next button and:

- Windows will search for the new hardware, and try to identify it and determine its proper settings.
- If the search is successful, Windows will display the results, asking you to confirm the listed information and perhaps supply a few more details. (The instruction manual may come in handy here.)
- You may then be asked to insert a certain diskette or CD-ROM in its drive so that the proper device driver can be copied to the hard disk.
- Windows may restart the computer to put the changes into effect. The installation process is now complete.

If Windows informs you that no new hardware was found, it will return you to the window shown in Figure 9.

6. If you select the No option button in Figure 9, you will have to complete all remaining steps in this procedure. Choose the Next command button, and the window shown in Figure 10 will appear.

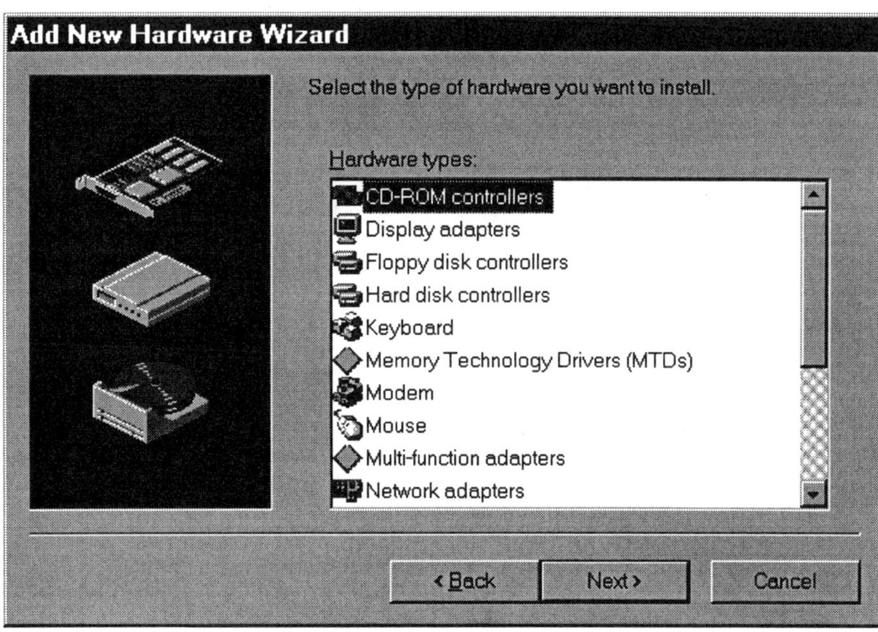


**Figure 10** Selecting the Type of Hardware to be Installed

7. Select the type of hardware you are installing and choose the Next command button. The window shown in Figure 11 will be displayed.

**TIP**

If you are not sure what "type" of hardware you are installing, select *Other devices* from the list. This selection will display all available hardware choices in the next window, the one shown in Figure 11. (Contrary to the statement in this window, there is no "Unknown Hardware" selection.)

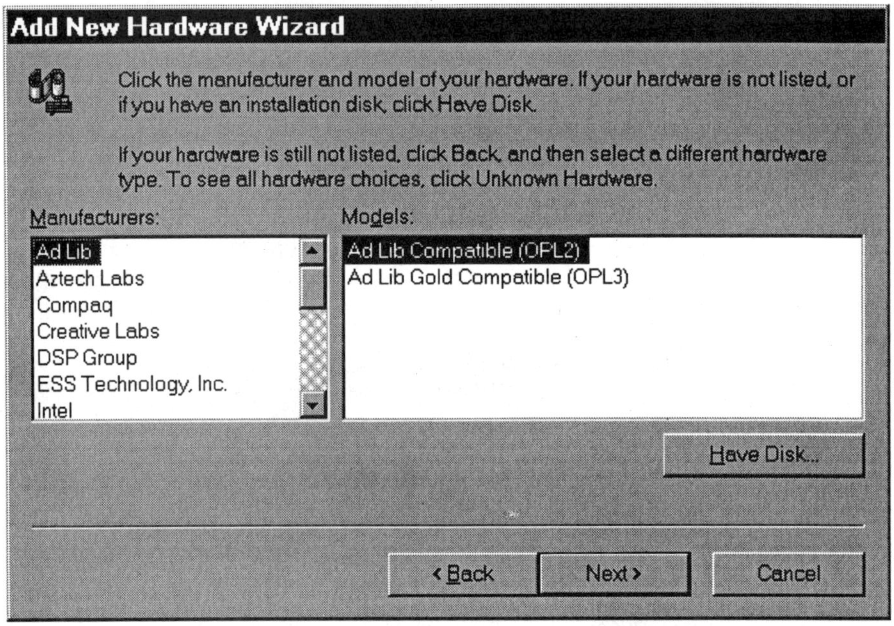


**Figure 11** Selecting the Particular Piece of Hardware to be Installed

8. Select the manufacturer of the new hardware in the left box and a list of corresponding models will appear in the right box. Select the appropriate model from this list and choose the Next command button.

**NOTE**

If the manufacturer has supplied an installation disk, insert it in its drive, choose the Have Disk command button, enter the appropriate drive in the resulting dialog box, and choose OK.

9. Depending on the device you are installing:
   - Windows may now display a list of settings for the device to be installed and it may be necessary for you to set certain switches or jumpers on the device to match these settings. If so, make these changes after you are finished with the Add New Hardware Wizard and have turned off your computer.
   - Windows may now ask that you insert a certain diskette or CD-ROM in its drive in order to copy relevant files to your hard disk.
   - Windows may advise you that there is a conflict between the new device and another device. To proceed, choose the Next button, follow the instructions, and see if the *Conflict Troubleshooter* can help. If you have any doubts about your ability to handle this situation, choose the Cancel button instead and get help from someone who is more experienced in this area.
10. When the process is complete, choose the Finish button. You may be asked to restart your computer at this point to put the changes into effect.

**5.2 TUTORIAL**

Try the following exercise on your own. It simulates the configuration of a mouse that you have supposedly just connected to your computer.

1. Turn on the computer (if necessary) to start Windows, and close any open windows.
2. Open the Control Panel window (from the Settings option on the Start menu) and double-click on the Add New Hardware icon. This starts the Add New Hardware Wizard.
3. Read the information displayed and then choose the Next command button.
4. Select the No option button, telling Windows that you will enter the information about the new device instead of having the system detect it automatically. Then, choose the Next button. A list of hardware types will be displayed.
5. Select Mouse from the list and choose the Next button. Two lists, of manufacturers and models, will be displayed.
6. Select Microsoft from the list on the left and Microsoft Serial Mouse from the list on the right. (In practice, you would get this information from the device's instruction manual.) Choose the Next button. A dialog box is displayed informing you that Win-

dows knows how to install this software.

7. Choose the Cancel button to abort the installation process. The Add New Hardware Wizard will close, returning you to Control Panel. (In practice, you would click on Finish and follow the on-screen instructions to complete the process.)
8. Close the Control Panel window.

# 5.3 Sounds and Multimedia

**What is multimedia?**

**Multimedia** is a catch-all term that refers to the use of sound, animation, and video to enhance computer software. For example, a multimedia encyclopedia not only contains the usual text and pictures, but also audio and video clips about certain subjects. Multimedia applications currently represent the fastest growing area of software development.

In order to run multimedia applications, your computer must be equipped with at least a CD-ROM drive, sound card (occupying one of the slots within the system unit), and speakers. Most desktop PCs sold nowadays come equipped with these components; moreover, they can usually be added fairly easily to most older computers. (Installing new hardware is discussed in Section 5.2.)

Windows support for multimedia can be found in two places. Several "accessories" allow you to create or play back multimedia files (see Chapter 9) and two Control Panel utilities, Sounds and Multimedia, let you customize the use or configuration of multimedia devices. In this section, we will discuss these two utilities.

## The Sounds Utility

If your computer is equipped with a sound card and speakers, you can specify that certain sounds be played at the occurrence of certain system "events", such as minimizing an application or exiting Windows. The assignment of a sound to a given event is made from within Control Panel's Sounds utility.

To start the Sounds utility:

1. Open the Control Panel window (by clicking on the Start button, pointing at the Settings option, and choosing the Control Panel item from the resulting submenu).

Sounds

2. Double-click on the Sounds icon. The Sounds Properties dialog box, shown in Figure 12, will open.

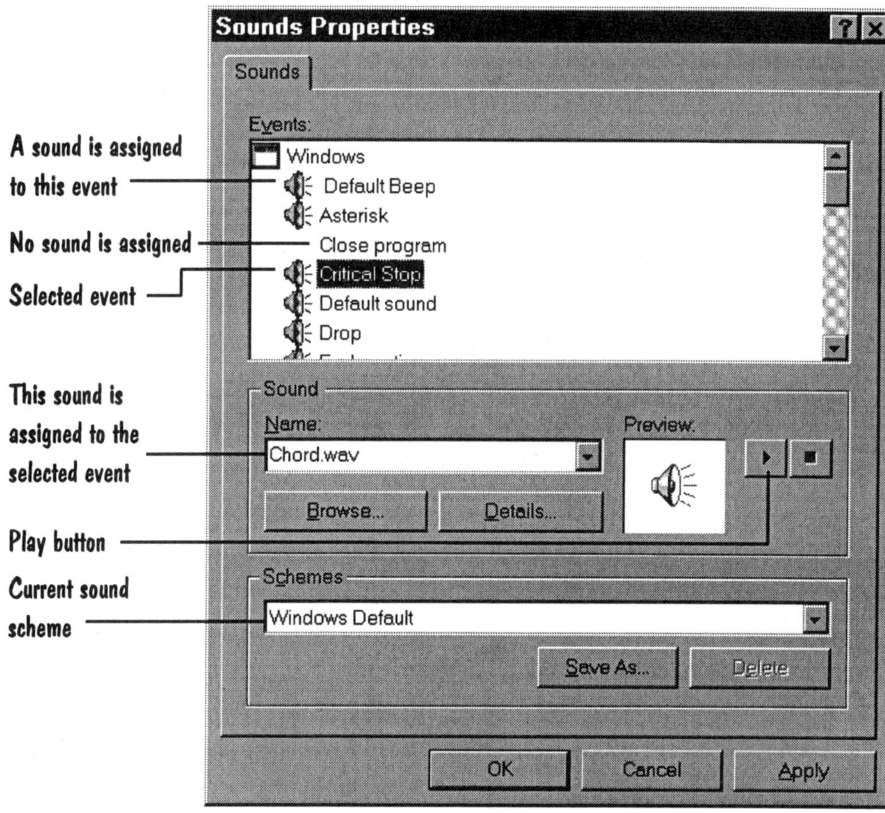


**Figure 12** The Sounds Properties Dialog Box

Using the Sounds Properties dialog box, you can:

- Choose a built-in *sound scheme*, consisting of a collection of sounds pre-assigned to system events, or choose not to use sounds at all.
- Create a custom sound scheme by assigning particular sounds to specific events.

**Selecting a Built-in Sound Scheme** Windows comes equipped with several sound schemes. To select one of them:

1. Open the Sounds Properties dialog box, as described above.

2. Select a sound scheme from the Schemes drop-down list. Select "No Sounds" from the list if you do not want to hear sounds at system events.

**Previewing sounds**

3. To listen to (*preview*) an assigned sound, select the associated event from the Events list box and click on the Play button. To terminate a sound file before it has finished playing, click on the Stop button.

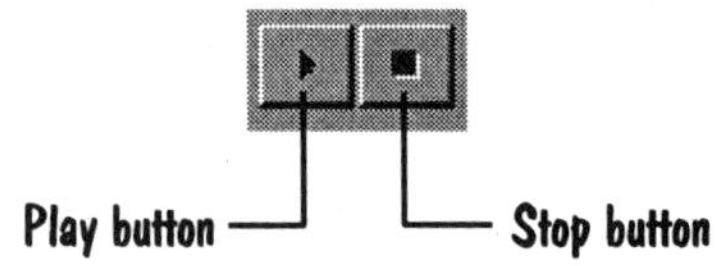


4. Choose the Apply command button, which puts the selected sound scheme into effect without closing the dialog box, or choose the OK button to put the scheme into effect and close the dialog box.

**Creating a Custom Sound Scheme** If you have the time and inclination, you can assign a sound of your choosing to each individual system event, creating a custom sound scheme. To do so:

1. Select a built-in sound scheme from the Schemes drop-down list that is similar to what you want.
2. Select a system event from the Events list box. (This box displays all events to which you can assign sounds; some events, such as Asterisk and Exclamation refer to dialog boxes of certain types.) The selected event will become highlighted.

   If the selected event is already associated with a sound, it will be preceded by the "speaker" symbol shown at the right, and the name of the corresponding sound file will be displayed in the Name text box. To preview the sound, click on the Play button.

3. To assign a new sound to the selected event, select another sound file from the Name drop-down list. (This list contains all files with extension *wav* in the default folder; to select a sound file from another folder, choose the Browse command button.)
4. Repeat steps 2 and 3 until your sound scheme is complete.
5. If you would like to save your new sound scheme (so that it will be added to the Schemes drop-down list), choose the Save As command button, enter a name for the scheme in the resulting dialog box, and choose the OK button.
6. Choose the Apply command button, which puts the new sound scheme into effect without closing the dialog box, or choose the OK button to put the scheme into effect and close the dialog box.

## *The Multimedia Utility*

The Multimedia utility allows you to adjust certain settings for the multimedia devices connected to your system. These may include audio, video, and MIDI (musical instrument digital interface) devices.

To start the Multimedia utility:

Multimedia

1. Open the Control Panel window.
2. Double-click on the Multimedia icon. The Multimedia Properties dialog box, shown in Figure 13, will open.

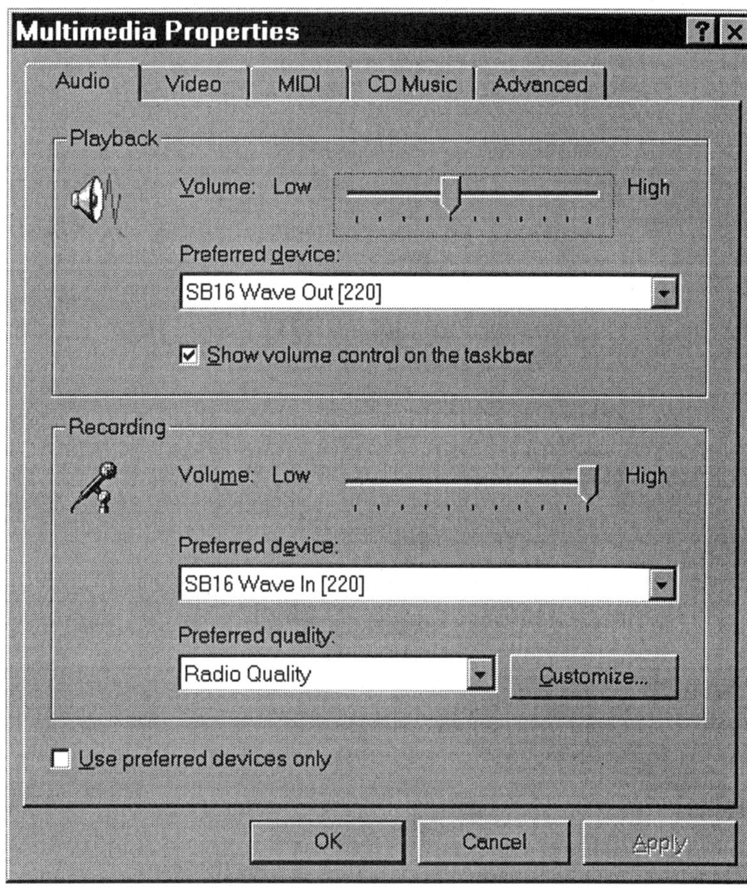


**Figure 13** The Multimedia Dialog Box — Audio Page

As you can see, this dialog box contains several pages, each corresponding to some aspect of multimedia.

**The Audio Page** The audio page (Figure 13) is divided into two main areas: Playback and Recording.

**The Playback section**

In the Playback section, you can:

- Adjust the volume of sound coming from the computer's speakers by dragging the Volume *slider* to the left (to decrease the volume) or to the right (to increase it). Alternatively, you can click on the desired spot to the left or right of the slider.

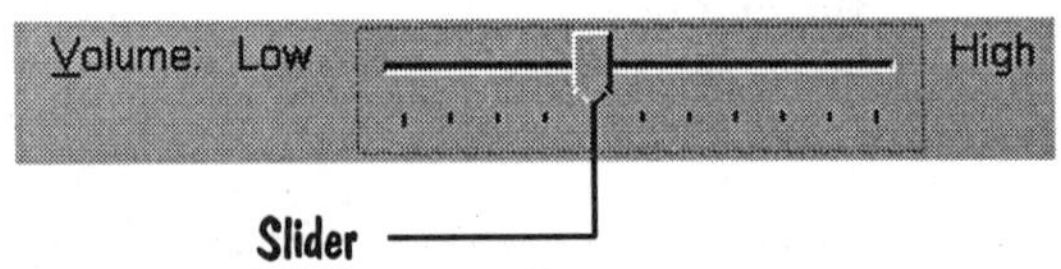


- Specify which of the audio devices connected to your computer will be the default device by selecting it from the *Preferred device* drop-down list.
- Choose to be able to access the volume control from the Taskbar by selecting the *Show volume control on the taskbar* check box. When this box is selected, a "speaker" symbol will appear next to the clock. Clicking on this symbol displays the volume control, as shown at the right.

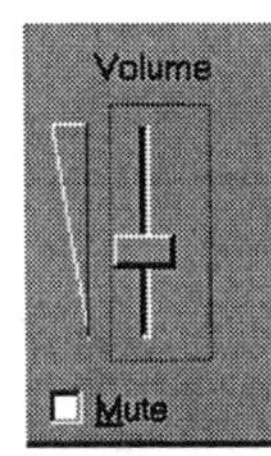


**The Recording section**

In the Recording section, you can:

- Adjust the microphone's sound level by using the Volume slider.
- Select the default audio recording device and the default quality at which it records by using the *Preferred device* and *Preferred quality* drop-down lists. (Typically, high, medium, and low quality settings are referred to as *CD*, *Radio*, and *Telephone* quality, respectively.) Be aware that high quality recordings may produce very large sound files.
- Change certain recording settings (such as whether a stereo or mono sound file is produced) by choosing the Customize command button.

**The Other Dialog Box Pages** Here is a brief rundown of the kinds of settings you can alter on the other Multimedia Properties dialog box pages.

- The *Video* page allows you to decide whether to run video clips full-screen or in a window and, if you select the latter, what size window to use. Be aware that video looks best when it is run in its original size window.

- The *MIDI* page lets you select the instrument on which Windows plays MIDI output. If several MIDI instruments are available, you can assign the instruments to different channels.
- The *CD Music* page lets you adjust the headphone volume setting for your CD-ROM drive.
- When you click on the *Advanced* tab, a list of multimedia categories is displayed on the corresponding page of the dialog box. Clicking on the "+" symbol to the left of a category (or double-clicking on the category name) displays all drivers installed for this type of device. (Recall that a *device driver* is a program that translates the various commands from the device into a language that Windows can understand.) Selecting a particular driver and choosing the Properties command button provides information about the driver and allows you to change some of its settings.

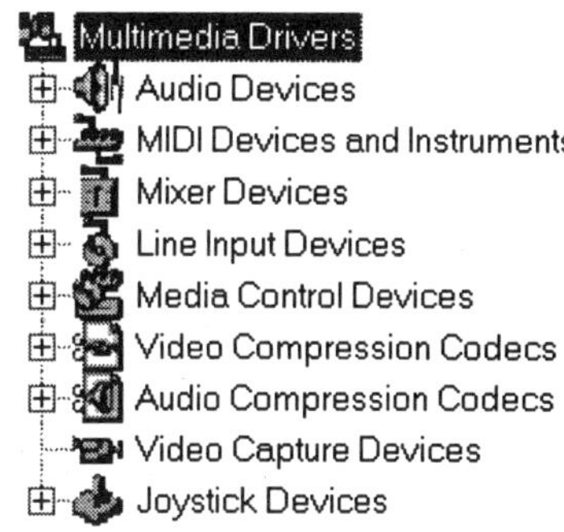


**5.3 TUTORIAL**

Try the following exercise on your own.

1. Turn on the computer (if necessary) to start Windows 95, and close any open windows.
2. Open the Control Panel window (from the Settings option on the Start menu) and double-click on the Sounds icon. The Sounds Properties dialog box will open.
3. Open the Schemes drop-down list and select the Windows Default sound scheme. (If a warning message box appears, choose No to close it.)
4. Play (preview) the sound associated with the Asterisk event by selecting it from the Events list and then clicking on the Play button (shown at the right).

5. Change the sound assigned to the Asterisk event: With Asterisk still selected, open the Name drop-down list and click on *tada .wav*. Preview this sound.
6. Choose the Cancel command button to close the Sounds Properties dialog box without putting your change into effect.
7. In the Control Panel window, double-click on the Multimedia icon to open the Multimedia Properties dialog box.

8. Experiment with the Playback volume control on the Audio page: Drag its slider to several different positions and listen to the sounds emitted when you release the mouse button.
9. Successively click on the other tabs in the Multimedia Properties dialog box. Notice the options available on each page.
10. Close the Multimedia Properties dialog box by choosing the Cancel command button, and then close Control Panel.

## *5.4 Accessibility Options*

Windows contains several features that make it easier for physically challenged people to use (or *access*) the computer. For example:

- For the visually impaired, text on the screen can be increased in size and given more contrast.
- For the hearing impaired, visual cues can be set up to accompany system sounds.
- For those who lack full dexterity, certain keystroke combinations can be made easier to manage and the keyboard can be set up to emulate mouse movements.

Most of these accessibility features are enabled from within Control Panel's Accessibility Options utility.

To start this utility:

1. Open the Control Panel window (by pointing at Settings on the Start menu and choosing Control Panel from the submenu).
2. Double-click on the Accessibility Options icon. The Accessibility Properties dialog box, shown in Figure 14, will be displayed.

**Accessibility Options**

As you can see this dialog box contains five tabs. In the remainder of this section, we will discuss the various options available on each of the corresponding pages. To put the options you select into effect, choose either the OK or the Apply command button. (The Apply command button leaves the dialog box open.)

### *Keyboard Options*

This set of options makes the keyboard easier to manage for those who lack some dexterity or only have the use of one hand. The changes made here affect all Windows applications.

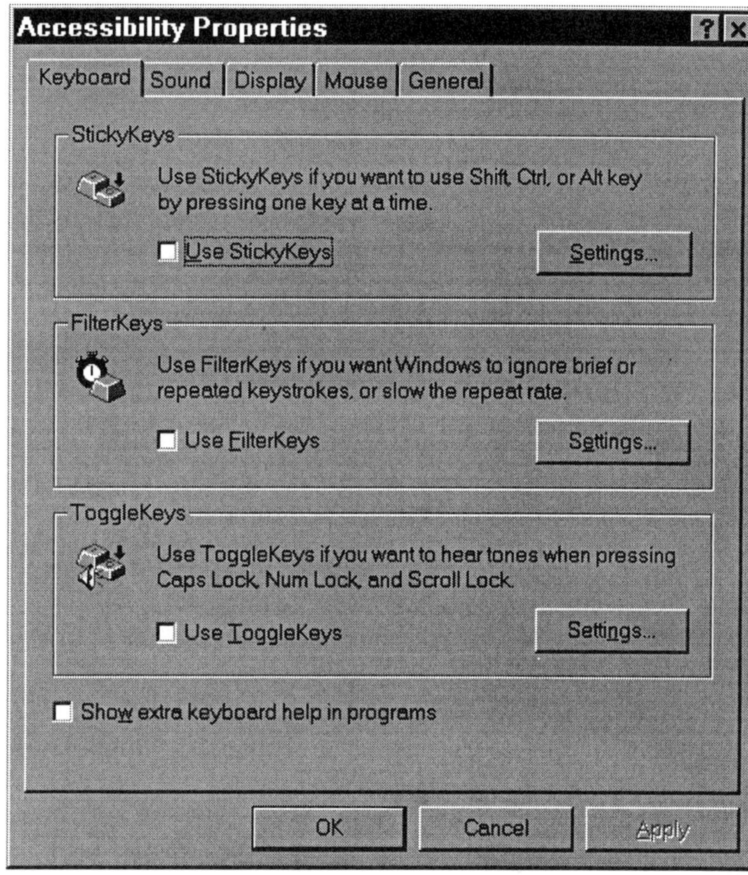


**Figure 14** The Accessibility Properties Dialog Box

**StickyKeys** As you know, many features of Windows and its applications can be accessed by means of keystroke combinations (such as Ctrl+Esc or Alt+Tab), which involve holding down one key while pressing another. Selecting the Use StickyKeys check box allows you to make these keystrokes one after the other, which is easier for some people to accomplish than pressing both keys simultaneously. For example, if StickyKeys is enabled, to open the Start menu, you would press (and release) the Ctrl key and then press (and release) the Esc key.

Choosing the Settings command button to the right of the check box allows you to select certain StickyKeys-related options, such as whether or not an icon appears on the Taskbar to show that StickyKeys has been enabled.

**FilterKeys** Selecting the Use FilterKeys check box instructs Windows to ignore quick keystrokes or ignore repeated keystrokes. (Enabling FilterKeys can help keep accidental keystrokes from being acted upon by Windows.) To select one of these options (and some others, as well), choose the Settings command button to the right of the check box.

**ToggleKeys** Many Windows users will find the ToggleKeys option useful. Selecting the Use ToggleKeys check box causes the speaker to emit a tone when one of the three "toggle keys" (Num Lock, Caps Lock, and Scroll Lock) is pressed. Enabling this option lets you know that you have (perhaps accidentally) pressed one of these keys.

Once you have selected the options you want to enable, choose the Apply or OK command buttons to put your selections into effect. (Choosing Apply leaves the dialog box open.)

**NOTE**

Control Panel's Keyboard utility (see Section 4.4) also provides options for changing the action of the keyboard. In addition, some Windows applications supply extra help for using the keyboard. To display this help (if available), select the *Show extra keyboard help in programs* check box at the bottom of the Keyboard page.

**TIP**

If you wish, any of the three keyboard accessibility options can be toggled on or off whenever Windows is running by using shortcut keys. To enable an option's shortcut key, choose the Settings command button for that option, select the *Use shortcut* check box in the resulting dialog box, and choose the OK button. The shortcut keys for these options are:

| | |
|---|---|
| StickyKeys: | Press the Shift key five times |
| FilterKeys: | Hold down the right Shift key for eight seconds |
| ToggleKeys: | Hold down the Num Lock key for five seconds |

## *Sound Options*

The Sound page of the Accessibility Properties dialog box provides options that may be useful for the hearing impaired. These options are shown in Figure 15.

**SoundSentry** Enabling SoundSentry (by selecting its check box and choosing the Apply or OK command button) causes Windows to flash part of the screen whenever the speaker emits a sound. The Settings command button opens a dialog box that allows you to select which part of the screen (for example, the active title bar) will flash.

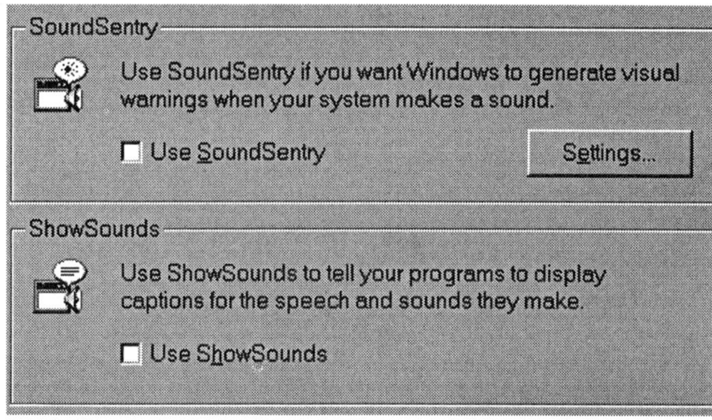


**Figure 15** Options Available on the Sound Page

**ShowSounds** SoundSentry informs a hearing impaired person that some kind of sound has been made. The ShowSounds option takes this idea a step further. When the Use ShowSounds check box is selected, certain applications will supply, usually by means of a message box on the screen, information related to the sound; for example, why it was made.

## *Display Options*

The Display page of the Accessibility Properties dialog box only contains one option; it allows you to put a high contrast display scheme into effect. Figure 16 shows this option displayed in high contrast black-on-white. (Notice that the usual gray-colored dialog box background is now white.) By choosing the Settings command button, you can select white-on-black or a custom scheme, instead.

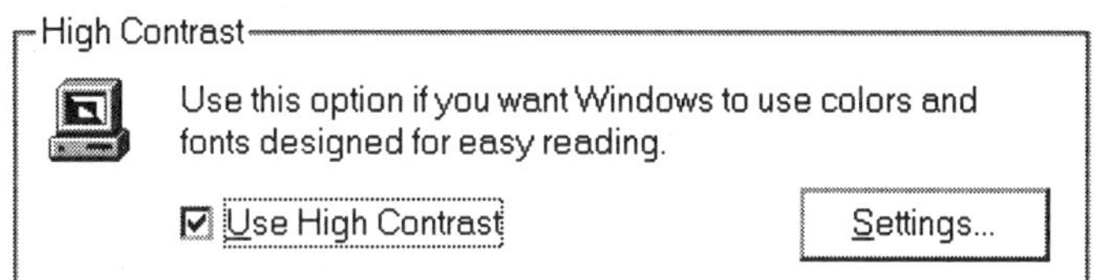


**Figure 16** High Contrast Display Option

TIP

Control Panel's Display utility offers much more control over the size and appearance of text (see Section 4.3). If a visually impaired person is going to make extensive use of this computer, it's a better idea to use the Display utility to set up the screen resolution and a window scheme to his or her liking. The only advantage of the Display page of the Accessibility Options utility (other than its simplicity) is that you can use a shortcut key to toggle high contrast mode on and off. To do so, choose the Settings command button, select the *Use shortcut* check box in the resulting dialog box, and choose the OK button. The High Contrast shortcut key is Left Alt + Left Shift + Print Screen.

## *Mouse Options*

The Mouse page of the Accessibility Properties dialog box only contains one option, MouseKeys (Figure 17). When the MouseKeys check box is selected, the numeric keypad can be used to move the mouse pointer around the screen and to simulate a mouse click, double-click, or drag:

- To move the mouse pointer horizontally or vertically, press the appropriate Arrow key (on the numeric keypad); to move the pointer diagonally, press the Home, End, PgUp, or PgDn key (on the numeric keypad).
- To simulate a mouse click, double-click, or right-click, on the numeric keypad press the 5 key, the + (plus) key, or the - (minus) key, respectively.
- To drag the mouse pointer to a new position, (on the numeric keypad) press the Ins key to start the drag operation, use the Arrow keys to move the pointer to the appropriate place, and then press the Del key to complete the operation.

**Figure 17** The MouseKeys Mouse Option

Choose the Settings command button to open a dialog box offering various options to be used with MouseKeys. These include:

- Enabling the shortcut key Left Alt + Left Shift + Num Lock to toggle MouseKeys on or off.
- Adjusting the pointer speed.
- Specifying whether MouseKeys will respond to the numeric keypad when Num Lock is on or Num Lock is off.

NOTE

Control Panel's Mouse utility provides additional options for configuring the mouse (see Section 4.4). Some of these, such as selecting left-handed or right-handed operation and enabling mouse trails, may be of particular interest to a person with a physical disability.

TIP

Keep in mind that Windows provides many keyboard alternatives to using the mouse. For example, as we pointed out in Chapter 1, you can select menu items and dialog box options, and resize or move a window using just the keyboard. Windows and most applications also use shortcut keys to provide alternatives to mouse clicks. For a list of important Windows shortcut keys, see Appendix A.

## *Other Accessibility Options*

The General page of the Accessibility Properties dialog box provides a few additional options. These are displayed in Figure 18.

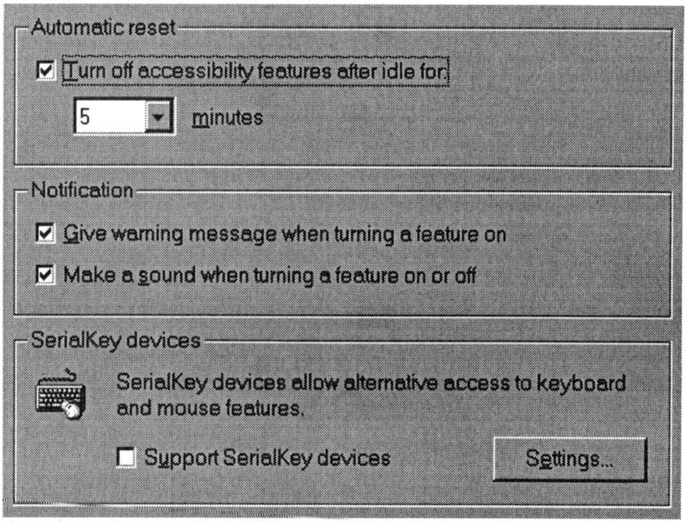


**Figure 18** Options on the General Page

The first two sets of options in this dialog box, *Automatic reset* and *Notification*, are fairly self-explanatory. The third, *SerialKey devices*, is used to configure (by choosing the Settings button) an alternate input device attached to the computer's serial port. These devices are intended for people who are unable to use a standard keyboard or mouse.

5.4 TUTORIAL

Try the following exercise on your own.

1. Turn on the computer (if necessary) to start Windows 95, and close any open windows.
2. Open the Control Panel window (from the Settings option on the Start menu) and double-click on the Accessibility Options icon. The Accessibility Properties dialog box will open.
3. On the Keyboard page, select the Use StickyKeys and Use Toggle-Keys check boxes, and choose the Apply command buttons. Now:
   - Press (and release) the Alt key, then the Tab key. Notice that (because StickyKeys is enabled), this works like Alt+Tab to switch the active window to Control Panel. Switch back to the Accessibility Properties dialog box.
   - Press the Caps Lock, Num Lock, and Scroll Lock keys twice each. Notice that (because Toggle Keys is enabled), an audible tone is emitted each time.

   Deselect the check boxes and choose the Apply button again.
4. Choose the Settings command button next to the FilterKeys check box. A Settings dialog box will open.
5. In this dialog box, select each of the two Filter options buttons and type in the test box to see the effect. (You may have to adjust the corresponding Settings to see a difference!) Cancel this dialog box.
6. Click on the Display tab, then select the Use High Contrast check box and choose the Apply button. Notice the dramatic difference in the screen's appearance. Deselect the Use High Contrast check box and choose the Apply button again.
7. Click on the Mouse tab, then select the Use MouseKeys check box and choose the Apply command button. Now:
   - Hold down the Up Arrow key on the numeric keypad. If the mouse pointer doesn't move, turn on (or off) the Num Lock key and try again. Use the Arrow keys to move the mouse pointer over the Settings command button.

- Simulate a right-click by pressing the + (plus) key on the numeric keypad. The one-item *What's This?* menu will open.
- Use the Arrow keys to position the mouse pointer over the menu item, and press the 5 key on the numeric keypad to simulate a click. Close the resulting pop-up box by pressing the Esc key. (The minus key on the numeric keypad simulates a *double*-click.)

8. Deselect the Use MouseKeys check box and choose the Apply button again.
9. Explore the various other options and settings in the Accessibility Properties dialog box with the help of context-sensitive help.
10. Close the Accessibility Properties dialog box and Control Panel.

# *5.5 Other Control Panel Options*

In this section, we will briefly discuss a few other common utilities housed within the Control Panel window. We will introduce the Modems and System utilities and then briefly describe the Network, Passwords, and Regional Settings options.

## *The Modems Utility*

A **modem** is a device that translates computer-generated data into signals that can be sent (usually over phone lines) to another computer. If your computer is equipped with a modem and the proper *communications software*, you have the potential to access the vast quantities of information found on **online services** (such as CompuServe and America Online) or the **Internet**, a world-wide system of interlinked computer networks.

Control Panel's Modems utility helps you to install and/or configure a modem. To start this utility:

Modems

1. Open the Control Panel window (from the Settings option on the Start menu).
2. Double-click on the Modems icon.

The Modems Properties dialog box, shown in Figure 19 on the next page, will open.

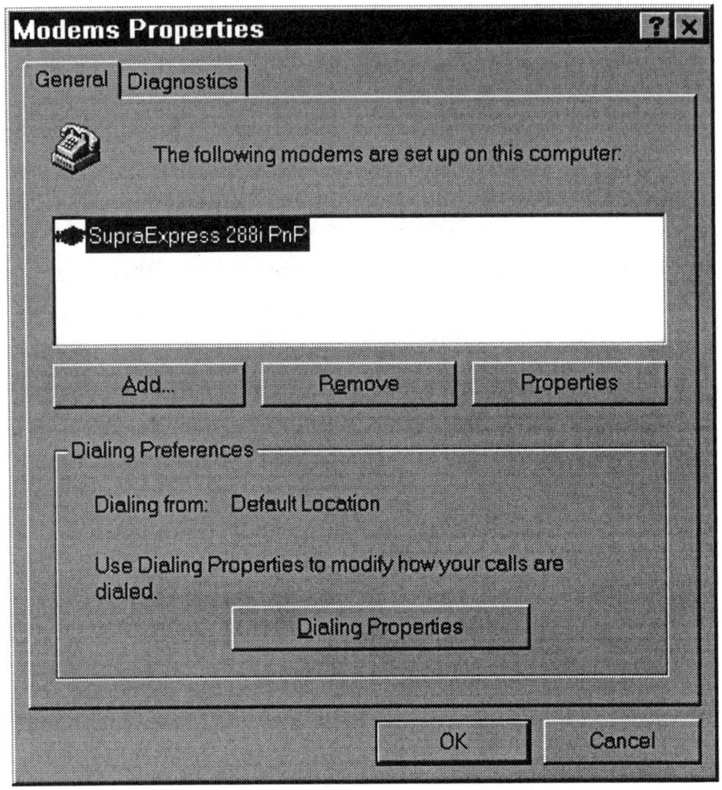


**Figure 19** The Modems Properties Dialog Box

The Modems utility has two basic functions: installing a new modem and configuring an existing one.

**Installing a Modem** To use the Modems Properties dialog box to install a new modem:

1. With the computer off, connect the modem to the computer:
   - If the modem is an *internal* type, insert it in a free slot within the system unit.
   - If the modem is an *external* type, attach it to a serial computer port with the appropriate cable and turn it on.
2. Turn on the computer, starting Windows, and open the Modems Properties dialog box, as described above.
3. Choose the Add command button. This starts the Install New Modem wizard.

4. Typically, you would now let Windows detect the new modem by choosing the Next command button, and if all goes well, the installation will proceed with little or no additional input on your part.
5. If, in carrying out step 3, Windows encounters problems in the installation process, select the *Don't detect my modem; I will select it from a list* check box, and choose the Next button. This option requires some information about the modem, so keep its instruction manual handy.
6. Follow the instructions, making selections and choosing Next (or Finish), until the process is complete. (For a more detailed description of the installation process, see the procedure in Section 5.2 for installing new hardware.)

**NOTE**

If your modem and computer support the *plug-and-play* standard, installation may be a lot simpler. Just physically connect the modem to your system, turn on the modem if it's an external one, and then turn on the computer. During start-up, Windows should indicate that it has detected and installed the new modem. (At some point in the process, you may have to insert a certain disk in its drive.)

If your modem is not of the plug-and-play variety, you should read through the instruction manual before installing it. If the manufacturer's instructions differ from the process outlined above, use the former!

**Configuring a Modem** The installation process installs a universal *driver*, a program that can be used by any Windows application to communicate with the modem. The Modems utility provides a central location to configure this driver by setting various parameters for its operation. This information can be entered or changed from the Modems Properties dialog box by choosing either the Properties or Dialing Properties command button (see Figure 19).

**The Properties command button**

Choosing the Properties button opens a dialog box that allows you to change information about the modem itself. This includes:

- The volume level of the modem's speaker.
- The maximum speed, measured in bits per second (bps), at which the modem can connect to a remote computer.
- Default connection parameters — the parity, and number of data and stop bits. (The settings for these parameters must match the requirements of the remote computer and can be changed, if

necessary, using communications software when making a particular connection.)

- Certain default calling preferences, such as how much time is allowed to elapse (between dialing a number and making the connection) before the call is canceled.
- Settings for the serial port that the modem is using.

**The Dialing Properties command button**

Choosing the Dialing Properties button opens a dialog box that allows you to express preferences for the way a call is made. For example:

- You can specify that a certain country code and area code be used, whenever necessary, in dialing a phone number.
- You can specify that "call waiting" be disabled while a call is in progress to prevent the connection from being lost should an incoming call come through.
- You can specify whether *tone* or *pulse* dialing is used to make the call. (Specify pulse dialing only if tone dialing is not available on your phone line.)

**Troubleshooting a Modem's Operation** The Modems Properties dialog box also contains a Diagnostics page that can help you to resolve conflicts with other serial (communications) devices. The information supplied on this page is fairly technical and we won't discuss it further in this text.

## *The System Utility*

The Windows System utility displays information about the various components of your computer and allows you to make changes in the way that some of them operate. To start this utility, either:

System

- Open the Control Panel window, as described earlier in this section, and double-click on the System icon.

*or*

- Right-click on the My Computer icon (on the Desktop) and choose the Properties item from the resulting pop-up menu.

In either case, the System Properties dialog box, similar to the one shown in Figure 20, will be displayed.

As you can see, the first page of this dialog box displays some general information about the computer system. The other three pages, which are discussed below, allow you to make changes to certain system parameters.

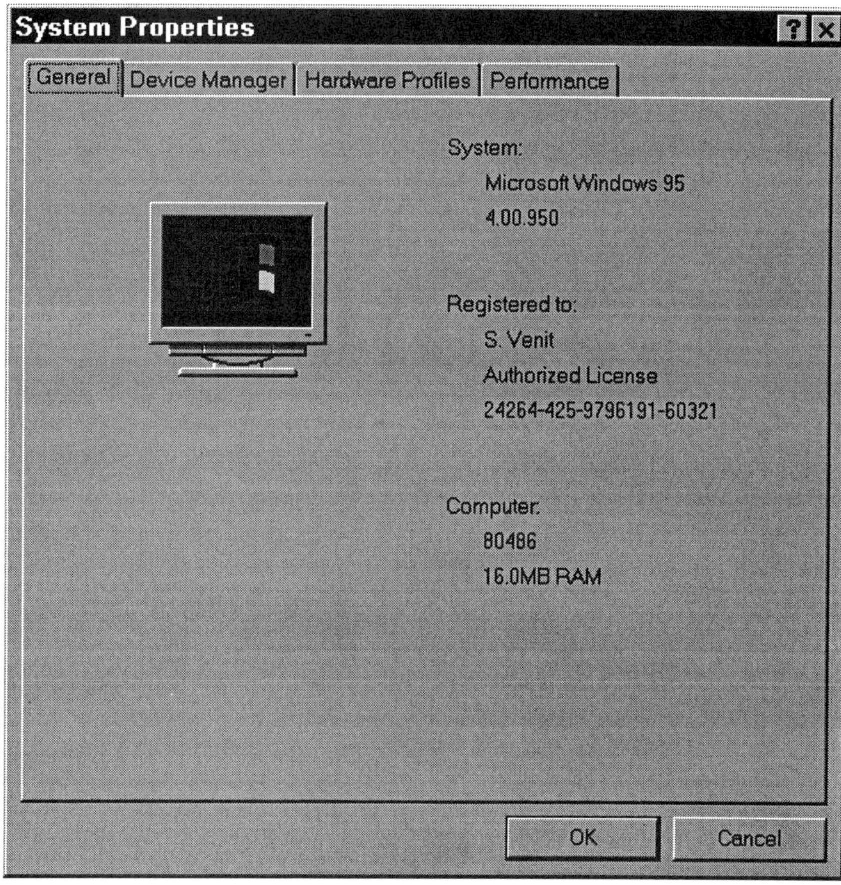


**Figure 20** The System Properties Dialog Box

WARNING

The System utility should be treated with respect. Changing certain settings in the System Properties dialog box can sometimes have unfortunate consequences. For example, after making a modification, a piece of hardware may stop working or Windows itself may fail to run. So, do not make any changes here unless you are sure of what you are doing.

**Device Manager** Clicking on the Device Manager tab in the System Properties dialog box displays a list of the types of hardware connected to your computer. If you want to see the hardware devices within a particular category, click on the plus sign next to the category name, or double-click on the latter. (The diagram at the right shows the result of clicking on the plus sign next to the CD-ROM icon.)

Now, if you double-click on a particular device (or select it and choose the Properties command button), a dialog box with information about that device will open. In most cases, you will also be given the opportunity to change certain settings for the given device.

**Hardware Profiles** A **hardware profile** consists of a set of *device drivers*, programs that help Windows communicate with the corresponding hardware devices. Normally, the hardware attached to a computer does not change from session to session, so only one hardware profile, created automatically by Windows, is necessary.

In certain special circumstances, however, you may want to use a couple of different hardware configurations on a regular basis. The most common case of this sort occurs with a portable computer. Most of the time, you will probably use the portable's built-in screen, keyboard, and pointing device. However, at times, you may find it more convenient to connect a regular monitor, keyboard, and mouse to the portable. In such a case, you would need different drivers for these components. This set of drivers can be set up as a hardware profile.

**Creating a new hardware profile**

To create a new hardware profile:

1. Open the System Properties dialog box, as described above, and click on the Hardware Profiles tab to display the corresponding page.
2. Select an existing profile that is close to the one you want, choose the Copy command button to copy its contents, type the new profile's name in the resulting dialog box, and choose OK.
3. To enable or disable a specific device for this profile, click on the Device Manager and:
   - Click on the plus sign next to the desired hardware type and then double-click on the device that you want to enable or disable.
   - In the Device Usage area of the resulting dialog box, select or deselect the new hardware profile, depending on whether you want to enable or disable the selected device.
   - Choose the OK command button to return to the System Properties dialog box.
4. Choose the OK button in the System Properties dialog box.

If more than one hardware profile has been set up for your computer, when Windows starts up, you will be asked which profile you want to use.

**Improving System Performance** When Windows 95 is installed or a new device is added, Windows tries to set up the hardware so that it operates in an optimal manner. The Performance page of the System Properties dialog box displays information about memory and hard disk use and allows you to change a few related settings to enhance performance "manually". However, in most cases, it is best not to make changes here; they are more likely to *adversely* affect performance.

**File System Properties**

Choosing the File System command button opens the File System Properties dialog box, which has three tabs:

- On the Hard Disk page, you can change the *read-ahead buffer* size allotted to the hard disk. When a hard disk read takes place, Windows will not only copy the requested information to RAM, but also *read-ahead* — transfer the data stored in the next disk sectors, as well. The amount of additional data sent to the hard disk — the read-ahead buffer size — is normally set to "Full", the largest available amount.
- On the CD-ROM page, you can change the *supplemental cache* size allotted to the CD-ROM drive. A *cache* is an area in RAM set aside to temporarily store information read from a hard disk or CD-ROM. Then, if this information is needed again, it can be quickly retrieved from RAM, instead of using the much slower process of reading again from the disk or CD. This setting is normally set to "Large".
- On the Troubleshooting page, you can disable certain performance-enhancing features if they appear to be causing trouble.

**Graphics settings**

Choosing the Graphics command button on the Performance page allows you to adjust the amount of *hardware acceleration* used by Windows. (*Acceleration* is accomplished through routines that speed up the display of new information on the screen.) This setting is normally set to "Full".

**Virtual Memory settings**

*Virtual memory* refers to Windows' practice of using the hard disk as if it were additional RAM. Windows 95 normally determines the amount of hard disk space to be used for this purpose, and it's best to accept this setting. If you want to change it (perhaps to use a different hard disk to hold the *swap file*), choose the Virtual Memory command button on the Performance page.

## *Other Control Panel Utilities*

Here are brief descriptions of a few other Control Panel utilities.

Network

**The Network Utility** This utility installs Network drivers and sets up other network components. To be more specific:

- The Configuration page is used to add, remove, and set up network components (such as adapters, protocols, and devices) on your system. It also allows you to share your files and/or printer with other network users.
- The Identification page allows you to provide a name for your computer ("workstation") and the "workgroup" in which it is located.
- The Access Control page provides ways to restrict access to your computer's shared resources. There are two general types of access control:
    1. *Share-level* access control creates a password for each shared resource.
    2. *User-level* access control creates passwords that allow individual users to gain access to shared resources.

Passwords

**The Passwords Utility** Using this utility:

- You can change passwords for both starting Windows and logging onto a network.
- You can set up a password that allows someone at another (*remote*) computer to access your computer.
- You can set up *user profiles* — collections of user-specific preferences, such as the icons present on the Desktop or the fonts and colors in which various items are displayed. User profiles are useful when a machine is shared by several people.

Regional Settings

**The Regional Settings Utility** This utility customizes the way Windows displays numbers, currencies, dates, and times. Its settings affect Windows itself and those Windows applications that elect to make use of them. Although the primary use of Regional Settings is to customize Windows for use in another country, you might want to change the default formats for numbers, dates, or times, even if you live in the United States.

# *Review Exercises*

**Section 5.1**

1. To ___________ a print job means to have it temporarily stored on the hard disk before it is transferred to the printer.
2. A ___________ is a program that translates your document's text, graphics, and special codes into a language that the printer can understand.
3. The "print manager" window displays the current print jobs in a list that is known as the print ___________.
4. To start the Add Printer Wizard, double-click on the ___________ icon in the Printers folder window.
5. True or false: The Printers folder can be opened from the Start menu's Settings option without starting Control Panel.
6. True or false: A separator page is a page that Windows automatically inserts between print jobs.
7. True or false: If a document is printed in portrait orientation, its text runs parallel to the long side of the page.
8. True or false: To interchange the order in which the first two jobs in the print queue will be printed, drag the first document's name and icon just below that of the second document.
9. If a printer is "paused", as indicated on the title bar of the print manager window, you can restart it by choosing
    a. Pause Printing from the Printer window.
    b. Unpause Printing from the Printer menu.
    c. Pause Printing from the Document menu.
    d. Unpause Printing from the Document menu.
10. The computer's primary parallel port is referred to as
    a. COM1
    b. COM2
    c. LPT1
    d. File

**Section 5.2**

11. The term ___________ refers to an industry-wide standard that makes the configuration of certain hardware devices easier.
12. Configuring a new hardware device can be accomplished from Control Panel's ___________ utility.
13. True or false: A device driver is a program that translates the signals from the device into a language that Windows can understand.

14. True or false: When you use the Add New Hardware Wizard to configure a newly-installed device, it is recommended that you let Windows try to detect the new hardware.

15. Before you use the Add New Hardware utility to help install a new device, you should

    a. Physically connect the device to your computer.
    b. Open Control Panel and then restart Windows.
    c. Start the Add/Remove Programs utility.
    d. Make sure that the device's driver is installed.

16. The Add New Hardware Wizard

    a. Will always automatically appear when Windows starts if a new device has been installed in your computer.
    b. Must be used to install a plug-and-play device.
    c. Only works with plug-and-play devices.
    d. Will try to detect and configure a new device, if you instruct it to do so.

**Section 5.3**

17. To associate particular sounds with certain system events, open Control Panel and double-click on the ___________ icon.

18. To put a predefined sound scheme into effect, open the Sounds Properties dialog box, select the scheme from the ___________ drop-down list, and choose the OK or Apply button.

19. The term ___________ refers to the use of sound, animation, and video to enhance computer software.

20. True or false: If a sound is associated with an event, a "speaker" icon appears next to this event in the Sounds Properties dialog box.

21. True or false: To hear the sound you have just assigned to an event, you must first close the Sounds Properties dialog box.

22. True or false: You can use the Sounds utility to place a volume control icon on the Taskbar.

23. Which of the following tasks cannot be accomplished using the Sounds utility?

    a. Assigning a new sound to a system event.
    b. Removing an assigned sound from a system event.
    c. Creating a sound to be assigned to a system event.
    d. Previewing a sound that is assigned to a system event.

24. Which of the following tasks cannot be accomplished using the Multimedia utility?

    a. Increasing the volume level of the computer's speakers.

b. Adjusting the bass and treble settings for the computer's speakers.
c. Adjusting the sound level of the computer's microphone.
d. Changing the size of the window that shows video clips.

**Section 5.4**

25. The Control Panel utility that can help some physically challenged people use the computer is called ___________.

26. If you want to open the Start menu by pressing Ctrl and Esc in sequence, select the ___________ option button in the Accessibility Properties dialog box.

27. The Use MouseKeys option in the Accessibility Properties dialog box allows you to use the Arrow keys on the ___________ area of the keyboard to move the mouse pointer.

28. True or false: The StickyKeys, FilterKeys, and ToggleKeys keyboard options can, if you want, be turned on and off using shortcut keys.

29. True or false: The Accessibility Properties dialog box allows you to specify the size of type used for text in dialog boxes.

30. True or false: The Accessibility Properties dialog box allows you to use the keyboard to move the mouse pointer, but not to simulate a mouse click or double-click.

31. If you want the computer to emit a sound when the Caps Lock, Num Lock, and Scroll Lock keys are pressed, in the Accessibility Properties dialog box, select the

    a. Use StickyKeys check box.
    b. Use FilterKeys check box.
    c. Use ToggleKeys check box.
    d. Use SoundSentry check box.

32. If you select the Use MouseKeys check box in the Accessibility Properties dialog box, you can use the keyboard to

    a. Move the mouse pointer on the screen.
    b. Simulate a mouse click.
    c. Simulate a mouse drag.
    d. Perform all of the above actions.

**Section 5.5**

33. A ___________ is a device that translates computer-generated data into signals that can be sent over phone lines to another computer.

34. If you frequently use your laptop computer with an auxiliary monitor, you should set up a ___________ that tells Windows, on your command, to load the proper driver for this device.

35. A ___________ is a portion of RAM set aside to temporarily store

information read from a hard disk or CD-ROM so that, if the information is needed again, it can be quickly retrieved.

36. True or false: The term *virtual memory* refers to RAM that has been added to your computer after the initial purchase.
37. True or false: The Passwords utility allows you to set up passwords to limit access to your shared network resources.
38. True or false: The Regional Settings utility allows you to adjust the time on the Taskbar clock.
39. Which of the following tasks cannot be accomplished using the Modems utility?
    a. Install a driver for a newly-connected modem.
    b. Set the maximum connection speed for your modem.
    c. Set up an "address book" of phone numbers that can be dialed from your modem.
    d. Specify that pulse dialing be used by your modem.
40. You can fine-tune your computer's hard disk and CD-ROM performance using Control Panel's
    a. System utility.
    b. Network utility.
    c. Regional Settings utility.
    d. Hardware Profiles utility.

## Lab Exercises

Work each of the following exercises at your computer. Begin by turning the machine on (if necessary) to start Windows 95. If you want to produce a written record of your answers, review the material on WordPad and capturing screens in Sections 2.2 and 2.3.

**Lab Exercise 1 (Section 5.1)**

a. Open the Printers folder window. How many printers are listed there?

b. Open the Properties dialog box for the printer that you normally use. What is the name of this printer?

c. Print a test page. Did it print in portrait or landscape orientation?

d. Click on the Details tab. What is the name of the port to which this printer is connected?

e. By locating the appropriate feature in the Properties dialog box, answer each of the following questions and give the location (for example, "Details page" or "Setup dialog box") of the feature. If a feature cannot be located, answer "Not found".

- Is paper orientation set to portrait or landscape?
- What paper size is currently selected?
- What is the current printing resolution?
- Are any font cartridges installed?
- How much printer memory is installed?

f. Close the printer's Properties dialog box and the Printers folder.

**Lab Exercise 2 (Section 5.1)**

*Note*: You may not be able to do this exercise if you are using a network printer.

a. Open the Printers folder window and select the printer you normally use.

b. Open the "print manager" window for this printer (by double-clicking on it). What is the actual title of this window?

c. Pause the printer (so that it will accept print jobs, but not print them). How did you accomplish this?

d. Start the WordPad word processor (from the Accessories submenu of the Start menu's Programs option). Type your name, your class, and the date on separate lines.

e. Choose the Print command from the File menu, and in the resulting dialog box, choose the Properties command button. Is portrait or landscape orientation selected?

f. Close the Properties dialog box and choose the OK button in the Print dialog box to send the document to the printer. Was it printed?

g. Insert the Lab Exercises disk in its drive and open the Preamble document in WordPad. (Answer "No" to the warning message.) Now, send this document to the printer.

h. Switch to the "print manager" window. How many print jobs are in the queue? What is the first job called? *Optional*: Size the window so that it has no extra "white space" and capture it.

i. Cancel all print jobs and restart ("unpause") the printer. How did you accomplish these tasks?

j. Close the print manager window, the Printers folder, and WordPad, and remove the diskette from its drive.

**Lab Exercise 3 (Section 5.2)**

a. Open the Control Panel window and start the Add New Hardware utility. What is the name of the resulting dialog box?

b. Choose the Next command button. You are going to simulate setting up a printer that has just been connected to your computer, so select the No option button and then choose the Next button.

c. Select Printer from the hardware types list and choose the Next button. What is the dialog box called now?

d. Suppose that the Printer is made by Epson and its model designation is "LQ-850". Select the appropriate items from the Manufacturers and Printers lists. What is the exact name of the item in the Printers list?

e. Choose the Next button to display the "ports" page. Which computer port is highlighted?

f. Choose the Next button. Select, if necessary, the No option button so that the new printer does not become the default one. What *is* the name of your default printer?

g. Choose the Next button and then the Cancel button.

h. Close the Control Panel window.

**Lab Exercise 4 (Section 5.3)**

*Note*: This exercise requires that your computer be equipped with a sound card.

a. Open the Control Panel window and start the Sounds utility. What is the name of the resulting dialog box?

b. Select the Windows Default sound scheme. (If necessary, answer "No" to the warning message.) What event, if any, is highlighted in the Events list?

c. Preview the sounds for the Start Windows and Exit Windows events. Are they the same sound?

d. Assign the "Chimes" sound to the Maximize event. Did a speaker icon automatically appear next to Maximize when you did this?

e. Choose the Cancel command button to close the dialog box.

f. Start the Multimedia utility from Control Panel. Which page of the resulting dialog box is displayed?

g. On the Audio page, drag the volume slider to High, then to Low. Was a sound emitted in both cases when you released the mouse button?

h. Use the Multimedia Properties dialog box to help answer the following questions:

- How many choices are there for the size of the window in which video clips will be shown? Which size is highlighted?
- What drive letter is assigned to your CD-ROM drive?

i. Choose the Cancel command button to close the dialog box and then close the Control Panel window.

**Lab Exercise 5 (Section 5.4)**

a. Open the Control Panel window and start the Accessibility Options utility. What is the name of the resulting dialog box?

b. On the Keyboard page, enable (turn on) StickyKeys and choose the Settings button next to it. Using context-sensitive help, state the function of the *Show StickyKeys status on the screen* check box.

c. Select this check box, then the OK button, and finally, the Apply button. Describe the StickyKeys status icon.

d. Disable (turn off) StickyKeys. Choose the Settings button next to the FilterKeys check box. What is the shortcut key for FilterKeys?

e. Select the *Ignore repeated keystrokes* option button and choose the Settings button next to it. In the resulting dialog box, move the slider to Long. How much time must now elapse between keystrokes before the second keystroke is recognized by Windows? (Try it in the test box!)

f. Choose Cancel twice to return to the Keyboard page. Enable ToggleKeys and then choose the Apply button. Now, press the Caps Lock key twice. Is the same sound emitted both times? What other keys are affected by ToggleKeys?

g. Disable ToggleKeys and choose the OK button to close the dialog box.

h. Close the Control Panel window.

**Lab Exercise 6 (Section 5.4)**

a. Open the Control Panel window and start the Accessibility Options utility.

b. Click on the Display tab, enable (turn on) High Contrast, and then choose the Settings command button. Did the screen go into high contrast mode?

c. Select the *White on black* option, choose OK, and then Apply. What is the color of the dialog box background? Of its title bar?

d. Select the *Black on white* option, choose OK, and then Apply. What is the color of the dialog box background? Of its title bar?

e. Disable (turn off) High Contrast and choose the Apply button. Then, click on the Mouse tab.

f. Enable MouseKeys and choose the Settings button. What is the shortcut key for MouseKeys?

g. Select the Num Lock *On* option and elect to show MouseKey status on the screen. Choose OK to return to the Mouse page. Did the MouseKeys icon appear on the Taskbar?

h. Choose the Apply button and then use the numeric keypad to drag the dialog box to another part of the screen. Give the steps you took to accomplish this.

i. Use the numeric keypad to disable MouseKeys. How did you accomplish this?

j. Close the dialog box and the Control Panel window.

**Lab Exercise 7 (Section 5.5)**

a. Open the Control Panel window and start the Modems utility. How many pages are there in the resulting dialog box?

b. If your computer is equipped with a modem, use this utility to answer the following questions:

- What is the name and maximum speed for this modem?
- What are the current settings for data bits, parity, and stop bits?
- Is the modem using tone dialing or pulse dialing?

c. Close the Modems utility and start the System utility. Use the latter to answer the following questions:

- What kind of processor and how much RAM does your computer have?
- What type of display adapter and monitor does it have?
- What are the names of the available hardware profiles?
- Is the hard disk making use of disk compression?

d. Close the System utility and start the Regional Settings utility. Use the latter to show how Windows would display:

- The current time
- The current date in both short and long format

e. Close the Regional Settings utility and the Control Panel window.

CHAPTER 6

# Using Windows Efficiently

In Chapters 2 and 3, we presented basic information about working with applications, documents, files, folders, and disks. You will probably make use of some of this material every time you use Windows. In this chapter, we present additional information about these topics. Although none of this new material is critical, it should help you to use Windows more productively. You will learn:

1. To move the Taskbar to another location, increase its size, and hide it from view.
2. To rearrange (tile or cascade) open application windows, or minimize them all at once, if so desired.
3. To customize the Start button menus by adding or deleting items from them.
4. To use the Windows Find utility to search for files and folders on your hard disk.
5. To manipulate (for example, move or copy) the files or folders found by the Find utility.
6. To associate a file type (extension) with a specific application so that certain actions (such as open or print) can be performed on a document without first starting the corresponding application.
7. To display the property sheet for a file, folder, or shortcut, and interpret the information provided on it.

# 6.1 Tricks with the Taskbar

The **Taskbar** (Figure 1) is a key element in the Windows 95 interface. As you know, it contains the Start button, which makes it easy to open certain programs and documents (see Section 2.1) and a button for each open application, which makes it easy to switch from one to another (see Section 2.3). Your Taskbar may contain other items as well: perhaps a digital clock or a few small icons for, say, adjusting speaker volume or monitoring print jobs. In this section, we will discuss additional features of the Taskbar.

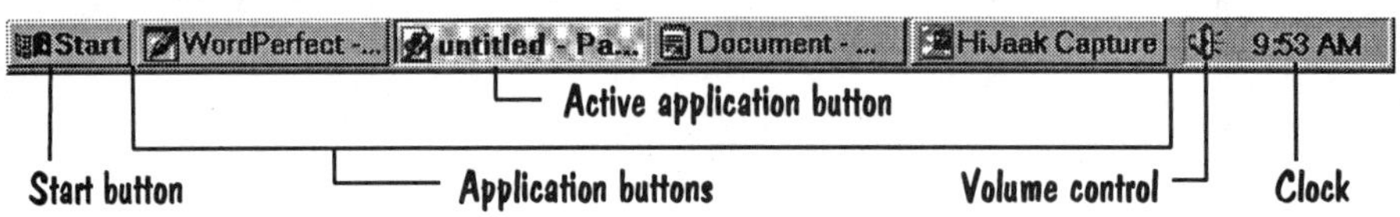


**Figure 1** A Typical Taskbar

## Changing the Way the Taskbar is Displayed

By default, the Taskbar is positioned at the bottom of the screen and is always visible, even when application windows are maximized. If you wish, you can:

- Increase the size of the Taskbar.
- Reposition the Taskbar at the left, right, or top edge of the screen.
- Hide the Taskbar from view.
- Remove the clock from the Taskbar.

We will now describe how to perform each of these tasks.

**Increasing the Size of the Taskbar** If several applications are running, their Taskbar buttons will be reduced in size to fit on the Taskbar. This, in turn, limits the amount of text that can be displayed on each. For example, in Figure 1, notice how the text on the first three application buttons has been truncated, as indicated by the ellipses (...). To increase the size of the Taskbar, and restore its buttons to their normal size:

1. Move the mouse cursor over the top edge of the Taskbar. It will become a double-headed arrow when positioned properly.
2. Drag the cursor up until the Taskbar is the desired height, as indicated by the moving outline. The Taskbar buttons will be

resized and repositioned when you release the mouse button.

A two-row high Taskbar is shown here:

TIP

The size and style of the text on the Taskbar buttons is determined by the font selected for the active window's title bar. You can change this font and, in so doing, the button font as well, from within the Display Properties dialog box. See Section 4.3 for the details of this procedure.

**Repositioning the Taskbar** The Taskbar can be positioned at any of the four edges of the screen. To move the Taskbar from its current location to another edge of the screen:

1. Position the mouse cursor over an empty part of the Taskbar.
2. Hold down the left mouse button and drag the cursor toward one of the other screen edges. As you approach this edge, an outline will appear indicating where the Taskbar will be repositioned.
3. Release the mouse button; the Taskbar will be displayed in the new location. The following figure shows it at the left screen edge.

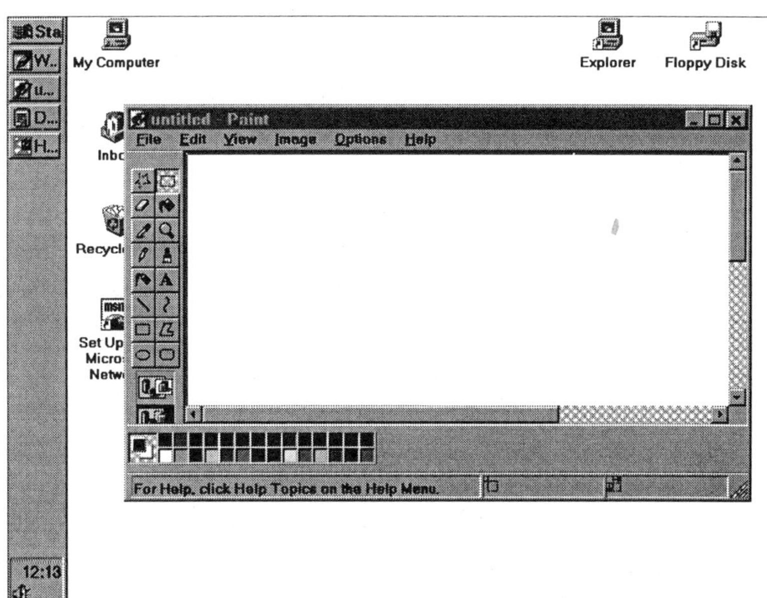

**Hiding the Taskbar** The Taskbar is convenient to have around, but it does take up space on the Desktop. At times, you may want to hide the Taskbar so that application windows can use the entire screen. To hide the Taskbar (or redisplay it if it is currently hidden):

1. Click on the Start button to open the Start menu, point at the Settings option, and choose the Taskbar item on the resulting submenu. The Taskbar Properties dialog box, shown in Figure 2, will be displayed. (You can also open the Taskbar Properties dialog box by right-clicking on an empty part of the Taskbar and choosing Properties from the resulting pop-up menu.)

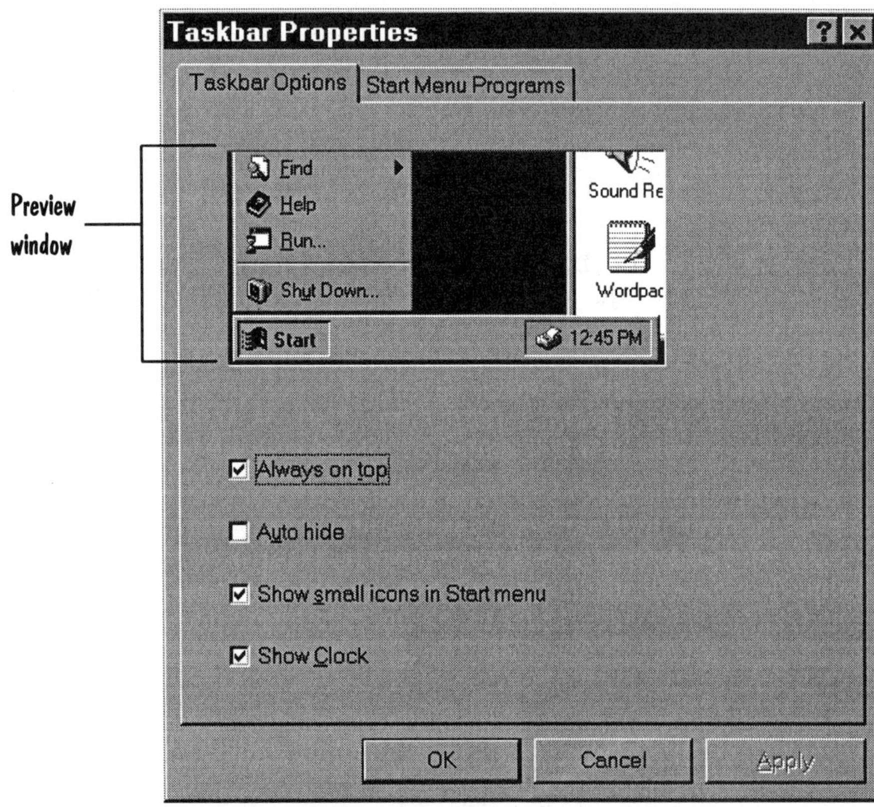


**Figure 2** The Taskbar Properties Dialog Box

2. Select the *Always on top* check box to prevent the Taskbar from being obscured by windows that might otherwise cover it.
3. Select the *Auto hide* check box to hide the Taskbar. When Auto hide is selected, the Taskbar is reduced to a thin line at the edge

of the screen. To temporarily redisplay the Taskbar, point the mouse at this thin line. Moving the mouse pointer away from that edge of the screen will cause the Taskbar to disappear again.

4. Choose the OK command button to put your changes into effect and close the dialog box, or choose the Apply button to put your changes into effect without closing the dialog box.

NOTE

Selecting the "auto hide" feature is a convenient way to increase the amount of screen real estate available to your running applications. Be aware, however, that if *Always on top* is not selected and an application is running full-screen, pointing at the Taskbar "line" will not display the Taskbar; it will still be obscured by the application window! Also keep in mind that you can *always* display the Taskbar (and simultaneously open the Start menu) by pressing the Ctrl+Esc keystroke combination.

**Hiding the Clock** To hide the Taskbar clock (which provides a little more room for application buttons):

1. Open the Taskbar Properties dialog box (Figure 2), as described above.
2. Deselect the *Show clock* check box. (Reselecting this check box will, of course, redisplay the clock if it is currently hidden.)
3. Choose the OK command button.

## *Manipulating Application Windows from the Taskbar*

Using the Taskbar, you can also:

- Minimize all open windows simultaneously, or restore all windows that have been minimized in this way.
- Rearrange windows by *cascading* or *tiling* them on the Desktop.

These operations are carried out by:

1. Right-clicking on an empty part of the Taskbar, which opens the menu shown in Figure 3.
2. Choosing the desired option from this menu. (Recall that choosing the Properties item displays the Taskbar Properties dialog box.)

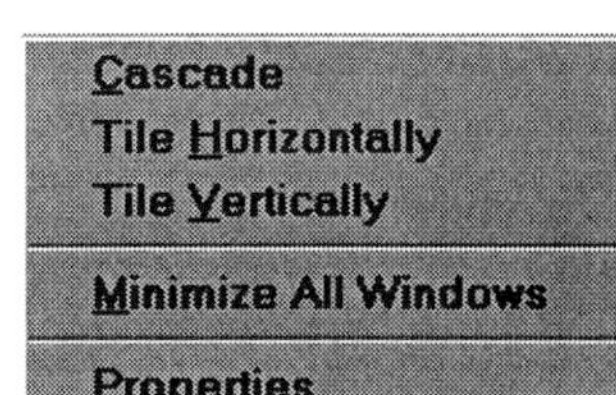


**Figure 3** The Pop-up Taskbar Menu

**Arranging Windows on the Desktop** The first three items on the pop-up menu shown in Figure 3 affect the way open application windows are grouped on the Desktop:

- Choosing the Cascade command overlaps the windows in such a way that little more than the title bars of the back windows can be seen (Figure 4). The window that was active when this command was issued becomes the one in front. To bring another window to the front, just switch to the corresponding application.
- Choosing the Tile Horizontally command arranges the windows in a non-overlapping fashion, one above the other. The effect is shown in Figure 5.
- Choosing the Tile Vertically command arranges the windows side-by-side in a non-overlapping fashion. See Figure 6.

**NOTE**

The Cascade and Tile commands only apply to the windows that are open when the command is issued. If another window is opened or restored later on, it will not be included in the grouping. However, if you maximize or minimize one of the grouped windows and then restore it, the original cascading or tiling will also be restored.

**Minimizing All Open Windows** The Minimize All Windows command on the pop-up Taskbar menu (shown in Figure 3) does just

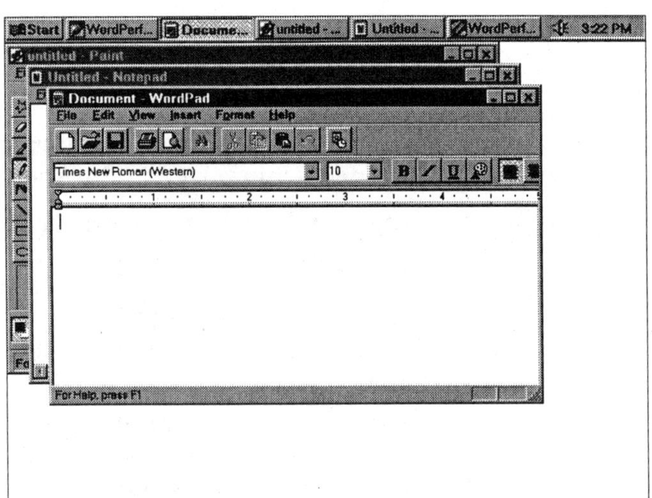


**Figure 4** Cascading Windows

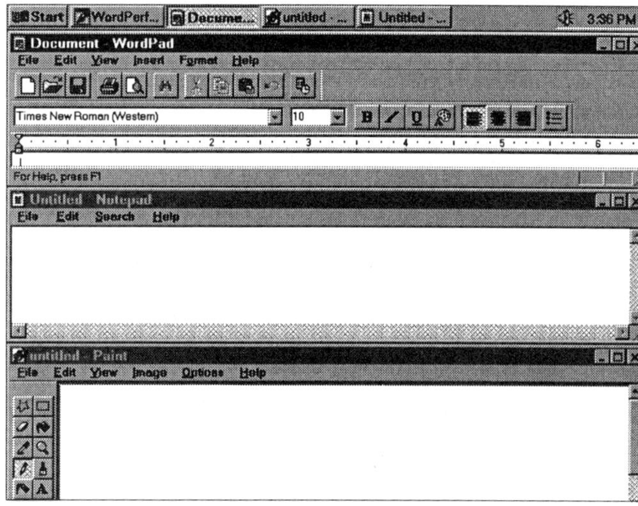


**Figure 5** Windows Tiled Horizontally

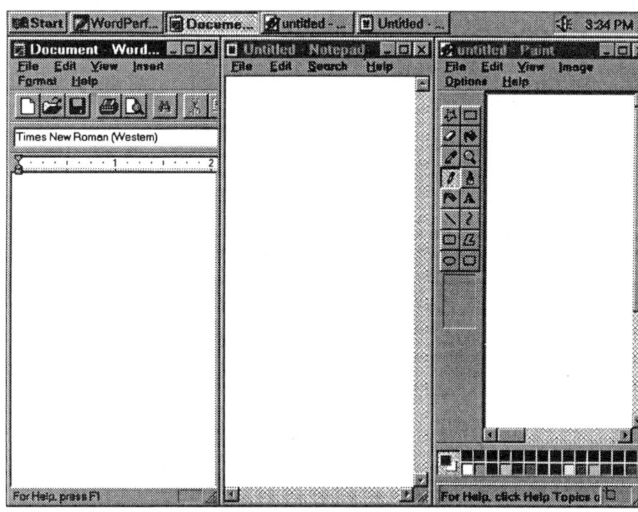


**Figure 6** Windows Tiled Vertically

that — it minimizes all open windows. When you reopen the pop-up Taskbar menu after issuing this command, you will notice another available option — Undo Minimize All. As you might guess, choosing this command restores all windows that were reduced to Taskbar buttons by the previous Minimize All Windows command.

6-1 TUTORIAL

Try the following exercises on your own.

1. Turn on your computer, if necessary, to start Windows 95 and close any open windows.
2. If the Taskbar is not visible on the screen, press Ctrl+Esc to display it and the Start menu; then press Esc to close the latter.
3. Reposition the Taskbar at another edge of the screen by dragging it there; that is, position the mouse pointer over an empty part of the Taskbar, press (and hold down) the mouse button, move the pointer to the desired edge of the screen, and release the button.
4. Position the Taskbar at the bottom edge of the screen.
5. Change the size of the Taskbar: Position the mouse pointer over the top edge of the Taskbar (the pointer will become a double-headed arrow), drag the pointer upward (the Taskbar will grow in size), and release the mouse button. Now, return the Taskbar to its former size by a similar process.
6. Open the Taskbar Properties dialog box by clicking on the Start button, pointing at the Settings option, and choosing the Taskbar command from the resulting submenu.
7. Select the *Auto-hide* check box and choose the Apply command button. The Taskbar will disappear from the screen. To redisplay it, move the mouse pointer past the bottom edge of the screen. Move the pointer away from the bottom edge of the screen, and the Taskbar will disappear again.
8. Deselect Auto-hide and choose the OK command button to close the dialog box.
9. Open the WordPad application (from the Accessories submenu of the Start menu's Programs option) and maximize it. Then, open the Paint application (also on the Accessories submenu) and maximize it.
10. Right-click on an empty part of the Taskbar, successively choose each of the following commands from the resulting pop-up menu, and notice the effect. (You will have to reopen this menu before issuing a new command.)
    - Cascade
    - Tile Horizontally
    - Tile Vertically
    - Minimize All Windows
    - Undo Minimize All
    - Properties
11. Close all open windows.

# 6.2 Customizing the Start Button Menus

When Windows 95 was installed on your computer, it automatically created several Start menu submenus and placed various items on them. Moreover, if a Windows application was installed later on, it created additional items on one of the submenus. In this section, we will demonstrate how you can "manually" add items to, or remove them from, the Start menu or one of its Programs option's submenus[*].

## The What and Why of the Start Button Menus

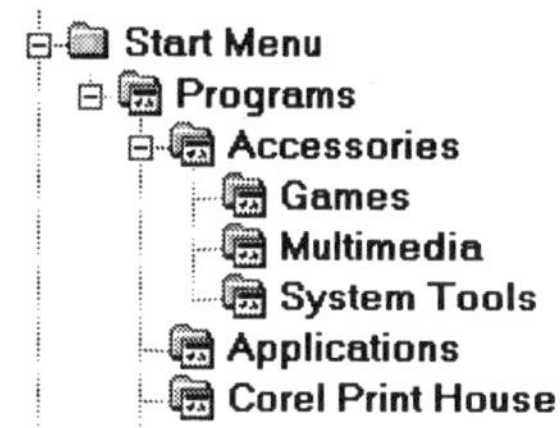


Each item on a Start button menu is actually a *shortcut* (see Section 3.4) to a file or folder. The shortcuts on the Start button menus are themselves small files stored in various related folders. The shortcuts on the Start menu itself are located in the Start Menu subfolder of the Windows folder, and those in the Programs option submenu are located in the Programs subfolder of the Start Menu folder. Similarly, each submenu of the Programs option corresponds to a subfolder of the Programs folder. Part of the folder tree is shown above.

The shortcuts on the Start button menus may represent applications, documents, or folders. In fact, any file or folder listed in Explorer can be placed on these menus. Clicking on a menu item (shortcut) opens the corresponding file or folder. To be more specific, clicking on

- A shortcut to a program file starts the corresponding application.
- A shortcut to a document starts the application associated with it and then opens the document within that application.
- A shortcut to a folder opens the corresponding folder, displaying its contents in a window.

Thus, the Start button menus can be configured to provide easy access to your most-used applications, documents, and folders. The Start menu itself is an especially convenient location for shortcuts to your favorite things. Although Desktop icons can be used for the same purpose, they are often buried beneath an open window or two. The Start menu, on the other hand, is always a mouse click (or, at worst, the Ctrl+Esc keystroke) away from the task at hand.

---

[*]For simplicity's sake, we will refer to the Start menu itself or any of its Programs option's submenus as a "Start button menu".

## *Adding Menu Items by Drag-and-Drop*

If you want to add an item to the Start menu itself, the easiest way to do it is by dragging the relevant file or folder (or a shortcut to it) onto the Start button. To be more specific:

1. Locate the file or folder you want to add to the Start menu:
   - If you are seeking a particular folder, it's usually easiest to start Explorer and find it by "brute force" — scroll down the folder tree pane, expanding the various branches if necessary, until you spot the folder you want.
   - If you are seeking a document, a relatively easy way to determine its location is to start the application that created it and display the Open dialog box. You will either see the desired file listed there or be able to find it with a little browsing.
   - If you are seeking a particular program file, you should be able to discover its name and the folder containing it by checking the application's documentation.
2. Drag its icon onto the Start button and release the mouse button.

TIP

Often, the easiest way to locate a particular file or folder is to use the Windows Find utility, which is described in Section 6.3. Find will search your entire hard disk, if necessary, for the desired object while you sit back and relax.

The next time you click on the Start button, you will see the new item displayed near the top of the Start menu. In fact, if you add several items to the Start menu, they will be grouped, in alphabetical order, in a section at the top of this menu. A typical example is shown at the right.

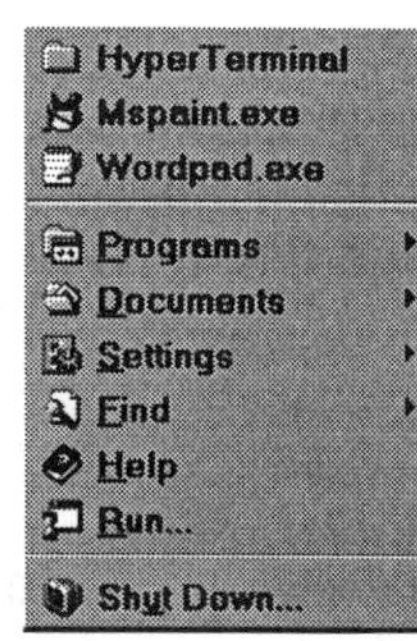


NOTE

After adding a shortcut to the Start menu, you may want to rename it. Unfortunately, this takes some work. To rename the new shortcut, start Explorer or My Computer and open the folder in which all Start menu shortcuts are stored — the Start Menu subfolder of the Windows folder. Locate the desired shortcut and rename it using one of the techniques described in Section 3.4.

## *A More Flexible Way to Add Menu Items*

Although the drag-and-drop technique that was just described is easy to carry out, it can only be used to add items to the Start menu itself. At times, you will want to add an item to a specific submenu of the Start menu's Programs option. In this case, you cannot use drag-and-drop. Instead, proceed as follows:

1. Open the Taskbar Properties dialog box by either:
   - Pointing at the Settings option on the Start menu and choosing Taskbar from the resulting submenu.

   *or*
   - Right-clicking on an empty part of the Taskbar and choosing Properties from the resulting pop-up menu.
2. Click on the Start Menu Programs tab. The corresponding page of dialog box will be displayed, as shown in Figure 7.

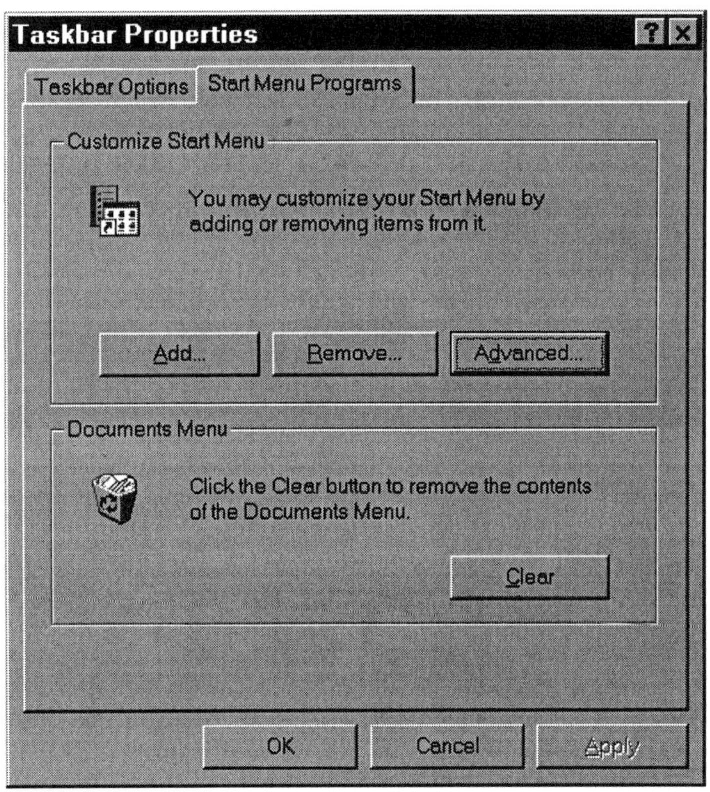


**Figure 7** Clicking on the Start Menu Programs Tab

3. Choose the Add command button. This action starts a Create Shortcut "wizard" and opens the corresponding dialog box.
4. If you know the path name (see Section 3.1) of the file or folder for which you want to create a shortcut, type it in the Command line text box and skip to step 6.
5. If you don't know the desired object's path name, choose the Browse command button, which opens a Browse dialog box (Figure 8) to help you locate the file or folder. (Browsing folders is discussed in Section 3.5.)

   By default, this Browse dialog box lists only folders and program files. If you are looking for a document, select the "All files" item from the *Files of type* drop-down list to display all files contained in the current folder.

   When you locate the file or folder you are seeking, double-click on it or select it and activate the Open command button. The Browse dialog box will close and the path name of the object you have selected will appear in the Command line text box of the Create Shortcut dialog box.
6. Click on the Next command button. The Select Program Folder dialog box will open (Figure 9) and display a folder tree showing the Start Menu folder (which contains the shortcuts on the Start menu) and its subfolders (which correspond to the Programs option menu and its submenus).

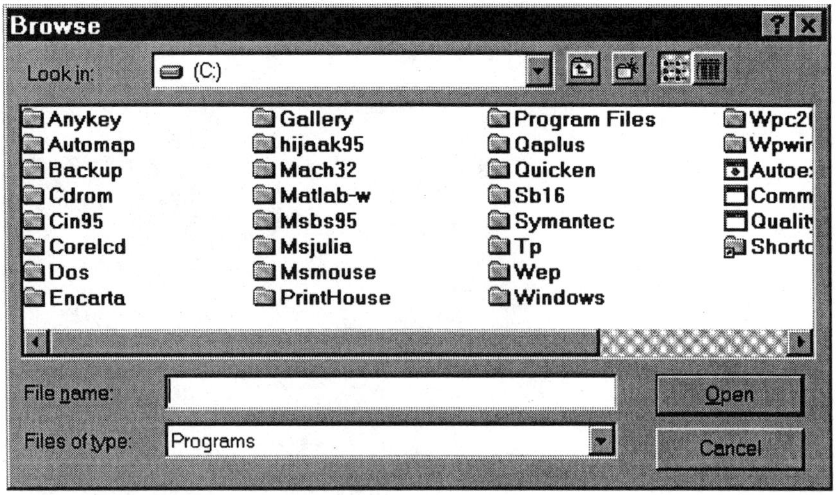


**Figure 8** A Browse Dialog Box

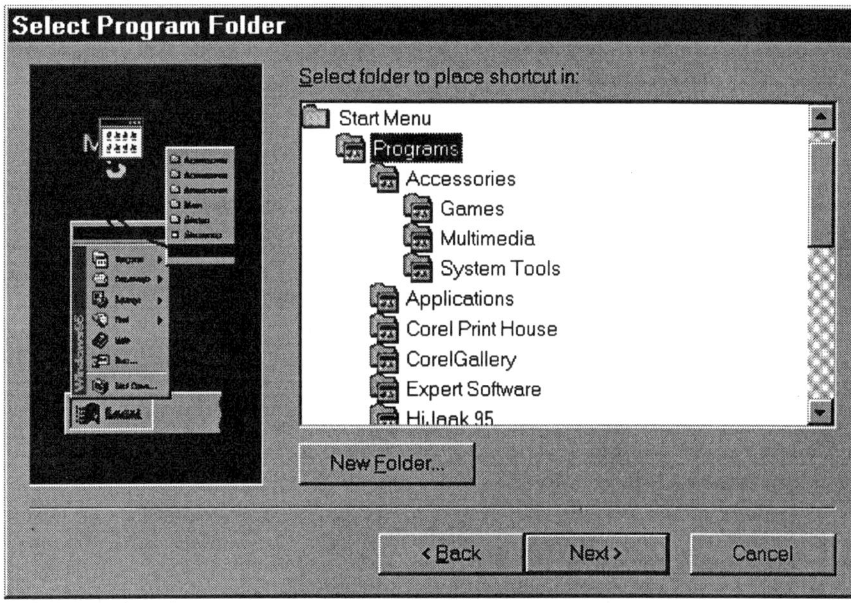


**Figure 9** The Select Program Folder Dialog Box

7. If you want to create a new submenu, select the folder corresponding to the menu on which you want your new submenu to appear, and activate the New Folder command button. (At the right, we show the result of selecting Accessories and then choosing New Folder.) A new subfolder will be displayed. To rename it, just type a new name.

8. Select (click on) the folder that corresponds to the menu in which you want the new shortcut to appear.
9. Choose the Next command button. A new dialog box will appear allowing you to select a name for the new shortcut. If you don't want to use the default name, type a new name in the text box.
10. Choose the Finish command button, which returns you to the Taskbar Properties dialog box.
11. Choose the OK command button to close this dialog box.

TIP

The Windows\Start Menu\Programs folder contains a special subfolder called StartUp. Each application, document, and folder contained in the StartUp folder automatically opens every time you start Windows.

Thus, if you run certain applications whenever you use Windows, you might consider adding their shortcuts to the StartUp folder.

## *Removing Items from the Start Button Menus*

A menu item can be removed from a Start button menu in the following way:

1. Open the Taskbar Properties dialog box as described above.
2. Click on the Start Menu Programs tab. The dialog box page shown in Figure 7 will be displayed.
3. Choose the Remove command button. This action opens the Remove Shortcuts/Folders dialog box shown in Figure 10.

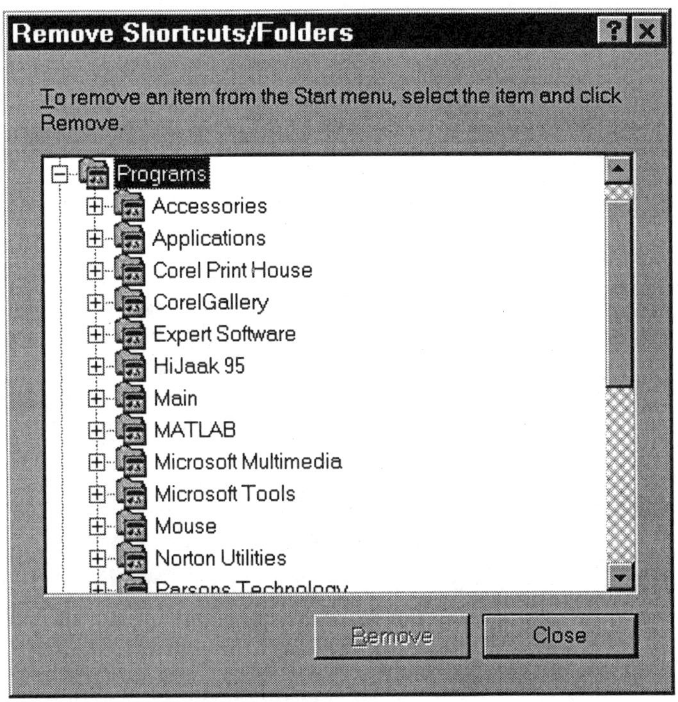


**Figure 10** Remove Shortcuts/Folders Dialog Box

4. Select (click on) the folder corresponding to the menu on which the desired item is located. (You may have to expand a branch of the tree to display a particular subfolder.)

5. Choose the Remove command button. Be aware that when you remove a folder, all shortcuts within it are removed as well! (You may see a warning message at this point.)
6. Choose the Close command button. The Remove Shortcuts/Folders dialog box will close and you will be returned to the Taskbar Properties dialog box.
7. Choose the OK command button to close the Taskbar Properties dialog box, completing the process.

## *Other Ways to Add or Remove Menu Items*

If you examine the Start Menu Programs page of the Taskbar Properties dialog box (Figure 7), you will notice two additional command buttons: Advanced and Clear.

**The Advanced command button**

Choosing the Advanced button starts Explorer, displaying a folder tree with the Start Menu folder at its root. Then, using the techniques described in Sections 3.3 and 3.4, you can:

- Place a shortcut in the Start Menu folder or any of its subfolders. This action adds an item to the corresponding menu.
- Delete an existing shortcut from a folder, which removes the corresponding item from its menu.
- Move or copy a shortcut from one folder to another, thus moving or copying the corresponding item from one menu to another.

If you are especially comfortable with Explorer and the way it works, you may find that using the Advanced button is preferable to the other methods for customizing the Start button menus.

**NOTE**

Since the Advanced button does nothing more than start Explorer, the techniques just described for adding, removing, or moving menu items can be accomplished without opening the Taskbar Properties dialog box. Just start Explorer in the usual way, or right-click on the Start button and choose Explore from the pop-up menu, which starts Explorer and opens the Start Menu folder.

**The Clear command button**

Choosing the Clear command button in the Taskbar Properties dialog box removes all items from the Documents submenu of the Start menu. No warning message is given.

**TIP**

If you would like to remove *selected items* from the Documents menu, start Explorer and open the Recent subfolder of the Windows folder. This folder contains the shortcuts on the Documents submenu. To selectively delete items from this submenu, just delete the corresponding shortcuts from the Recent folder!

**6-2 TUTORIAL**

Try the following exercises on your own.

1. Turn on your computer, if necessary, to start Windows 95 and close any open windows.
2. Start Explorer (from the Programs option submenu of the Start menu) and open the Accessories subfolder of the Program Files folder.
3. Add a shortcut for the WordPad application to the Start menu by dragging the Wordpad file name from the contents pane onto the Start button. (If you now click on the latter, you will see "Wordpad" listed toward the top of the Start menu.)
4. Now, add a shortcut for the Paint application to the Programs option submenu of the Start menu:
   - Open the Taskbar Properties dialog box by right-clicking on an empty part of the Taskbar and choosing Properties from the resulting submenu.
   - Click on the Start Menu Programs tab in this dialog box.
   - Choose the Add command button, which starts the Create Shortcut wizard.
   - Now enter the path name for Paint in the *Command line* text box by choosing the Browse command button, opening the Accessories subfolder of the Program Files folder, selecting "Mspaint", and pressing the Enter key.
   - Choose the Next command button, which opens the Select Program Folder dialog box.
   - To tell Windows that you want the shortcut on the Programs submenu, select the Programs folder in the tree and choose the Next command button, which opens another dialog box.
   - Finally, select a name for the new menu item: Type *Paint* in the text box and choose the Finish command button. (You can check, if you want, that a Paint item now appears on the Programs submenu of the Start menu.)
5. Remove the WordPad item from the Start menu:
   - On the Start Menu Programs page of the Taskbar Properties dialog box, choose the Remove command button.
   - In the resulting folder tree, select Wordpad (which is listed as a subfolder of Start Menu, toward the bottom of the tree).

- Choose the Remove command button; then choose Close.

6. Now remove the Paint item from the Programs submenu in another way:
   - On the Start Menu Programs page of the Taskbar Properties dialog box, choose the Advanced command button. Explorer will start, opening the Start Menu folder.
   - Open the Programs subfolder (by clicking on it) in the left pane; then select the Paint shortcut in the right pane.
   - Press the Delete key (or choose Delete from the right-click pop-up menu), answer Yes to the query in the resulting dialog box, and the process is complete.
7. Close all open windows.

# *6.3 The Windows Find Utility*

A typical hard disk contains thousands of files spread across dozens of folders. As a result, locating a particular file or folder (say, to create a shortcut for it) can be a daunting task. Fortunately, Windows provides a powerful utility, called **Find**, that helps you with the search. In this section, we will discuss how to use Find to locate files and folders. (If your computer is connected to a network, Find can also help you search for computers on the network.)

## *The Find Utility Window*

There are several ways to start the Find utility:

- Click on the Start button, point at the Find option, and choose Files or Folders from the resulting submenu.
- Right-click on the Start button, the My Computer icon, or any folder icon, and choose the Find command from the pop-up menu.
- Click on an empty part of the Desktop and then press the F3 function key.
- In Explorer, either press the F3 function key, or point at the Find command on the Tools menu and choose Files or Folders from the resulting submenu.

In any case, the Find window (Figure 11, on the next page) will open.

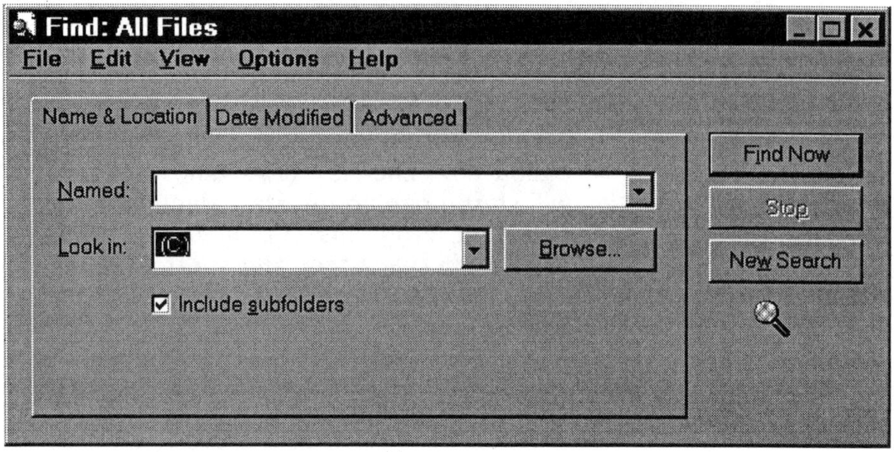


**Figure 11** The Find Window

Since Find is an application, its window can be resized, minimized, or maximized. Notice (in Figure 11) that the Find window contains both pull-down menus and tabs. The menus provide capabilities that are similar to those of Explorer; the tabs supply options that help narrow the search for a particular file or folder.

## *Performing a Simple Search*

Typically, we use the Find utility to locate a file or folder because:

- We have forgotten its name.

*or*

- We don't know in which folder it is located.

**If you know the name of the file or folder ...**

If you know the name (or at least part of the name) of the file or folder you are seeking, proceed as follows:

1. Start the Find utility, as described above.
2. Type the name (or partial name) of the file or folder in the *Named* text box. (The *Named* drop-down list contains the entries for recent searches.)
3. If you know the folder that contains the object you are seeking, enter that folder in the *Look in* text box. As an alternative, you can choose the Browse button and then select the desired folder from the folder tree. If you don't know in which folder to look, enter the drive designation of the disk you are searching — for example, C: — in the *Look in* text box.

4. Select the *Include subfolders* check box if you want to search, not only the *Look in* folder, but all its subfolders as well.

5. Choose the Find Now command button to start the search. All files and folders in the specified folders whose names contain the text entered in the *Named* text box will be displayed in a Search Results window in the lower part of the Find window; the Status bar indicates the number of files found (Figure 12).

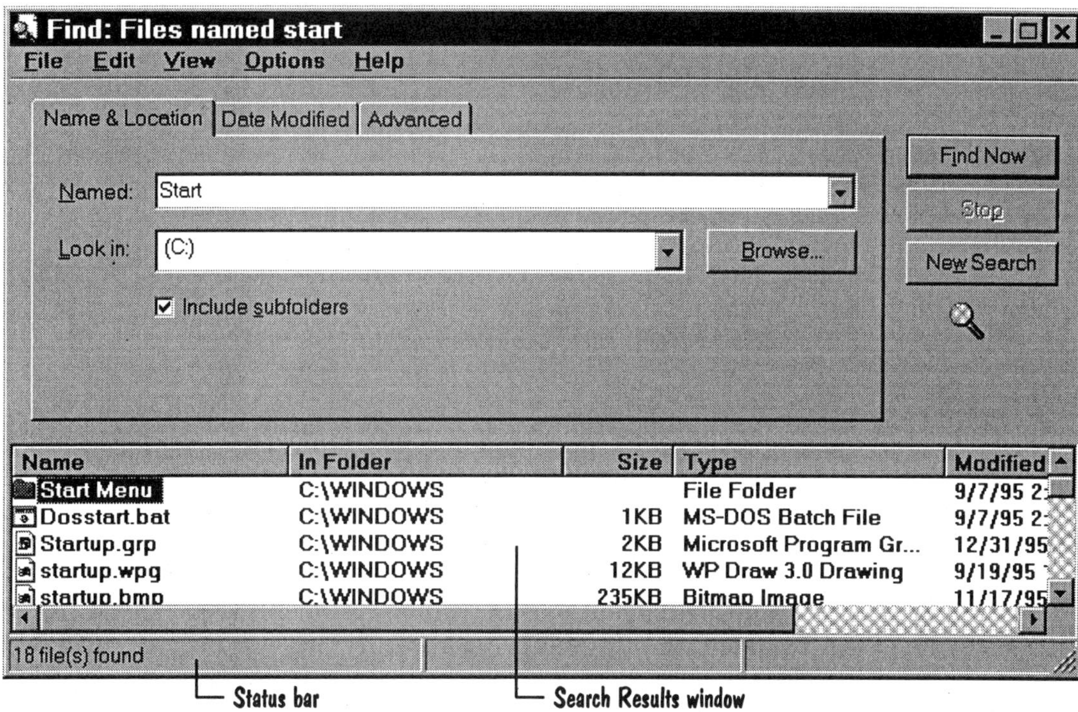


**Figure 12** The Find Window After a Search

TIP

You can use *wildcards* in the *Named* text box to narrow the search. A **wildcard** is a symbol that represents one or more characters of any kind. Windows uses two wildcards:

- The symbol * represents any number of consecutive characters.
- The symbol ? represents any single character.

For example, in the *Named* text box, entering

| | |
|---|---|
| *.* | displays all files and folders. |
| *.exe | displays all files with extension *exe*. |

start??.* displays all files with names that contain *start*, followed by two characters and any extension.

?s? displays all files and folders with *s* somewhere in the name from the second to the next-to-last character.

?s?.* displays all files with a three-letter name and *s* as the second letter.

## *Refining the Search Criteria*

If you do not know the name of the file you are seeking or just want to narrow the search (so that fewer files will be found), use the Date Modified and/or Advanced pages of the Find window.

**The Find windows's Date Modified tab**

The Date Modified page is most useful in finding a *document* when:

- You know the approximate date that the file was last saved (perhaps because you have a dated paper copy of the document).

*or*

- The document was created or modified recently.

To start a search in one of these cases:

1. Start the Find utility, if necessary.
2. Fill in information on the Name & Location page, as described above. If you do not know certain information, leave the corresponding text box blank.
3. Click on the Date Modified tab to display the options shown in Figure 13.

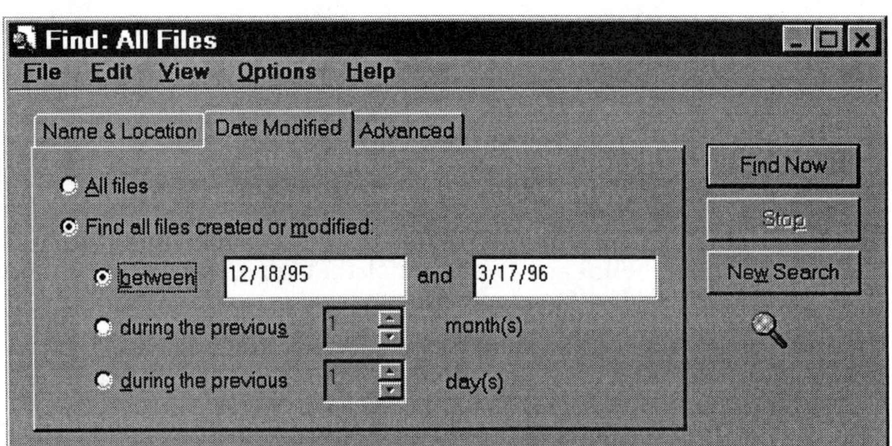


**Figure 13** The Date Modified Page of the Find Window

4. Select the *Find all files created or modified* option button.
5. If you know the approximate date that the file was last saved, select the *between* option button and, in the two text boxes, enter dates that bracket the date the document was last saved.

   If the document was modified recently, you could select either the *during the previous days* or the *during the previous months* option button (depending on how recently the document was modified); then enter an appropriate number in the corresponding text box.
6. Begin the search by choosing the Find Now button. All files that match the search criteria will be displayed in the Search Results window, as shown in Figure 12.

**The Find window's Advanced tab**

The Advanced page of the Find window allows you to refine a search in a few additional ways. After providing as much information as possible on the Name & Location and Date Modified pages, click on the Advanced tab to display the options shown in Figure 14. Then:

- You can restrict the search to files of a specified type by selecting it from the *Of type* drop-down list.
- You can search for a piece (*string*) of text in a document by entering that string in the *Containing text* box. (This is an extremely useful option for locating a document. Just supply any piece of text that is unique to that document!)
- You can specify the minimum or maximum sizes for the files to be included in the search by using the *Size is* drop-down list and text box.

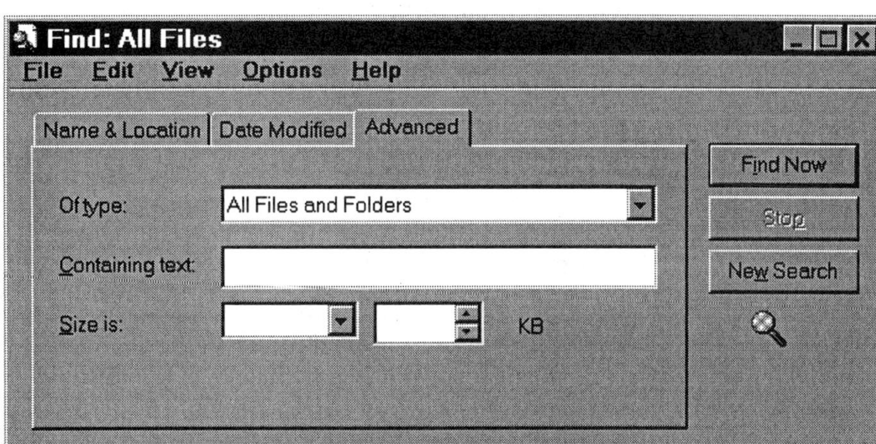


**Figure 14** The Advanced Page of the Find Window

NOTE

In addition to Find Now, there are two other command buttons in the Find window:

- While a search is taking place, choosing the Stop button discontinues the search.
- Choosing the New Search button resets all search criteria to their defaults and clears all files and folders (if any) from the Search Results window.

## *Using the Results of a Search*

As you know, when a search is complete, the files and folders found are displayed in the Search Results window at the bottom of the Find window (see Figure 12). For all practical purposes, this window can be used as if it were a My Computer window or the contents pane of an Explorer window. To be more specific:

- You can display the files in the Search Results window in different ways by choosing Large Icons, Small Icons, List, or Details from the View menu. The advantages of each view option are discussed in Section 3.2. (In Figure 12, the Details option is turned on.)
- You can select objects in the Search Results window using the techniques described in Section 3.3.
- Selected objects can be cut or copied to the Clipboard (so they can be pasted into other folders or onto the Desktop) by choosing Cut or Copy from the Edit menu, or by right-clicking on a selected object and choosing Cut or Copy from the resulting pop-up menu.
- You can drag-and-drop objects from the Search Results window to another folder, onto the Desktop, or onto the Recycle Bin.
- You can create a shortcut for an object in the Search Results window using the techniques described in Section 3.4.
- You can delete, rename, or open a selected object by choosing the corresponding command from either the File menu or the menu that pops up when you right-click the object. (An object can also be opened by double-clicking on it.)
- You can print selected documents by choosing Print from the File menu or the right-click pop-up menu.

6-3 TUTORIAL

Try the following exercises on your own.

1. Turn on your computer, if necessary, to start Windows 95 and close any open windows.

2. Start the Find utility by clicking on the Start button, pointing at the Find command, and clicking on Files or Folders.
3. Try to find the file that starts the Paint application. It is located somewhere on the drive that contains the Windows folder.
   - Enter this drive (for example, C:) in the *Look in* text box and type `Paint` in the *Named* text box.
   - Select (if necessary) the *Include subfolders* check box.
   - Choose the Find Now command button. After a few moments a list of files will appear in the lower part of the Find window, all of which include "paint" as part of their names. The file that you are seeking is called `Mspaint` and is of type "Application".
4. Start Paint by double-clicking on its file name. (Other operations, such as move and copy, can also be performed on any file listed in the Find window.) Now, close the Paint application.
5. Close the Find utility as you would any application.
6. Start Find again, this time by right-clicking on the Start button and choosing the Find command from the resulting pop-up menu.
7. Determine if any files were saved to the C: drive today:
   - Enter `C:` in the *Look in* text box, click on the Date Modified tab, and select the *Find all files created or modified* option button.
   - Click on the *between* option button and enter today's date in both of the corresponding text boxes.
   - Choose the Find Now command button. All files saved today to the C: drive will be listed at the bottom of the Find window.
8. Determine if there is a document on the Lab Exercises disk that contains the word *people*.
   - In the Find window, choose the New Search command button to reset the search parameters. (Click on OK when the warning message appears.)
   - Insert the Lab Exercises disk in its drive.
   - Click on the Name & Location tab and enter the appropriate drive designation (for example, A:) in the *Look in* text box.
   - Click on the Advanced tab and type `people` in the *Containing text* box.
   - Choose the Find Now command button. After the search, the file Preamble should be displayed (twice) in the Find window.
9. Remove the Lab Exercises disk from its drive and close the Find utility.

# 6.4 Associating File Types with Applications

To a certain extent, Windows 95 is a document-oriented operating system. For example, as you know, you can open certain documents by double-clicking on their icons (on the Desktop or in Explorer, My Computer, or any folder window). When you double-click on such an icon, the associated application starts and the document opens within it. In this section, we will discuss how a document becomes associated with an application and how you can create or modify such an association.

## File Types

Windows assigns a *file type*, based on the file's extension, to every file stored on your disks. File types are displayed in the Type column of Details view in Explorer or any folder window (see Figure 15).

- If the file extension is *registered* (as described below), and is thus recognized by Windows, the corresponding file type is displayed (see, for example, "Bitmap Image" in Figure 15).
- If the file has an extension but it is not registered, its type is the extension itself (see "LOG File" in Figure 15).
- If the file has no extension, then it is typed as simply "File".

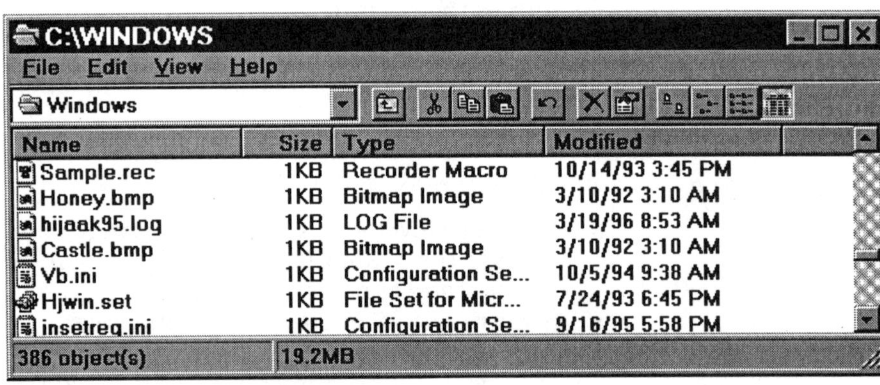


**Figure 15** Some File Types

**How extensions are registered**

When a file extension is **registered** with Windows, it is associated with a particular application. These associations can occur in several ways:

- When Windows 95 was installed, it set up certain associations; for example, the extensions BMP and TXT are normally associated with Paint and Notepad, respectively. (The corresponding file type descriptions are "Bitmap Image" and "Text Document".) Moreover, if Windows 3.1 was present on the machine at the time Windows 95 was installed, any existing associations were carried over to Windows 95.

- Most Windows applications register at least one extension as part of their installation process.
- You can "manually" register an extension that is not yet associated with a particular application. We will discuss how to carry out this process, and how to modify or remove existing associations, later in this section.

**NOTE**

When an extension is registered, it is normally associated with a distinctive icon, often the icon of the corresponding application. All documents with that extension inherit this icon, which makes them easy to spot in Explorer and My Computer windows, especially in Large Icons view. In the figure below, the files `Charmap.hlp` and `Chimes.wav` have registered extensions, whereas `charmap.GID` does not; the latter has a generic icon.

**Why register an extension?**

Once an extension is registered with Windows, all documents with that extension become associated with a particular application. As a result, you can perform certain actions directly on these documents. For example, double-clicking on the document's icon (normally) opens the associated application, as well as the document. Moreover, additional actions can be specified on the menu that pops up when you right-click on the document's icon. From the right-click menu, you might be able to:

- Open the document within another specified application.
- View the document without opening its application.
- Print the document.
- Play the document, if it represents a sound file.

As you will see, some of the options that are available on a particular right-click menu depend on how the association between the file extension and the application was set up.

NOTE

The extension of a file having a registered file type may or may not be displayed as part of its file name in Explorer or a folder window. For example, since bmp is a registered extension, the file Arcade.bmp may be listed in the \Windows folder as `Arcade.bmp` or simply as `Arcade`. To display registered extensions (or hide them if they're currently displayed), choose Options from the View menu and click on the View tab in the resulting dialog box. Then, either select or deselect the *Hide MS-DOS file extensions for file types that are registered* check box.

## *Creating a New Registered File Type*

Windows allows you to create new file types by registering extensions that are currently unregistered. In doing so, you associate an extension with a particular application and also define some of the options that will be available on the menu that pops up when you right-click on a file with that extension. Here's how it's done:

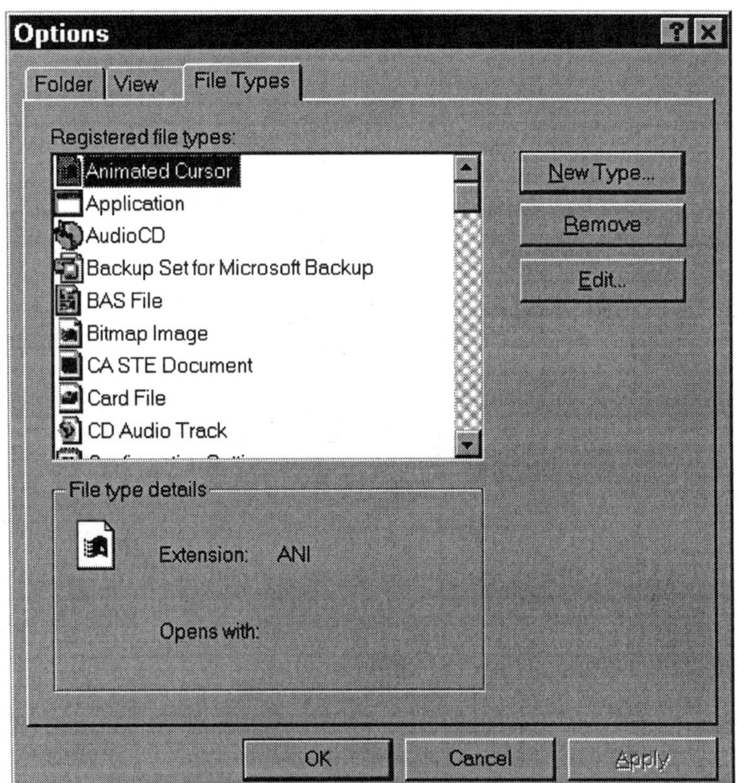


**Figure 16** File Types Page of View Options Dialog Box

1. Start Explorer or My Computer.
2. Choose the Options item from the View menu and click on the File Types tab in the resulting dialog box. A list of registered file types is displayed, as shown in Figure 16. Notice that the extension corresponding to the highlighted type and the application that opens these files (if any) is displayed below the list box.
3. Choose the New Type command button to display the Add New File Type dialog box, which is shown in Figure 17.

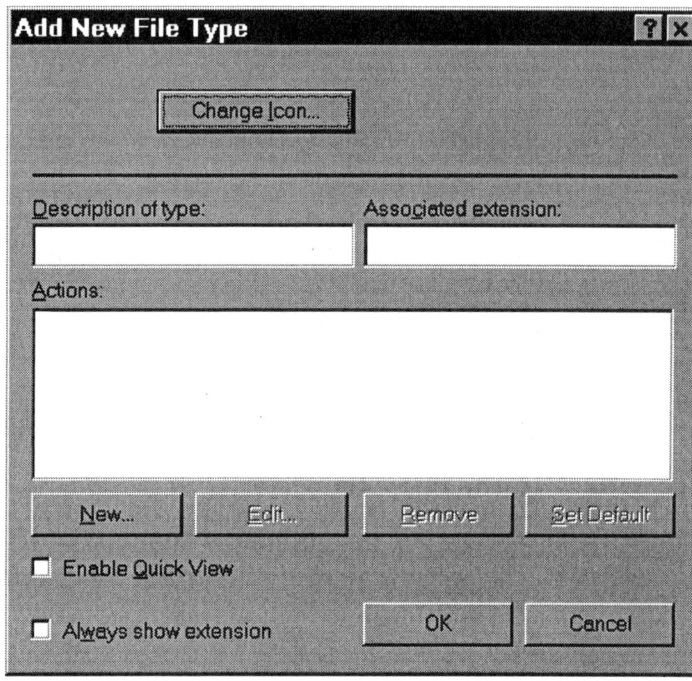


**Figure 17** The Add New File Type Dialog Box

4. Type the extension you wish to register in the *Associated extension* text box and its description in the *Description of type* text box. (The description will appear in the Type column of a folder's Details view.) For example, if you use the extension LTR for all letters you write using WordPerfect for Windows, you might use *Letters* for the description of this extension.
5. Now, you have to define *actions* (such as Open or Print) for this association. These actions will appear on the menu that pops up when you right-click on a file with the specified extension. To

specify an action, choose the New command button, which opens the New Action dialog box (Figure 18).

**Figure 18** The New Action Dialog Box

**Defining an action**

6. In the *Action* text box, type a name for the action. This name will appear on the right-click pop-up menu. For example, if you want to be able to open the document from the right-click menu, use "Open" or, perhaps, "Open with WPWin".
7. Now type the command that will perform the action specified in step 6 in the *Application used to perform action* text box. If you want to *open* the application, give the appropriate program file's path name (which can usually be found in the application's documentation); for example, C:\WPWin60\WPWin.exe. If you can't determine the appropriate path name, choose the Browse command button, and then try to track down the relevant exe file. (If you want to perform an action other than opening the file, you'll have to check the application's documentation for the appropriate start-up command.)
8. Choose the OK button to return to the Add New File Type dialog box; the description of the action you have just defined appears in the *Actions* box.
9. If you want to define another action for the current file type, click on the New command button and repeat steps 6 through 8.

**Selecting other options for the association**

10. Select the *Enable Quick View* check box (when this option is available) if you want to be able to view the contents of a document without starting its associated application. (A *Quick View* item will appear on the right-click pop-up menu.)
11. Select the *Always show extension* check box if you want the extension for files of this type to be displayed when they are listed in Explorer or a folder window, regardless of whether or not other

registered extensions are hidden.

12. Choose the OK command button to complete the file type creation process. The Add New File Type dialog box will close and you will be returned to the Options dialog box.

**The right-click pop-up menu**

When you right-click on a file name that has an extension you have registered, a menu will pop up listing (among other standard items) the actions you defined when that file type was created. The menu item displayed in bold type (which is "Open with WPWin" in the menu shown at the right) is the *default* action; double-clicking on the file's icon (say, in Explorer) causes the default action to be executed.

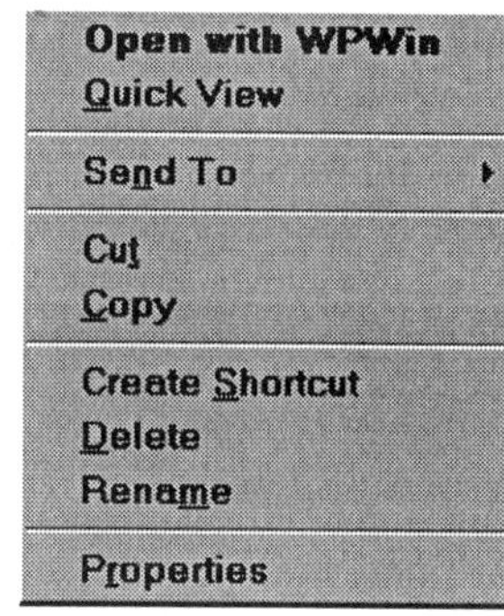


TIP

Here is a quick way to register a file type if the only action you want to associate with this type is opening the file:

1. Right-click on any file having the extension you want to register and choose the Open With command from the resulting pop-up menu. The Open With dialog box, shown below, will appear.

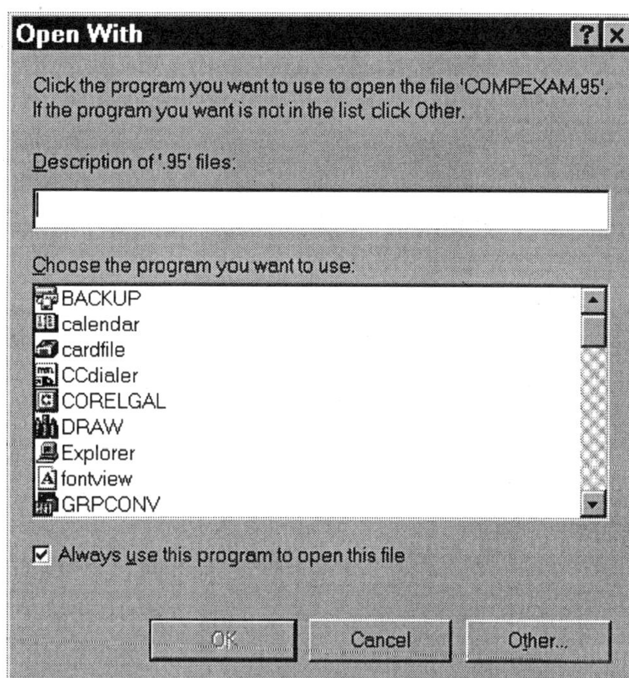

2. In the text box, provide a description of the file type; it will appear in the Type column of the Details view in Explorer or any folder window.
3. Select, from the list, the application you want to use to open files that have this extension, or choose the Other command button to browse for the desired application.
4. Be sure that the *Always use this program to open this file* check box is selected.
5. Choose the OK command button. (The selected application will start and the selected file will open within it.) The creation of the new file type is now complete.

## *Removing or Modifying a Registered File Type*

Windows allows you to remove or modify an existing registered file type; you can, for example, change the application associated with it or add a new action to its right-click menu. To remove or modify an existing registered file type:

1. Start Explorer or My Computer.
2. Choose the Options item from the View menu, and click on the File Types tab in the resulting dialog box. The dialog box page shown in Figure 16 (on page 220) will be displayed.
3. In the list of registered file types, select the one with which you want to work; it will become highlighted.
4. If you want to remove the registration of the highlighted file type (ending the association between the corresponding extension and application):
   - Choose the Remove command button.
   - Choose the Yes button in the resulting warning message box.
   - Choose the OK command button.
5. If you want to modify the properties of the highlighted file type, choose the Edit command button (which opens an Edit File Type dialog box, like the one shown in Figure 19), and follow the rest of the steps of this procedure.
6. To change the icon for all files of this type:
   - Choose the Change Icon command button. The Change Icon dialog box will open.

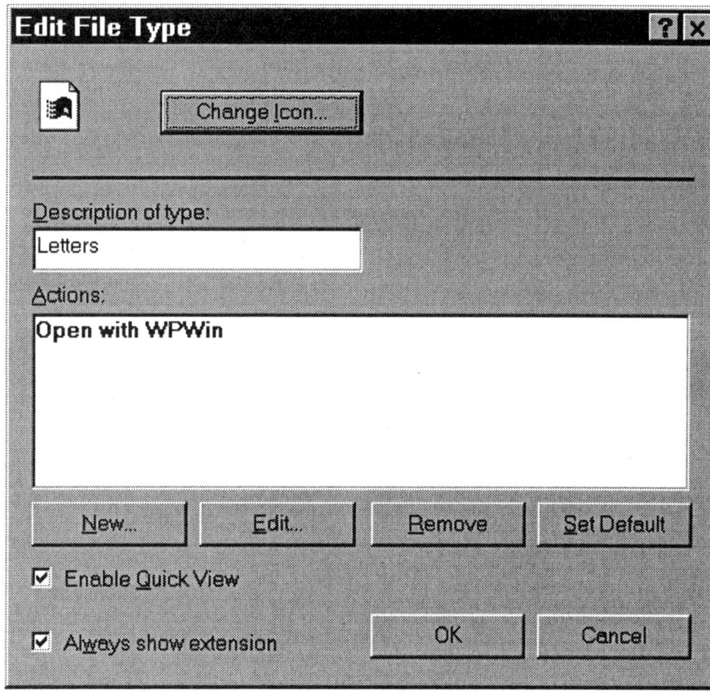


**Figure 19** The Edit File Type Dialog Box

- Type the path name of a file that contains icons in the text box, or choose the Browse button to locate such a file. (The file \Windows\System\Shell32.dll contains an extensive collection of icons.)
- Click on the icon you want and choose the OK button.

7. To add an action to the right-click menu for this type, choose the New command button and proceed as described earlier in this section, under the heading "Creating a New Registered File Type".
8. To edit an existing action, select it and choose the Edit command button. Then, proceed as you would for a "new" action.
9. To remove an action from the right-click menu for this type, select the desired action and choose the Remove command button.
10. To return the set of actions to the default list for this file type, choose the Set Default command button.

11. Choose the OK command button when you're done with your modifications, and you will be returned to the Options dialog box.

6.4 TUTORIAL

Try the following exercises on your own.

1. Turn on your computer, if necessary, to start Windows 95 and close any open windows.
2. Start Explorer, choose the Options command on the View menu, and click on the File Types tab.
3. Associate the extension NOT with the Notepad application:
   - Choose the New Type command button, which opens the Add New File Type dialog box.
   - In the *Description of type* text box, enter Notepad Document; in the *Associated extension* text box, enter NOT.
   - Select the *Enable Quick View* check box (if available) so that a Quick View item will appear on the menu that pops up when you right-click on a file name with extension NOT.
   - Choose the New command button, which opens the New Action dialog box.
   - In the *Action* text box, type `Open with Notepad`; in the *Application used to perform action* text box, type the path name for Notepad: `\windows\notepad.exe` Now, if you double-click on a file name with extension NOT (or right-click on it and choose Open with Notepad from the pop-up menu), Notepad will start and open the file within it.
   - Choose the OK command button to close the New Action dialog box; then choose the Close command button to exit the Add New File Type dialog box.
4. In the Options dialog box, choose the Edit command button to open the Edit File Type dialog box.
5. Change the current icon for the Notepad Document file type:
   - Choose the Change Icon command button, which opens the Change Icon dialog box.
   - Select another icon from the *Current icon* box and choose the OK command button.
6. In the Edit File Type dialog box, choose the Close command button to return to the Options dialog box.
7. With the Notepad Document file type still highlighted, choose the Remove command button and answer Yes to the query.
8. Close the Options dialog box and then close Explorer.

# 6.5 *Property Sheets*

Just about everything in Windows, or that interacts with Windows, has "properties" — files, folders, disks, and even hardware, like printers and the mouse. When you right-click on an icon representing one of these objects, the last item listed on the resulting right-click menu is Properties. Choosing this menu item opens the object's Properties dialog box, which is commonly known as its **property sheet**. In this section, we will discuss property sheets for files, folders, and shortcuts.

## *The Property Sheet for a File or Folder*

Figure 20 shows a typical file (or folder) property sheet. This particular dialog box was displayed by starting Explorer, right-clicking on the file name Internet.txt, and choosing Properties from the pop-up menu.

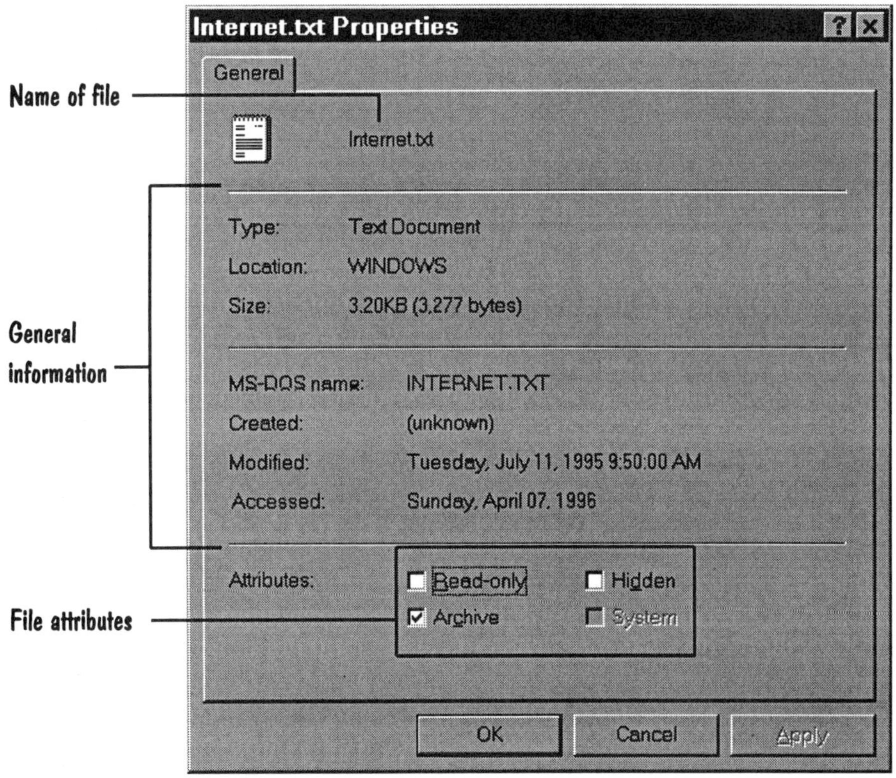


**Figure 20** A Typical Property Sheet

The contents of a property sheet varies depending on the type of object it represents, but always includes general information about the object. The property sheets for files and folders also allow you to change their *attributes* (see Figure 20). A check mark next to an attribute indicates that the attribute is *set* — it is currently in effect; otherwise, we say that the attribute is *clear* — it is not in effect.

**File Attributes**

- Putting the *Read-only* attribute into effect makes it harder to accidentally erase or modify the file. Setting this attribute for a file is analogous to write-protecting a floppy disk (see the Introduction); it reduces the likelihood of accidental erasure or modification of the contents.
- The *Archive* bit is used in conjunction with backup software (see Section 9.3). The Archive bit is normally set for a file that has never been backed up or that has been modified since the last backup.
- When the *Hidden* attribute is set, the given file's name is not normally displayed in Explorer or a folder window.
- Windows attaches the *System* attribute to certain files, called *system files*, that it uses to perform basic functions. This attribute cannot normally be set or cleared by the user. (Notice that *System* is dimmed in Figure 20, indicating that this option is not available.)

Some Properties dialog boxes have more than one tab, providing additional pages of information and possibly additional available options. For example, all documents created in the Microsoft Word word processor have property sheets with three tabs: one for general information, a second that displays an optional user-generated summary of the document, and a third that provides additional statistics about the file.

## *The Property Sheet for a Shortcut*

As you know, a shortcut is a small file that tells Windows where to find the associated (or *target*) object. When you right-click on a shortcut to a file or folder and choose Properties from the resulting pop-up menu, the property sheet for the shortcut (not for the target object) is displayed.

The property sheet for a shortcut normally contains two pages. The first page, which is displayed by clicking on the *General* tab, supplies information about the file in which the shortcut is defined; it provides the same information as the page shown in Figure 20. The second page, triggered from the *Shortcut* tab, supplies additional information and options. For example, if we display the Properties dialog box for a shortcut to the WordPad word processor and then click on the Shortcut tab, the resulting dialog box looks like the one in Figure 21.

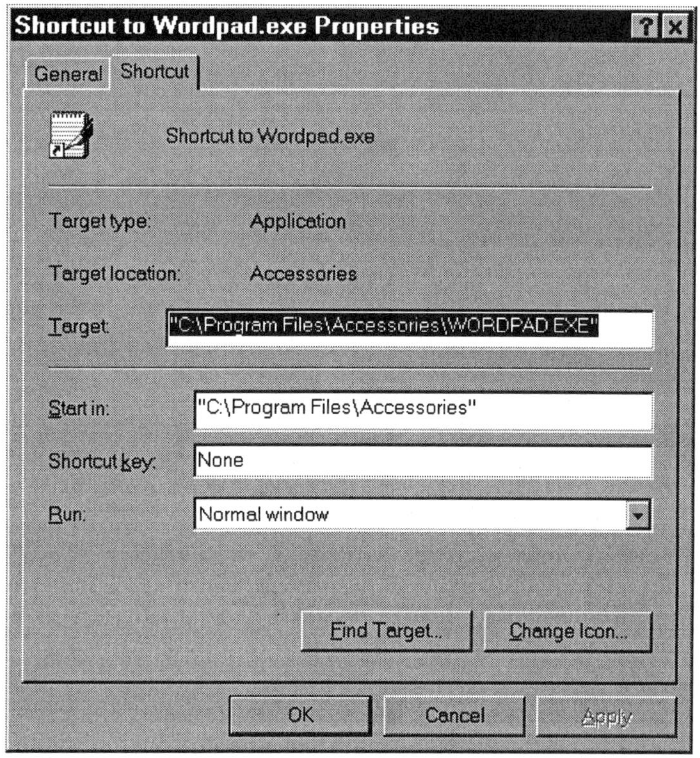


**Figure 21** The Shortcut Page of a Property Sheet

The shortcut's name and icon are displayed at the top of the Shortcut page, followed by the target's type and the folder in which it resides. The text boxes and drop-down list on this page allow the user to alter certain properties of the shortcut. To be more specific:

**Shortcut properties**

- The *Target* text box contains the full path name for the target. The path is defined at the time the shortcut is created and would normally only need to be changed if the target file or folder were subsequently moved to another location. In this case, you would want to supply the new path name in this text box so that the shortcut would continue to work.
- The *Start in* text box shows the folder that will be opened by default after the shortcut is used to start an application. For

example, if WordPad is started using the shortcut of Figure 21, and you choose Open or Save As from the File menu, the contents of the Accessories folder will be displayed in the corresponding dialog box.

**Shortcut keys**

- The *Shortcut key* text box allows you to define a keystroke combination to open the file or folder. The shortcut keystrokes must begin with Ctrl+Alt and be followed by a single character. For example, to define the shortcut key Ctrl+Alt+W to start WordPad:

  1. Display the property sheet for a WordPad shortcut and click on the Shortcut tab (see Figure 21).
  2. Click in the Shortcut key text box.
  3. Press the W key (Windows automatically inserts Ctrl+Alt in front of the W).
  4. Choose the OK command button.

  Now, when you press Ctrl+Alt+W from anywhere within Windows or one of its applications, WordPad will start.

- The *Run* drop-down list supplies three options for displaying the file or folder window when you use this shortcut to open it:

  1. *Normal* means that the initial window will be the same size it was when the target file or folder was last closed.
  2. *Maximized* means that the target file or folder window will automatically be maximized when it is opened.
  3. *Minimized* means that the target file or folder, when opened, will automatically be reduced to a button on the Taskbar.

NOTE

The Shortcut page also contains two command buttons:

- Activating Find Target opens the folder window that contains the target and highlights the latter.
- Change Icon opens the Change Icon dialog box. (See Section 6.4 for information about changing an icon.)

## *Creating a "Project Folder"*

Often, we use a computer to help us work on a project over an extended period of time. In this case, you can work more productively if you create a folder to house the tools and documents you need in working on the project. As you will see, shortcut properties are useful in this endeavor.

A project folder typically contains shortcuts to applications (and perhaps a few other objects) and subfolders containing data files. To illustrate the creation of a project folder, let's make some assumptions concerning the nature of our project:

- We anticipate needing to use the WordPad word processor and Paint graphics program.
- All the data files generated by the project will be stored in a single subfolder of the project folder called Data.
- We will frequently be printing documents and want to make this process as easy as possible.

Let's go through the steps in creating the appropriate project folder.

1. Create the project folder as a subfolder of the Desktop:
    - Right-click on the Desktop, point at the New command on the pop-up menu, and choose Folder from the submenu.
    - Rename the new folder *Project*.
2. Create shortcuts for WordPad and Paint:
    - Start Explorer and open the Accessories subfolder of the Program Files folder.
    - Select WordPad and Mspaint in the contents pane.
    - Right-drag these files onto the Project folder icon and choose Create Shortcuts(s) Here from the menu that appears when you release the mouse button.
3. Open the Project folder by double-clicking on its icon.
4. Rename the shortcuts in the Project folder *WordPad* and *Paint*.
5. Create a shortcut for the default printer:
    - In Explorer, open the My Computer folder, then double-click on the Printers icon, and select the appropriate printer.
    - Right-drag this printer's icon into the Project folder and choose Create Shortcut(s) Here from the pop-up menu.
    - Rename the new shortcut *Printer*.
6. Create a data folder as a subfolder of Project:
    - Right-click on an empty part of the Project folder, point at the New item on the pop-up menu, and choose Folder on the submenu.
    - Rename the new folder *Data*.
7. Change the default folder for the WordPad and Paint shortcuts to

the Data subfolder (so that all files will automatically be saved to this folder):

- Right-click on the WordPad shortcut, choose Properties from the pop-up menu, and click on the Shortcut tab in the resulting dialog box (see Figure 21).
- In the *Start in* text box, enter Desktop\Project\Data, and choose the OK command button.
- Repeat this process for the Paint shortcut.

8. Choose Large Icons view, remove the Toolbar (by choosing Toolbar from the View menu), and resize the Project folder window so that there is no unnecessary "white space". The resulting folder window is shown below.

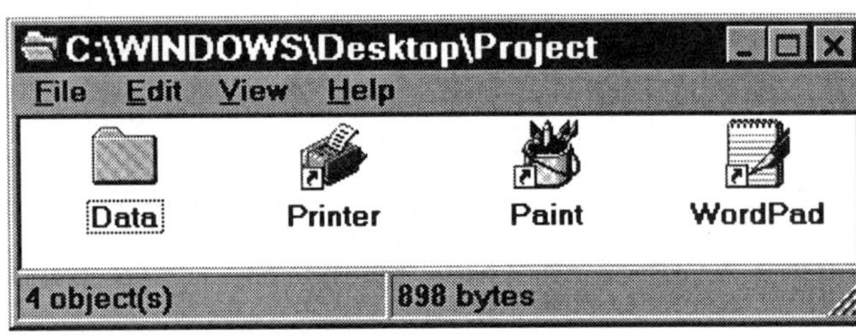


Now, all the tools and documents we need for our project are contained in one location. By opening the project window, we can start Paint or Wordpad, and all files created by these applications will be saved, by default, to the Data folder. Moreover, to print a Paint or WordPad file, all we need do is drag it from the Data folder onto the Printer icon.

TIP

If you want the Project folder to open whenever you start Windows:

- In Explorer, right-drag the Project folder onto the StartUp folder, which is a subfolder of \Windows\Start Menu\Programs.
- Choose Create Shortcut(s) Here from the pop-up menu.

## *Review Exercises*

**Section 6.1**

1. To increase the size of the Taskbar when it is located at the bottom of the screen, position the mouse cursor over its ___________ edge and drag it in an upward direction.

2. You can open the Taskbar Properties dialog box by right-clicking on the Taskbar and choosing ____________ from the pop-up menu.
3. When three windows are ____________ on the screen, each window occupies one-third of the available space.
4. True or false: When the auto-hide feature is in effect, the only way to display the Taskbar is to press Ctrl+Esc.
5. True or false: The Taskbar can be repositioned along any of the four edges of the screen.
6. True or false: To minimize all application windows simultaneously, right-click on the Taskbar and choose the Properties command.
7. Which of the following tasks cannot be accomplished using the Taskbar Properties dialog box?
   a. Ensuring that the Taskbar is "always on top".
   b. Hiding the Taskbar from view.
   c. Removing the Clock from the Taskbar.
   d. Repositioning the Taskbar at another edge of the screen.
8. Which of the following tasks cannot be accomplished by right-clicking on the Taskbar and choosing a command from the pop-up menu?
   a. Cascading the open application windows.
   b, Tiling the open application windows.
   c. Maximizing all open application windows.
   d. Minimizing all open application windows.

**Section 6.2**

9. The Windows Explorer item on the Programs submenu of the Start menu is actually a ____________ to a program file.
10. If you drag a file onto the Start button, a corresponding item is added to the ____________.
11. You can add items to the Programs submenu of the Start menu by using the ____________ page of the Taskbar Properties dialog box.
12. True or false: Choosing the Advanced command button in the Taskbar Properties dialog box starts Explorer.
13. True or false: The Clear command button in the Taskbar Properties dialog box removes all items from the Programs submenu.
14. True or false: If the \Windows\Start Menu\Programs\StartUp folder contains a shortcut to an application, that application will open every time Windows is started.

15. To add an item to the Programs submenu of the Start menu:
    a. Drop its shortcut onto the Start button.
    b. Drop its shortcut onto the Programs submenu of the Start button.
    c. Copy its shortcut into the \Windows\Start Menu folder.
    d. Copy its shortcut into the \Windows\Start Menu\Programs folder.
16. To delete one of the items on the Documents submenu of the Start menu
    a. Choose the Remove command button in the Taskbar Properties dialog box.
    b. Choose the Clear command button in the Taskbar Properties dialog box.
    c. Open the Recent subfolder of the Windows folder and delete the item from it.
    d. Open the Documents menu and drag the item onto the Recycle Bin.

**Section 6.3**

17. To use the Windows Find utility to locate a file, type its name in the ____________ text box on the Name & Location page.
18. After the Find utility completes a search, all files and folders found are displayed in the ____________ subwindow.
19. To open a folder located in a Find search, ____________ on its name in the Find window.
20. True or false: The Find utility can be used to locate all files and folders whose names contain the word *start*.
21. True or false: If the *Look in* text box contains C: and the *Include subfolders* check box is selected, the Find utility will search the entire C: drive for the specified file or folder.
22. True or false: You can copy a file from Find's Search Results window to the Clipboard by highlighting its name and choosing Copy from the Edit menu.
23. If you have forgotten a file's name but you know it contains the text "Dear Bob", you should enter this information on
    a. The Name & Location page of the Find window.
    b. The Date Modified page of the Find window.
    c. The Advanced page of the Find window.
    d. The Text page of the Find window.
24. If you have forgotten a file's name but you know that it was created in the last three days, enter this information on
    a. The Name & Location page of the Find window.

b. The Date Modified page of the Find window.
c. The Advanced page of the Find window.
d. The Recent page of the Find window.

**Section 6.4**

25. If double-clicking on a file's icon opens the file, then the corresponding file type is ____________ with Windows.

26. To associate an extension with an application, begin by choosing the ____________ command from Explorer's View menu.

27. True or false: An application cannot be associated with two different extensions.

28. True or false: The menu that pops up when you right-click on a file icon always contains a Print command.

29. The File Types page of the Options dialog box allows you to

    a. Create a new registered file type.
    b. Remove an existing registered file type.
    c. Edit an existing registered file type.
    d. Perform all of the above tasks.

30. Which characteristic of a file type registration cannot be changed in the Edit File Type dialog box?

    a. The icon associated with this file type.
    b. The extension associated with this file type.
    c. The actions associated with this file type.
    d. Whether or not Quick View is enabled for this file type.

**Section 6.5**

31. The Properties dialog box for an object is commonly known as its property ____________.

32. To open the Properties dialog box for an object, right-click on its icon and choose ____________ from the pop-up menu.

33. True or false: When a file's read-only attribute is set, that file cannot be modified.

34. True or false: The shortcut key assigned to a shortcut must begin with the Ctrl+Alt keystroke combination.

35. Which file attribute is cleared when the file is backed up using backup software?

    a. Archive
    b. Backup
    c. Hidden
    d. System

36. On the Shortcut page of the Properties dialog box for a shortcut to a folder, the word *target* refers to

a. The folder in which the shortcut resides.
b. The folder that opens when the shortcut is double-clicked.
c. The file that defines the shortcut.
d. None of the above is the target for a shortcut.

## *Lab Exercises*

Work each of the following exercises at your computer. Begin by turning the machine on (if necessary) to start Windows 95 and closing any open windows. If you want to produce a written record of your answers, review the material on WordPad and capturing screens in Sections 2.2 and 2.3.

**Lab Exercise 1 (Section 6.1)**

a. If the Taskbar is hidden, display it. Position the Taskbar at the left edge of the screen. Is the Start button at its top or bottom?

b. Increase the size of the Taskbar as much as possible. What percentage (roughly) of the entire screen does it occupy?

c. Remove the Clock from the Taskbar or, if it's currently hidden, redisplay it. Also, ensure that the *Always on top* check box is selected. What dialog box did you open to accomplish these tasks?

d. Start My Computer and maximize its window. Does it cover part or all of the Taskbar?

e. Hide the Taskbar. Does the My Computer window expand to fill the entire screen?

f. Temporarily redisplay the Taskbar by moving the mouse pointer to the left edge of the screen. Does the Taskbar cover part of the My Computer window?

g. Close My Computer, "unhide" the Taskbar and Clock (if necessary), move the Taskbar to the bottom of the screen, and reduce it to normal size.

**Lab Exercise 2 (Section 6.1)**

a. Start WordPad and maximize it; then start Paint (which is also on the Accessories submenu of the Start button) and maximize it.

b. Cascade the WordPad and Paint windows. Which one is in front?

c. Tile the two windows horizontally. Which is on top?

d. Tile the windows vertically. Which is on the left?

e. Issue the Minimize All Windows command (from the Taskbar's right-click menu), reducing WordPad and Paint to buttons on the Taskbar. Which button is highlighted?

f. Restore the WordPad window; then close it.

g. Issue the Undo Minimize All command (from the Taskbar's right-click menu). Does the Paint window occupy the entire Desktop?

h. Close the Paint window.

**Lab Exercise 3 (Section 6.2)**

a. Start Explorer and open the Windows folder.

b. Use drag-and-drop to add Calc and Charmap items to the Start menu. Which item is positioned higher on this menu?

c. Close Explorer.

d. Use the Add command button in the Taskbar Properties dialog box to add a Charmap shortcut to the Programs submenu of the Start menu. Name this shortcut CHARMAP (all capital letters). Does it appear on this menu in capital letters?

e. Choose the Advanced command button in the Taskbar Properties dialog box and open the Programs subfolder in the resulting folder tree. Move the CHARMAP shortcut from the Programs subfolder to the Start Menu folder. Did Windows allow you to do this? Do both Charmap and CHARMAP appear on the Start menu?

f. Close the folder window.

g. Use the Remove command button in the Taskbar Properties dialog box to delete the Calc, Charmap, and (if it exists) CHARMAP items from the Start menu. Was a warning message displayed at any time?

h. Close any open windows.

**Lab Exercise 4 (Section 6.3)**

a. Start the Find utility. What steps did you take to accomplish this?

b. Locate all files and folders in the Windows folder, but *not* in any of its subfolders, with names that contain the word *start*. How many are there?

c. Clear the Search Results window without closing Find. How did you accomplish this?

d. Now locate all files and folders in the \Windows\Start Menu folder and its subfolders that contain the letters *ter*. How many were found?

e. Create a shortcut for the file Character Map (displayed in the Search Results window) and place it on the Desktop. Can this be done by both copy-and-paste and drag-and-drop?

f. Delete the new shortcut.

g. Open the file Character Map (displayed in the Search Results window). Can this be done by

   Double clicking on it?
   Right-clicking on it and choosing a command from the pop-up menu?
   Choosing the appropriate command from Find's File menu?

h. Close the Find utility.

**Lab Exercise 5 (Section 6.3)**

a. Insert the Lab Exercises disk in its drive and start the Find utility.

b. Use Find to locate all files in the root folder of this disk which satisfy each of the following criteria. (Be sure to clear the Search Results window after each search is complete.)

   - Files that were last saved in the year 1995
   - Files of type Application
   - Files that are at most 10 KB in size

   In each case, how many files were found?

c. In the WordPad folder of the Lab Exercises disk, locate all files that contain the word *this*. Which files, if any, were found?

d. Use Find to determine all files on the entire Lab Exercises disk that satisfy *all* of the following criteria:

   - Their names contain the letters *file*.
   - They were saved between 1/1/95 and 12/31/96.
   - They are larger than one KB in size.

e. Close the Find utility and remove the Lab Exercises disk from its drive.

**Lab Exercise 6 (Section 6.4)**

a. Start Explorer and display the File Types page of the Options dialog box. How many pages are there in this dialog box?

b. Create a new registered file type with extension NOT and description *Notepad Document*. What is the name of the dialog box in which this information is entered?

c. Define the following two actions for the new file type:

   1. Open with Notepad (The path name for Notepad is \Win-

dows\Notepad.exe.)

2. Print (Add " /p" — without the quotes, but with the space — after Notepad's path name to define this command.)

d. Choose the OK command button twice to return to the Options dialog box, and close the latter. Were any warning messages issued?

e. Insert the Lab Exercises disk in its drive and select this drive in Explorer's folder tree.

f. Check that your printer is ready, right-click on the NoteDoc file, and choose Print from the pop-up menu. Does Notepad close after printing is complete? If not, close Notepad.

g. Use the Options dialog box to remove the registered file type NOT. Were any warning messages issued in the process?

h. Close Explorer and remove the Lab Exercises disk from its drive.

**Lab Exercise 7 (Section 6.5)**

a. Insert the Lab Exercises disk in its drive.

b. Start Explorer and open the root folder of this drive.

c. Display the property sheet for the Shortcut to WordPad file. How did you accomplish this?

d. Set the Read-only attribute for this file. Is the System attribute available (can it be set)?

e. Try to delete the Shortcut to WordPad file. What message is displayed?

f. Using the Shortcut page of this property sheet:

- Set the default folder ("Start in") to A:\.
- Set the shortcut key to Ctrl+Alt+W.
- Set the Run type to Minimized.

g. Press Ctrl+Alt+W. Does the WordPad window open? If not, open it.

h. Choose Open from the File menu. What is the current (active) folder in the Open dialog box?

i. Cancel the Open dialog box, close WordPad and Explorer, and remove the Lab Exercises disk from its drive.

CHAPTER 7

# Word Processing with WordPad

Windows supplies two applications whose primary purpose is to help you "process words"; that is, to create text-based documents. **Notepad** is little more than a *text editor*, with virtually no text formatting capability, and we will discuss it in Section 9.2. **WordPad**, which was introduced in Section 2.2, is more powerful and will be considered in depth in this chapter. To be more specific, you will learn:

1. Some additional ways to select and edit text in a WordPad document.
2. To change the typeface, font size, and font style of text.
3. To specify page margins and paper orientation for a WordPad document.
4. To format paragraphs by setting tabs and specifying text alignment and indentation.
5. To create a list of items automatically preceded by "bullets".
6. To insert graphics into a WordPad document.
7. To move, copy, resize, and delete graphics.
8. To use WordPad's Find and Replace utility.
9. To preview a document before printing it.
10. About the various file formats that WordPad can recognize.

# 7.1 WordPad Revisited

Using a word processor to create a document involves several steps. You have to:

1. Enter the text that makes up the document or open a previously created document.
2. Edit the document to correct errors, modify its content, or improve its style.
3. Format the document; for example, set margins and choose fonts.
4. Save the document to disk.
5. Print a copy of the document on paper.

In Section 2.2, we presented an introduction to the WordPad word processor that quickly covered a few of these points. In this section, we will review and expand upon some of this material.

## The WordPad Window

To start WordPad:

1. Click on the Start button (or press Ctrl+Esc) to open the Start menu.
2. Point at the Programs option and then at Accessories on the resulting submenu.
3. Click on the WordPad item on the Accessories submenu.

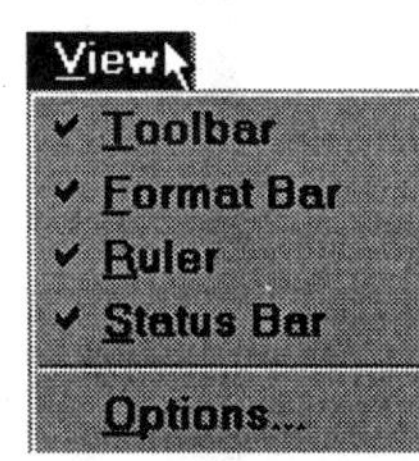


A window, similar to the one in Figure 1, will open. The Toolbar, Format bar, Ruler, and Status bar can all be toggled on or off by selecting or deselecting the corresponding item on the View menu. If you don't use one of these features, you can increase the size of the document window slightly by removing that feature from the screen.

Recall that to create a document, you just begin typing. The text you type will appear in the *document window* and also be stored in the computer's internal memory, RAM. The *insertion point* moves to indicate where the next character you type will appear on the screen. When you reach the end of a line, just keep typing; WordPad automatically *wraps* the text to the beginning of the next line. Press the Enter key to start a new line only if you want to begin a new paragraph or skip a line. When you reach the bottom of the document window, continue typing; the window will scroll to accommodate the new text.

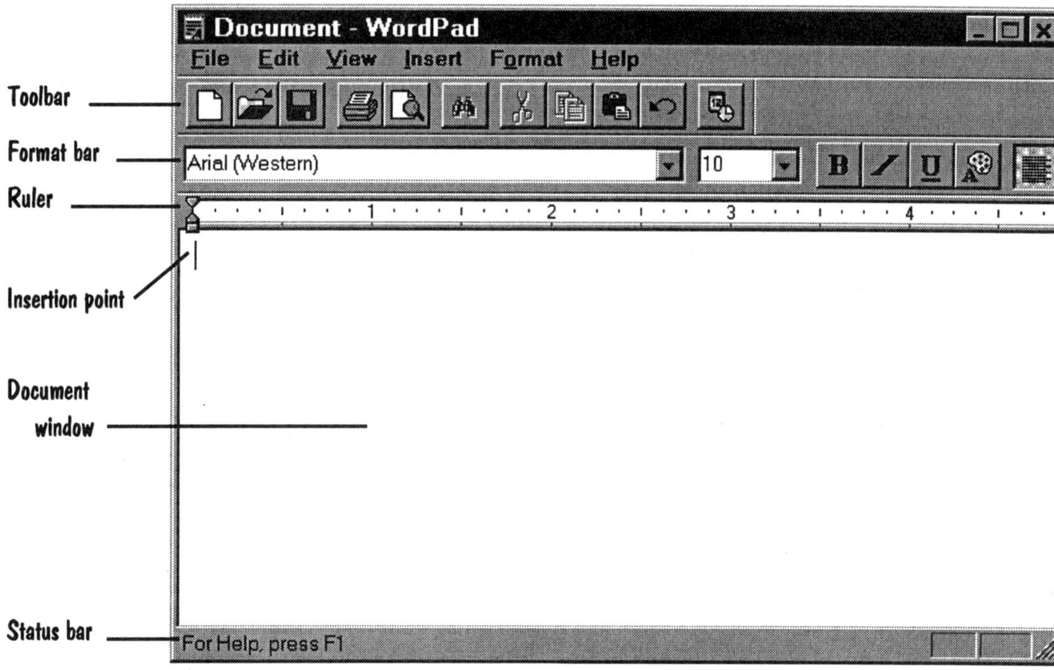


**Figure 1** The WordPad Window

## *Editing a Document*

It is inevitable that from time to time you will want to modify the content of the text you have typed. Making changes to existing text, for whatever reason, is called **editing** the document. To modify a piece (*block*) of text, you have to:

1. Move the insertion point to the text you are changing.
2. Delete the undesirable text and/or insert the new text.

In Section 2.2, we briefly discussed how to use the mouse or Arrow keys to move the insertion point within the document window or scroll the window. In some situations, using one of the keys or keystroke combinations given in the following table will move the insertion point more quickly to a desired location in the document.

**Insertion point movement keys**

| Key | Moves the insertion point . . . |
|---|---|
| Home | To the beginning of the current line |
| End | To the end of the current line |
| Page Up | One window up |
| Page Down | One window down |
| Ctrl + Left Arrow | To the previous word |
| Ctrl + Right Arrow | To the next word |
| Ctrl + Home | To the beginning of the document |
| Ctrl + End | To the end of the document |

**Deleting and inserting text**

Once you have moved the insertion point to the desired spot, you can:

- Delete the character to the *left* of the insertion point by pressing the Backspace key, or delete the character to the *right* of the insertion point by pressing the Delete key. If you want to delete a number of consecutive characters quickly, hold down the Backspace or Delete keys (as appropriate) until the block of text is erased from the screen.
- Insert text at the insertion point by typing it at the keyboard. If the new text just replaces (types over) existing characters, then WordPad is in *overwrite mode*. To return WordPad to the default *insert mode*, press the Insert key.

You can also delete or insert text by moving it from place to place within the document with the aid of the Windows Clipboard. In Section 2.3, we discussed how to select, cut, copy, and paste text. Recall that:

- To *select* a block of text, position the insertion point at the beginning of the block and then either hold down the Shift key while moving the insertion point to the end of the block or mouse-drag the insertion point to the end of the block. In either case, the selected block of text will become highlighted.

- To *cut* a block of text to the Clipboard, deleting it from its current location in the process, choose Cut from the Edit menu or click on the Toolbar's Cut button.

- To *copy* a selected block of text (which does not delete it from its current location), choose Copy from the Edit menu or click on the Toolbar's Copy button.

- To *paste* a block of text at the insertion point, choose Paste from the Edit menu or click on the Toolbar's Paste button.

These techniques work with every Windows-based application. In addition, WordPad provides some shortcuts for these procedures:

**Other ways to select text**

- To select a word, double-click on any letter in it.
- To select a paragraph, triple-click anywhere within it.

You can also select certain blocks of text by moving the mouse cursor (the I-beam) into the left margin. The cursor will become a right-facing pointer, called the *selection cursor* (see Figure 2). Then:

- To select the line of text at the cursor, click the mouse (see Figure 2). To select several consecutive lines of text, drag the mouse pointer down the left margin until all the desired lines have become highlighted.
- To select the paragraph at the cursor, double-click the mouse.
- To select the entire document, triple-click the mouse. (You can also select the entire document by choosing the Select All command from the Edit menu.)

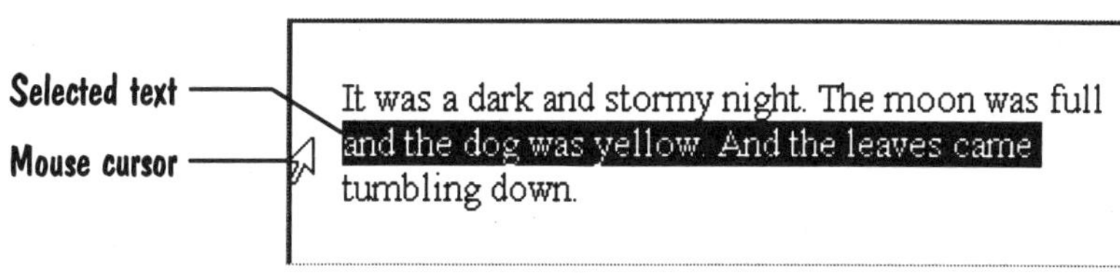


**Figure 2** Selecting a Single Line of Text

**Deselecting text**

To *deselect* a block of text, click the mouse anywhere on the screen or press a cursor movement key, such as an Arrow key. (Do not press any other kind of key while a block of text is selected; the corresponding character will *replace* the selected text!)

**Drag-and-drop move or copy**

You can also move or copy text from one place in a WordPad document to another using the *drag-and-drop* technique. (In Section 3.3, we used this technique to move and copy files or folders.) Here's the way it works:

1. Select the block of text to be moved or copied.
2. Position the mouse pointer anywhere in the highlighted text (the cursor will become a left-facing pointer).
3. If you want:

- To *move* the selected text, press (but do not release) the left mouse button and reposition the mouse pointer at the selected text's new location.
- To *copy* the selected text, hold down the Ctrl key and press the left mouse button as you move the pointer to the selected text's new location. (In this case, the mouse pointer displays a small box containing a plus symbol.)

The insertion point moves with the mouse cursor and indicates the exact place the text will be positioned (see Figure 3).

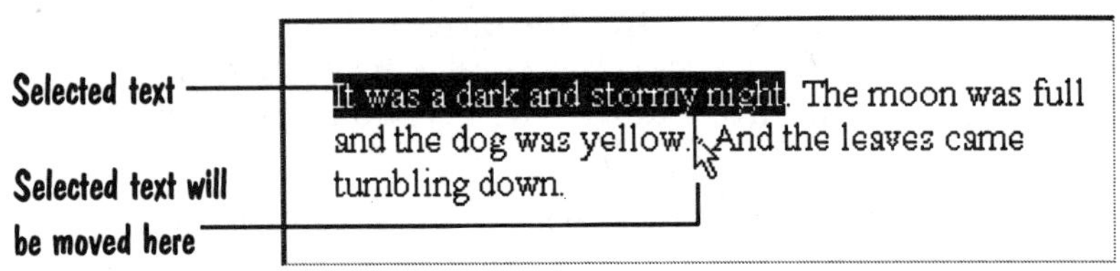


**Figure 3** Moving Selected Text by Drag-and-Drop

4. When the insertion point is positioned properly, release the mouse button (and Ctrl key, if copying). The selected text will appear in the new location.

NOTE

Once you have selected a block of text, in addition to moving or copying it, you can:

- Delete the text by pressing the Delete or Backspace key.
- Change the text's font, as described in Section 7.2.

To *undo* your last edit (such as moving or deleting some text), either choose the Undo command from the Edit menu or click on the Toolbar's Undo button.

TIP

When using a word processor, you may find it more convenient to perform editing operations using the keyboard rather than by clicking on menu commands or Toolbar buttons. Here are some shortcut keys for the operations discussed in this section:

Ctrl+A selects the entire document.
Ctrl+X cuts a selected block of text to the Clipboard.
Ctrl+C copies a selected block of text to the Clipboard.
Ctrl+V pastes the text on the Clipboard at the insertion point.
Ctrl+Z undoes the last editing operation.

**7.1**
**TUTORIAL**

Try the following exercise on your own.

1. Turn on the computer (if necessary) to start Windows 95 and open WordPad by clicking on the WordPad item on the Accessories submenu of the Start menu's Programs option.
2. Begin a document by typing the sentences "It was a dark and stormy night. The dogs were barking.", and then pressing the Enter key.
3. Select the first line of this document by moving the mouse cursor into the left margin, where it becomes a right-facing arrow, and clicking. (Because the first line happens to be a paragraph, you can also select it by either double-clicking while the mouse cursor is in the left margin or triple-clicking while the cursor is in the paragraph itself.) The first line of text will become highlighted.
4. *Copy* the selected text to the end of the document by dragging it there: Hold down the Ctrl key (if you forget to do this, the text will be *moved*, not copied), position the mouse cursor within the selected text, press the left mouse button, reposition the cursor (and insertion point) at the end of the document, and release the mouse button and Ctrl key.
5. Select the entire document by either
   - Repositioning the mouse cursor in the left margin and triple-clicking.

   *or*
   - Choosing Select All from the Edit menu (or pressing Ctrl+A).
6. Copy the selected text to the end of the document: Copy it to the Clipboard (press Ctrl+C), reposition the insertion point at the end of the document (press Ctrl+End), and paste the text there (press Ctrl+V). There should now be four lines of stormy nights and barking dogs.
7. Undo the last action (step 6): Either choose the Undo command from the Edit menu, click on the Undo Toolbar button, or press Ctrl+Z.
8. Close WordPad, responding No to the "save changes?" message.

# 7.2 Using Fonts in WordPad

In Section 7.1, we discussed some of the basic capabilities of the WordPad word processor. In this section, we will describe how you can control the way text appears on the screen and the printed page.

## *Fonts Revisited*

Nothing makes a bigger difference in the impact your words will have on the reader than the fonts you use to print them. In Section 4.5, we briefly discussed the nature of fonts; we will expand upon that material here and then show how fonts are implemented within a WordPad document.

Recall that a **font** is a collection of characters of a given design, size, and style.

- The *design* or **typeface** of a font refers to the general appearance of the characters, independent of their size, thickness, or other attributes. For example, Arial, `Courier New`, and Times New Roman are three of the typefaces supplied by Windows.
- The *size* of a font refers to its height, measured in **points**. There are 72 points per inch, so 18-point type, for example, is roughly 1/4-inch high on the printed page. Here are some examples of different sizes of the Arial typeface:

  8-point 12-point 18-point

- The *style* of a font is dictated by attributes such as **bold** or *italic*.

Some fonts are only supplied in discrete sizes, such as 10-point, 12-point, and so on. Others, called **scalable fonts**, can be scaled to any size. Microsoft includes several scalable typefaces, known as *TrueType fonts*, with the Windows 95 software. These fonts are available for use in any Windows-based application.

**WYSIWYG** When you type text in WordPad, the corresponding characters appear on the screen in the current font (which is displayed on the Format bar). If you print the document, the fonts that appear on the screen will also be used by the printer. We say that WordPad is a WYSIWYG (What You See Is What You Get, pronounced "whizzywig") word processor. WYSIWYG means that the appearance of the document on the screen, including fonts, graphics, spacing, and so on, previews the way it will appear on the printed page.

**Changing the font** There are several ways to change the current font in WordPad. With any of these techniques, the font change will apply to either:

- The currently selected block of text, if text is selected when the change is made.

*or*

- The text you type after the change is made, if no text is currently selected.

## *Using the Font Dialog Box*

The most flexible way to change the current font is to make use of the Font dialog box, which allows you to change not only the typeface, style, and size of the font, but also other attributes such as underline (underline), strikeout (~~strikeout~~), and color. Here's how to use this dialog box:

1. If you want the new font to apply to existing text, select that block of text. (Otherwise, the new font will apply to the text you type after the change is made.)
2. Choose the Font command from the Format menu. The Font dialog box, shown in Figure 4, will be displayed. The current font's typeface, style, and size are shown in the Font, Font style, and Size text boxes, respectively; a sample of this font is displayed in the Sample box. As you make selections to change this font, the sample text changes accordingly.

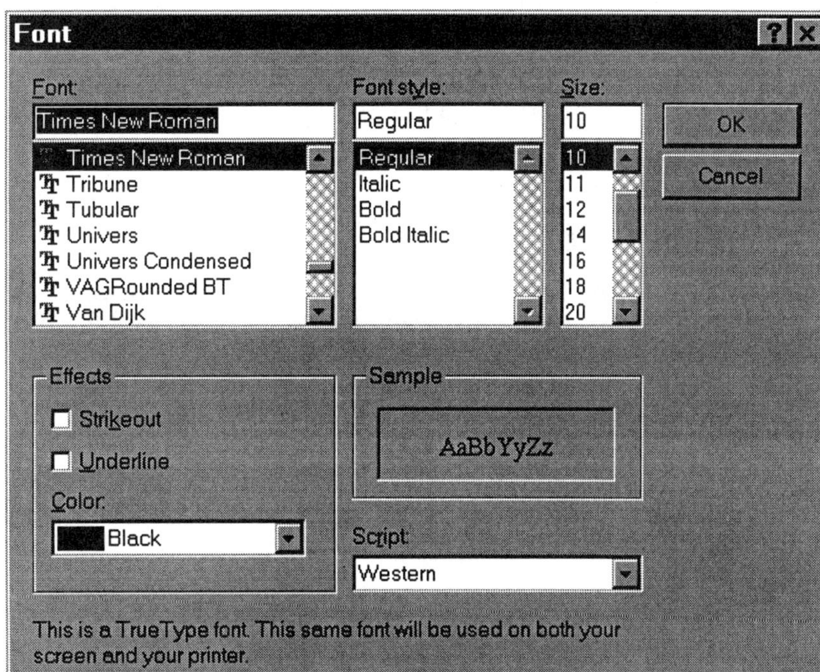


**Figure 4** The Font Dialog Box

3. Select a typeface for the new font from the Font list box. Instead of scrolling to the desired name, you might save time by typing its

first few letters in the Font text box at the top of the list. For example, to change to Arial, type "ar" in the text box and the Font list box will scroll to display Arial and other "nearby" typefaces.

4. Select bold, italic, or bold italic, if you wish, from the Font style list. Selecting Regular turns off (cancels) a current style.
5. Select a font size (in points) from the Size list. You can select any (whole number) size that your printer can print, even if it doesn't appear in this list. Just click on the text box at the top of the Size list and enter the desired size.
6. If you want to add an underline and/or strikeout line to the text, select the appropriate check boxes.
7. You can select a text color from the Color drop-down list. Of course, to print the resulting text in this color, you need a color printer. (Some non-color printers print text colors in various shades of gray.)
8. The Script drop-down list is used to select an alternate character set for use with a language other than English. If Windows has not been configured for another language, you can ignore this feature.
9. To put your font changes into effect, choose the OK command button. To ignore these changes, choose Cancel.

## *Using the Format Bar*

The Format bar provides a quicker, though less flexible, way of changing fonts and their attributes. (Remember: If the Format bar is not displayed in your WordPad window, choose the Format Bar item from the View menu to display it.) The functions of the Format bar buttons that alter the current font are identified in Figure 5. Notice that the typeface and font size of the current font are displayed on the Format bar; if the current font has bold, italic, or underline attributes, the corresponding buttons will appear to be "pressed in".

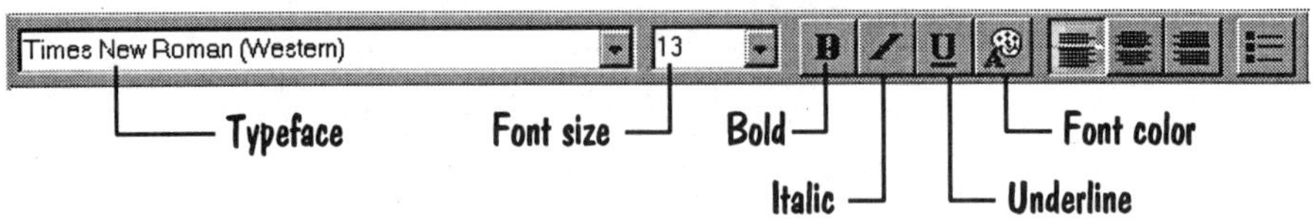


**Figure 5** Font Attributes on the Format Bar

To use the Format bar to change the font of selected text or the text that you are about to type:

1. Select a new typeface or font size from the appropriate drop-down list.
2. Select or deselect bold, italics, or underline by clicking on the corresponding button.
3. Change the font color by clicking on the Font Color button and selecting the desired color from the drop-down list.

TIP

The easiest way to turn the bold, italics, or underline attribute on or off is to use the keystroke combinations Ctrl+B, Ctrl+I, or Ctrl+U, respectively. For example, to bold a word you are about to type, press Ctrl+B, type the word, and press Ctrl+B again. Or, to remove italics from a word you have already typed, select the word and press Ctrl+I.

7.2 TUTORIAL

Try the following exercise on your own.

1. Turn on the computer (if necessary) to start Windows 95.
2. Open WordPad from the Start button's Accessories submenu and maximize its window.
3. Insert the Lab Exercises disk in its drive and open the document named Preamble. (For information on opening documents, see Section 2.2.)
4. If the Format bar is turned off, display it by choosing the Format Bar command from the View menu. Notice (from the Format bar) that 14-point Arial type is used for the title of the document.
5. Change the title's font to 12-point bold italic Times New Roman:
   - Select the title (by, for example, clicking in the left margin).
   - Choose the Font command from the Format menu to open the Font dialog box.
   - In the dialog box, select Times New Roman from the Font list, Bold Italic from the Font style list, and 12 from the Size list.
   - Choose the OK command button.
6. Change the text for the preamble from 12-point Times New Roman to 11-point Arial:
   - Select the text of the preamble (by, for example, double-clicking in the left margin next to this paragraph).
   - Select "Arial (Western)" and "11" from the drop-down lists on the Format bar.

7. Deselect the selected text by clicking elsewhere in the WordPad window.
8. Italicize the words "United States of America":
   - Select these words.
   - Either press Ctrl+I or click on the Format bar's Italic button to italicize them. 
   - Deselect these words.
9. Add the words THE END at the end of the document in bold type:
   - Reposition the cursor at the end of the document and press the Enter key twice.
   - Turn on boldface by clicking on the Format bar's Bold button (or pressing Ctrl+B). 
   - Type the words THE END and turn off boldface by clicking on the Bold button (or pressing Ctrl+B) again.
10. Close WordPad (responding No to the "save changes?" message) and remove the Lab Exercises disk from its drive.

# 7.3 Formatting Text in WordPad

**Formatting** a document changes, in some manner, the way the text in that document is arranged on the page. In this section, we will discuss WordPad's formatting features.

## Formatting the Document as a Whole

WordPad provides several formatting features that apply to the entire document. When one of these commands is issued, it doesn't matter where the insertion point is positioned; the command affects all text that has already been typed and will be typed in the current document. These features include:

**Document-oriented features**

- Placing text on the page in either portrait or landscape orientation.
- Specifying the size of the left, right, top, and bottom page margins.

To access either of these formatting features, choose Page Setup from the File menu. The Page Setup dialog box, shown in Figure 6, will be displayed.

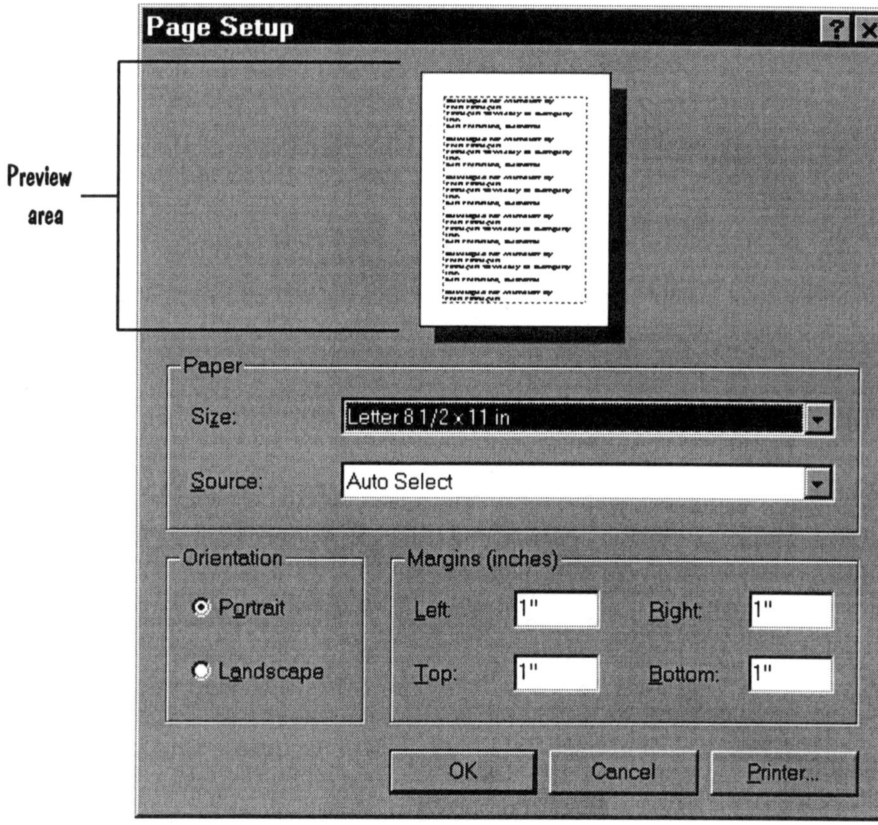


**Figure 6** The Page Setup Dialog Box

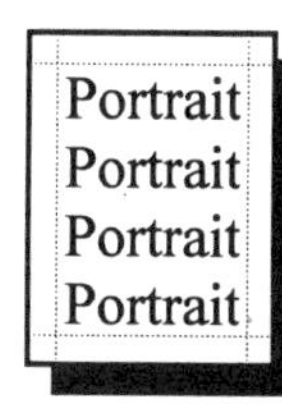


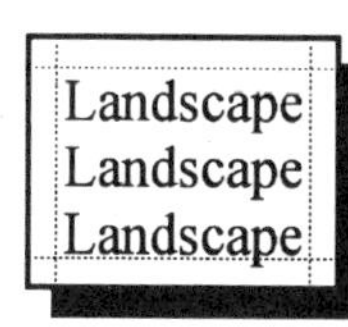


**Specifying Page Orientation** You can choose to print your document in either portrait or landscape orientation. In **portrait** orientation, the document's text is printed parallel to the short side of the paper. For example, the page you are now reading is printed this way. In **landscape** orientation, the text is printed parallel to the long side of the paper. Landscape orientation is usually used for certificates and diplomas. The figures at the right further illustrate this concept.

To specify page orientation:

1. Open the Page Setup dialog box (Figure 6) from the File menu.
2. Select the Portrait or Landscape option button. (The "page" shown

in the preview area will appear in the selected orientation.)

3. Choose the OK command button.

**Specifying Margins** By default, WordPad leaves the margin settings for a new document the same as they were in the previous one. To specify different margins for the current document:

1. Open the Page Setup dialog box (Figure 6) from the File menu.
2. Enter the desired margins in the Left, Right, Top, and Bottom text boxes. (The "page" shown in the preview area will indicate the new margins.)
3. Choose the OK command button.

NOTE

The width and height of a page's text area depend not only on its margins and orientation, but also on the size of the paper being used. For example, suppose that all margins are set to one inch and the orientation is portrait. Then, on a standard 8½" × 11" ("letter size") piece of paper, all text is enclosed in an imaginary box that is 6½ inches wide and 9 inches high. However, for "legal size" paper (which is 8½" × 14"), our imaginary box becomes 6½ inches wide and 12 inches high. Thus, WordPad needs to know the size of paper you are using. This setting is also specified in the Page Setup dialog box, by selecting the appropriate item on the Paper Size drop-down list.

## *Formatting Paragraphs*

When you press the Enter key while typing text in WordPad, a paragraph marker code, which is not visible on the screen, is placed in the document file. To WordPad, a *paragraph* is the text lying between two paragraph markers, or between a paragraph marker and the beginning or end of the document. In other words, every time you press the Enter key, WordPad interprets it as the beginning of a new paragraph.

WordPad has several formatting features that apply either to the paragraphs containing selected text, or (if no text is selected) to the paragraph that contains the insertion point. These features include:

**Paragraph-oriented features**

- Centering the text or aligning it with the left or right margin.
- Indenting a paragraph of text from the left and/or right margin, or the first line of a paragraph from the rest of the paragraph.
- Setting tabs to help create columns of text.
- Automatically placing a "bullet" before each item in a list.

**NOTE** When you start typing a new paragraph, it automatically inherits all the formatting characteristics of the previous one. For example, suppose the current paragraph is centered between the margins. If you press the Enter key and start typing, you'll see that the new text is still centered.

**Changing Text Alignment** WordPad provides three options for aligning (or *justifying*) text relative to the left and right margins:

The text in this paragraph is *left-justified.* All lines in this paragraph align on the left margin.

This text is *centered.* All lines in this paragraph are centered between the margins.

The text in this paragraph is *right-justified.* All lines in this paragraph align on the right margin.

The default alignment option is left-justification. To change text alignment, place the insertion point in the desired paragraph or select the paragraphs to be aligned and:

1. Choose the Paragraph item from the Format menu.
2. Select the desired option (Left, Right, or Center) from the Alignment drop-down list.
3. Choose the OK command button.

**TIP** It is a little easier to select an alignment option using the Format bar. To do so, place the insertion point in the desired paragraph or select the paragraphs to be aligned and click the appropriate Format bar button, as shown below:

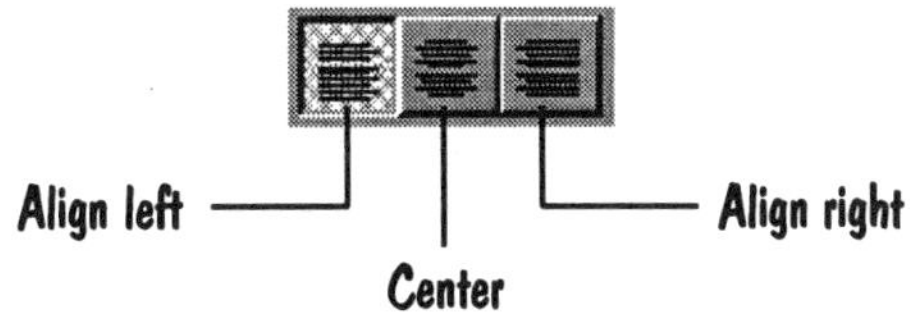


The button that appears to be "pressed in" (*Align left*, in the diagram above) indicates the justification of the current paragraph.

**Changing Paragraph Indentation** As you know, when you change the margins for a document, that change applies to the entire document. To change the left or right margin for a particular paragraph in WordPad, you change its *indentation* relative to the given margin. The indentation feature also allows you to indent the first line of the paragraph relative to the rest of the paragraph.

For example, in Figure 7:

- The first paragraph is not indented.
- The second paragraph is indented 1 inch on the left, 0.5 inches on the right, and the indent for the first line is 0 inches. Since the first line indent is measured relative to the rest of the paragraph, it is indented the same amount as the rest of the paragraph.
- The third paragraph is indented 1 inch on the left, 1.5 inches on the right, and has a first line indent of -0.5 inches. Since the indent for the first line is *negative* and is measured relative to the rest of the paragraph, it starts one-half inch to the *left* of the rest of the paragraph. (*Positive* first line indents start this line to the *right* of the rest of the paragraph.)

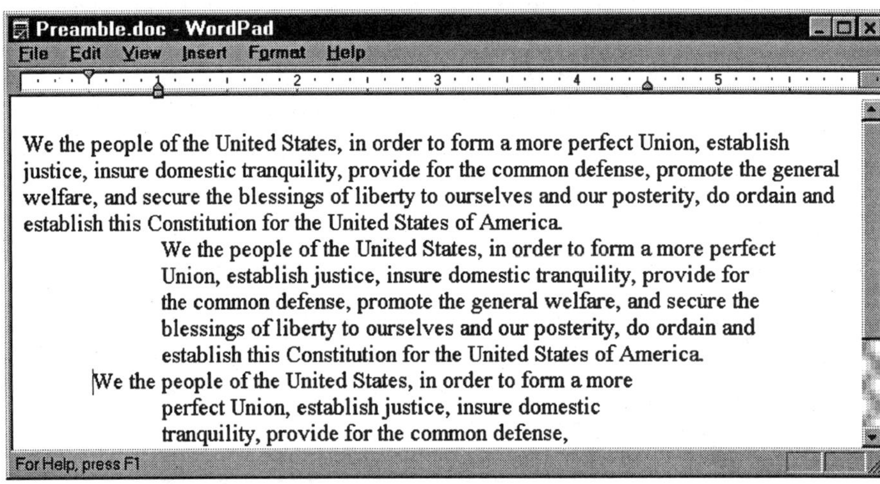


**Figure 7** Examples of Indented Paragraphs

To change indentation, place the insertion point in the desired paragraph, or select text in the paragraphs to be changed, and:

1. Choose Paragraph from the Format menu. The Paragraph dialog box, shown in Figure 8, will open.
2. Type the desired numbers in the *Left*, *Right*, and *First line* indentation text boxes.
3. Choose the OK command button.

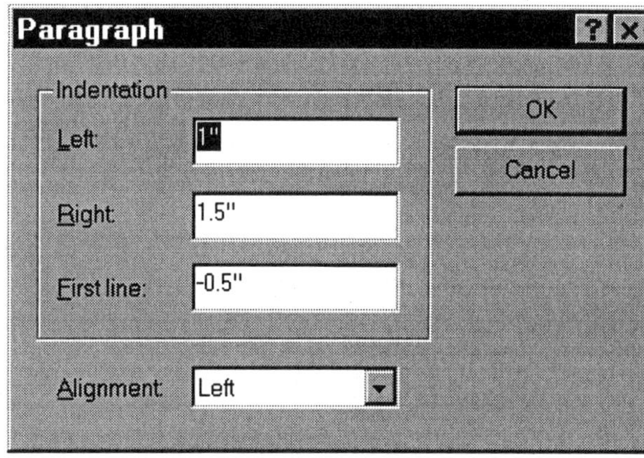


**Figure 8** The Paragraph Dialog Box

You can also use the WordPad Ruler to change paragraph indenting. (Remember: If the Ruler is hidden, you can display it by choosing the Ruler item from the View menu.) To change indentation this way:

1. Place the insertion point in the desired paragraph, or select text in the paragraphs to be changed.
2. Use the mouse to drag the left-, right-, and/or first-line-indent markers to the appropriate positions on the Ruler.

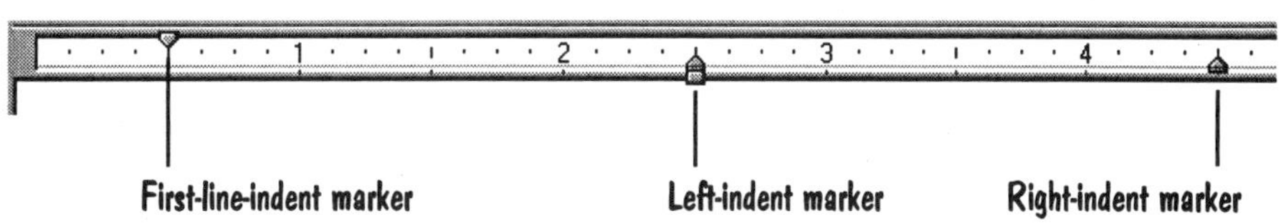


Figure 7 shows the markers set for the third paragraph's indentation.

**Changing the Tab Settings** When you press the Tab key while working in a WordPad document, the insertion point moves to the right and is positioned at the next tab setting (or *tab stop*). By default, the tab stops are set at half-inch intervals, beginning at the left margin. Thus, if you press the Tab key when the insertion point is 2.75" from the left margin (and the default tab stops are in effect), it will move to a position on the same line 3" from the margin.

Tab stops can be very useful in creating columns of text in a document. To add or remove tab stops for a given paragraph:

1. Place the insertion point in the desired paragraph, or select text in the desired paragraph.
2. Choose the Tabs item from the Format menu. The dialog box shown in Figure 9 will open.

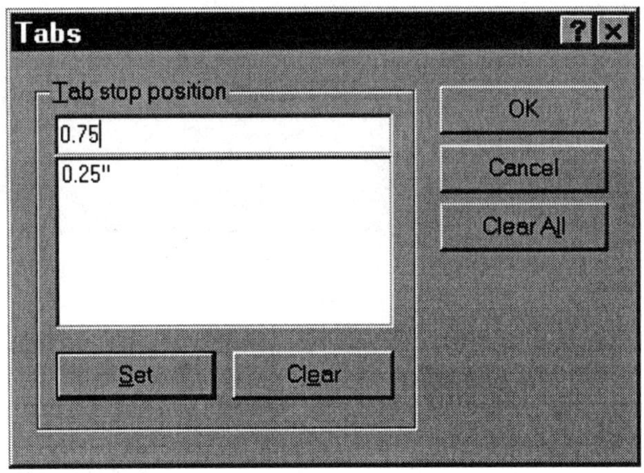


**Figure 9** The Tabs Dialog Box

3. To add a new tab stop:
   - Enter its position (relative to the left margin) in the *Tab stop position* text box.
   - Choose the Set command button. The new tab stop will be displayed in the *Tab stop position* list box and all *default* tab stops to its left will be removed. For example, adding a tab setting of 0.75 removes the default tab stop at 0.5.
4. To remove all tab stops displayed in the *Tab stop position* list box, choose the Clear All command button. To remove one of the tab stops displayed in the list box, select it and choose the Clear command button.
5. Choose the OK command button to close the dialog box and put the new settings into effect. If the Ruler is currently displayed in the WordPad window, L symbols will appear on it in the appropriate positions.

TIP

The WordPad Ruler provides an easier way to add and remove tab stops. To use the Ruler for these purposes:

1. Position the insertion point (or select text) in the desired paragraph.
2. To add a tab stop, click on the appropriate location on the Ruler. An L symbol will appear there.

3. To remove an existing tab stop, drag that L symbol off the Ruler.

**Creating a Bulleted List** If your document contains a list of important points, you can add emphasis by preceding each item on the list by a "bullet". A **bullet** is a small symbol, often round or square, used for this purpose. Here are some examples of typical bullets: • ■ ○ ☛ ✔

WordPad has a *bullet style* feature that allows you to easily create a bulleted list. When this feature is in effect, new paragraphs will begin with a solid round bullet followed by a tab. To turn the bullet style on, either

- Choose the Bullet Style item from the Format menu.

*or*

- Click on the Format bar's Bullets button, which is shown at the right.

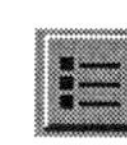

Once you have completed your list, press the Enter key, moving the insertion point to the next line and inserting a new bullet. Then, either choose Bullet Style from the Format menu (it's a toggle) or click on the Toolbar's Bullets button. The last bullet will disappear.

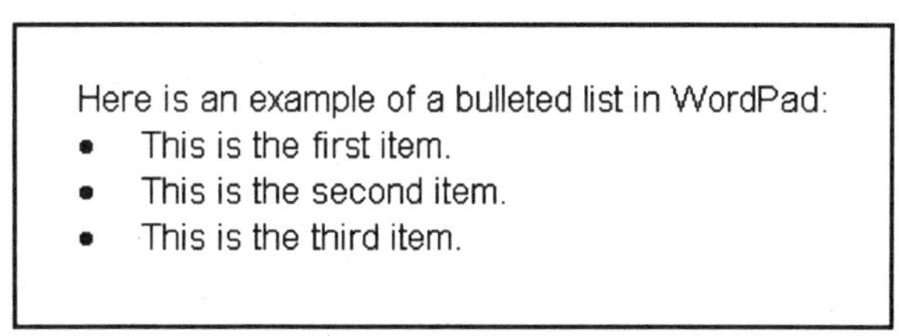

Here is an example of a bulleted list in WordPad:

- This is the first item.
- This is the second item.
- This is the third item.

TIP

The amount a bullet and the corresponding list item is indented is governed by the first-line-indent and left-indent, respectively, for that paragraph. Thus, to change the positions of the bullets and list items relative to the left margin, just change these indentation options (as described earlier in this section) for all lines of the list.

If you want to use another symbol for your bullets, you can do so with the help of the Character Map accessory, which is discussed in Section 9.5. However, with this technique, you will have to manually insert each bullet and then press the Tab key before typing the corresponding list item.

7-3 TUTORIAL

Try the following exercise on your own.

1. Turn on the computer (if necessary) to start Windows 95.
2. Open WordPad from the Start button's Accessories submenu and maximize its window.
3. Insert the Lab Exercises disk in its drive and open the document named History.
4. Display the Page Setup dialog box, by choosing this item from the File menu, and:
   - Set the margins for the History document to 1.5" on the left and right and 1.25" on the top and bottom by entering these numbers in the appropriate text boxes.
   - Select the Portrait option button (if necessary) so the document's text will print parallel to the short side of the page.

   Choose the OK button to put these changes into effect.
5. Center the title by positioning the insertion point within it and clicking on the appropriate button on the Format bar. In a similar way, right-align the first paragraph of the document. (This step can also be carried out by choosing Paragraph from the Format menu and selecting the proper option from the Alignment drop-down list.)

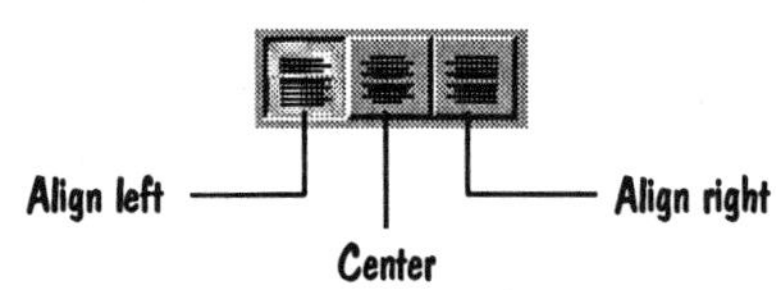


6. Indent the second and third paragraphs 1 inch on the left and right (relative to the margins), with a first-line-indent of 0.5 inches: Select both paragraphs, choose Paragraph from the Format menu, enter these figures in the Indentation text boxes, and choose OK. (These settings can also be made using the Ruler's indent markers; see the TIP on page 257.)
7. Remove all tabs for the second paragraph of the document and set a new tab stop at 2.25 inches for this paragraph:
   - Click the mouse within the second paragraph.
   - Choose Tabs from the Format menu to open this dialog box.
   - Choose the Clear All button to remove the existing tabs.
   - Enter 2.25 in the *Tab stop position* text box.
   - Choose the OK button.

   (An existing tab can also be removed by dragging the corresponding **L** symbol off the Ruler; similarly, a new tab can be set by clicking on the appropriate spot on the Ruler.)

8. To see the effect of your new tab stop, position the insertion point in front of the first letter in the second paragraph and press the Tab key.
9. Close WordPad (responding No to the "save changes?" message) and remove the diskette from its drive.

# 7.4 Using Graphics in a WordPad Document

WordPad lets you do more than just process words. It allows you to insert **graphics** (pictures) into a document and then, if you wish, to move or resize them. In this section, we will describe how to perform these operations.

## Inserting a Graphic into a Document

Although WordPad itself cannot be used to create graphics, you can insert (or *import*) a graphic created by another application into a WordPad document. There are two ways to accomplish this task.

**Using the Clipboard** As we mentioned in Section 2.3, the Windows Clipboard can be used to transfer a graphic from one document to another. Here's the way the process works:

1. Use a graphics program (such as Paint, which is discussed in Chapter 8) to create the picture or to open an existing graphics file.
2. Select the graphic and copy it to the Clipboard.
3. Switch to WordPad.
4. Place the insertion point where you want the graphic to appear.
5. Choose Paste from the Edit menu or click on the Toolbar's Paste button. The graphic will be displayed in your document at the insertion point.

TIP: If the graphic does not display satisfactorily in WordPad when you issue the Paste command, delete the graphic (by pressing the Del key), and choose the Paste Special command from the Edit menu. A dialog box will open allowing you to choose from among several image formats. Now, try these one at a time (by selecting a format from the list box and choosing the OK button) to get the most satisfactory image. However, be aware that some formats will not let you edit the graphic (see below) after it has been imported into WordPad.

**Using the Insert Object Command** There is an another way to import a graphic into a WordPad document. This method works especially well if the graphic is stored on disk, but it does require some familiarity with the Windows 95 file system (Chapter 3). To use this technique:

1. Place the insertion point in the WordPad document where you want the graphic to appear.
2. Choose the Object item from the Insert menu. The Insert Object dialog box, shown in Figure 10, will open.

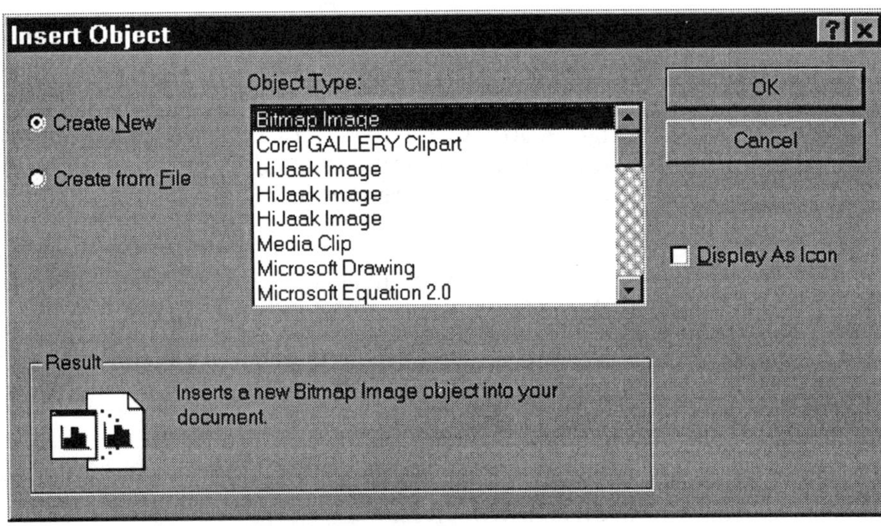


**Figure 10** The Insert Object Dialog Box

3. If you want to create the graphic (using another application), select the Object Type corresponding to that application and then choose the OK command button. A box will open (at the insertion point) in the WordPad window, in which you can draw the graphic using the selected application's tools. When you are done, just click the mouse anywhere outside of the box.

   As an example, selecting Bitmap Image and choosing OK invokes the Paint application, and the WordPad window looks as pictured in Figure 11. (Although the title bar says "WordPad", the menus and available tools are those of Paint.)

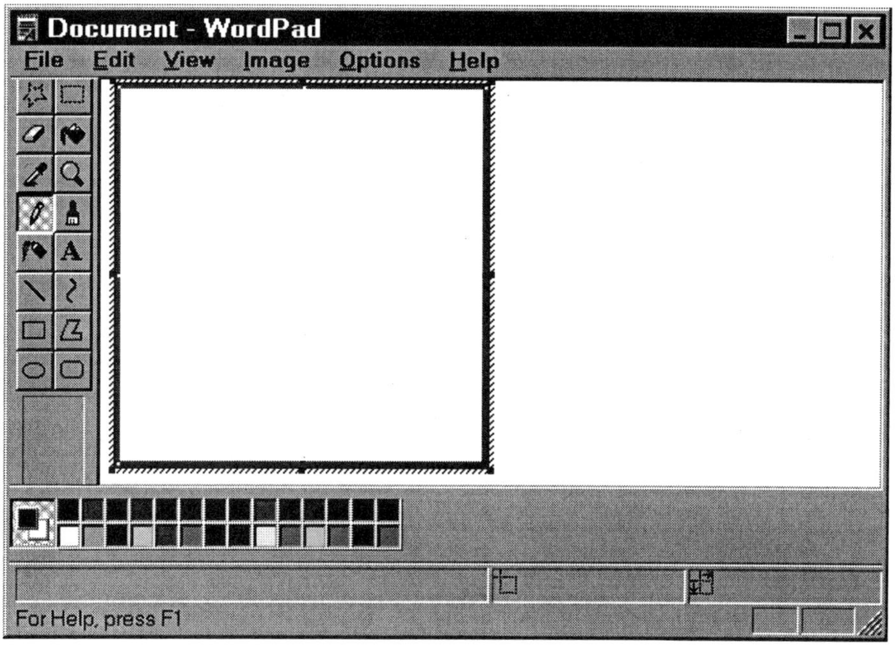


**Figure 11** Working with Paint Inside the WordPad Window

4. If, instead of creating a graphic, you want to retrieve one from disk, select the *Create from file* option button. The Object Type list in the Insert Object dialog box will be replaced by the following display:

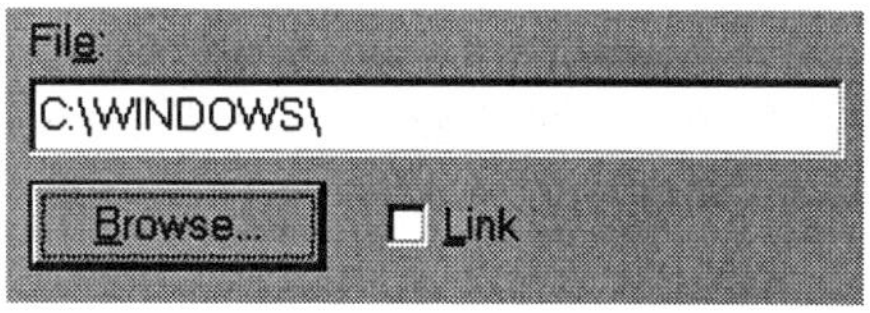


Now, either type the path name (see Section 3.1) for the desired file in the *File* text box or choose the Browse button to locate the desired file by browsing folders (see Section 3.5). Then, in either case, choose the OK command button in the Insert Object dialog box, and the graphic will be inserted into the WordPad document at the insertion point.

## *Editing a Graphic*

When you **edit** a graphic, you modify the way it looks. WordPad has no graphics editing capabilities of its own. However, you may be able to edit a graphic contained in a WordPad document using a Windows feature known as **Object Linking and Embedding**, or **OLE**.

If the object was pasted or inserted into the document from an application that supports OLE (such as Paint), then it can be edited using that application's tools. To edit such a graphic:

1. Right-click on the graphic and point at the last item on the resulting pop-up menu. (This item has a name of the form *object-type* Object; for example, Bitmap Image Object.)
2. Choose either Edit or Open from the submenu:
   - If you choose Edit, the graphic will be enclosed in a box and the WordPad window will take on the look of the application that is being used to edit the image (see Figure 11).
   - If you choose Open, the application that is being used to edit the graphic will start and the graphic will open within it.

   (Double-clicking on a graphic achieves the same result as right-clicking on it, pointing at the "Object" item, and choosing Edit.)
3. Edit the graphic as you wish using the graphics application's tools.
4. When you are done, to return to WordPad:
   - If you chose Edit to begin the process, just click outside the graphic's box.
   - If you chose Open to begin, now choose Exit & Return to Document from the File menu.

## *Deleting, Moving, and Resizing a Graphic*

Although you need to make use of another application to *edit* a graphic, WordPad can be used to delete, move, copy, or resize it.

TIP

If you are unhappy with the result of any of these operations, you can undo it: Either press Ctrl+Z, click on the Toolbar's Undo button (shown at the right), or choose the Undo command from the Edit menu.

**Selecting a Graphic** In most cases, before you can delete, move, copy, or resize a graphic, you must first select it. To select a graphic, just click on it. The graphic will become enclosed in a box containing small squares, known as *sizing handles*, at each of its corners and at the midpoint of each side. (See the figure at the right.)

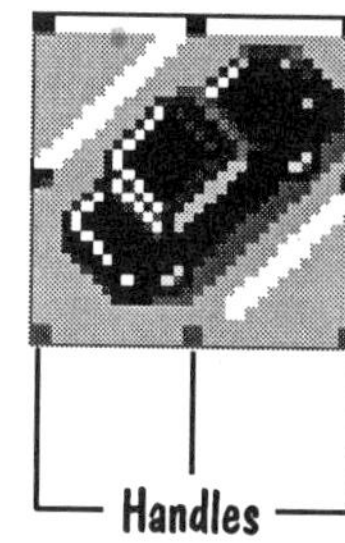


To deselect a graphic just click anywhere else in the document window.

**Deleting a Graphic** To delete a graphic from a WordPad document, either

- Select the graphic and press the Delete key.

*or*

- Position the insertion point just before or just after the graphic and press the Delete key or Backspace key, respectively.

**Moving or Copying a Graphic** To some extent, a graphic acts as if it were a character of text. (For example, as you have just seen, it can be deleted by positioning the insertion point just to the right of it and pressing the Backspace key.) This feature also provides a means for moving a graphic within a document.

**Moving a graphic like a piece of text**

- The graphic can be left-aligned, centered, or right-aligned (relative to the left and right margins) by selecting it and clicking on the appropriate button on the Format bar:

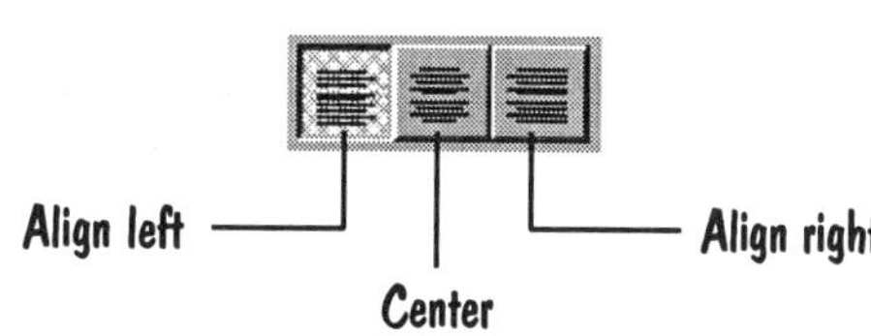


- The graphic can be "pushed" to the right or down the page by positioning the insertion point just to the left of the graphic and pressing the Spacebar, Tab key, or Enter key.
- You can select the graphic, cut or copy it to the Clipboard, and then paste it into another part of the document.

In addition to these text-oriented ways of moving a graphic, you can use the mouse to drag it to another part of the document. To be more specific:

**Using drag-and-drop**

1. Select the graphic.
2. Position the mouse pointer over the graphic, press and hold down

the mouse button, and reposition the pointer at the desired place within the document. (If you want to *copy* the graphic, instead of moving it, hold down the Ctrl key during this process.)

3. Release the mouse button (and, if necessary, the Ctrl key). The graphic will be displayed in the new location.

**NOTE** If you use drag-and-drop to move or copy a graphic, be aware that the graphic must be dropped at some location *within* the existing document. For example, if the graphic is located at the end of the document and you try to move it down the page, you *will* be able to drag the mouse cursor downward, but when you release the button, the graphic will remain in its original position.

**Resizing a Graphic** To enlarge or reduce the size of a graphic within a WordPad document:

1. Select the graphic.
2. Position the mouse pointer over one of the eight handles:
   - Use the top side or bottom side midpoint handle to change the height of the graphic without changing its width.
   - Use the left side or right side midpoint handle to change the width of the graphic without changing its height.
   - Use a corner handle to change both height and width at the same time.
3. Drag the handle in the desired direction. An outline of the graphic's box will move with the cursor to show you the corresponding size, as shown below.

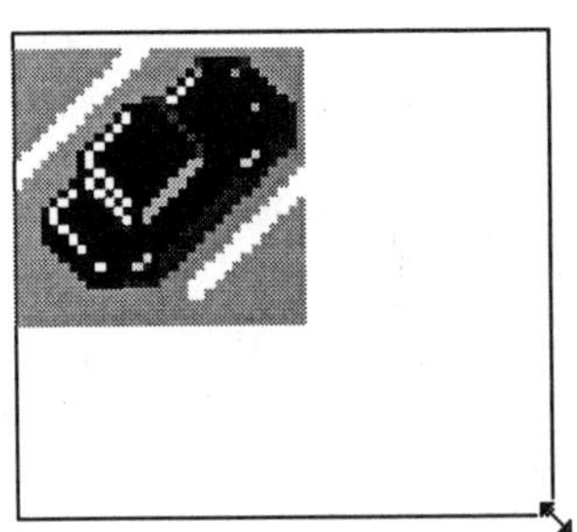

4. Release the mouse button when the graphic is the desired size. (To abort the process, press the Escape key before releasing the mouse button.)

**7-4 TUTORIAL**

Try the following exercise on your own.

1. Turn on the computer (if necessary) to start Windows 95.
2. Open WordPad from the Start button's Accessories submenu and maximize its window.
3. Insert the Lab Exercises disk in its drive.
4. Insert a graphic into the empty WordPad document:
   - Choose Object from the Insert menu.
   - Select the Create from File option button.
   - Erase the text in the *File* box and type: `A:\shapes`
   - Choose the OK command button. A graphic will be displayed in the document window.
   - Deselect the graphic by clicking elsewhere in the document window. The box around the graphic, together with its eight "sizing handles", will disappear.
5. Press Ctrl+Home to move the insertion point to the beginning of the document, just to the left of the graphic. Press the Enter key twice to "push" the graphic down two lines and then click on the Center Format bar button to center the graphic between the left and right margins.
6. Select the graphic by clicking on it; a box with "handles" will appear around the graphic. Now:
   - Reduce its size: Drag the handle in the lower-right corner of the selection box (the mouse pointer will become a two-headed arrow when it's positioned properly) about half-way toward the upper-left corner.

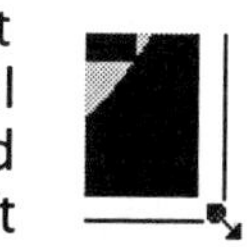

   - Increase its width without increasing its height: Drag the middle handle on the right side of the box to the right about one inch.
7. Add six blank lines to the bottom of the document by positioning the insertion point at the end of the document and then pressing the Enter key six times.
8. Create a copy the graphic at the bottom of the document:
   - Select the graphic.
   - Position the mouse pointer over the graphic and hold down the Ctrl key (for *copying*).
   - Drag the cursor to the end of the document, and release the mouse button and Ctrl key.
9. While the copy of the graphic is still selected, delete it by pressing the Delete key.

10. Right-click on the remaining graphic, point at Bitmap Image Object on the resulting submenu, and choose Open. The Paint graphics program will start, allowing you to edit the graphic.
11. Close Paint and WordPad (responding No to the "save changes?" message), and remove the diskette from its drive.

# 7.5 *Other Features of WordPad*

In the first four sections of this chapter, we have discussed how to create, edit, format, and add graphics to a WordPad document. In this section, we will introduce a few more assorted features of WordPad.

## *Find and Replace*

Occasionally, you may want to locate an occurrence of a particular word in a given document, perhaps to replace it with another word. You can accomplish this in WordPad using the Find and Replace utility. As its name implies, this utility performs two functions:

- It can be used to locate a particular piece of text within a document.
- It can be used to automatically replace a particular piece of text with something else.

**Finding text** To locate a desired piece of text:

1. Choose Find from the Edit menu or click on the Toolbar's Find button. The Find dialog box, shown in Figure 12, will open.

2. Type the text you wish to locate in the *Find what* text box, and:

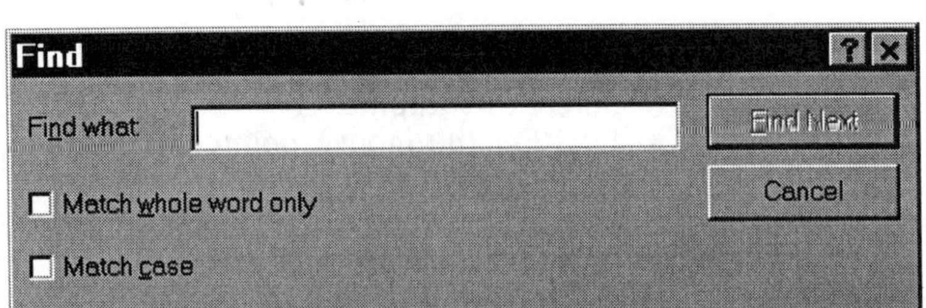


**Figure 12** The Find Dialog Box

- Select the *Match whole word only* check box if you do not want the utility to search for longer words that contain the text you've typed. For example, suppose your document contains the words *all*, *small*, and *allow*, and you type *all* in the *Find what* text box. If the *Match whole word only* check box is selected, only the word *all* will be located. If it is not selected, all three words will be found.
- Select the *Match case* check box if you want to locate text that has the same combination of upper- and lower-case letters as the *Find what* text. For example, if this check box is selected and you type *all* in the *Find what* box, then *all* will be searched for, but not *All*; if this check box is not selected, both *all* and *All* (and, for that matter, *ALL*) will be sought.

3. Choose the Find Next command button. The next occurrence of the *Find what* text will be located and highlighted. (The search starts at the insertion point and, if the end of the document is reached before the text is found, the search continues at the beginning of the document.) If the *Find what* text is not found, a message to this effect will appear on the screen.

The Find dialog box will not close when the desired text is found, so that you can locate the next occurrence of the text, if so desired. To close this dialog box, choose the Cancel command button, press the Escape key, or click on the close button.

**Replacing text** The Find and Replace utility can also replace the next occurrence of a particular piece of text (or *all* occurrences, if you wish) with text that you specify. To perform this operation:

1. Choose the Replace command from the Edit menu. The Replace dialog box, shown in Figure 13, will be displayed.

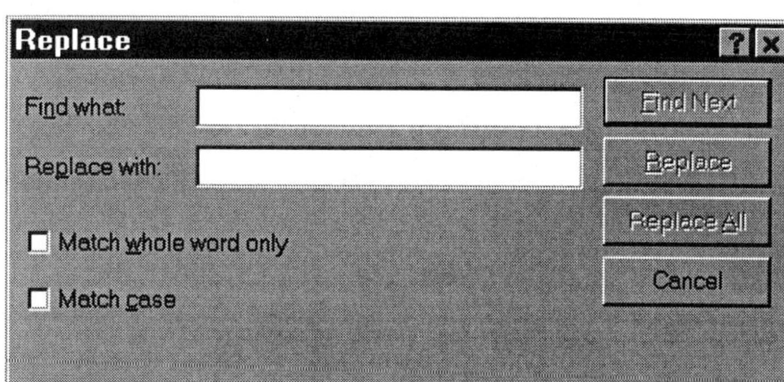


**Figure 13** The Replace Dialog Box

2. Type the text you want to change in the *Find what* box and select the *Match whole word only* and/or *Match case* check boxes, if desired (their functions are described above).
3. Type the replacement text in the *Replace with* box.
4. Choose one of the command buttons:
   - Find Next locates the next occurrence of the *Find what* text and highlights it, but does not replace it.
   - Replace automatically replaces the highlighted word (if any) with the *Replace with* text, and then finds the next occurrence of the *Find what* text and highlights it.
   - Replace All automatically replaces every occurrence of the *Find what* text with the *Replace with* text.
   - Cancel terminates the find and replace operation and closes the dialog box.

TIP

You can use Find and Replace to speed up the entry of text into a document that has many occurrences of the same long word or phrase. For example, suppose you are writing a report on the Mediterranean region of Italy. Instead of typing the phrase *Mediterranean region of Italy* over and over again, simply type (say) *Med* each time. Then, when you're done, use Find and Replace to automatically replace all occurrences of *Med* with the longer phrase.

## *Print Preview*

WordPad does not show certain formatting features, such as margins and page breaks, in the document window. However, it does provide a *print preview* feature to give you a better idea of what a document will look like when it's printed. This feature can sometimes save lots of time and paper.

To open the print preview window, either

- Choose the Print Preview command from the File menu.

*or*

- Click on the Toolbar's Print Preview button (as shown at the right).

In either case, the window shown in Figure 14 will open, displaying the first two pages of the document. (The page numbers are given on the status bar at the bottom of the window.) The margins are shown as "white space" outside the dashed lines that enclose the text.

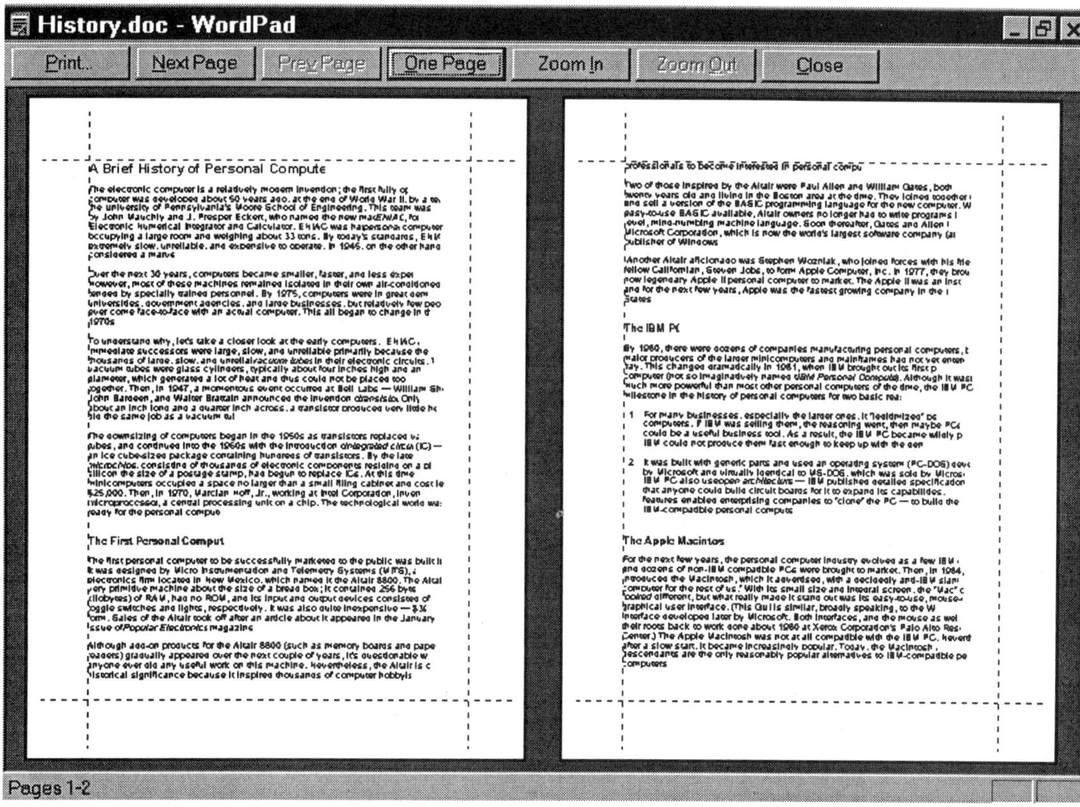


**Figure 14** WordPad's Print Preview Window (Two-Page View)

**Paging through the document**

You can get an overall view of the appearance of the entire document by paging through it.

- To display one page at a time click on the One Page button at the top of the window. (It will be relabeled *Two Page.*)
- To display the next page, click on the Next Page button or press the Page Down key (on the keyboard).
- To display the previous page, click on the Prev Page button or press the Page Up key.

**Zooming in and out**

As you can see, it is difficult (sometimes, impossible) to read the text displayed in the preview window. (The situation does not improve if you switch to One Page view.) To deal with this problem, WordPad provides three levels of magnification, the default view and two "zoom" modes.

To *zoom in*, so that text appears larger (but with less of it displayed at once), either

- Click on the part of the page that you would like to enlarge. (In the preview window, the mouse cursor takes the shape of a magnifying glass, as shown at the right.)

*or*

- Click on the Zoom In button (at the top of the window). Then, use the scroll bars to display the desired part of the page.

In either case, the window will switch to One Page view (if necessary) and the text will be displayed in a larger font.

Clicking on the page or the Zoom In button again displays the second Zoom mode, increasing the magnification even more. At this point, the Zoom In button is dimmed, and clicking again on the page will return the display to the default magnification level. While in one of the two Zoom modes, clicking on the Zoom Out button changes the display to the next lower magnification level.

The relative magnification levels are shown below; each figure displays the same amount of screen area.

When you are done using the print preview window, either choose the Close button to return to the WordPad document window or choose the Print button to print the document.

## *Specifying a File Format*

When a word processor (or, for that matter, any program) saves a document, it does so using a certain *file format* — a scheme for encoding the document's text, fonts, formatting symbols, and graphics, so that this information can be stored on disk. Unfortunately, every word processor uses a different file format for storing the documents it produces. Thus, if you want to be able to open a document created by WordPad in another word processor, or vice-versa, you may have to specify a particular file format when it is saved. WordPad recognizes (opens documents in) four different file formats, offers a different default view option for each such format, and saves files in three of these formats.

**File formats recognized by WordPad**

WordPad is able to open documents that were saved in the following file formats; the conversion process is done automatically:

- *Microsoft Word for Windows (version 6)* Because Word contains a greater number of formatting features than WordPad, some of a document's original formatting may be lost when it is saved in Word and then opened in WordPad.
- *Windows 3.1 Write* Again, some formatting may be lost.
- *Rich Text Format (RTF)* This is a common format, recognized by most word processors. If you are transferring a formatted document from a word processor other than Word for Windows or Write, save it (in that word processor) in RTF.
- *Text* WordPad opens any file whose format it does not recognize as a plain text file, consisting of letters, numbers, punctuation marks, and a few other symbols. If, in fact, the file was saved in a format other than Text, you will see a lot of strange characters on the screen.

**File format view options**

When WordPad opens a document, it displays the document in a certain way and makes certain "tool bars" available, depending on the format in which the file was saved. For example, by default, Text files are displayed in the Courier New typeface with no alignment choices other than left-justification, and the Ruler and Format bar are hidden. You can specify which view option defaults are used for each format in the following way:

1. Choose the Options item from the View menu, which displays the Options dialog box, shown in Figure 15 (on the next page).
2. Click on the tab corresponding to the file format for which you wish to set the default view. (The last tab, *Embedded*, is used for text that is exported to another document via Object Linking and Embedding; the first tab, *Options*, applies to all formats and will be discussed later in this section.)
3. Select a *Word wrap* option by clicking on the appropriate button:
   - If you select *No wrap*, the text you type will continue on the same line until you press the Enter key. This option is often used with Text files.
   - *Wrap to window* does just that; it starts a new line when the text reaches the right window border. This option is useful when viewing text in a small document window.

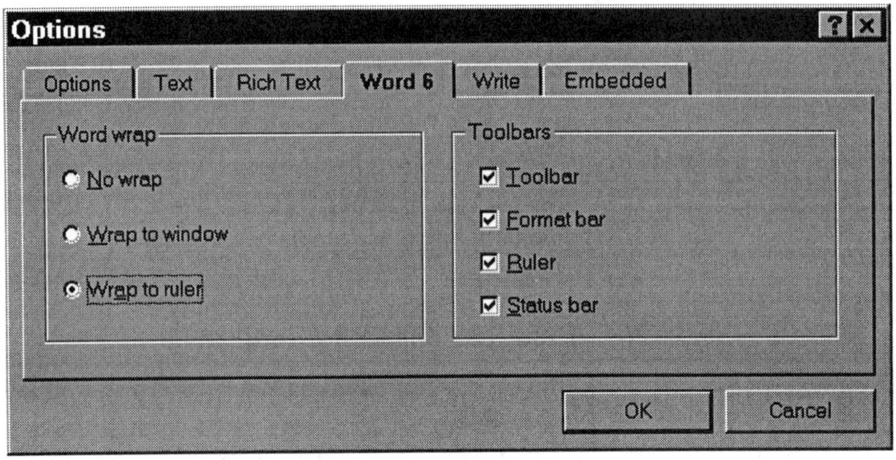


**Figure 15** The (View) Options Dialog Box

- *Wrap to ruler* begins a new line as determined by the margins and indents specified for the document and paragraph.

Note that regardless of which word wrap option is in effect, when a document is printed, the specified margins and indents will be used to determine where lines are broken.

4. In the *Toolbars* area, select the check box of each "bar" that you want displayed in the WordPad window.
5. Choose the OK command button to close the dialog box and put the new defaults into effect.

NOTE

When you choose the New command from the File menu, a dialog box (pictured below) opens from which you can select a "document type".

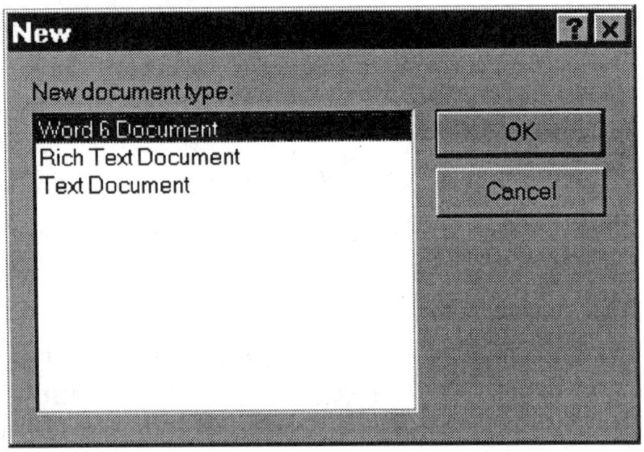

The type selected determines the way the document is displayed and the kinds of "bars" available (as specified in the Options dialog box), just as if the document were opened with that file format. It is a good idea to select *Word 6 Document* unless you have a particular reason to do otherwise.

**File format save options**

WordPad can *save* files in Word for Windows 6.0, RTF, or Text formats, regardless of which one was used to open or view the document. To save a document in one of these formats:

1. With the document displayed in the WordPad window, choose Save As from the File menu. The Save As dialog box will open, as shown in Figure 16.

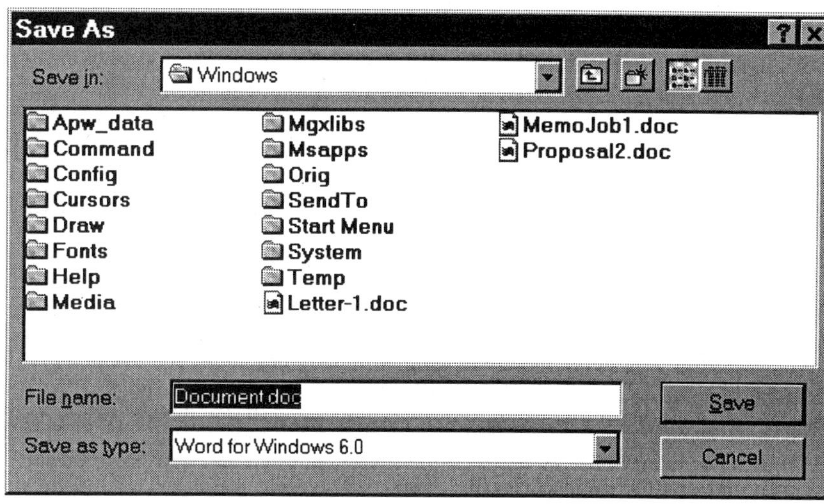


**Figure 16** The Save As Dialog Box

2. Select a file format from the *Save as type* drop-down list.
3. Now, proceed as usual: Type a name for the document in the *File name* box, select a location (disk and folder) for the file, if necessary, and choose the Save command button.

## *And a Few Frills ...*

We will close this section with a look at a few minor (but nice) WordPad features.

**Inserting the Date or Time** WordPad provides a very easy way to insert the current date or time into a document at the insertion point:

1. Choose the Date and Time item from the Insert menu or click on the Date/Time button, shown at the right, on the Toolbar. The Date and Time dialog box (Figure 17) will open.

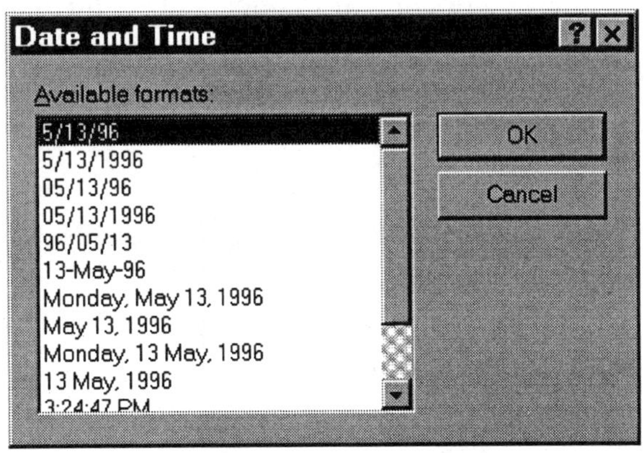


**Figure 17** The Date and Time Dialog Box

2. Select the format you want for the date or time and either double-click on it or click on it and choose the OK command button. The date or time selected will be inserted into the document at the insertion point.

**Opening Recently Saved Documents** This is a very handy, time-saving feature: To open one of the last four documents saved by WordPad, just display the File menu and choose that document from the list at the bottom of the menu (see the figure at the right).

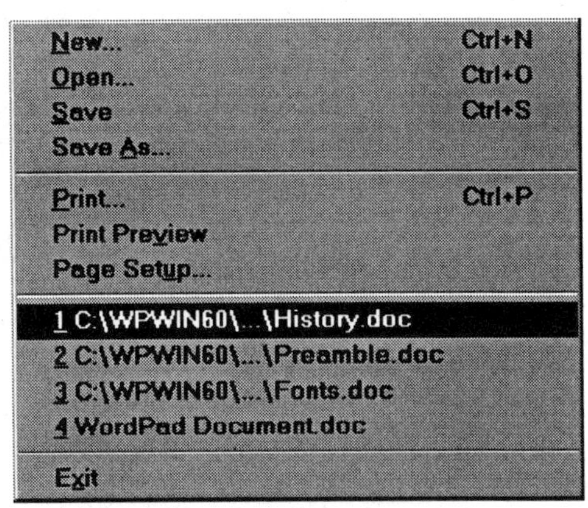

**Specifying Units of Measurement** By default, all measurements shown on the Ruler and in the Paragraph and Tabs dialog boxes are given in inches. If you want to use another unit of measurement:

1. Choose the Options command from the View menu. The Options dialog box will open.
2. Click on the Options tab in this dialog box and the page shown in Figure 18 will be displayed.

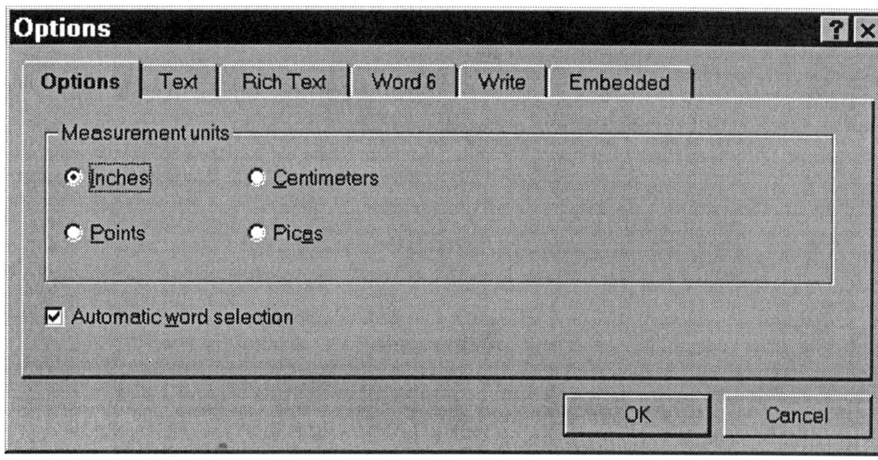


**Figure 18** The Options Page of the (View) Options Dialog Box

3. Select the appropriate *Measurement units* option button. (In one inch, there are 2.54 centimeters, 72 points, and 6 picas.)
4. Deselect the *Automatic word selection* check box if you want to be able to select parts of words. Otherwise, leave it selected; it will be easier to use the mouse to select blocks of text.
5. Choose the OK command button to put your changes into effect and close the dialog box.

7.5 TUTORIAL

Try the following exercise on your own.

1. Turn on the computer (if necessary) to start Windows 95.
2. Open WordPad and maximize its window.
3. Insert the Lab Exercises disk in its drive and open the document named *History*.

4. Use the Find and Replace utility to locate the first occurrence of the word *chip* and replace it with *microchip*:
   - Choose the Replace command from the Edit menu.
   - In the *Find what* and *Replace with* boxes, enter *chip* and *microchip*, respectively.
   - Select the *Match whole word only* so you don't locate longer words that contain the letters *chip*, but leave *Match case* deselected so that you do find *Chip* or *chip*.
   - Choose the Find Next command button. The first occurrence of the word *chip* will be highlighted.
   - Choose the Replace command button. The replacement will be made and the next occurrence of *chip* will be highlighted.
   - Choose the Close command button to close the dialog box.
5. Choose the Print Preview item from the File menu and check out the features of this command:
   - Display a single page at a time by clicking on the One Page button. (Notice that its label changes to Two Page.)
   - Page through the document by clicking on the Next Page button twice. Now, page backwards by clicking on the Prev Page button twice.
   - Try the Zoom feature by observing what happens when you click on the Zoom In button twice, then click on the Zoom Out button twice, and finally click (slowly) on the displayed page three times.
   - Click on the Close button to return to the document window.
6. Choose the Options item from the View menu and then click on the Text tab. Click on the *No wrap* option button, deselect the *Format bar* check box, and select the *Ruler* check box. Then, choose the OK button.
7. Choose the New command from the File menu, select Text Document from the list, and choose the OK button. (Respond No to the "save changes?" message.) Notice that, due to the selections made in step 6, the Format bar is hidden and the Ruler is displayed.
8. Type something (without pressing the Enter key) until you see that the line continues past the right margin marker on the Ruler (because word wrap is off).
9. Close WordPad (responding No to the "save changes?" message) and remove the diskette from its drive.

# Review Exercises

**Section 7.1**

1. In WordPad, to move the insertion point to the beginning of the current line, press the ____________ key.
2. To select a word in a WordPad document, ____________ the mouse on any letter within it.
3. To undo the last editing change in WordPad, choose Undo from the Edit menu or just press the ____________ keystroke combination.
4. True or false: To move the cursor to the end of a WordPad document, press the End key.
5. True or false: To select an entire WordPad document, move the insertion point into the left margin and double-click the mouse.
6. True or false: You can copy a selected block of text by dragging it to its new location while holding down the Ctrl key.
7. To paste a block of text into a WordPad document, click on the Toolbar button that looks like:

   a. 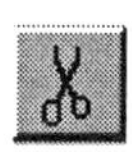 b.  c.  d. 

8. Which of the following keystroke combinations can be used to select an entire WordPad document?
   a. Ctrl+A
   b. Ctrl+V
   c. Ctrl+X
   d. Ctrl+Z

**Section 7.2**

9. To print type that is about one inch high, use a ____________ point font size.
10. To change the current typeface in WordPad, select one from the Format bar's drop-down list or choose the ____________ command from the Format menu.
11. True or false: If text is selected when you make a font change in WordPad, the font change applies only to the selected text.
12. True or false: The "strikeout" attribute (selected in the Font dialog box) causes the affected text to become unreadable.
13. Which of the following text formatting features is not accessible from WordPad's Format bar?
    a. Changing the font size.

b. Changing the font color.
c. Changing the font style to bold, italic, or underline.
d. All the above features are accessible from the Format bar.

14. Which of the following keystroke combinations will not affect the style of currently selected text?

a. Ctrl+A
b. Ctrl+B
c. Ctrl+I
d. Ctrl+U

**Section 7.3**

15. When a document is printed with the text running parallel to the long side of the page, we say it is in ____________ orientation.

16. If the left-indent for a paragraph is 1.5" and the first-line-indent is 0.5", then the text on the first line of that paragraph will begin ____________ inch(es) to the right of the left margin.

17. The default tab stops for WordPad are set every ____________ inch(es) across the page.

18. You can select an alignment option in the dialog box that opens when you choose the ____________ command from the Format menu.

19. True or false: In WordPad, it is not possible to align text in a given paragraph with both the left and right margins.

20. True or false: If you set a tab stop at the beginning of a WordPad document, then (unless you remove it later on) this tab setting will apply to the entire document.

21. True or false: When using WordPad's bullet style feature, you can elect to use either round or square bullets.

22. Which formatting feature is not available in WordPad?

a. Changing tab settings.
b. Changing page margins.
c. Changing line spacing.
d. Changing page orientation.

23. Assuming that no text is currently selected, which of the following format changes applies to all text in a WordPad document?

a. Changing the margins.
b. Changing the tab settings.
c. Changing the text alignment.
d. Changing the paragraph indentation.

24. Which of the following WordPad format settings is not displayed on the Ruler?

a. The right margin for the document.
b. The left indent for the current paragraph.
c. The alignment option for the current paragraph.
d. Custom tab stops for the current paragraph.

**Section 7.4**

25. To insert a graphic from a disk file into a WordPad document, begin by choosing the ____________ item on the Insert menu.

26. The feature of Windows that allows you to edit a graphic from *within* a WordPad document is called ____________.

27. True or false: You can delete a graphic from a WordPad document by positioning the insertion point just to the right of the graphic and pressing the Backspace key.

28. True or false: Once you have inserted a graphic into a WordPad document, it cannot be resized.

29. Which of the following techniques cannot be used to reposition a graphic at the beginning of a WordPad document?

    a. Using the mouse to drag it there.
    b. Cutting it to the Clipboard and pasting it there.
    c. Choosing the Move command from the Edit menu and then moving the graphic there using the Arrow keys.
    d. All of the above actions can be used to move the graphic.

30. After a graphic is inserted into a WordPad document, you cannot

    a. Enlarge its size.
    b. Move it to another place in the document.
    c. Copy it to another place in the document.
    d. All of the above operations can be performed on a graphic.

**Section 7.5**

31. If you want to see where the page breaks occur in a WordPad document, you must either print the document or choose the ____________ item from the File menu.

32. To change the units of measurement on the Ruler from inches to centimeters, begin by choosing the ____________ command from the View menu.

33. True or false: In the Find dialog box, if you type *the* in the *Find what* text box, select the *Match whole word only* check box, and choose the Find Next button, WordPad will search the current document for any word that contains the letters *the.*

34. True or false: To turn word wrap off for the current WordPad document, begin by choosing Options from the View menu.

35. True or false: You can have WordPad automatically insert the current date in a document by clicking on the Toolbar's Date/Time button and making a selection in the resulting dialog box.

36. The Find command on WordPad's Edit menu can be used to
    a. Locate all occurrences of the word *rich* in a document.
    b. Automatically replace the first occurrence of *rich* with *poor* in a document.
    c. Automatically replace all occurrences of *rich* with *poor* in a document.
    d. Perform all of the above tasks.
37. In WordPad's print preview window, you can
    a. Type new text.
    b. Edit existing text.
    c. Format existing text.
    d. Perform none of the above tasks.
38. Which of the following file formats does not preserve any of the text formatting features of the document being saved?
    a. Word for Windows 6.0 format
    b. Rich Text Format
    c. Text format
    d. Windows 3.1 Write format

# Lab Exercises

Work each of the following exercises at your computer. Begin by turning the machine on (if necessary) to start Windows 95 and closing any open windows.

**Lab Exercise 1 (Section 7.1)**

a. Start WordPad and maximize its window.
b. Type your name and class on separate lines, and skip a line (by pressing the Enter key twice).
c. Type the sentence: This is a test of the copy and paste operations. Then, press the Spacebar to insert a blank space after the period.
d. Select the sentence and the space that follows it. Describe how you accomplished this.
e. Copy the selected text to the Clipboard. What menu command or mouse actions did you use?
f. Paste the text from the Clipboard onto the end of the document. What menu command or mouse actions did you use?
g. Repeat step *f* four times. Try pasting the text without reselecting and recopying it. Did this work?

h. Print the document. (See Section 2.2, if necessary, for information about printing a document.)

i. Save the document if you wish and exit WordPad.

**Lab Exercise 2 (Section 7.2)**

a. Start WordPad and maximize its window.

b. Insert the Lab Exercises disk in its drive and open the document on this disk named Preamble. (See Section 2.2 for information on opening a document.)

c. Display the Format bar (if it's not currently visible) and use it to help determine the two fonts used in the Preamble document. What are they?

d. Break the title into two lines (after "Constitution"), select both lines, and center them. Describe how you centered the lines.

e. Change the font for the entire title to 19-point Arial bold. Do you have to use the Font dialog box to do this?

f. Within the preamble itself:

- Bold the phrase *We the people.*
- Italicize the word *Constitution.*
- Underline the last four words, *United States of America.*

What keystroke combination can be used to accomplish each of these text enhancements?

g. Skip a line at the bottom of the document and type your name.

h. Print the revised document (see Section 2.2, if necessary).

i. Save the modified document under another name if you wish, exit WordPad, and remove the diskette from its drive.

**Lab Exercise 3 (Section 7.2)**

a. Start WordPad and maximize its window.

b. Insert the Lab Exercises disk in its drive and open the document on this disk named Fonts.

c. Follow the instructions on the screen.

d. Skip a line at the bottom of the document and type your name.

e. Print the revised document.

f. Save the modified document under another name if you wish, exit WordPad, and remove the diskette from its drive.

**Lab Exercise 4 (Section 7.3)**

a. Start WordPad and maximize its window.

b. Insert the Lab Exercises disk in its drive and open the document on this disk named History.

c. Set all margins to 1.25" and the page orientation to landscape.

d. Type your name at the top of the document and skip a line.

e. Center the title of the document and right-align its first paragraph.

f. In the second paragraph, set the left-, right-, and first-line indents equal to 0.5".

g. In the third paragraph:

- Remove the existing tabs at 0.35" and 0.7".
- Set a tab stop at 1.25".
- Move the insertion point to the beginning of this paragraph and press the Tab key.

h. Print the *first page* of the revised document.

i. Save the modified document under another name if you wish, return the page orientation to portrait, exit WordPad, and remove the diskette from its drive.

**Lab Exercise 5 (Section 7.3)**

a. Start WordPad and maximize its window.

b. Create a document similar to the one in Figure 19:

- Set all margins to 1.5"and orientation to portrait.
- Center the title in 18-point bold Arial type.
- Use 12-point Arial type for everything else, with bold for the column headings.
- Use the bullet style feature to create the list.
- Set tab stops to create the table columns at 1.5" and every 0.75" after that.

c. At the bottom, skip two lines and type your name.

d. Print the resulting document.

e. Save the document if you wish, exit WordPad, and remove the diskette from its drive.

**Lab Exercise 6 (Section 7.4)**

a. Start WordPad and maximize its window.

b. Insert the Lab Exercises disk in its drive and open the document on this disk named Title-3.

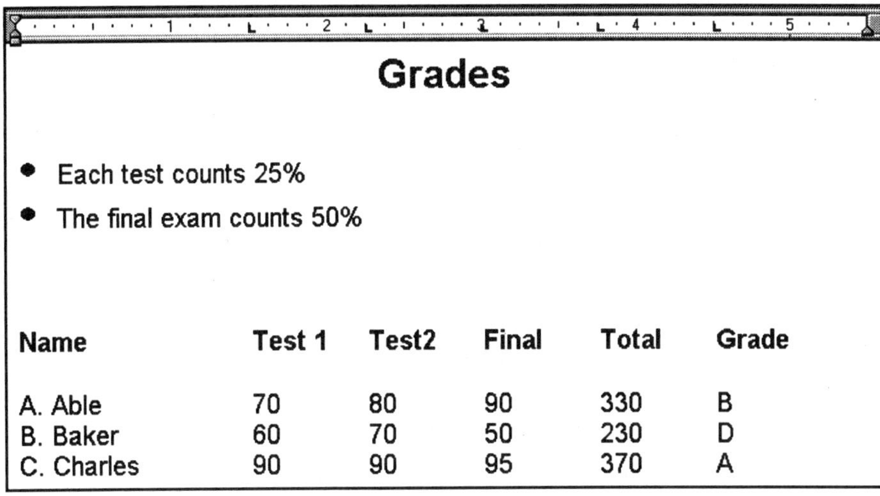

**Grades**

- Each test counts 25%
- The final exam counts 50%

| Name | Test 1 | Test2 | Final | Total | Grade |
|---|---|---|---|---|---|
| A. Able | 70 | 80 | 90 | 330 | B |
| B. Baker | 60 | 70 | 50 | 230 | D |
| C. Charles | 90 | 90 | 95 | 370 | A |

**Figure 19** The Document for Lab Exercise 5

c. Set all margins to 1.25" and the page orientation to portrait, and display the Ruler if it's currently hidden.

d. Reduce the graphic's size so that the width of its "selection box" is about 1.5" (as measured on the Ruler).

e. Create a copy of this smaller graphic, positioned just to the right of the original (on the same line).

f. Position the insertion point between the two graphics and use the Spacebar to "push" the second graphic to the right about 1".

g. Center this configuration of graphics between the margins.

h. Center the document's title and replace the given name, class, and date by your name, your class, and the current date.

i. Skip a line and insert the Shapes graphic on the Lab Exercises disk into the document at the insertion point.

j. Print the revised document.

k. Save the modified document under another name if you wish, exit WordPad, and remove the diskette from its drive.

**Lab Exercise 7 (Section 7.5)**

a. Start WordPad and maximize its window.

b. Insert the Lab Exercises disk in its drive and open the document on this disk named History.

c. Set all margins to 1" and the page orientation to portrait.

d. Use the print preview feature to determine the last word on page one of this document. (You may have to zoom in!) What is it?

e. Use WordPad's Find command to locate all occurrences of the words *computer* and *computers.*

- What word should you type in the *Find what* box so that both of these words will be searched for simultaneously?
- How many occurrences of these words were there?
- Were boldfaced words found? Were italicized words found?

f. Use the WordPad Replace command to replace (one-by-one) all occurrences of the word *chip* (but not *Chip*) with *microchip.* Which check boxes in the Replace dialog box did you select?

g. Now find all occurrences of the word *microchip*? How many are there?

h. Determine the file format of the History document. (Open the Options dialog box; this format will be the active page.) What is this format?

i. Click on the Options tab. Which wrap option is in effect?

j. Exit WordPad (responding No to the "save changes?" message) and remove the diskette from its drive.

CHAPTER 8

# Creating Graphics with Paint

Often, the best way to impart a large amount of information in a small amount of space is to use a **graphic** — a picture, diagram, graph, or other illustrative material. Windows supplies a drawing program called **Paint** to help you create graphics. In this chapter, we will describe how to use this application. You will learn:

1. How to start Paint and select the colors and tools needed to draw a graphic.
2. To use Paint's drawing tools to create lines, curves, and shapes.
3. To place text in a Paint graphic.
4. To erase portions of an existing graphic.
5. To magnify part of a graphic so that you can create or edit fine details.
6. To select part of a graphic and move, copy, flip, rotate, stretch, skew, or resize the resulting "cutout".
7. To set up the printed page and preview it before printing takes place.

# 8.1 An Introduction to Paint

Creating a *graphic* (a picture) using the Paint application is not unlike creating one using conventional artist's tools. (In fact, some Paint tools have familiar names, such as the Pencil, Brush, and Eraser.) Instead of using an artist's brush to apply paint to a canvas or other surface, Paint allows you to manipulate the tiny dots of light (*pixels*) that make up the screen image, coloring them as you wish to create various shapes. In this section, we will provide an introduction to the graphics-creation process.

## The Paint Window

To start Paint:

1. Click on the Start button to open the Start menu.
2. Point at the Programs option on this menu and at Accessories on the resulting submenu.
3. On the Accessories submenu, click on the Paint item. The Paint window, shown in Figure 1, will open.

In addition to the usual components, such as title and menu bars, the Paint window is broken into three main parts:

1. The *Tool Box* contains icons that represent the tools you use to create the graphic. The names of these tools are given in Figure 2; we will describe their use later in this chapter. Below the icons is a box (see Figure 1) that displays the options, if any, available for the selected tool. For example, for the Line tool, the Options Box (shown at the right) displays the available line widths with the current width highlighted. To select another drawing width, click on it.

2. The *drawing area* (or *work area*) is the window in which you compose the graphic. Often, the graphic is larger than the drawing area, so only part of it is displayed. In such a case, you can view other parts of the graphic by scrolling the window. To minimize scrolling:
   - Maximize the Paint window.
   - Remove the Tool Box, Color Box, and/or Status Bar from the screen by choosing the corresponding command from the View menu. (Each command is a toggle; choosing it again returns the corresponding object to the screen.)

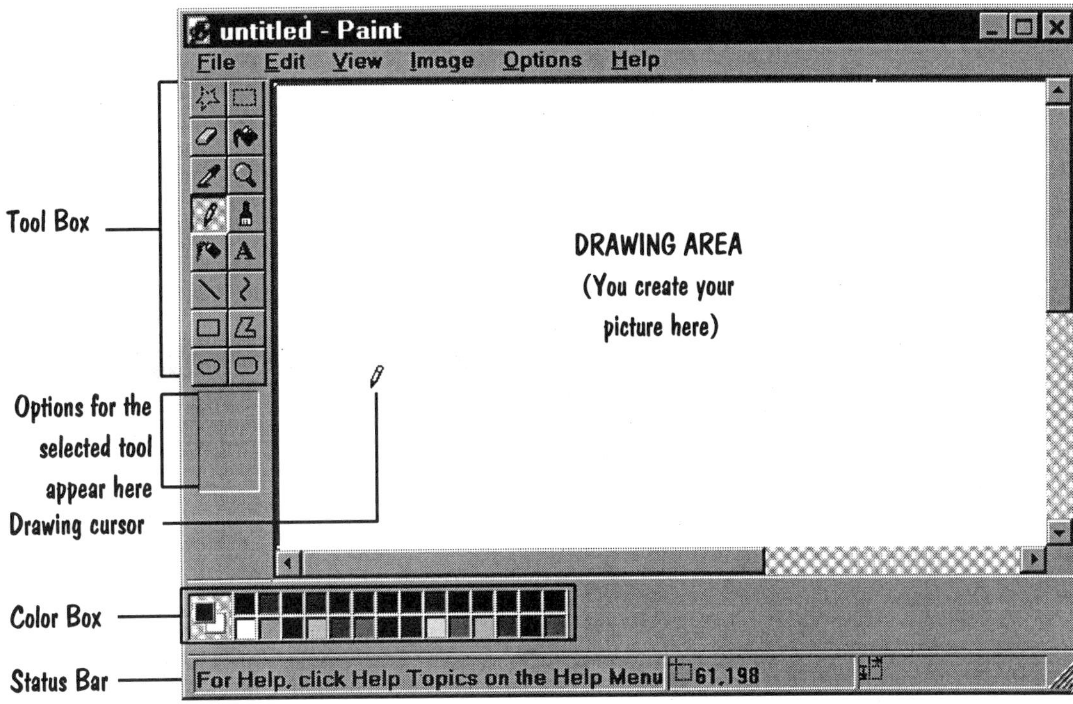


**Figure 1** The Paint Window

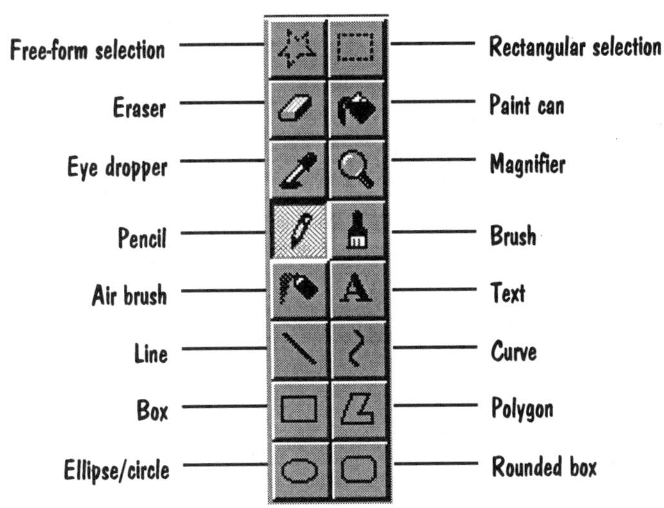


**Figure 2** The Paint Tool Box

- To expand the graphic to fill the entire screen (whether or not the Paint window is maximized), choose the View Bitmap command from the View menu. (Unfortunately, you cannot work on your drawing while View Bitmap is in effect.) Clicking anywhere on the screen returns it to "normal".

3. The *Color Box* allows you to select the colors for the object you are about to draw (by clicking on them). It also displays the current foreground and background colors (Figure 3).

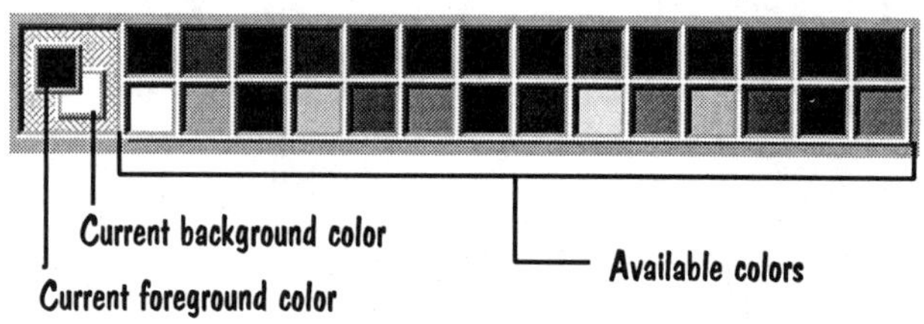


**Figure 3** The Color Box

## *Drawing a Graphic*

Using Paint to draw a graphic involves these general steps:

1. Select a *background color*, the color of the drawing area, by *right*-clicking on the desired color in the Color Box. Then, choose the New command from the File menu, which clears the drawing area and colors it as you specified.
2. For the object you are about to draw:
   - Select a drawing tool by clicking on its icon in the Tool Box. (The selected icon will appear to be "depressed".)
   - Select an option for this tool (when applicable) from the Options Box.
   - Select a *foreground color*, the color with which the object will be drawn, by *left*-clicking on the desired color in the Color Box. In some cases, you may also select a background color, which is used in different ways by different tools; this selection will not affect the color of the drawing area.

TIP

Paint makes it easy to select a foreground or background color that matches a color already present in your graphic. To do so, select the Eye Dropper tool from the Tool Box, position the mouse cursor (an "eye dropper") over an object that has the desired color, and select it as the foreground or background color by clicking the left or right button, respectively.

3. Draw the object:
   - Position the cursor at the location in the work area where you want to begin drawing.
   - Drag the cursor to draw the object; release the mouse button when you're done.
4. Repeat steps 2 and 3 until the drawing is complete.

**An example** To illustrate the drawing process, let's create the graphic image of a signature. (An example of the finished graphic is shown in Figure 4.)

- Leave the foreground and background colors at their default settings: black and white, respectively. 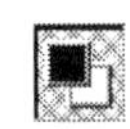
-  Select the Brush tool by clicking on its Tool Box icon. The options for Brush are various sizes and styles of "brush tips". Choose the smallest available tip from the Options Box; the one on the right end of the first row. 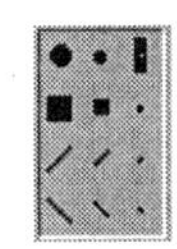
- Move the cursor (cross hairs) into the work area and position it where you want to begin drawing your first name.
- Drag the cursor to form your first and last names. (To move the

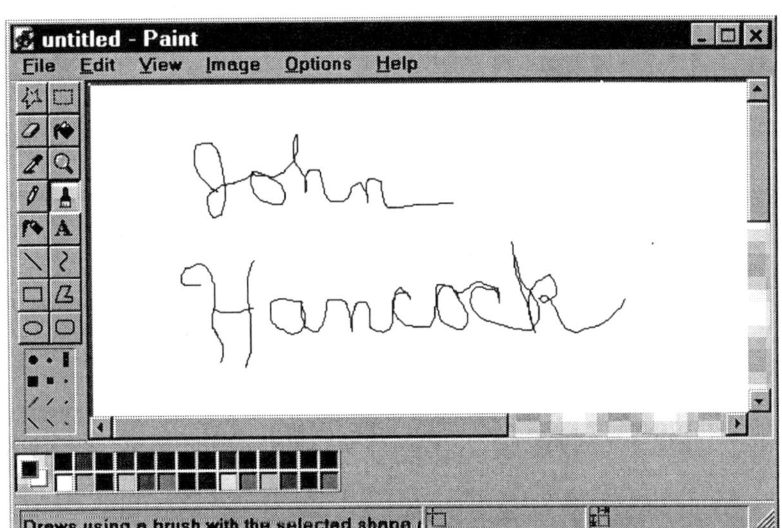


**Figure 4** Graphic Image of a Signature

cursor from one place to another without drawing, just release the mouse button, reposition the cursor, and start dragging again.)

It takes some practice to use the Brush tool. If you want to delete the part of the graphic you just drew, choose Undo from the Edit menu or press Ctrl+Z.

**NOTE**

From Windows' point of view, the graphic you are creating is a "document". It is saved, opened, and printed in the same ways as a WordPad document (see Section 2.2). Moreover, as in WordPad, the last four graphics saved in Paint are displayed at the bottom of the File menu. To open one of these files, just click on it.

**8-1 TUTORIAL**

Try the following exercise on your own.

1. Turn on the computer (if necessary) to start Windows 95.
2. Start Paint by selecting it from the Accessories submenu of the Start button, and maximize its window.
3. If the Tool Box or Color Box (see Figure 1) is not visible on the screen, display it by choosing the corresponding item from the View menu.
4. Set the foreground color to red by left-clicking on the red square in the Color box; set the background color to yellow by right-clicking on the yellow square in the Color Box.
5. Color the entire drawing area in the background color by choosing the New command from the File menu.
6. Select the Brush tool from the Tool Box by clicking on its icon. The "brush tip" options will be displayed in the Options Box.
7. Select the smallest round brush tip by clicking on the right-most icon in the top row of the Options Box.
8. Position the mouse cursor inside the drawing area (it will become a pair of cross hairs) and draw a line across the screen by dragging the cursor horizontally to the right.
9. Delete the line you have just drawn by choosing the Undo command from the Edit menu (or by pressing Ctrl+Z).
10. Experiment with the Brush tool by choosing different brush tips to see their effect while drawing whatever you want. Select a different foreground color now and then. Note the following points:

- To clear the entire picture from the screen, choose the New command from the File menu.
- To print your graphic, choose the Print command from the File menu (see Section 2.2 for information about printing).
- To save your graphic, choose the Save command from the File menu (see Section 2.2 for information about saving a file).

11. Close the Paint window. Respond No to the "save changes?" message unless you want to save your graphic.

# *8.2 Using the Drawing Tools*

Most of the tools in the Paint Tool Box (Figure 2) are used to create the curves, shapes, and text that make up your graphic. We will describe how to use these kinds of tools in this section. Tools that are used in modifying the graphic will be discussed in Section 8.3.

## *Creating Lines, Curves, and Other Strokes*

The Pencil, Brush, Airbrush, Line, and Curve tools are used to form the lines, curves, and other "paint strokes" in the graphic. Each of these tools is used in the same basic way:

**The basic technique**

1. Select the tool by clicking on its icon in the Tool Box.
2. Select a drawing option (if available) from the Options Box.
3. Select a new foreground or background color, if you want.
4. Position the cursor in the drawing area where you want the paint stroke to begin. (The shape of the cursor depends on the tool selected; it may be cross hairs, a stylized pencil, or a tiny spray can.)
5. If you want to paint with the foreground color, press the left mouse button; to paint with the background color, press the right mouse button.
6. Continuing to depress the mouse button, create the stroke by dragging the cursor to another position in the drawing area.
7. When the stroke is complete, release the mouse button.

Of course, each tool has its own special capabilities; we will discuss them on the following pages.

TIP

To some extent, creating graphics with Paint is a trial-and-error process. Occasionally, while creating an object, it will become clear that you are not getting the desired effect. In such a case, to cancel the operation while you are still dragging the cursor, just tap the other mouse button or press the Escape key. Also, remember that you can undo an operation that you have just completed by choosing Undo from the Edit menu. (The last three changes can be undone in reverse order.)

**The Pencil Tool** The **Pencil** is a basic drawing tool. It is used to draw fine free-form curves, just as if you were using a pencil on paper. There are no options for this tool; all lines drawn with it are one pixel ("dot") wide. The Pencil does have a nice feature, though. If you hold down the Shift key while dragging the cursor, the result will be a straight line that is perfectly horizontal, vertical, or diagonal (inclined at a 45° angle), depending on the direction you move the mouse.

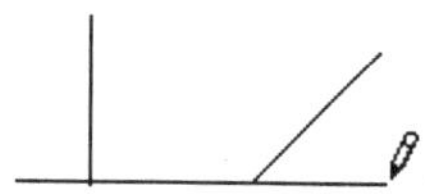

**The Brush Tool** The **Brush** tool is used like an artist's paint brush; it creates free-form curves using several different brush widths and styles, which are selected from the Options Box. The effect of selecting a particular option is shown in Figure 5.

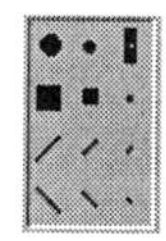

**Figure 5** Brush Tip Effects for the Brush Tool

**The Airbrush Tool** The **Airbrush** tool draws a free-form figure made up of a spray of dots. The faster you move the Airbrush, the finer the spray, as illustrated below:

The Options Box for the Airbrush tool, which is shown at the right, allows you to select from among three different spray widths.

**The Line Tool** The **Line** tool is used to draw straight lines (it can *only* draw straight lines). Several line widths are available, and are selected in the Options Box (shown at the right). Holding down the Shift key while dragging the Line cursor creates perfectly horizontal, vertical, or diagonal (inclined at 45°) lines.

**The Curve Tool** Although the Pencil and Brush can draw curves, the result is a *free-form* curve. Unless you have a very steady hand, the result may not be as smooth as you might like. The **Curve** tool (which has the same available line widths as the Line tool) draws smooth, uniform curves, but is somewhat tricky to use.

In using the Curve tool, you first construct a line and then deform this line into the desired curve by "bending" the former once or twice with the aid of the mouse. To be more specific, after selecting the tool and the appropriate line width and drawing color:

1. Position the cursor (cross hairs) in the drawing area where you want the curve to begin, press the mouse button, drag the cursor to the other endpoint, and release the button. A straight line now connects the curve's two endpoints.
2. Drag the cursor away from the line in the direction you want it to bend. As you do, you will see a curve forming. Continue to drag the cursor around, until this part of the curve has the desired shape; then release the mouse button. If the curve's appearance is satisfactory, double-click the mouse to complete the operation.
3. If you want the curve to bend in a second direction, drag the cursor in this direction. When the curve has the desired appearance, release the mouse button. The curve is now anchored in place.

Let's try a specific example. Select the Curve tool from the Tool Box and the second thinnest line width from the Options Box. Now:

- Drag a vertical line that is about two inches in length (as shown in

Figure 6a).

- Position the cursor about one-half inch below the top of the line, drag it to the right as in Figure 6b, and release the mouse button. Notice that the curve bends to the right as you drag the cursor.
- Position the cursor about one-half inch above the bottom of the current curve, drag the cursor to the left as in Figure 6c, and release the mouse button. Notice that the curve has bent back to the left. When you release the button this time, the curve becomes anchored in place.

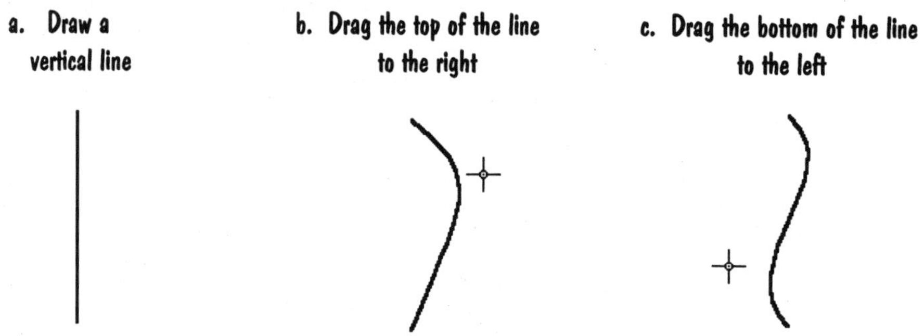


**Figure 6** Using the Curve Tool

## *Creating Geometric Shapes*

The Box, Rounded Box, Circle/Ellipse, and Polygon tools are used to create the corresponding geometric figures. To use one of these tools:

1. Select the tool by clicking on its icon in the Tool Box.
2. From the Options Box (shown at the right), select one of three border/fill options:

**Border/fill options**

   - *Hollow* — Only the border of the figure will be drawn (see the left box in Figure 7).
   - *Filled* — The border will be drawn and the figure will be filled with color (see the center box in Figure 7).
   - *Borderless* — The figure will be filled with color, but the border will not be drawn (see the right box in Figure 7).
3. Select new foreground and background colors (if you want) from the Color Box. These are used to color the figure, as follows:

**Figure 7** Hollow, Filled, and Borderless Boxes

**Drawing colors**

- If you create the figure using the left mouse button, the current foreground color is used to draw the figure's border; the current background color is used to fill its interior.
- If you create the figure using the right mouse button, the current background color is used to draw the figure's border; the current foreground color is used to fill its interior.

**Border width**

4. If the figure is to have a border, select its width by clicking on the Line tool and selecting from among the five choices shown in the Options Box. (If you do this, you will have to reselect the tool you want to use to create the geometric shape.)
5. Position the cursor (cross hairs) in the drawing area and draw the figure. The way in which this is done varies a little from tool to tool and will be described below, when each tool is discussed.

**The Box Tool** The **Box** tool draws rectangles and squares. (Examples of shapes drawn with the Box tool are shown in Figure 7.) To use this tool:

1. Select the Box icon from the Tool Box; then select a border/fill option, drawing colors, and a border width, as described earlier.
2. Position the mouse cursor at one corner of the box-to-be and drag the cursor toward the opposite corner. As you do, the corresponding rectangle will be displayed on the screen. To draw a perfectly square box, hold down the Shift key while dragging the cursor.
3. When the box is the correct size, release the mouse button.

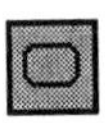

**The Rounded Box Tool** The **Rounded Box** tool draws a rectangle (or square, if you hold down the Shift key while dragging the cursor) with rounded corners. This tool is used in exactly the same way as the Box tool.

**The Ellipse/Circle Tool** The **Ellipse/Circle** tool is used to draw ellipses and circles. Here are a few examples:

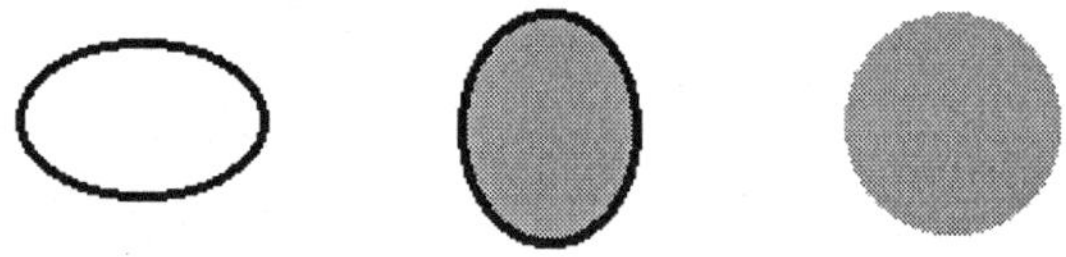

To use the Ellipse/Circle tool:

1. Select the Ellipse/Circle icon from the Tool Box; then select a border/fill option, drawing colors, and a border width, as described earlier.
2. Picture the ellipse-to-be enclosed in an imaginary box. Now, position the mouse cursor at one corner of this box and drag the cursor toward the opposite corner. As you do, the corresponding ellipse will be displayed on the screen. To draw a circle, hold down the Shift key while dragging the cursor.
3. When the ellipse or circle is the correct size, release the mouse button.

**The Polygon Tool** The **Polygon** tool helps you draw a many-sided enclosed figure. Here are some examples of the kinds of figures you can draw using the Polygon tool:

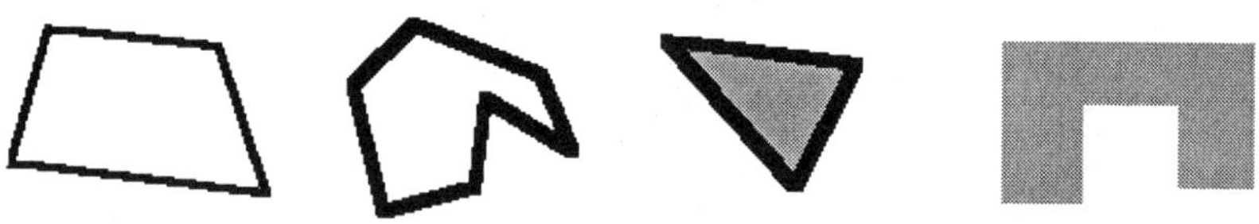

Although the same border/fill options are available as for the Box tool, the Polygon tool is used in a very different way. Here's how it works:

1. Select the Polygon icon from the Tool Box; then select a border/fill option, drawing colors, and a border width, as described earlier.
2. Position the mouse cursor (cross hairs) at one of the polygon's vertices, drag the cursor to form the first side, and release the mouse button.
3. To construct the rest of the sides, except the last, click the mouse on each successive vertex. As you do, the side joining the previous vertex to the new one will be displayed.
4. To construct the last side of the polygon (the one that encloses the figure), double-click the mouse on the last vertex. It will automatically be joined to the first vertex by a straight line.

If you want to construct a side that is horizontal, vertical, or inclined at a 45° angle, hold down the Shift key while dragging or clicking.

**The Paint Can Tool** All the tools we have discussed so far draw objects on the screen. The **Paint Can** does not; it fills an existing enclosed figure with color or changes the color of a previously filled region. To use this tool:

1. Select the Paint Can icon from the Tool Box.
2. In the Color Box, set either the foreground or background color to the desired color.
3. Position the mouse cursor (a tiny paint can) anywhere within the figure to be colored. For small regions, make sure the tip of the "pouring paint" is inside the region.
4. Click a mouse button to color the region. If you click the left mouse button, the figure will be filled with the foreground color; if you click the right mouse button, the background color will be used.

TIP

Graphics programs like Paint are not usually used for precision work, such as technical drawing. Nevertheless, Paint supplies a very useful tool for aligning and correctly sizing objects. The Status bar at the bottom of the Paint window constantly displays *cursor coordinates,* (shown on the left in the figure below), which give the precise location of the mouse cursor relative to the upper-left corner of the drawing area. For example, the coordinates shown here indicate that the cursor is 416 pixels from the left border of the drawing area and 214 pixels down from the top border. (The use of cursor coordinates is demonstrated in the Tutorial at the end of this section.)

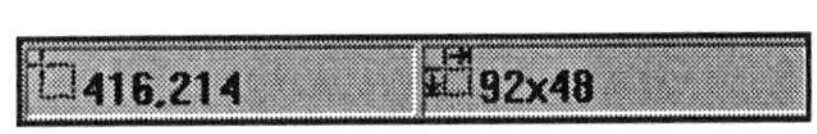


A second set of coordinates is displayed on the Status bar when you are creating a box, rounded box, ellipse/circle, or polygon. They give the width and height of the object being drawn. For example, in the figure above, the current width of the object is 92 pixels and its current height is 48 pixels.

## Inserting Text into a Graphic

Although a graphic can often convey a thought without any explanatory text, it sometimes needs a few words to clarify the message. Through the use of the **Text** tool, Paint allows you to place text in a graphic in your choice of color, design, style, and size. To use this tool to insert text:

1. Select the Text icon from the Tool Box.
2. Select a foreground color from the Color Box (by clicking on it) for the color of the text to be inserted. (You should also select a background color from the Color Box if you want the new text displayed on a colored background.)
3. Drag the mouse cursor (cross hairs) to form a box in the drawing area within which you will place the text. Don't be overly concerned about sizing this window to fit the given text; its size (and position) can be adjusted later.
4. Release the mouse button. After a few moments, the Fonts window (which is usually referred to as the *Text Toolbar*) will open somewhere on the screen. (If it doesn't, choose the Text Toolbar item from the View menu.)

The text frame you have created will sprout eight "sizing handles" and an insertion point will appear in its upper-left corner.

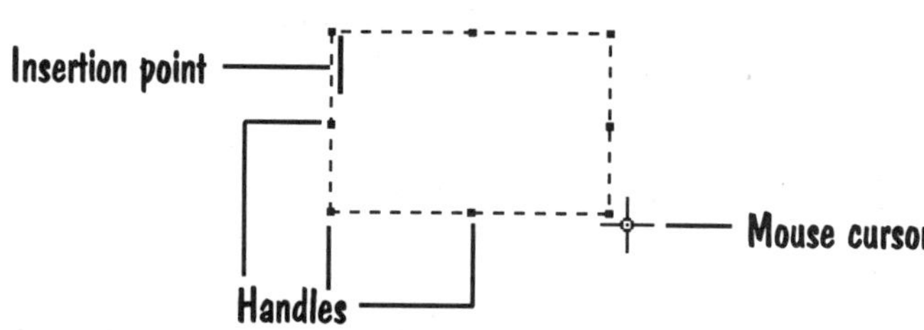


5. Using this Text Toolbar (Fonts window):
   - Select a *typeface* for the text from the first drop-down list. The typeface determines the overall design or "look" of the characters. (The typeface selected in the figure above is *Arial*.)
   - Select a *font size* for the text from the second drop-down list. The font size is (roughly) the height the characters will be on the printed page, measured in *points*, where 72 points equal one inch.

- Select *attributes* for the text (if you want) by clicking on one or more of the buttons. Here are examples of the resulting effects:

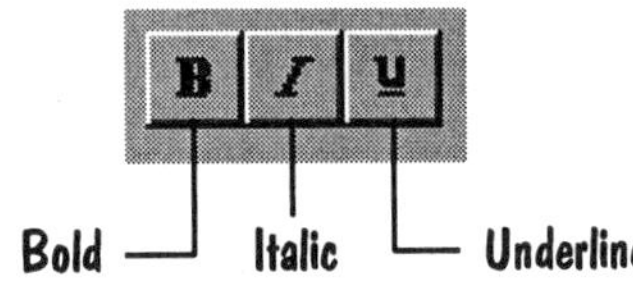


**Bold** *Italic*

Underline

6. From the Options Box, select either *opaque* mode, the top option, or *transparent* mode, which is the one selected in the figure at the right. (As an alternative, you can toggle between these modes by choosing the Draw Opaque command from the Options menu.)

- If you use opaque mode, the text you type will appear within a frame that is colored in the current background color, as shown at the right.

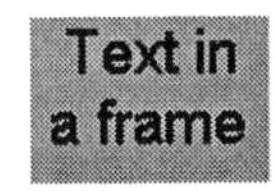


- In transparent mode, the text is displayed without the colored frame.

7. Click inside the text frame and type the desired text. When the text reaches the right frame border, it will wrap (possibly in the middle of a word) to the next line. (The text box will extend, if necessary, in the vertical direction to accommodate the text you are typing.) You can start a new line manually by pressing the Enter key.
8. To complete the text-insertion operation (to "paste down" the text), click anywhere outside the text frame.

TIP

Until you paste the text in place (that is, while the frame outline is still visible), it is possible to make changes to the text and its background. You can:

- Modify the text as you would in WordPad (see Section 2.2).
- Change the frame mode from transparent to opaque or vice-versa.
- Change the color of the text or its background (if any).
- Increase the size of the text frame by dragging one of its handles in the desired direction away from the existing "box". For example, to widen the box, position the mouse cursor over the middle handle on the right side of the frame (it will become a two-headed arrow when it's positioned properly), and drag it to the right. When you release the mouse button, the frame will redraw to the new size and the text that had been wrapped to a new line will rearrange itself accordingly within the new frame (see below).

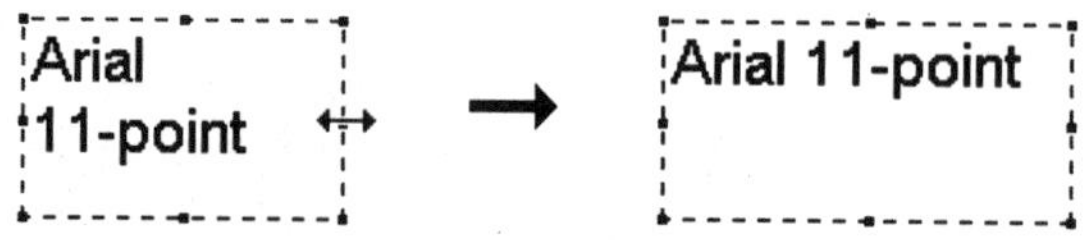


- Move the text frame (and enclosed text) by positioning the mouse pointer over any part of the border that is not a handle and dragging the frame to its new location.

After the text-insertion operation is complete, the text (and its background, if applicable) becomes a single object in the graphic. At this point, the block of text can be moved (as described in Section 8.4), but none of the other operations listed above can be carried out.

TUTORIAL

Try the following exercise on your own, creating a drawing of the truck shown in Figure 8. Remember: To start over while creating an object, press the Escape key; to undo the last change to the graphic, press Ctrl+Z.

1. Start Windows 95 (if necessary) by turning on the computer.
2. Start Paint by selecting it from the Accessories submenu of the Start button, and maximize its window.
3. Draw the road:

   - Select the Line tool from the Tool Box (see Figure 2) by clicking on it and select the second smallest line thickness in the Options Box (see Figure 1) by clicking on it.
   - Position the Line cursor in the drawing area about one inch from the lower-left corner, hold down the Shift key (for a horizontal line), and drag the cursor to the right side of the drawing area.

   - Select the Airbrush tool from the Tool Box, and select a medium thickness from the Options Box.
   - Position the Airbrush cursor just under the left edge of the line you've just drawn and drag the cursor slowly across the screen under this line.

4. Draw the truck tires:

   - Select the Ellipse/Circle tool from the Tool Box and the hollow (top) option from the Options Box.
   - Draw the rear tire by positioning the cursor about one inch above the road, holding down the Shift key (for a circle), and dragging the cursor down and to the right until the circle touches the road.
   - Use the cursor coordinates on the Status bar to help create a

**Figure 8** Truck Graphic for Tutorial 8.2

front tire of exactly the same size: Position the cursor at the top of the rear tire and note the second cursor coordinate. Then, for the front tire, position the cursor so that its second coordinate has this value, hold down the Shift key, and drag a circle until it touches the road.

5. Draw the truck's trailer:

   - Select the Box tool from the Tool Box and the "filled box with border" option (the middle one) from the Options Box.
   - Select a foreground of black (by clicking on this color in the Color Box) and a background of light gray (by *right*-clicking on this color in the Color Box).
   - Start near the rear wheel and drag a box that makes a rectangle about 2" high and 4" long.

6. Draw the lower (shaded) part of the cab of the truck:

   - Select a background color of white from the Color Box.

   - Select the Polygon tool from the Tool Box and the "hollow" option from the Options Box.
   - Hold down the Shift key (for horizontal, vertical, and diagonal lines) and drag the Polygon cursor from corner to corner of the polygon that makes up the lower cab. At each corner, click the mouse to end the previous line segment before dragging the next one. Double-click on the last corner to close the polygon.

   - Fill the polygon with color: Select a foreground color of dark gray from the Color Box, select the Paint Can tool, and click inside your polygon.

   - Select a foreground color of black, select the Line tool, hold down the Shift key, and draw the vertical line that forms the door.

7. Continuing to use the Line tool, draw the four lines that make up the window area of the cab.
8. Insert the text (Sam's Delivery Service) on the truck's trailer using 24-point, boldface type:

   - Select the Text tool from the Tool Box.
   - Drag the cursor to form a box (a text frame) just within the trailer rectangle. When you release the mouse button, the Fonts window will appear.
   - In the Fonts window, select Arial from the first drop-down list, "24" from the second, and click on the Bold button.
   - Click within the text frame and type *Sam's*, *Delivery*, and *Service*, pressing the Enter key after each of the first two words. (If the text doesn't fit, select a smaller font size from the Fonts window.) Now, center each word on the trailer by inserting spaces (using the Spacebar) before that word.
   - Click outside the text frame to complete the operation.
9. Save and/or print the graphic, just as you would in WordPad, and exit Paint.

# 8.3 Editing a Graphic

At some point in the process of creating a graphic, you will probably want to *edit* it — to alter the graphic to correct mistakes or improve its looks. We have already described one way to edit a graphic: You can use the Undo command on the Edit menu to undo the last three operation you have carried out. This section discusses other, more specialized editing features of Paint.

## Erasing Mistakes

The **Eraser** is the editing tool you're likely to use the most. It works on your electronic graphic in the same general way that an ordinary eraser works on a penciled drawing. However, the Eraser tool is more powerful:

**Basic operation of the Eraser tool**

- If you left-drag the Eraser's cursor, it wipes out everything in its path; if you right-drag the cursor, it removes only the current foreground color.
- The area that is erased is replaced with the current background color, which need not be the color of the graphic's background.

More specifically, here's how to use this tool:

1. Select the Eraser tool from the Tool Box by clicking on its icon.
2. Select an eraser size from the Options Box (shown at the right) by clicking on it. The smaller sizes are best for fine work; the larger ones are best at erasing large areas.

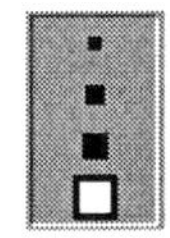

3. Set the background color as desired by right-clicking on the corresponding square in the Color Box. (This color will replace the ones erased.)
4. If you only want to erase one specific color, set the foreground to this color by left-clicking on the corresponding square in the Color Box.
5. Position the mouse cursor (a small square) where you want to begin erasing, and drag it across the area to be erased. Remember:
   - Left-dragging the cursor replaces everything in its path with the current background color.
   - Right-dragging the cursor replaces only the current foreground color with the current background color.

**An example** Figure 9 shows the two ways the Eraser tool can be used. In both erasures, the background color was set to white and the foreground color was set to black. The left erasure was accomplished with a left-drag; it replaces everything with white. The right erasure is the result of a right-drag; only black is replaced with white.

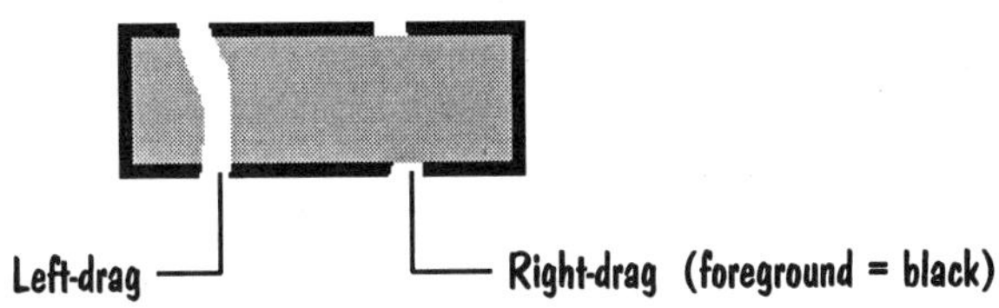


**Figure 9** Using the Eraser Tool

## *Zooming In on the Graphic*

At times, you may want to change small details in a graphic. For these occasions, Paint supplies the Zoom command, which allows you to magnify a small part of the graphic so that it fills the Paint window. Once the graphic is suitably enlarged, you can even edit it pixel by pixel. (Recall that *pixels* are the small dots of light that make up the screen image.)

To zoom in on a graphic, point at the Zoom command on the View menu. The resulting submenu has five options. Choosing:

**Zoom menu options**

- *Normal Size* returns the graphic to its original size if it currently magnified.
- *Large Size* magnifies the image by a factor of four (400 percent). When you choose Large Size, scroll bars may appear in the Paint window so that you can view the entire image. Figure 10b shows the result of applying the Large Size command to the graphic in Figure 10a and then scrolling to display the dog's nose.
- *Custom Size* opens the following dialog box:

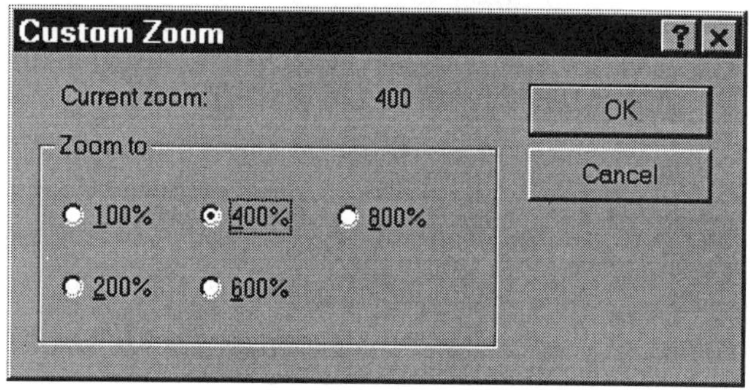


By selecting the appropriate option button and choosing the OK command button, you can magnify the original graphic one, two, four, six, or eight times. (Figure 11a shows the original dog graphic enlarged 600 percent.)

**Figure 10a** "Normal" Zoom Size

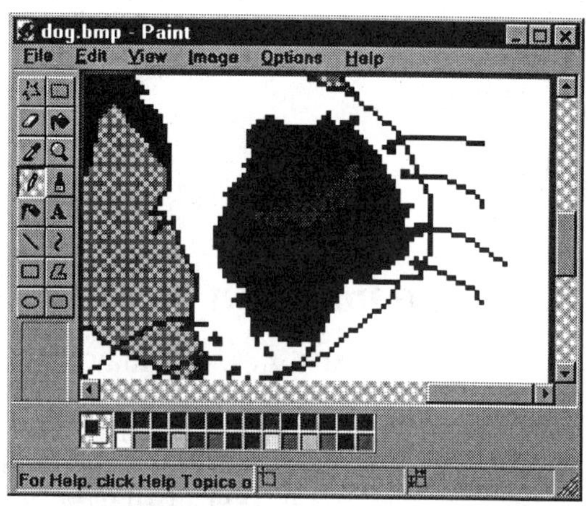


**Figure 10b** "Large" Zoom Size

- *Show Grid* is a toggle that turns the pixel grid on or off (Figure 11b shows the grid displayed). By magnifying to a relatively large size (600% or 800%) and turning on the grid, you can edit the graphic pixel by pixel, obtaining the finest detail possible.
- *Show Thumbnail* is also a toggle; it turns the Thumbnail window on and off. Displaying this window gives you an overall view of the normal-sized graphic as you work on the close-up. The Thumbnail window can be moved around the screen and resized, if so desired.

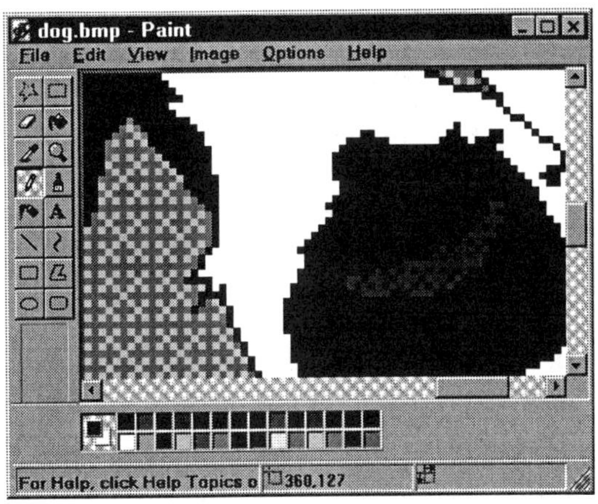


**Figure 11a** Custom Zoom — 600%

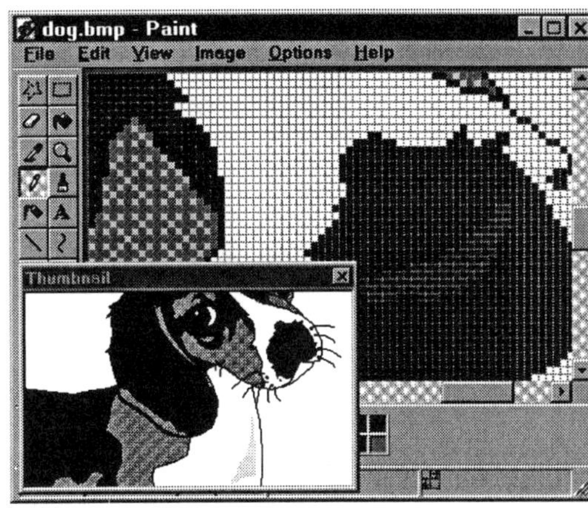


**Figure 11b** Grid and Thumbnail On

TIP

Here is perhaps the easiest way to edit individual pixels in a graphic:

1. Use the Custom Size option on the Zoom menu to magnify the image to 600 or 800 percent.
2. Scroll to the part of the image you wish to edit.
3. Select the Pencil tool from the Tool Box.
4. In the Color Box, set the foreground color to the color you want to paint in, set the background color to the that of the background area in which you are working.
5. Then, using the Pencil cursor as a pointer, just left-click in any grid square that you want to add to the graphic, and right-click in a grid square if you want to erase it from the graphic.

To edit larger areas, involving a relatively large number of pixels, you may want to use other tools, such as the Brush, Eraser, or Paint Can.

**Magnifier tool** The **Magnifier** tool provides another way to zoom in on your graphic. It is a little easier to use, but not as versatile as the Zoom command. To use this tool:

1. Click on the Magnifier icon in the Tool Box.
2. You now have two choices. Either
   - Click on the desired magnification factor in the Options Box (shown at the right). Notice that you can magnify the image two, six, or eight times (but not four times, as with the Zoom command).

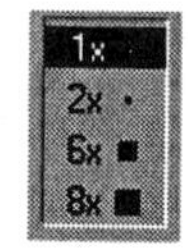


   *or*

   - Move the mouse cursor into the drawing area. A box containing a magnifying glass icon will appear. Position the box around the part of the graphic you wish to magnify and click the mouse button. (The size of the box and the degree of magnification depend on the last option button selected in the Custom Zoom dialog box.)

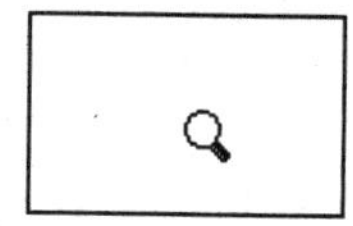

## *Selecting Part of a Graphic*

One of the major advantages of Paint over conventional drawing is its ability to move, copy, and resize any object in the graphic. Before performing one of these operations, you must select the object to be manipulated; in Paint parlance, you must "define a cutout". A **cutout** is a region in the graphic that has been selected using one of Paint's two selection tools:

- The **Rectangular Selection** tool is the easier of the two to use, but it is less versatile. This tool is used when you can place a rectangular box around the object to be selected without including part of another object (see Figure 12a).
- The **Free-form Selection** tool is generally used in situations where

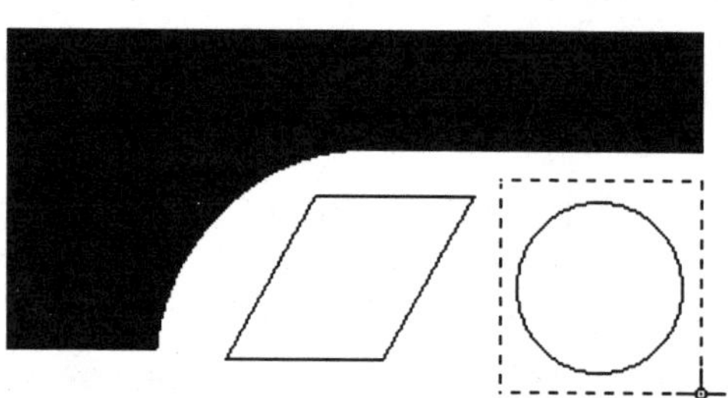

**Figure 12a** Rectangular Selection

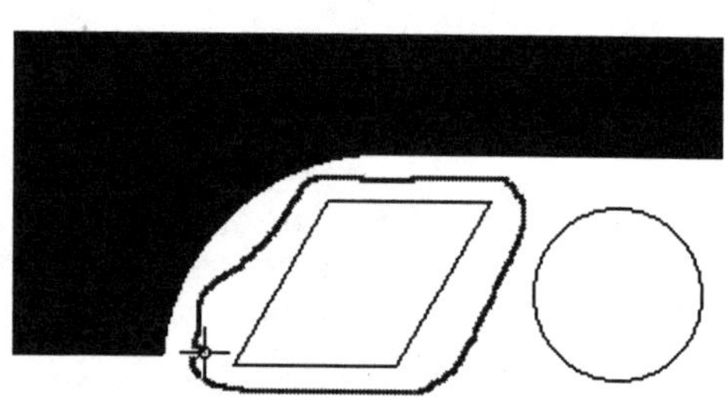

**Figure 12b** Free-form Selection

rectangular selection doesn't work; free-form selection creates an irregularly shaped cutout (Figure 12b).

**Rectangular selection**

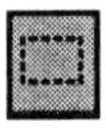

To use the Rectangular Selection tool:

1. Select its icon from the Tool Box.
2. From the Options Box, select either *opaque* mode, the top option, or *transparent* mode, which is the one selected in the figure at the right. (As an alternative, you can toggle between these modes by choosing the Draw Opaque command from the Options menu.)

   - If you use opaque mode, the resulting selection will consist of everything within the selected region, both foreground and background colors.
   - In transparent mode, the resulting selection does not include anything colored in the background color. This is the mode that is normally used with cutouts.

   We will provide examples of the two selection modes in Section 8.4, while discussing how cutouts are moved and copied.
3. Position the mouse cursor (cross hairs) at one corner of the cutout, the region that contains the object(s) to be selected.
4. Press the mouse button and drag the cursor to the opposite corner of the cutout. As you drag, a box will move with the cursor, indicating the selected region (see Figure 12a).
5. When the cutout is defined as you want, release the mouse button. A "dashed" rectangular box delineates the selected region.

**Free-form selection**

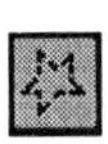

To use the Free-form Selection tool:

1. Select its icon from the Tool Box.
2. From the Options Box, select either *opaque* mode, the top option, or *transparent* mode, which is the one selected in the figure at the right. (See the description of the two modes under "rectangular selection".) The transparent mode is almost always used with free-form selection.

3. Position the mouse cursor in the drawing area where you want to start the cutout, the region that contains the object(s) to be manipulated.
4. Press the mouse button and drag the cursor, creating a free-form curve that defines the cutout (see Figure 12b).
5. Release the mouse button. A "dashed" rectangular box, like the one in rectangular selection, delineates the selected region.

**NOTE**

Whether you use rectangular or free-form selection:

- To abort the selection process while you are dragging the cursor to define the cutout, press the Escape key.
- To deselect the selected object, which causes the selection box to disappear, click anywhere outside the box.

**Deleting a cutout**

Here's a simple example of how cutouts are used. Suppose you want to delete an object from a graphic; say, the circle in Figure 12a. Usually the easiest way to do this is to select the circle (that is, define a cutout that includes the circle), as in Figure 12a, and then press the Delete key. The cutout and the object it contains will be replaced by the current background color, so be sure that this color is set properly before pressing the Delete key.

We will discuss many other ways in which cutouts can be manipulated in Section 8.4.

**8-3 TUTORIAL**

Try the following exercise on your own.

1. Start Windows 95 (if necessary) by turning on the computer.
2. Start Paint, maximize its window, and insert the Lab Exercises disk in its drive.
3. Open the Truck-2 bitmap image on this disk.
4. Use the Zoom submenu of the View menu to:
   - Choose the Large Size command.
   - Turn off (if necessary) the Show Grid option.
   - Turn on (if necessary) the Show Thumbnail option.
5. Scroll the Paint window so that the front end of the truck is visible.
6. Modify the slanted part of the hood, as follows:

   - Erase the slanted line: Select the Eraser tool from the Tool Box, select the smallest size in the Options Box, set the background color to white, and drag the cursor over the line.

   - Using the Curve tool with the second thinnest line option, put a curved line in its place. (See section 8.2.)
   - Turn on the Show Grid command on the Zoom submenu of the View menu.

   - Fill in the modified area with color: Set the foreground color to dark gray (top row, second from the left), select the Brush tool from the Tool Box and a medium brush tip from the

Options Box, and drag the cursor over the appropriate white squares in the grid to turn them gray.

7. Return the magnification to normal size: Select the Magnifier tool from the Tool Box and click on "1x" in the Options Box. (You can also do this by choosing Normal Size from the Zoom submenu of the View menu.) 

8. Delete the word *Sam's* from the side of the truck:

   - Set the background color to light gray.
   - Select the Rectangular Selection tool from the Tool Box. 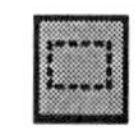
   - Use the mouse to drag a box around the word to be deleted and then release the mouse button.
   - Press the Delete key.

9. Exit Paint, responding No to the "save changes?" message.

# 8.4 Manipulating Cutouts

Once you have *defined a cutout* — selected an area in the graphic — using either the Free-form or Rectangular Selection tool (as described in Section 8.3) you can:

- Delete the cutout.
- Cut or copy the cutout to the Clipboard.
- Save the cutout in a graphic file on disk.
- Move, copy, or sweep the cutout to another part of the graphic.
- Resize the cutout.
- Flip, rotate, stretch, or tilt the cutout, or invert its colors.

In this section, we will describe how to perform these operations.

## Basic Operations on Cutouts

**Deleting a cutout**

As we mentioned in Section 8.3, a convenient way to remove objects from your graphic is to select them (using one of the selection tools), defining a cutout, and then delete the cutout. To delete a cutout, perform any of the following actions:

- Press the Delete key.
- Choose the Clear Selection command from the Edit menu.

- Right-click inside the cutout and choose the Clear Selection command from the resulting pop-up menu.

NOTE

When you "delete" a cutout, you actually replace it with the current background color, as indicated in the Color Box. Unless you're trying for some special effect, you'll want to make sure that the current background color matches the color behind the cutout. If you forget this fact, you may wonder why the rectangular cutout you just deleted was replaced by, say, a red box on the screen.

**Cut, copy, and paste**

A cutout, like any other selected information, can be cut or copied to the Clipboard, and then pasted into Paint or another Windows application (see Section 2.3). Recall that when information is *cut* to the Clipboard, it is deleted from the current document, but when it is *copied* to the Clipboard, the current document remains unchanged. Here's how these procedures work in Paint.

- To *cut* a cutout to the Clipboard, choose the Cut command from the Edit menu or right-click inside the cutout and choose the Cut command from the pop-up menu. The cutout will be deleted from the current graphic (and replaced by the current background color).
- To *copy* a cutout to the Clipboard, choose the Copy command from the Edit menu or the right-click pop-up menu.
- To *paste* a cutout from the Clipboard into a Paint graphic, choose the Paste command from the Edit menu or the right-click pop-up menu. The cutout is pasted into the upper-left corner of the drawing area and remains *active*, as indicated by the selection box enclosing it. An active cutout can continue to be manipulated; in particular, it can be moved (as described shortly) to another location in the drawing area.

TIP

Once it is selected, a cutout remains active, outlined by the selection box, until it is *pasted down* (anchored in place). To paste down a cutout, perform any of the following actions:

- Click the mouse outside the cutout.
- Define (select) a new cutout.
- Select any tool from the Tool Box.

When a cutout is anchored in place, its selection box disappears.

**Saving and retrieving a cutout**

Paint allows you to save a cutout as a separate file on disk. It can then be opened at a later time as a graphic of its own or as part of another graphic. In this way, you can create a *library* of graphic components. For example, if you frequently draw pictures of houses, you can create and save types of windows, doors, and other "house components" for use in all your drawings.

To save an active cutout to disk:

1. Choose the Copy To command from the Edit menu or right-click inside the cutout and choose the Copy To command from the pop-up menu. The Copy To dialog box, which is virtually identical to the Save As dialog box (Section 2.2), is displayed.
2. Proceed as you would to save any file to disk.

If you want to *retrieve* a graphic that is stored on disk and place it in your current drawing, you must use the Paste From command. If you use the Open command, the new graphic *replaces* the current one in the drawing area. To insert a graphic file into the current drawing:

1. Choose the Paste From command from the Edit menu. The Paste From dialog box, which is virtually identical to the Open dialog box (Section 2.2), is displayed.
2. Proceed as you would to open any file stored on disk.

The retrieved graphic will be pasted, as an active cutout, into the upper-left corner of the current graphic. You can then move it anywhere in the drawing area, as we will now demonstrate.

## *Moving, Copying, and Sweeping a Cutout*

Paint makes it easy to transfer a cutout from one location in the drawing area to another. There are three types of "transfer" operations:

**Move**

- When you *move* a cutout, it is transferred to the new location and deleted from the original one. (The region occupied by the original cutout takes on the current background color.) To move an active cutout, position the cursor inside the selection box (it will become a four-headed arrow), press the mouse button, drag the cutout to the new location, and release the mouse button.

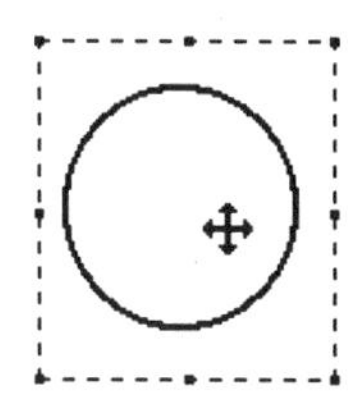

**Copy**

- When you *copy* a cutout, it is transferred to the new location without being deleted from the original one. To copy an active cutout, follow the *move* procedure, but hold down the Ctrl key as you drag the cutout.

**Sweep**

- When you *sweep* a cutout, it is transferred to the new location, leaving a series of copies in its path. To sweep an active cutout, follow the *move* procedure, but hold down the Shift key as you drag the cutout. Shown below is the result of sweeping a square (with a black border and gray interior) from one location to another:

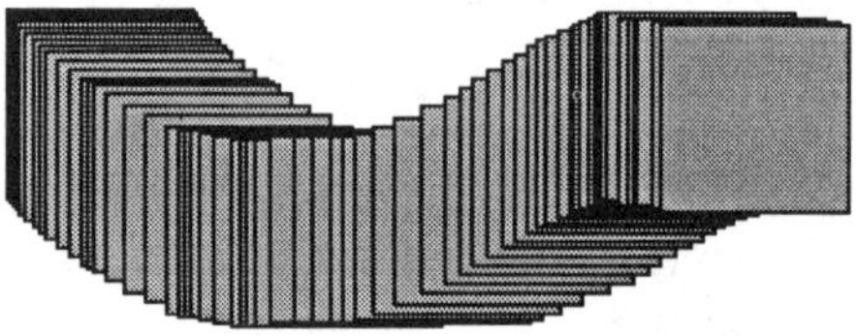

**Opaque vs. transparent transfers**

When you perform a transfer operation (move, copy, or sweep), the image of the cutout may obscure whatever is beneath it. This is called an *opaque* transfer. When the part of the graphic lying beneath the copy shows through, we call it a *transparent* transfer. Figure 13 illustrates the difference between the two types of transfers. The original figures, circles, are shown on the left. They were selected with the Rectangular Selection tool and copied over the picture of the car on the right. In Figure 13a, the copy is opaque — the copied cutout obscures the car; in Figure 13b, the copy is transparent — the car shows through the copied circle.

a. Opaque Copying b. Transparent Copying

**Figure 13** Opaque versus Transparent Transfer

**Selecting transparent or opaque mode**

To transfer a cutout opaquely, select the top option from the Options Box before moving, copying, or sweeping the cutout. To transfer a cutout transparently, select the bottom option. Alternatively, you can turn on opaque mode by selecting (placing a check mark on) the Draw Opaque item on the Options menu; to turn on transparent mode, deselect Draw Opaque.

## *Resizing a Cutout*

To change the size of a cutout (and all of the objects contained within it):

1. Position the mouse pointer over one of the eight *handles*. The pointer will become a two-headed arrow when positioned properly (Figure 14a).

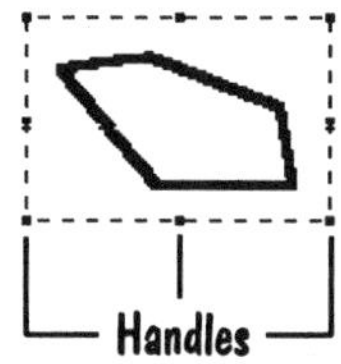


   - Use the middle handle on the top or bottom side to change the height of the cutout without changing its width.
   - Use the middle handle on the left or right side to change the width of the cutout without changing its height.
   - Use a corner handle to change both height and width at the same time.

2. Drag the handle away from the selection box to increase the size of the cutout, or drag it inside the box to decrease its size. An outline of the selection box will move with the cursor to show you the resulting effect (Figure 14b).

3. When the selection box is the desired size, release the mouse button. The cutout will be redrawn in the new size, as shown in Figure 14c. (To abort the process, press the Escape key before releasing the mouse button.)

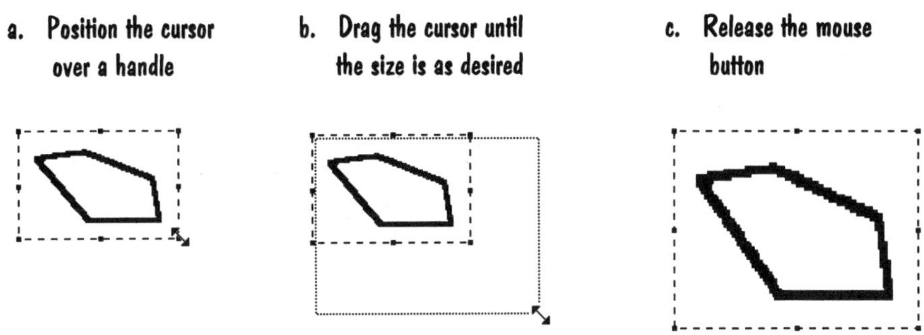


**Figure 14** Resizing a Cutout

**NOTE**

When the cutout is resized, the original selection box may take on the current background color, so select an appropriate background color from the Color Box before starting the process.

When the cutout is made larger and opaque mode is in effect, part of the existing graphic may be obscured. If you don't want this to happen, be sure that transparent mode (the bottom option) is selected in the Options Box before beginning the process.

## *Other Operations on Cutouts*

Paint provides several other ways to manipulate cutouts, all of which are accessible from the Image menu (as well as from the right-click pop-up menu).

**Flips and Rotations** You can *flip* an active cutout from left to right (a *horizontal flip*) or from top to bottom (a *vertical flip*). Here is an example of each type of flip; in an actual graphic, the triangle on the right would *replace* the one on the left.

**Flipping a cutout**

To flip an active cutout:

1. Choose the Flip/Rotate command from either the Image menu or the menu that pops up when you right-click inside the cutout. The Flip and Rotate dialog box, shown in Figure 15, will be displayed.

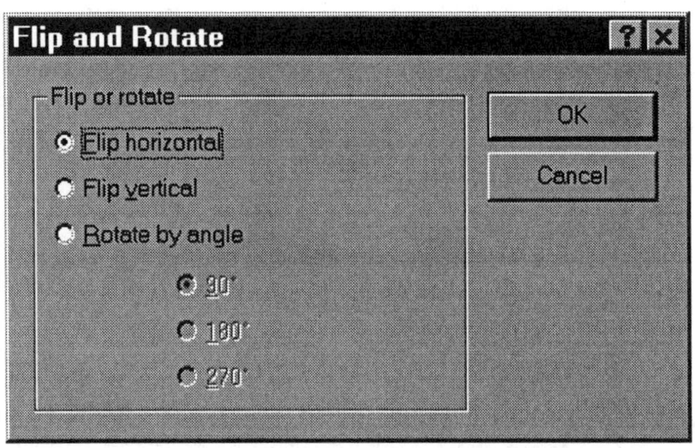


**Figure 15** The Flip and Rotate Dialog Box

2. Select the *Flip horizontal* or *Flip vertical* option button, as appropriate.
3. Choose the OK command button.

**Rotating a cutout**

Paint provides the ability to *rotate* a cutout a quarter turn (90°), a half turn (180°), or a three-quarter turn (270°). Here's an example (as with a flip, the rotated cutout replaces the original):

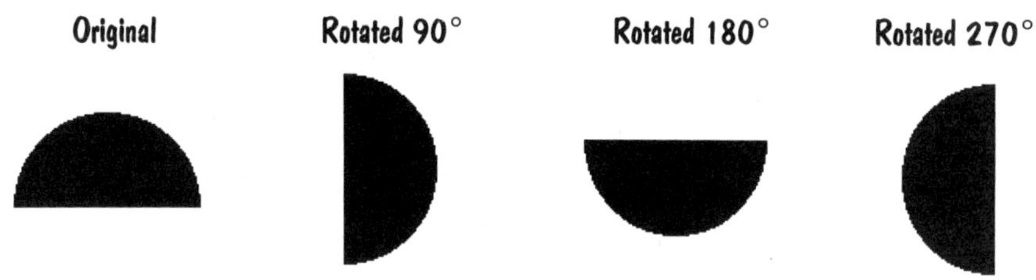


To rotate a cutout:

1. Choose the Flip/Rotate command from either the Image menu or the menu that pops up when you right-click inside the cutout. The Flip and Rotate dialog box, (see Figure 15) will be displayed.
2. Select the *Rotate by angle* option button and then select the option button that gives you the desired amount of rotation. (The rotation takes place in a clockwise direction.)
3. Choose the OK command button.

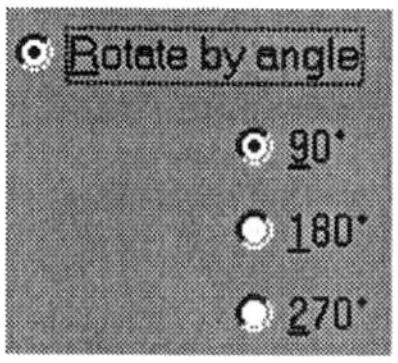


**Stretching or Skewing a Cutout** *Stretching* a cutout changes its size in either the horizonal or vertical direction. For example, stretching a circle creates an elliptical shape, as shown below:

**Stretching a circle**

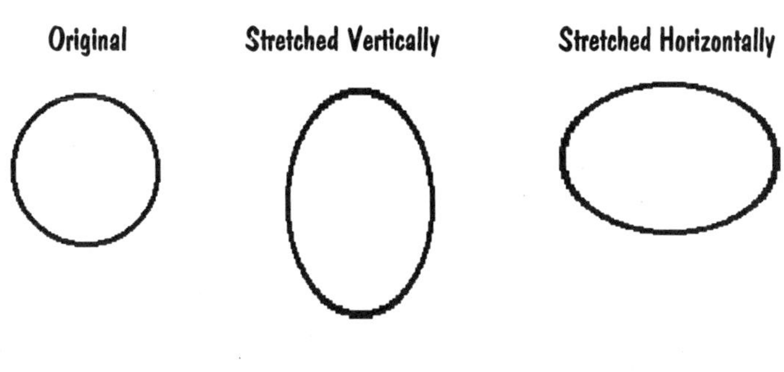


*Skewing* a cutout tilts it in a horizontal or vertical direction. For example, skewing a square creates a parallelogram, as shown in the figure below:

Skewing a square

To stretch and/or skew an active cutout:

1. Choose the Stretch/Skew command from either the Image menu or the menu that pops up when you right-click inside the cutout. The dialog box shown in Figure 16 will open.

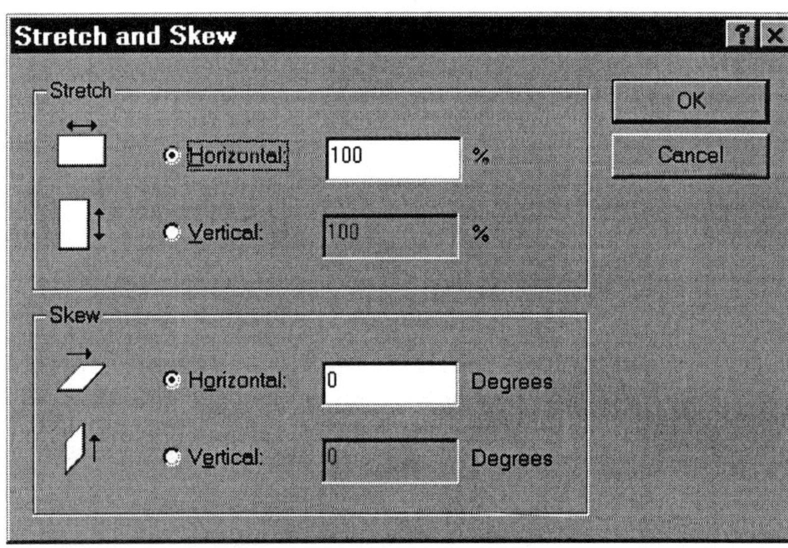


**Figure 16** The Stretch and Skew Dialog Box

2. If you want to stretch the cutout, select the Horizontal or Vertical option button in this part of the dialog box and enter a percentage in the corresponding text box. For example, entering "200" in the Horizontal text box will double its size in that direction; entering "25" will reduce its size by a factor of four. (The circle on the previous page was stretched 150%.)

3. If you want to skew the cutout, select the Horizontal or Vertical option button in this part of the dialog box and enter a number of degrees in the corresponding text box. (You may have to experiment here to get the desired effect.) For example, the square on the previous page was skewed 30°.
4. Choose the OK command button to complete the process.

**Inverting the Colors in a Cutout** To *invert* the colors in a cutout means to replace each one by its *complement*, the opposite color on the color wheel. For example, whites are changed into blacks, blues into browns or yellows, and reds into greens (and vice-versa). As a specific example, the object shown below on the left has a blue border, black interior, and white stripes. When its colors are inverted, the object on the right (which has a brown border, white interior, and black stripes) replaces it.

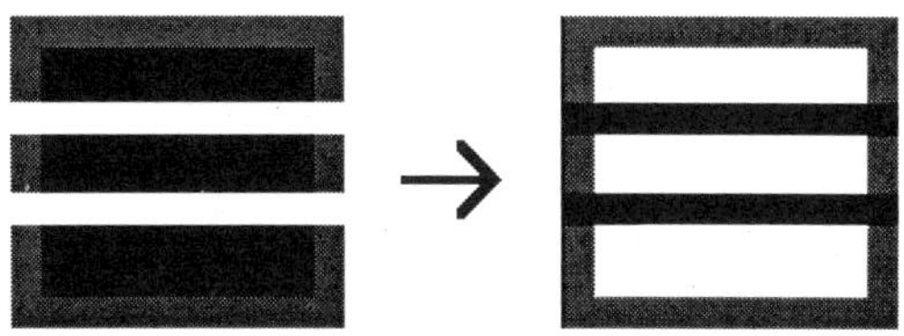

To invert the colors in the active cutout, choose the Invert Colors command from either the Image menu or the menu that pops up when you right-click inside the cutout.

TIP

You can issue the Flip/Rotate, Stretch/Skew, and Invert Colors commands even if no cutout is active. In this case, the operation applies to the entire graphic! However, be aware that the result of applying one of these operations to the entire graphic is sometimes difficult to predict. (If you don't like the effect, just choose the Undo command from the Edit menu to return the graphic to its former state.)

8.4 TUTORIAL

Try the following exercise on your own, creating a drawing of the factory shown in Figure 17 (on the next page).

1. Start Windows 95 (if necessary) by turning on the computer.
2. Set the line width by selecting the Line tool from the Tool Box and, in the Options Box, selecting the second option from the top.
3. Draw the factory building at the bottom of the drawing area: Use the Box tool and the "hollow" (top) option in the Options Box.

**Figure 17** Graphic for Tutorial 8.4

4. Draw the smokestack with the Box tool, using the "borderless" (bottom) option and dragging with the *right* mouse button so that it is colored black.
5. Draw the right-most window: Use the Box tool with the hollow option for the outside and the Line tool for the crosspieces. (Remember that holding down the Shift key results in horizontal or vertical lines.)
6. Create the middle window:
   - Select the existing window using the Rectangular Selection tool, position the mouse cursor inside the resulting cutout, hold down the Ctrl key, and drag the cutout's outline to the left of the existing window.
   - Reduce the size of the copy by dragging one of the corner handles toward the center of the new window until it is the proper size; then release the mouse button.
   - Move the new, smaller window into position by placing the mouse cursor inside the cutout and (without holding down Ctrl), dragging it to the proper place.
7. Create the triangular piece above the middle window (the one that was just created) using the Line tool.
8. Copy the middle window and place it to the left of the original (see step 6).

9. With the left-most window still selected, flip it horizontally so that it faces in the proper direction: Choose the Flip/Rotate command from the Image menu (or from the menu that pops up when you right-click inside the cutout), select the Flip horizontal option button in the resulting dialog box, and choose the OK command button.
10. Select a light gray foreground color and paint the building this color: Choose the Paint Can tool and click on a part of the building that is not a window.
11. Draw the smoke — use the Airbrush tool, with a medium brush width selected from the Options Box.
12. Close Paint, saving the graphic if you want.

# 8.5 Other Features of Paint

In the first four sections of this chapter, we have discussed how to use the Paint application to create and edit a graphic. In this section, we will introduce a few additional features of Paint. These include:

- Setting page orientation and margins.
- Previewing the way the graphic will look on the printed page.
- Changing image attributes, such as the size of the drawing area.
- Using Paint to create Desktop wallpaper.

## Setting Up the Page

Before printing your graphic, you should specify the size of the paper you are using, and its orientation and margins. These settings are entered in the Page Setup dialog box (Figure 18, on the next page). To open this dialog box, choose the Page Setup command from the File menu. Then, you can:

**Paper size**

- Specify the size of the paper on which you will be printing by selecting a size from the Paper Size drop-down list.

**Margins**

- Specify the top, bottom, left, and right page margins by entering the appropriate numbers in the Margins text boxes. The margin settings determine the size of the blank border around the graphic. By increasing the top and left margins, you can "push" the graphic down and to the right, perhaps to center it on the page.

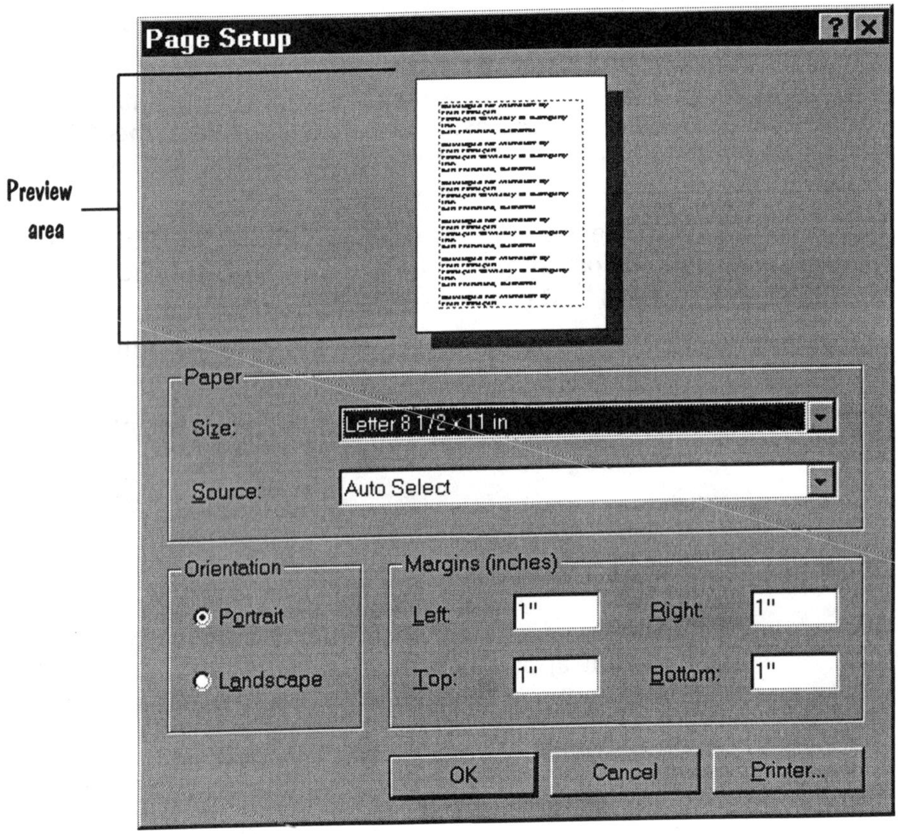


**Figure 18** The Page Setup Dialog Box

**Orientation**

- Specify the paper's orientation, either *portrait* or *landscape*, by selecting the corresponding option button. In **portrait** orientation, the graphic is viewed holding the page so that the long side is vertical; in **landscape** orientation, the graphic is viewed with the long side horizontal. The following figures further illustrate this concept:

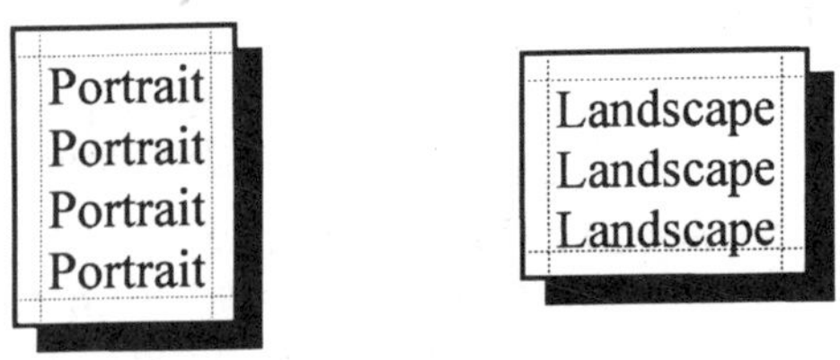


When you change a setting, the sample page in the preview area will also change to indicate the effect of the new setting. After you have entered all the needed information, choose the OK button to put the changes into effect.

## Print Preview

If you would like to see how the graphic will appear on the printed page before it is actually printed, choose the Print Preview command from the File menu. The **print preview** window will open (Figure 19), not only displaying the graphic as it appears in the drawing area, but also taking into account paper size, orientation, and margins. For example, the graphic in Figure 19 was positioned in the upper-left corner of the drawing area and the page settings were 8½" × 11" paper size, landscape orientation, and margins of 2" left and right, 1" top and bottom.

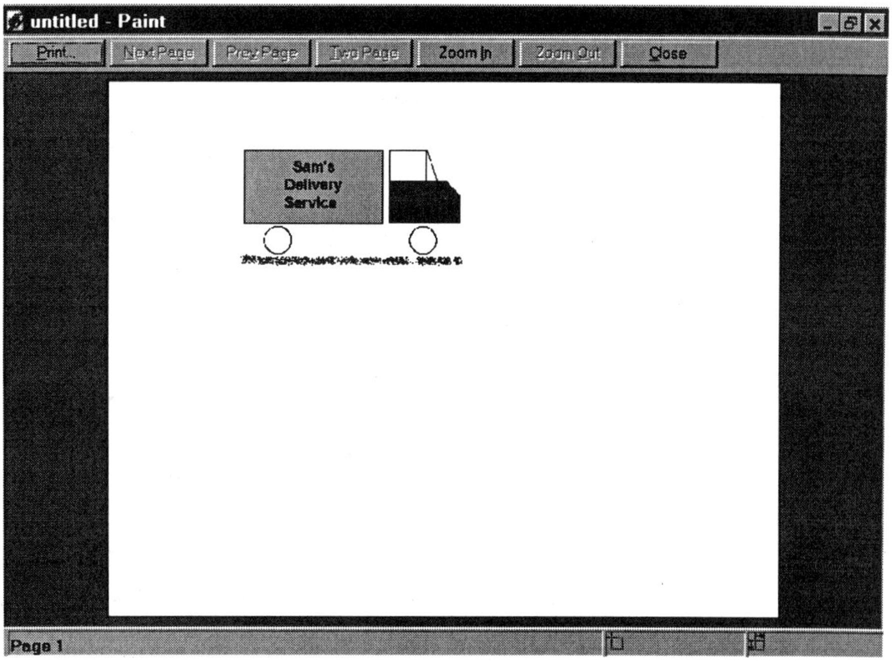


**Figure 19** The Print Preview Window

**Zooming in and out**

Although you cannot edit the graphic while it is in the print preview window, you can magnify parts of it to see finer detail. In addition to the full-page view shown in Figure 19, there are two "zoom" modes. To *zoom in*, magnifying the graphic:

- Click on the part of the page that you would like to enlarge. (In the preview window, the mouse cursor takes the shape of a magnifying glass, as shown at the right.) 

*or*

- Click on the Zoom In button (at the top of the window). Then, use the scroll bars to display the desired part of the page.

Clicking on the page or the Zoom In button again displays the second Zoom mode, increasing the magnification even more. At this point, the Zoom In button is dimmed, and clicking again on the page will return the display to the default magnification level. While in one of the two Zoom modes, clicking on the Zoom Out button changes the display to the next lower magnification level.

The relative magnification of the full-page view (on the left) and the two zoom modes is shown below:

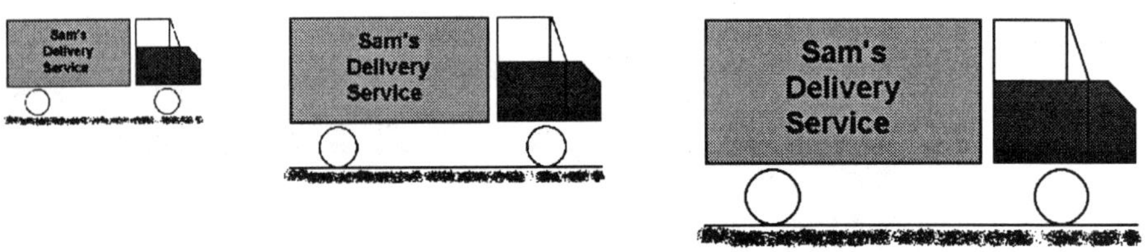


When you are done using the print preview window, either choose the Close button to return to the drawing window or choose the Print button to print the document.

## *Changing the Size of the Drawing Area*

Paint uses a default drawing size that is 6.67" wide and 5" high (on the printed page). When you start Paint, however, the drawing area will be set to the same size it was when you last exited. To return to the default dimensions, or to change to another drawing size:

1. Choose the Attributes command from the Image menu. The dialog box pictured in Figure 20 will be displayed.
2. To return to the default drawing size, choose the Default command button.
3. To set another drawing size, enter the desired dimensions in the Width and Height text boxes. (The units of measurement are determined by which option button is currently selected.)
4. Choose the OK command button to close the dialog box and put the changes into effect.

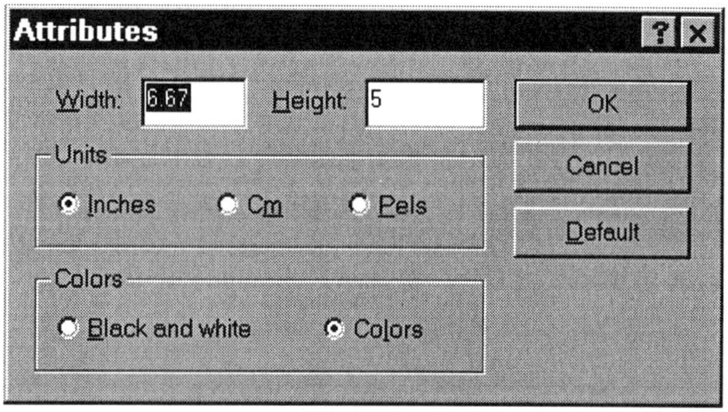


**Figure 20** The Image Attributes Dialog Box

If the specified dimensions are *larger* than the Paint window can accommodate, scroll bars will appear. (A larger drawing size uses more RAM and it takes more disk space to store the graphic.) If the specified dimensions are *smaller* than the Paint window, a rectangular box will be displayed in its upper-left corner marking off the new drawing area.

NOTE

As you can see, the Image Attributes dialog box also allows you to:

- Specify units of measurement — inches, centimeters (cm), or pixels (pels) — for the drawing size.
- Elect to use patterns of black and white for your palette, instead of colors. Here's how the Color Box will look if you select the *Black and white* option button and choose the OK command button:

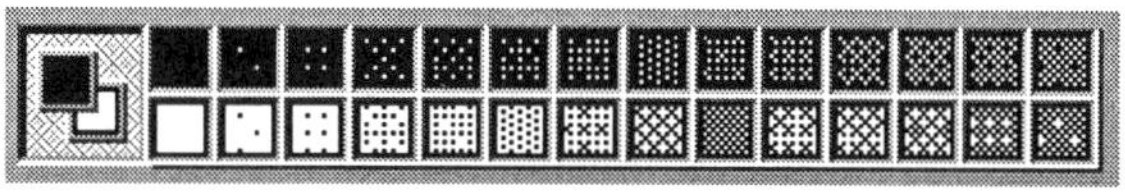

Be aware that if you switch to black and white while creating a graphic, all colors will be changed to patterns and you will not be able to restore its original colors!

## *Creating Wallpaper*

*Wallpaper* is a graphic image that covers the Desktop. It acts as a background for the icons, windows, and other objects that occupy the Desktop during a typical Windows session. Although wallpaper is normally selected using Control Panel's Display utility (see Section 4.2), you can also set up a Paint graphic to be the current wallpaper. To do so:

1. Use Paint to create or open the graphic.
2. Save it to disk (if the latest version has not already been saved).
3. Choose one of the *Set as Wallpaper* commands from the File menu:
   - If you choose *Set as Wallpaper (Tiled)*, the graphic will be repeated as many times as necessary to cover the entire Desktop (see Figure 21a).
   - If you choose *Set as Wallpaper (Centered)*, a single copy of the graphic will be centered on the Desktop (see Figure 21b).

In order to see the new wallpaper, you may have to first minimize all windows.

a. **Tiled Wallpaper** b. **Centered Wallpaper**

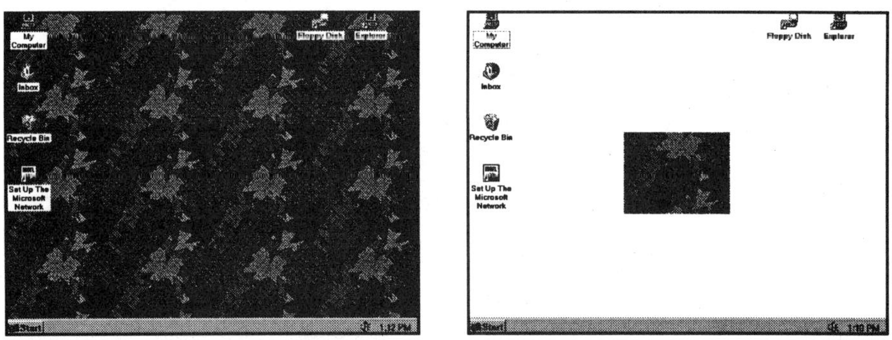


**Figure 21** Examples of Wallpaper

**NOTE**

When you set a graphic as wallpaper, it not only becomes the current Desktop background, but its file name is also added to the list of wallpapers on the Background page of Control Panel's Display utility. Consequently, at any time in the future you can:

- Change this wallpaper from tiled to centered, or vice-versa.
- Reselect this wallpaper, if another one is currently in use.

For more information about wallpaper, see Section 4.2.

# Review Exercises

**Section 8.1**

1. To select red as the foreground color in a Paint graphic, click the ____________ mouse button on that color in the Color Box.
2. To expand Paint's drawing area so that it fills the entire screen, choose the ____________ command from the View menu.
3. True or false: If you select a new background color from the Color Box after drawing a graphic, the background of that graphic will change to the new color.
4. True or false: Paint's Eye Dropper tool can be used to change both the foreground and background colors.
5. To select blue as the foreground color in Paint:

   a. Click the left mouse button on blue in the Color Box.
   b. Double-click the left mouse button on blue in the Color Box.
   c. Click the right mouse button on blue in the Color Box.
   d. Double-click the right mouse button on blue in the Color Box.

6. Which of the following tools cannot be found in Paint's Tool Box?

   a. Eraser
   b. Pencil
   c. Pen
   d. Brush

**Section 8.2**

7. To draw a horizontal line with Paint's Line tool, hold down the ____________ key while dragging the cursor.
8. When you use Paint's __________ tool, a spray of dots is produced.
9. When you use Paint's Box tool to create a hollow box (using the left mouse button), it is drawn in the current ____________ color.
10. An existing polygon can be filled with color by using Paint's ____________ tool.
11. True or false: Paint's Brush tool can only produce curves of a single line thickness.
12. True or false: To draw a perfect circle with Paint's Ellipse/Circle tool, hold down the Ctrl key while dragging the cursor.
13. True or false: The Tool Box icon for Paint's Text tool is the capital letter "T".
14. True or false: Paint's Rounded Box tool is used to create a rectangular shape with rounded corners.
15. Which of the following Paint tools cannot draw an "L-shaped" pair of lines?

a. The Polygon tool
b. The Line tool
c. The Pencil tool
d. The Brush tool

16. To fill an irregularly shaped region in a Paint graphic with color
    a. Double-click on that color in the Color Box.
    b. Use the Filled Box tool.
    c. Use the Paint Can tool.
    d. Use the Airbrush tool.

17. To draw a square using Paint's Box tool, while dragging the cursor, hold down the
    a. Alt key.
    b. Ctrl key.
    c. Shift key.
    d. Spacebar.

18. In the Text tool's Fonts window, you cannot select
    a. The color for the current text.
    b. The typeface for the current text.
    c. The point size for the current text.
    d. A bold and italic style for the current text.

**Section 8.3**

19. To erase a green circle that is enclosed in a red square using Paint's Eraser tool, set the background color to ___________.

20. You can magnify a part of your graphic using Paint's ___________ tool.

21. True or false: To define an irregularly-shaped cutout, use Paint's Free-form Selection tool.

22. True or false: You can use the Custom Size command (on Paint's Zoom submenu) to magnify the current graphic by any factor you want.

23. To delete the current (active) cutout in Paint, you can
    a. Press the Delete key.
    b. Choose the Clear Selection command from the Edit menu.
    c. Right-click inside the cutout and choose Clear Selection from the resulting pop-up menu.
    d. Carry out any of the above actions.

24. You cannot use the Zoom command (on Paint's Edit menu) to:
    a. Magnify the graphic by 400%.
    b. Show the graphic as it will appear on the printed page.
    c. Turn the (pixel) grid on and off.

d. Display a thumbnail view of the graphic.

**Section 8.4**

25. To *sweep* a cutout in Paint, hold down the ___________ key while dragging the cutout.
26. To flip a cutout in Paint from top to bottom, begin by choosing the ___________ command from the Image menu.
27. To save a cutout to disk, choose the Copy To command from Paint's ___________ menu.
28. True or false: To move a cutout transparently in Paint, select the bottom option in the Options Box.
29. True or false: Paint allows you to rotate a cutout by 90°, 180°, or 270°.
30. To paste down (anchor) a cutout in Paint:
    a. Choose Paste from the Edit menu.
    b. Choose Clear Selection from the Edit menu.
    c. Reposition the cursor.
    d. Click outside the cutout.
31. To copy a cutout from one location to another:
    a. Drag it to the new location.
    b. Drag it to the new location while holding down the Ctrl key.
    c. Drag it to the new location while holding down the Shift key.
    d. Drag it to the new location while holding down the Spacebar.
32. Which operation on cutouts is not performed by issuing a menu command?
    a. Resizing
    b. Flipping
    c. Rotating
    d. Skewing

**Section 8.5**

33. To see how your Paint graphic will look on the printed page before it is actually printed, choose the ___________ command from the File menu.
34. You can replace the colors in a Paint drawing by black-and-white patterns by choosing the ___________ item from the Image menu.
35. True or false: You can edit a Paint graphic that is displayed in the print preview window.
36. True or false: When you use one of the Set as Wallpaper commands on Paint's File menu, the resulting wallpaper is immediately put into effect.
37. Which of the following operations cannot be carried out using

Paint's Page Setup dialog box?

a. Setting the page margins.
b. Setting the page orientation.
c. Placing a header or footer on the page.
d. Selecting a paper size.

38. Paint's Image Attributes dialog box can be used to specify the size of

a. The page margins.
b. The text font.
c. The drawing area.
d. The screen resolution.

## Lab Exercises

Work each of the following exercises at your computer. Begin by turning the machine on (if necessary) to start Windows 95 and closing any open windows.

**Lab Exercise 1 (Section 8.2)**

a. Start Paint and maximize its window.

b. Use the 24-point Arial Bold font to insert the words Greek Flag at the top of the drawing area.

c. Create a drawing that resembles the blue-and-white Greek flag pictured at the right.

d. Insert your name, your class, and the date under the drawing in your choice of font.

e. Save the graphic to a floppy disk under the name Flag and print the graphic.

f. Exit Paint and remove the diskette from its drive.

**Lab Exercise 2 (Section 8.2)**

a. Start Paint and maximize its window.

b. Create a drawing that resembles the 5¼" floppy disk pictured at the right. Make it as large as you can, yet ensuring that the entire disk can be viewed without scrolling.

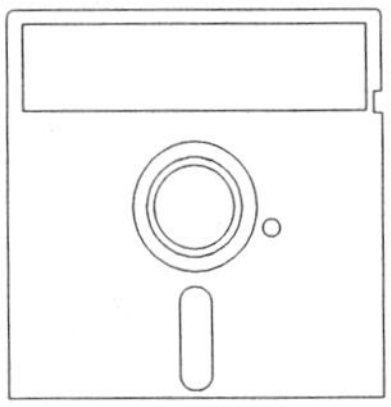

c. Insert your name, your class, and the date on the diskette's label (the rectangle at the top) in an appropriately-sized font.

d. Save the graphic to a floppy disk under the name Floppy and print the graphic.

e. Exit Paint and remove the diskette from its drive.

**Lab Exercise 3 (Section 8.3)**

a. Start Paint and maximize its window.

b. Insert the Lab Exercises disk in its drive and open the Graph1 graphic on this disk.

c. Edit the Graph1 graphic, so that the revised version resembles the one pictured at the right, using your class in the title. (Use the 10-point Arial font for all the text.)

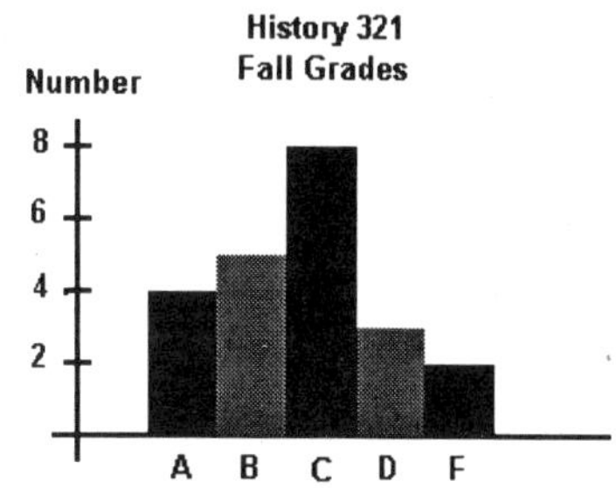


d. Insert your name and the date below the revised graphic in your choice of font.

e. Save the revised graphic to a floppy disk under the name Graph2 and print the graphic.

f. Exit Paint and remove the diskette from its drive.

**Lab Exercise 4 (Section 8.3)**

a. Start Paint and maximize its window.

b. Create the Palette graphic shown below. Here are a couple of hints so that your graphic will look right:

- Use the cursor coordinates on the Status bar to help create even subdivisions in the palette.
- Zoom in at 800% magnification on the line intersections and "clean them up" so that the lines meet perfectly.
- Use the Paint Can tool to fill each compartment with a different color from the Color Box.

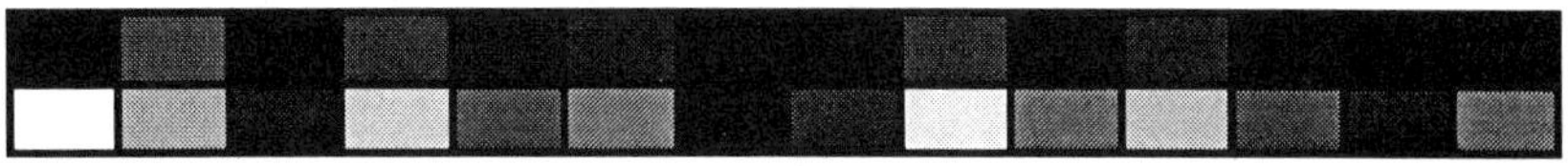

c. Insert your name, your class, and the date under the palette in your choice of font.

d. Save the graphic to a floppy disk under the name Palette and print the graphic.

e. Exit Paint and remove the diskette from its drive.

**Lab Exercise 5 (Section 8.3)**

a. Start Paint and maximize its window.

b. Insert the Lab Exercises disk in its drive and open the Factory1 graphic on this disk.

c. Edit the Factory1 graphic, so that the revised version resembles the one pictured in Figure 22, by:

- Using the Eraser tool to erase the triangular part of the two existing windows.
- Using the Box tool to create the new rectangular window and second smokestack.
- Using the Airbrush tool to create the new smoke.

d. Insert your name, your class, and the date to the left of the smokestacks in your choice of font.

e. Save the revised graphic to a floppy disk under the name Factory2 and print the graphic.

f. Exit Paint and remove the diskette from its drive.

**Figure 22** Final Graphic for Lab Exercise 5

**Lab Exercise 6 (Section 8.4)**

a. Start Paint and maximize its window.

b. Create a drawing that resembles the house shown at the right. Make use of the copy and resize operations to simplify your work.

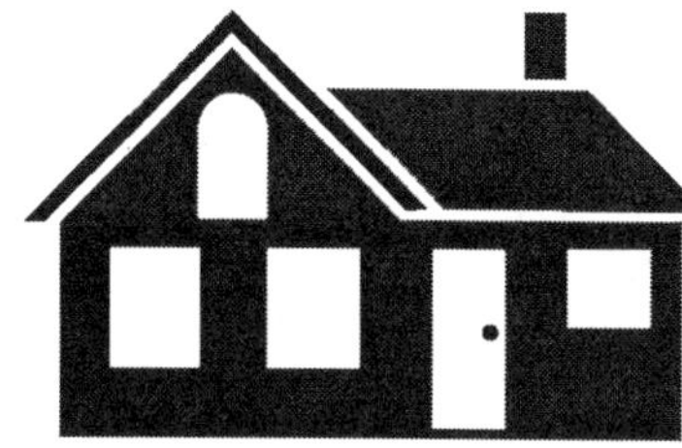

c. Insert your name, your class, and the date below the graphic in your choice of font.

d. Save the graphic to a floppy disk under the name House and print the graphic.

e. Exit Paint and remove the diskette from its drive.

**Lab Exercise 7 (Section 8.4)**

a. Start Paint and maximize its window.

b. Create a drawing that resembles the locomotive shown at the right. Make use of the copy and resize operations to simplify your work.

c. Insert your name, your class, and the date below the graphic in your choice of font.

d. Save the graphic to a floppy disk under the name Loco and print the graphic.

e. Exit Paint and remove the diskette from its drive.

CHAPTER 9

# Using Other Windows Accessories

In Chapters 7 and 8, we discussed two of the applications, WordPad and Paint, included with the Windows 95 package. These applications are sometimes referred to as *accessories* because they appear on the Accessories submenu of the Start menu's Programs option. In this chapter we will describe how to use other Windows accessories. More specifically:

- Section 9.1 introduces a simple, but useful accessory called Calculator, which includes two types of on-screen calculators.
- Section 9.2 discusses the Notepad text editor.
- Section 9.3 describes how to back up your files using the Windows Backup utility.
- Section 9.4 discusses several tools (ScanDisk, Disk Defragmenter, and DriveSpace) that help maintain your hard disk.
- Section 9.5 briefly describes the Character Map utility and introduces Windows built-in multimedia and communications applications.

The topics in this chapter are independent of one another, so you can read them in any order, or skip any you want.

# 9.1 The Windows Calculators

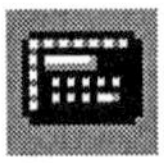

Windows' **Calculator** accessory provides two types of on-screen calculators — a basic *standard* calculator and a more powerful *scientific* calculator. To start Calculator:

1. Click on the Start button to open the Start menu.
2. Point at the Start menu's Programs option and then at the Accessories item on the resulting submenu.
3. Click on the Calculator item on the Accessories submenu.

**Switching between the calculator types**

The Calculator window will open, displaying the calculator type (standard or scientific) that was active when you last exited this accessory. To switch from one type to the other, choose Standard or Scientific, as desired, from the View menu.

## The Standard Calculator

If you know how to use a conventional calculator, then you'll be able to use Windows' Calculator; it works in a completely analogous way! In standard mode (Figure 1), Calculator contains all the keys usually found on a basic calculator, but instead of pressing a key with your finger, you click on it with the mouse. For example, to multiply 365 by 23:

1. Click on the 3, 6, and 5 buttons. As you do, the corresponding digits appear in the calculator's "display".

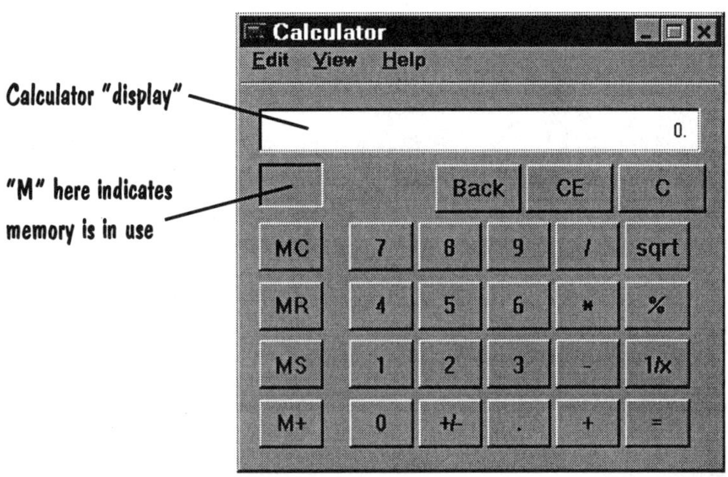


**Figure 1** Standard Calculator

2. Click on the multiplication key (*).
3. Click on the 2 and 3 buttons; 23 appears in the display.
4. Click on the equals key (=). The product, 8395, appears in the display.

In addition to the number and operation (/, *, +, -, =) keys, the standard calculator contains all the keys usually found on a basic calculator (and one atypical key, *Back*). The following table provides a quick rundown of their functions.

| Key | Symbol | Function |
|---|---|---|
| Back | Back | Deletes the last digit entered into the display. |
| Clear entry | CE | Clears the number in the display. |
| Clear | C | Clears the entire current computation. |
| Memory clear | MC | Clears the number stored in memory. |
| Memory recall | MR | Replaces the displayed number by the one in memory. |
| Memory store | MS | Stores the displayed number in memory, replacing the currently stored number. |
| Memory plus | M+ | Adds the displayed number to the number in memory. |
| Plus/minus | +/- | Reverses the sign of the number in memory. |
| Reciprocal | 1/x | Replaces the displayed number by its reciprocal. |
| Percentage | % | Multiplies the result of a multiplication by 100. |
| Square root | sqrt | Replaces the displayed number by its square root. |

**Table 1** Standard Calculator Keys

**TIP**

If you use Calculator a lot, you can speed up data entry by using *keyboard equivalents*. For example, the number keys and operation symbols can be activated by pressing the corresponding keys on the keyboard. (If you use the numeric keypad to do this, make sure the

Num Lock light is on; if it isn't, press the Num Lock key.) Here are a few other useful keyboard equivalents; instead of clicking on:

- The Back button — press the Backspace key.
- The CE button — press the Delete key.
- The C button — press the Escape key.

To discover the rest of the keyboard equivalents, right-click on the key in question and chose *What's This?* from the resulting pop-up menu.

**Copy and paste with Calculator**

You can transfer numbers between the Calculator display and another application with the aid of the Clipboard:

- To copy the displayed number to the Clipboard, choose the Copy command from the Edit menu.
- To transfer a number from the Clipboard to the Calculator display, choose Paste from the Edit menu.

## *The Scientific Calculator*

In scientific mode (Figure 2), Calculator supplies an impressive array of advanced functions, in addition to the basic operations provided by standard mode.

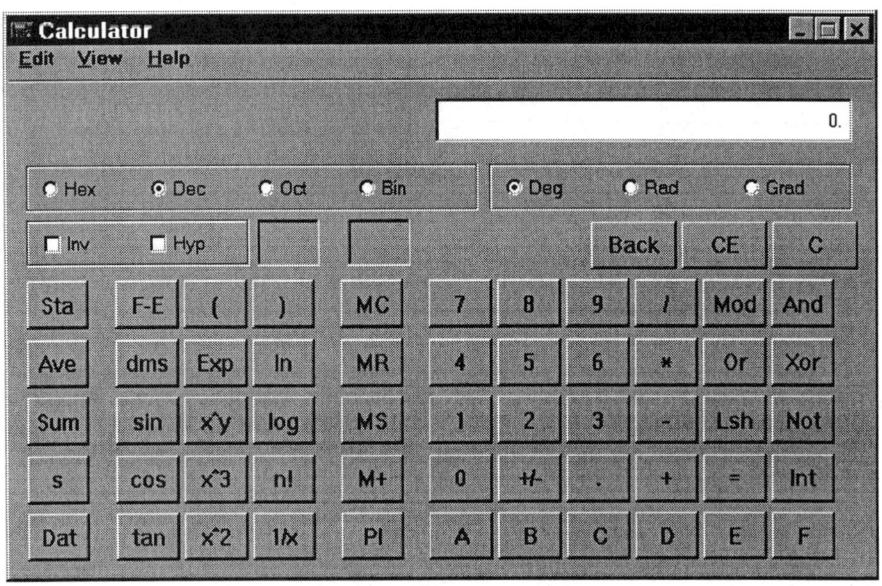


**Figure 2** Scientific Calculator

**Dealing with Numbers** In scientific mode, you can choose to enter and manipulate numbers in four different number systems. Calculator defaults to our everyday *decimal* (base 10) number system. If you want to set Calculator to work in the *hexadecimal* (base 16), *octal* (base 8), or *binary* (base 2) system, select the corresponding option button:

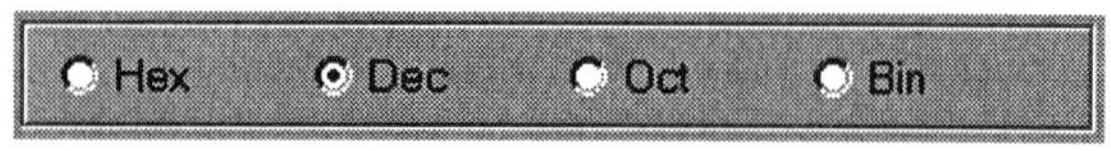


Calculator will only accept numbers that are valid for the selected system. For example, if *Bin* is selected and you try to enter anything but a 0 or 1 into the display, you will hear a "beep" and nothing will happen. At the other extreme, the hexadecimal system uses the digits 0, 1, ..., 9, A, B, C, D, E, and F and the additional "digits" are entered by using the corresponding calculator (or keyboard) keys:

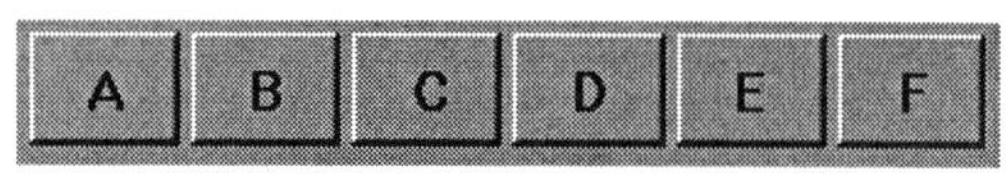


TIP

You can use the number system option buttons to convert a number from one system to another. To do so:

1. Select the option button for the system to be converted *from*.
2. Enter the desired number (actually, its representation in the current system) into the display.
3. Select the system to be converted *to*. The numeral in the display will change to the correct representation in the new system.

**Performing Statistical Calculations** Calculator can compute the sum, mean (average), and standard deviation of a given set of numbers. To perform one of these operations:

1. Click on the *Sta* button. The Statistics Box window will open.
2. Click on the RET (return) button in the Statistics Box to close this window.
3. Enter the data (the numbers with which you want to work) into the display one at a time, clicking on the *Dat* button after each number is entered. (Each time you click on Dat the displayed number is added to the list in

the Statistics Box, even though the latter is hidden from view.)

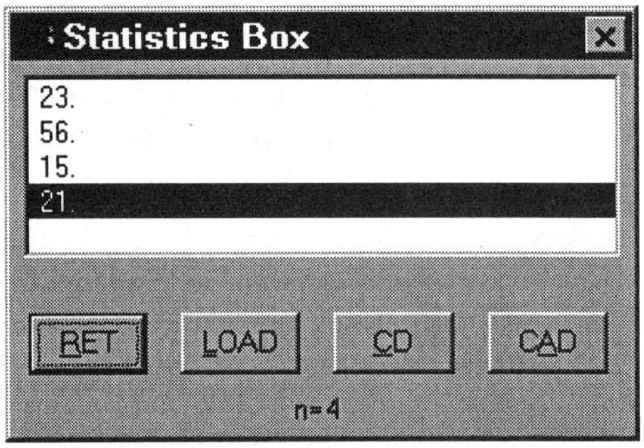


4. If you wish to review the numbers you have just entered, click on the *Sta* button again. The Statistics Box window will open, displaying the data and the total number (*n* =) of items.
5. To delete a number, select it and click on CD. To clear the window, click on CAD. To replace the number in the Calculator display by the one currently selected in the Statistics Box, click on LOAD.
6. Click on RET to close the Statistics Box. Now, to display:
   - The mean of the data — click on the *Ave* button.
   - The sum of the data — click on the *Sum* button.
   - The standard deviation of the data — click on the *s* button.

**Trigonometric Functions** Calculator allows you to compute trigonometric and hyperbolic functions and their inverses. Moreover, in working with trig functions, you can elect to have the angle measured in degrees (*Deg*), radians (*Rad*), or gradients (*Grad*) by selecting the appropriate option button prior to the calculation:

Table 2 gives the functions of the trigonometric keys. Selecting the *Inv* (Inverse) and/or *Hyp* (Hyperbolic) check boxes prior to clicking on a trig button, modifies its function as described in the table. We will use the following notation with regard to these check boxes:

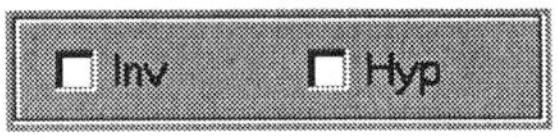


- Inv+*button* (or Hyp+*button*) means select the *Inv* check box (or *Hyp* check box), then click on the indicated button. For example, Inv+cos means select *Inv*, then click on *cos*.
- Inv+Hyp+*button* means select both check boxes, then click on the indicated button. For example, Inv+Hyp+cos means select *Inv*, select *Hyp*, then click on *cos*.

| Key | Function |
|---|---|
| dms | Converts the displayed angle from decimal degree format to degree-minute-second format. Inv+dms does the reverse. |
| sin | Calculates the sine of the displayed angle. Inv+sin calculates the inverse sine (arcsin) of the displayed number. Hyp+sin and Inv+Hyp+sin calculate the hyperbolic sine (sinh) and its inverse, respectively. |
| cos | Calculates the cosine of the displayed angle. Inv+cos calculates the inverse cosine (arccos) of the displayed number. Hyp+cos and Inv+Hyp+cos calculate the hyperbolic cosine (cosh) and its inverse, respectively. |
| tan | Calculates the tangent of the displayed angle. Inv+tan calculates the inverse tangent (arctan) of the displayed number. Hyp+tan and Inv+Hyp+tan calculate the hyperbolic tangent (tanh) and its inverse, respectively. |

**Table 2** Calculator's Trig-related Functions

**Other Scientific Calculator Functions** We conclude this section by briefly discussing the other functions provided in scientific mode.

- *F-E* toggles the display between ordinary (floating point) and scientific (exponential) notation.
- *Exp* allows you to enter numbers using scientific notation.
- The keys, *(* and *)*, allow you to insert parentheses into a calculation.
- The keys *ln* and *log* calculate the logarithm (base *e* and 10, respectively) of the displayed number. (Inv+ln and Inv+log calculate $e^x$ and $10^x$, respectively, where *x* is the displayed number.)
- The key *n!* calculates the factorial of the displayed integer.
- The key *x^y* calculates the value of *x* raised to the *y* power. (Inv+x^y calculates the $y^{th}$ root of *x*.)
- The keys *x^2* and *x^3* square and cube, respectively, the displayed number. (Inv+x^2 and Inv+x^3 calculate square and cube roots.)

- *Pi* inserts the value of π into the display.
- *Mod* calculates the remainder in an integer division.
- *Int* displays the integer part of a decimal number. (Inv+Int displays the decimal part.)
- *And*, *Or*, *Xor* (exclusive or), *Lsh* (left shift), and *Not* perform the corresponding logical operations on binary numbers.

9.1 TUTORIAL

Try the following exercise on your own.

1. Turn on the computer (if necessary) to start Windows 95 and display Calculator by clicking on the Calculator item on the Accessories submenu of the Start menu's Programs option.
2. Switch to the Standard calculator (if necessary) by choosing this item from the View menu.
3. Calculate the value of the expression 21(15 - 3.67):
   - Enter 15 into the calculator's display by clicking on the "1" and "5" calculator buttons.
   - Click on the minus (-) button.
   - Enter 3.67 by clicking on the appropriate buttons.
   - Click on the multiply (*) button.
   - Enter 21 by clicking on the appropriate buttons.
   - Click on the equals (=) button. The answer (237.93) will appear in the display.
4. Clear this calculation by clicking on the C (clear) button.
5. Perform the same calculation as in step 3, but this time use the keys on the computer's keyboard. (Hopefully, your answer will be the same as before.)
6. Clear this calculation.
7. Enter the number 2345. Now, click on the Back button to delete the last digit entered (5); then, click on the CE (clear entry) button to clear the resulting number from the display.
8. Determine the reciprocal of the square root of 10, $1/\sqrt{10}$:
   - Enter 10 into the display.
   - Take its square root by clicking on the *sqrt* button.
   - Take the reciprocal of the displayed number by clicking on the *1/x* button. (The answer, 0.316..., will appear in the display.)
9. Use the calculator's memory keys to add the integers from 1 to 5:

- Enter 1 into the display.
- Store the displayed number in memory by clicking on the MS button. (An "M" appears in the box above the memory buttons to indicate that the memory is in use.)
- Enter 2 into the display and add it to the number in memory by clicking on the M+ button.
- Repeat the previous step for the numbers 3, 4, and 5.
- Transfer the number currently in memory (the sum of 1, 2, 3, 4, and 5) to the display by clicking on the MR button.
- Clear the calculator's memory by clicking on the MC button. (The "M" disappears from the box above the memory buttons.)

10. Switch to scientific mode by choosing the Scientific item from the View menu. If you are familiar with the use of a conventional scientific calculator, explore this electronic version by performing various calculations. Remember: To get help with a particular button or feature, right-click on it and choose the *What's This?* item from the pop-up menu.

11. Close Calculator by clicking on its close button.

## *9.2 The Notepad Text Editor*

**Notepad** is a very simple type of word processor called a **text editor** because its capabilities are limited to entering and editing (modifying) text. Unlike more sophisticated word processors, such as WordPad, Notepad cannot *format* text (you have no choice of fonts and no alignment or indentation options) or insert graphics into a document.

**Advantages of Notepad**

Notepad's major virtue is simplicity; it loads more quickly and takes up less memory than WordPad. Notepad is (arguably) more convenient than WordPad for taking quick notes and editing text files. A **text file**, which is also known as an **ASCII** (pronounced "askey") file, is the simplest and most universal format for storing text. A text file is made up solely of characters you can type on the keyboard; it does not contain any special symbols (such as £ or ©) or formatting codes. Some system files (such as autoexec.bat and config.sys) and program files are stored in ASCII format.

**Starting Notepad**

To start Notepad:

1. Click on the Start button to open the Start menu.
2. Point at the Start menu's Programs option and then at the Accessories item on the resulting submenu.

3. Click on the Notepad item on the Accessories submenu. Notepad will open and display its window, as shown in Figure 3.

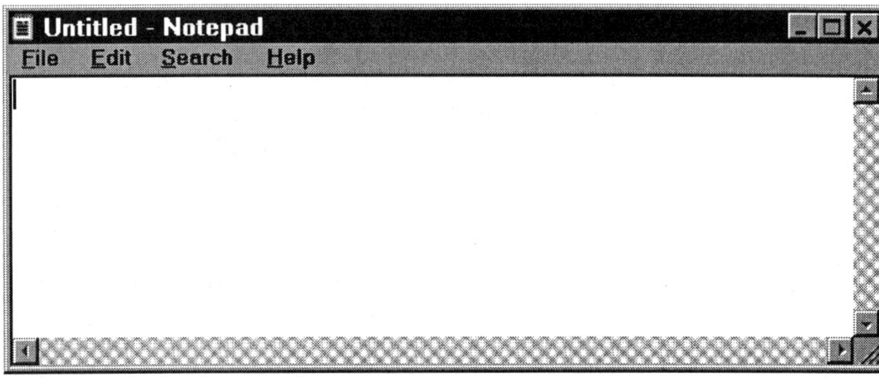


**Figure 3** The Notepad Window

## *Basic Features*

At a basic level, Notepad creates, edits, and operates on documents the way you would expect from any Windows-based word processor.

**Entering text** You enter text into a Notepad document in the same general way as you would in WordPad — just type, and the words appear on the screen. However, when you start Notepad, *word wrap* is turned off, which means that the text you type continues on the same line until you press the Enter key. If you turn word wrap on (by choosing this item from the Edit menu), text will wrap to the beginning of the next line when it reaches the right edge of the Notepad window.

**TIP** One of the Notepad's few frills gives you the ability to enter the current time and date into a document. To insert this text at the insertion point, choose the Time/Date command from the Edit menu or just press the F5 function key. (Unlike WordPad, you cannot select the format in which the time and date will be displayed.)

**Editing text** Simple editing is done in much the same way as with WordPad; the Backspace and Delete keys work in exactly the same way, as does the Undo command on the Edit menu (see Section 2.2). Moreover, text is selected, cut or copied to the Clipboard, and pasted from the Clipboard in the usual Windows-compliant way (see Section 2.3). Notepad also supplies a quick way to select all the text in a document; just choose the Select All command from the Edit menu. (However, Notepad lacks the other, more sophisticated ways of selecting text that are available in WordPad, which were described in Section 7.1.)

**Standard File menu commands** The New, Open, Save, Save As, Print and Exit commands on Notepad's File menu work in the same way as in most Windows applications (see Section 2.2) with one major exception: When you issue the Print command, printing begins immediately; the Print dialog box does not appear. As a result, you do not have access to some of the usual print features, such as specifying a range of pages to be printed.

## *Beyond the Basics*

Notepad does provide two relatively advanced features: It can locate any specified piece of text within a document and has page layout options to enhance the look of the printed page.

**Searching for Text** One of Notepad's most useful features when editing a long or complicated document is its ability to search for a specified word or other sequence of characters. To search a Notepad document:

1. Choose the Find command from the Search menu. The Find dialog box (Figure 4) will open.

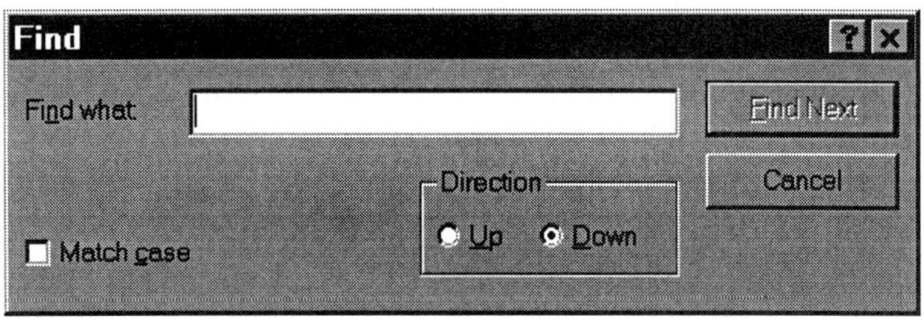


**Figure 4** The Find Dialog Box

2. Type the text you are seeking in the *Find what* box. Notepad will search for this sequence of characters, whether or not it is part of a word, an entire word, or spans more than one word. For example, if you enter the win in the *Find what* box, Notepad may locate "the winner" or "the window", but not "a window".
3. Select the *Match case* check box if you want to search for text that

has the same combination of upper and lower case letters as that entered in the *Find what* box. For example, if you leave this box *de*selected and search for able, then "able", "Able", and "ABLE" will be located (if they appear in the document); if the box is selected, then only "able" will be located.

4. The search commences at the insertion point. Select the *Down* option button if you want the search to proceed forward through the document; select the *Up* button to proceed backward.
5. Choose the Find Now command button. Notepad will locate and highlight the next occurrence (in the specified direction) of the *Find what* text. If this text is not found, a message to this effect will be displayed.

TIP

You can use Find to locate the last text entered in the *Find what* box even if the Find dialog box is no longer on the screen. To do so, choose the Find Next command from the Search menu or press the F3 function key.

**Setting Up the Page** Although Notepad provides no choice of fonts, alignment, or indentation, it does allow you to specify certain page layout options prior to printing. These features are accessed from the Page Setup dialog box (Figure 5), which is opened by choosing the Page Setup command from the File menu.

In the Page Setup dialog box:

- You can specify the size of the paper on which you will be printing by selecting the appropriate item on the Paper Size drop-down list. (When you select a new size, the "page" shown in the Preview area will reflect the change.)
- You can specify the printer bin from which the blank paper will be fed by selecting an item from the Paper Source drop-down list.
- You can choose to print your document in either portrait or landscape orientation. In **portrait** orientation, the document's text is printed parallel to the short side of the paper. In **landscape** orientation, the text is printed parallel to the long side of the paper. The figures at the right illustrate this concept.

  To specify page orientation, select the Portrait or Landscape option button. The "page" shown in the Preview area will appear in the selected orientation.

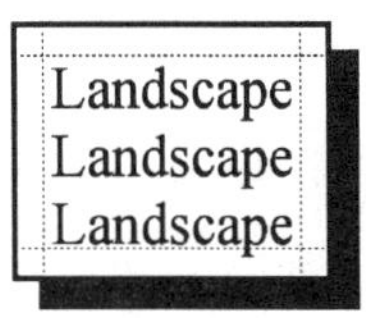

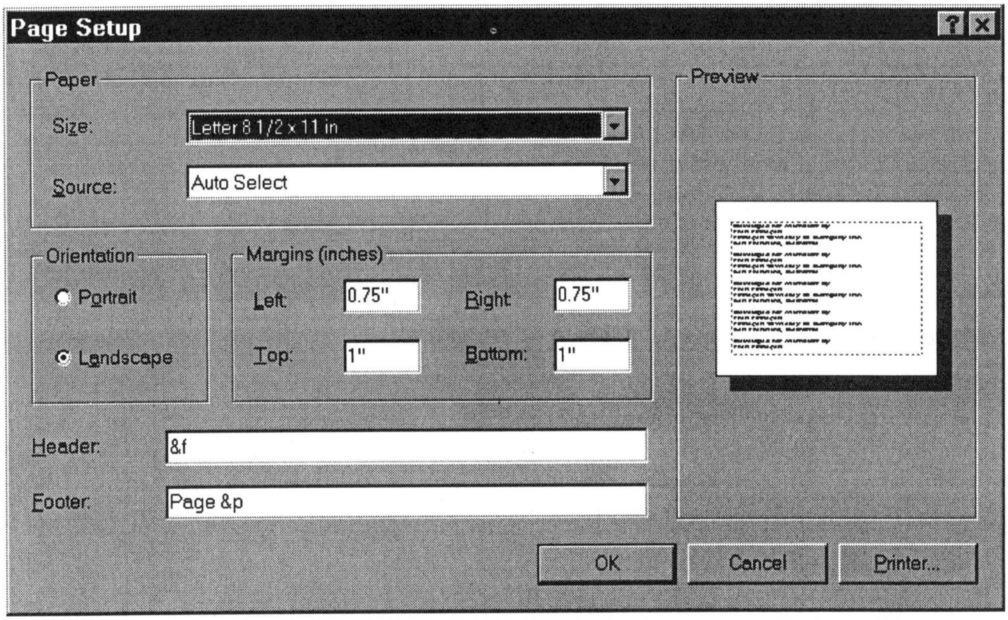


**Figure 5** Notepad's Page Setup Dialog Box

- You can change the margins for the current document by entering the desired margins in the Left, Right, Top, and Bottom text boxes. (The "page" shown in the Preview area will indicate the new margins.)
- You can create headers and footers for the document. A **header** is text that is automatically placed in the top margin of every page of a document. Similarly, a **footer** appears in the bottom margin of every page. To create a header or footer for the current document, enter text in the Header or Footer boxes. The text is printed as entered except for letters that are preceded by an ampersand (&) symbol. These codes have the following meaning:

| | |
|---|---|
| &c | centers the text that follows this code |
| &d | inserts the current date |
| &f | inserts the document's file name |
| &l | aligns the text that follows with the left margin |
| &p | inserts the current page number |
| &r | aligns the text that follows with the right margin |
| &t | inserts the current time |

If no alignment code is present, the header or footer text is centered on the line. Thus, in Figure 5: the text in the Header box (&f) will cause the document's file name to be printed at the top center of every page; the Footer text will print the current page number, preceded by the word Page and a blank space, at the bottom center of each page. As another example, the Header text &l&p&cWindows 95&r&d produces a header (when the document is printed) like the following one:

```
1                    Windows 95                    1\7\96
```

9.2

**TUTORIAL**

Try the following exercise on your own.

1. Turn on the computer (if necessary) to start Windows 95 and open Notepad by clicking on the Notepad item on the Accessories submenu of the Start menu's Programs option.
2. Insert the Lab Exercises disk in its drive and open the `History2` document on this diskette. (See Section 2.2 for more information about opening a document.)
3. Maximize the Notepad window.
4. Use Notepad's Find utility to search for all occurrences of the word *computer* in the History2 document:
   - Choose the Find command from the Search menu to open the Find dialog box.
   - Type the word *computer* in the *Find what* box, deselect the *Match case* check box (so that capitalized spellings of *computer* will be found), and select the *Down* option button (so that the search, which begins at the insertion point, will proceed in a forward direction).
   - Choose the Find Next command button. The first occurrence of *computer* will be located and highlighted.
   - Continue to search for additional occurrences of *computer* by repeatedly choosing the Find Next button. When the last occurrence is found, close the resulting message box and choose the Cancel command button to close the dialog box.
5. Prepare the document for printing:
   - Choose the Page Setup command from the File menu to open the corresponding dialog box.
   - Select (if necessary) "Letter 8 1/2 × 11 in" from the Paper Size drop-down list and the Portrait option button.
   - Set the page margins to 1" left and right and 1.5" top and bottom by entering these numbers in the corresponding text boxes. (Notice how the "page" in the Preview area reflects these changes.)
   - Place the following text and codes in the Header and Footer boxes so that the indicated text will appear at the top and

bottom, respectively, of each page of the printed document (a list of the available codes precedes this tutorial):

Header: `&lHistory &r&d`

(The word "History" aligned with the left margin; the current date aligned right.)

Footer: `&c&p`

(The current page number, centered.)

- Choose the OK command button.

6. Print the revised document by choosing the Print command from the File menu.
7. Exit Notepad and remove the diskette from its drive.

# *9.3 Backing Up Your Hard Disk*

To **back up** a file on your hard disk simply means to copy it to another medium; for example, a floppy disk or tape. You should back up your newly created or just-modified data files at the end of every session at the computer. Then, if a file becomes inaccessible or you accidentally erase it at some time in the future, you can easily copy that file from your backup to the hard disk, instead of having to recreate it from scratch.

In addition to daily backups of individual files, many users also make more extensive backups, of key folders or even the entire disk, every once in a while. Then, should a major disaster occur and your hard disk (or a large part of it) become inaccessible, you can recreate its contents after it has been repaired or replaced.

## *Starting the Backup Utility*

Simple backups can be made using the Copy or Send To commands in Explorer or My Computer (see Chapter 3). For more extensive backups, Windows supplies the **Backup utility**. To start Backup:

1. Click on the Start button to display the Start menu.
2. Point at Programs, then at Accessories, and finally at System Tools on each resulting submenu.
3. Click on Backup on the System Tools submenu, which starts the Backup utility and displays the window shown in Figure 6, on the next page. (You may first see one or two informational dialog

boxes. If one of them appears, choose its OK command button to clear it from the screen.)

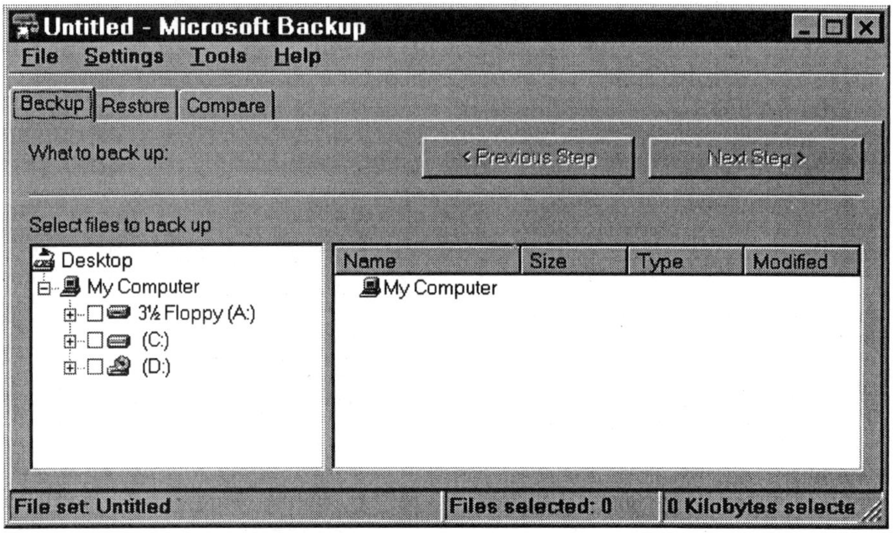


**Figure 6** The Main Backup Window

The three tabs in the Backup window correspond to the three main functions of this utility:

- The Backup page allows you to back up the desired files.
- The Restore page enables you to copy files from the backup media (floppies or tapes) to their original location, when needed.
- The Compare page allows you to compare the original files with their backups.

## *The Backup Procedure*

The basic backup procedure consists of three steps:

1. Select the files to be backed up.
2. Select a destination to which they will be backed up.
3. Start the copying process.

Carrying out these steps is easy if you're familiar with Explorer's way of navigating the Windows folder system (see Section 3.2). Here's a more detailed description of the backup process:

1. Start the Backup utility, as described above.
2. If you want to back up an entire folder, click on the little box to the left of the folder's icon. A check mark will be displayed indicating that this folder is selected. If you want to back up specific files in a given folder, open that folder (by clicking on its icon) and click on the boxes next to the desired files. (In either case, you may have to scroll and/or expand the folder tree in the left pane, just as you would in Explorer.)

   Figure 7 shows the result of clicking on the box to the left of the "Chap-2" icon in the folder tree. All files in the contents (right) pane were automatically selected when this was done. The shaded, checked box next to the parent folder (Win95Txt) indicates that part, but not all, of this folder has been selected. Notice that the status bar indicates the number of files that have been selected and the total number of kilobytes they contain.

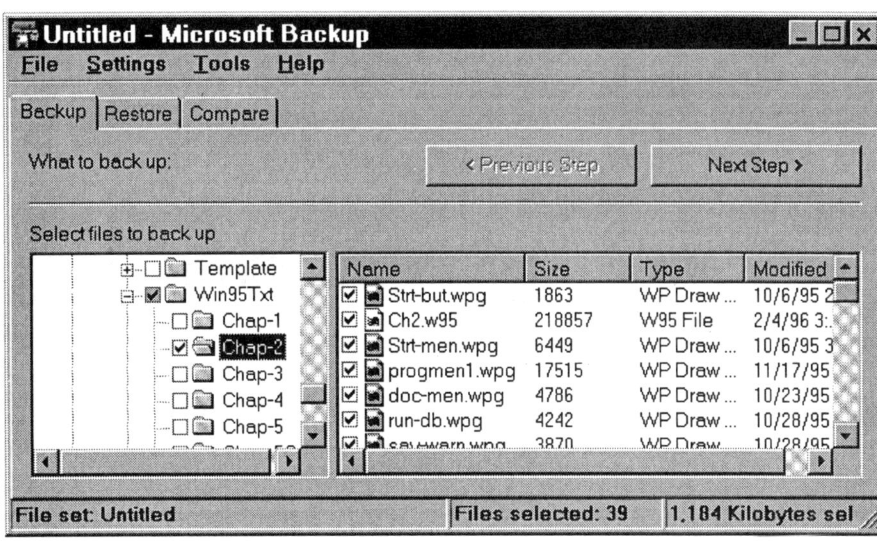


**Figure 7** Selecting the "Chap-2" Folder in Backup

3. Click on the Next Step command button. The Backup window will take on the look shown in Figure 8, on the next page.
4. Select the destination to which the files are to be copied in the folder tree by clicking on the desired drive or folder name. It will become highlighted. In Figure 8, the selected destination is the disk in the 3½" floppy drive.

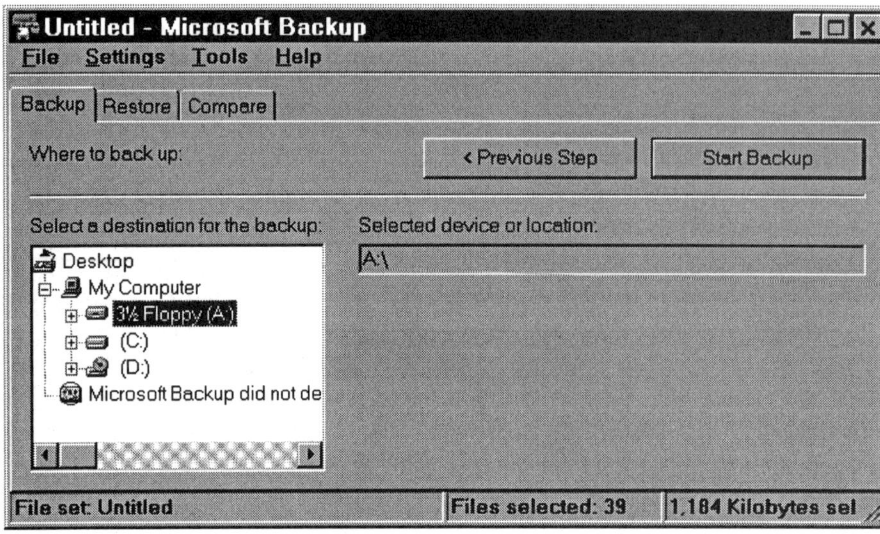


**Figure 8** Selecting a Destination for the Backup

5. Insert a diskette or tape cartridge in the appropriate drive.
6. Now choose the Start Backup command button. The Backup Set Label dialog box will open:

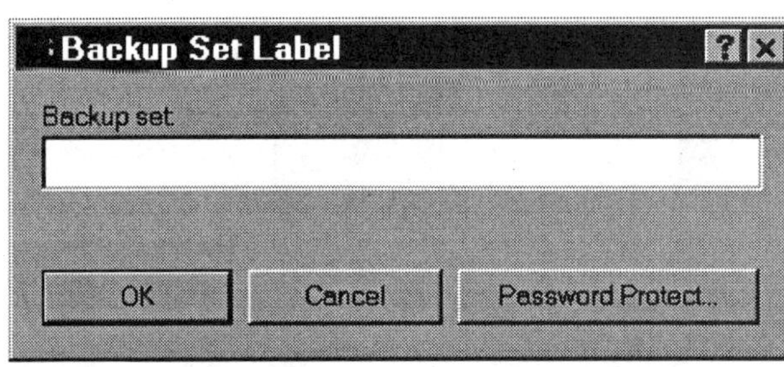


7. In the *Backup set* text box, type a name for the set of files you are backing up. Choose a meaningful name. For example, for the collection of files shown selected in Figure 7, the name "Chapter 2 of Win95 Text" would be appropriate. You should use the same name when you write a label on the actual disks or tape used in the backup.
8. Choose the OK command button and the copying process will begin. The animated Backup dialog box will show the progress of the backup. If a destination diskette becomes full, you will be prompted to insert another one. When the backup process is

complete, a message to this effect will appear on the screen.

**NOTE**

If you are backing up particularly important files and you want to be sure that the backups exactly match the originals, you can compare the two. To do so:

1. Click on the Compare tab in the Backup window.
2. Insert the disk or tape in its drive that contains the file set you want to compare.
3. Select that drive in the *Compare from* folder tree.
4. Select the backup set you want to compare in the right pane of the window and choose the Next Step command button.
5. In the *Select files* folder tree, select (by clicking on the appropriate boxes) the (original) files and folders you want to compare.
6. Choose the Start Compare command button. The animated Compare dialog box will indicate the progress of the operation. When the process is complete, a message to this effect will be displayed.

**TIP**

If you intend to back up the same files or folders in the future, you can save the *file set* — the set of selected objects together with the destination folder. To do so, after your selections have been made, choose Save As from the File menu. A Save As dialog box will open (see Section 2.2), allowing you to save the file set. Then, whenever you want to back up that set of files, start Backup, choose the Open File Set command from the File menu, and select the appropriate file set from the resulting Open dialog box.

To further simplify the process, you can place a shortcut to the saved file set on the Desktop, as described in Section 3.4. Then, double-clicking on this shortcut icon will start Backup, make the specified selections, and begin the copying process!

## *Restoring Backed Up Files*

Backups are worth their weight in gold when something goes wrong and the original files become unusable. In such a case, it is an easy matter to *restore* the backups — copy them to their original locations. Here's how the process works:

1. Start Backup, as described earlier in this section, and click on the Restore tab. The resulting page of the Backup dialog box is shown in Figure 9.

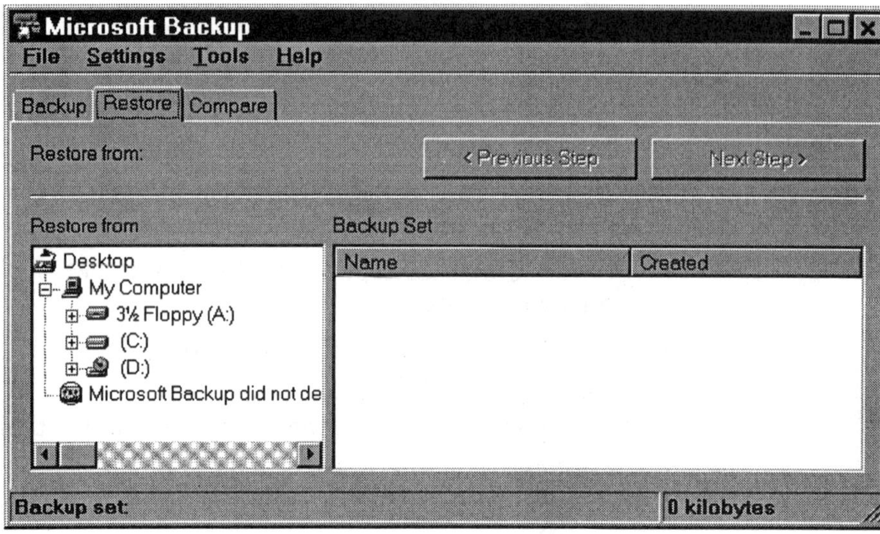


**Figure 9** The Restore Page of the Backup Window

2. Insert the appropriate backup diskette or tape cartridge in its drive. (This is the point at which careful labeling pays off!)
3. Select this drive in the *Restore from* folder tree. The names of the backup sets on the disk or tape in this drive will appear in the right pane.
4. Select the desired backup set from the right pane.
5. Choose the Next Step command button.
6. Select the files and/or folders to be restored (by clicking on the corresponding boxes).
7. Choose the Start Restore command button, and the copying process will begin. The animated Restore dialog box will appear, indicating the progress of the operation. When the process is complete, a message to this effect will be displayed.

## *Some Options for the Backup Process*

The Backup utility offers quite a few options for the way the backup, restore, and compare processes are carried out. These options are selected by choosing the Options command from the Settings menu. The dialog box that results has four tabs — one for general options and one for each of the three processes. We will only discuss the

Backup options page here. It is shown in Figure 10.

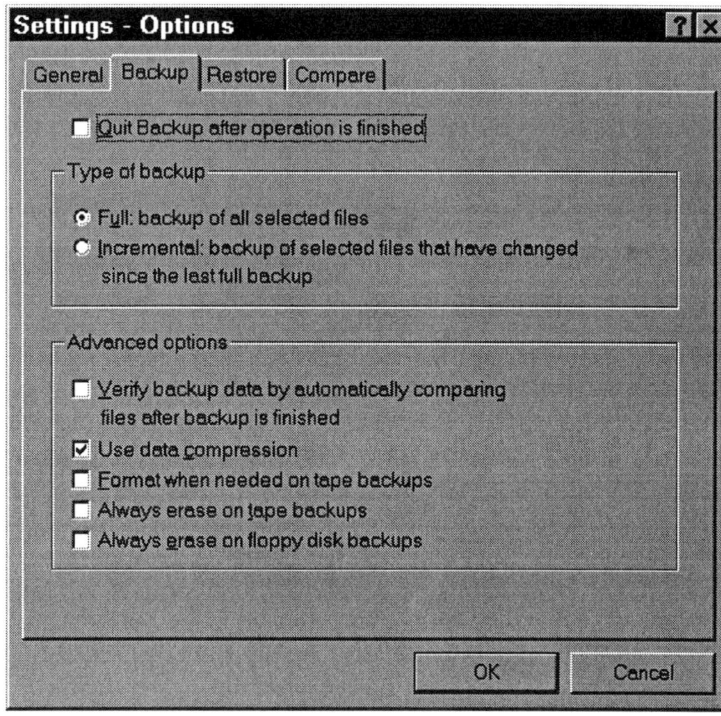


**Figure 10** The Backup Page of the Options Dialog Box

- Select the *Quit Backup after operation is finished* check box at the top of the dialog box if you want the Backup utility to close when the current operation is complete.
- An *incremental backup* copies only those selected files that have been modified since the last backup. Thus, selecting this *Type of backup* option button may save time if the current file set has been backed up before.
- In the *Advanced options* section of the dialog box:

  Selecting *Verify backup data by automatically comparing files after backup is finished* does just that.

  *Use data compression* works with tapes only; when selected, this feature reduces the space used by the backed up files.

  Selecting *Format when needed on tape backups* will automatically format unformatted tapes before backup begins.

Selecting *Always erase on tape backups* erases the tape in the drive before backup begins. If not selected, the new files are added to those already on the tape.

Selecting *Always erase on floppy disk backups* erases the diskette in the drive before backup begins. If not selected, the new files are added to those already on the disk.

9.3 TUTORIAL

Try the following exercise on your own.

1. Turn on the computer (if necessary) to start Windows 95 and open the Backup utility: Click on the Start button, successively point at Programs, Accessories, and System Tools, and finally click on the Backup item on the last submenu.
2. Place a formatted diskette in its drive.
3. Select files to be backed up:
   - In the *Select files to back up* subwindow, open the Programs subfolder of the Start Menu folder: Successively click on the plus (+) symbols next to the C:, Windows, and Start Menu icons; then click on the Programs icon.
   - In the right-hand window, select the Accessories subfolder and the Windows Explorer and MS-DOS Prompt shortcuts by clicking on the box to the left of these icons.
4. Select a destination for the backup:
   - Choose the Next Step command button.
   - In the window, click on the icon for the floppy drive in which you inserted the diskette.
5. Start the backup:
   - Choose the Start Backup command button. The Backup Set Label dialog box will open.
   - Type a name for the set of backup files, say "My Backup", and choose the OK command button. The animated Backup dialog box will show the progress of the backup operation.
6. Complete the operation by clicking on the OK buttons to clear the "operation complete" and Backup dialog boxes from the screen.
7. Restore the backed up files to their original locations (which could be necessary if the originals became unusable):
   - Click on the Restore tab in the Backup window.
   - Select the floppy drive in the *Restore from* subwindow and the My Backup item in the *Backup Set* subwindow.
   - Choose the Next Step command button. The right-hand

window will display the contents of the My Backup set.
- Select (by clicking on the check box) all the listed items.

8. At this point, you would normally choose the Start Restore command button to begin the restoration. Here, however, close the Backup window and remove the diskette from its drive.

# 9.4 *Using Other System Tools*

In this section, we will discuss several accessories that help you to maintain and make more efficient use of your disks. Like Backup (which was introduced in Section 9.3), these utilities are located on the System Tools submenu of the Start button's Accessories menu. We will discuss:

- *ScanDisk*, which finds and repairs (when possible) certain disk problems.
- *Disk Defragmenter*, which rearranges the data on a disk so that its files occupy contiguous sectors.
- *DriveSpace*, which compresses the data stored in files so that they occupy less space on the disk.

## *ScanDisk*

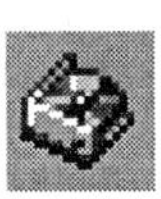

Considering their complexity, disk drives and disk drive controllers are amazingly reliable devices. Nevertheless, every once in a while, data are not stored properly and, as a result, become unusable or needlessly take up disk space. You should periodically use the **ScanDisk** accessory to detect and repair these problems.

**Running ScanDisk** To have ScanDisk check one of your disks:

1. Click on the Start button to display the Start menu.
2. Point at Programs, then at Accessories, and finally at System Tools on each resulting submenu.
3. Click on the ScanDisk item on the System Tools submenu. This utility will start and display the window shown in Figure 11, on the next page.
4. In the ScanDisk window, select the drive you want to check for errors.

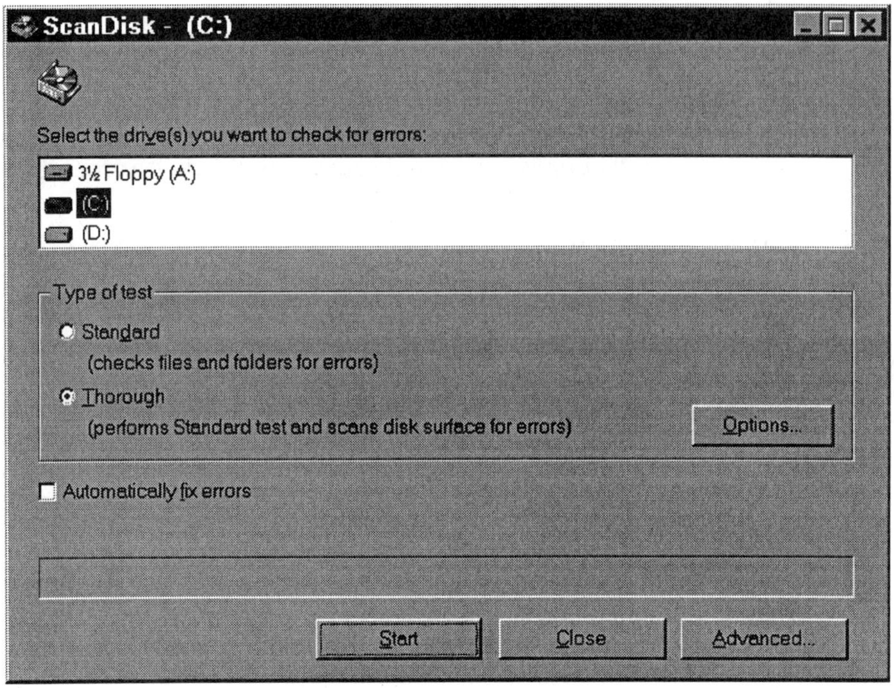


**Figure 11** The ScanDisk Window

5. Select either the *Standard* or the *Thorough* option button. The Standard option checks for errors in the way files and folders have been stored on disk. The Thorough option not only runs these tests, but also checks the physical integrity of the selected disk. The Thorough option takes *much* longer and, as a practical matter, need not be run as frequently as the Standard one.
6. If you select the *Automatically fix errors* check box, ScanDisk will not only detect and report any errors, but also attempt to repair them. It is safer to deselect this box. You can always have ScanDisk try to fix the reported errors later.
7. You can select additional options for the ScanDisk run by choosing the Advanced button (for both Standard and Thorough test modes) and the Options button (which is available only if the Thorough mode is selected). There is normally little reason to change most of these options, and we will discuss them later.
8. Choose the Start command button to activate ScanDisk. The progress of the testing process will be indicated at the bottom of the ScanDisk window. (You can abort the process at any time by choosing the Cancel button.) When testing is complete, a message

to this effect or a report summarizing ScanDisk's findings will be displayed.

9. Choose the Close command button to exit ScanDisk.

**ScanDisk Options** As we mentioned earlier, you can select options for ScanDisk testing by choosing either the Advanced or Options (in Thorough test mode only) command buttons. You should be aware that the defaults chosen for these options tend to emphasize safety over speed; think twice before changing them.

**Choosing the Advanced button**

When you choose the Advanced command button in the ScanDisk window, the dialog box shown in Figure 12 is displayed:

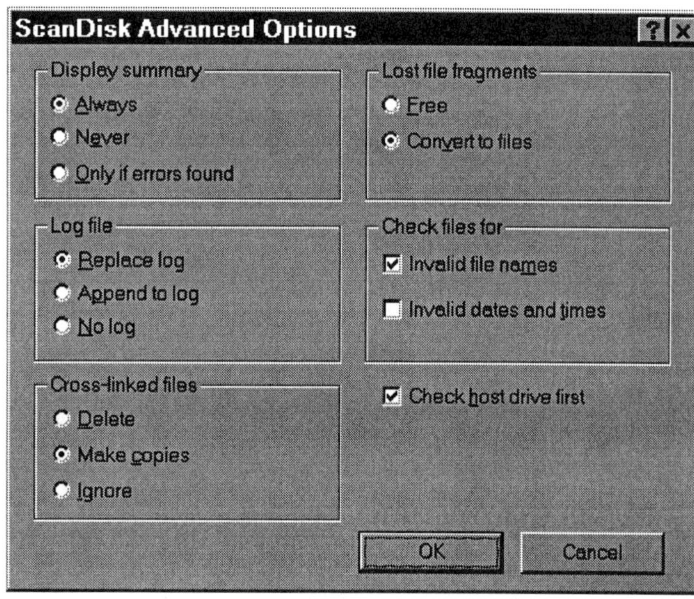


**Figure 12** "Advanced" ScanDisk Options

Here's a description of some of these options:

- The *Log file* option buttons determine whether or not a report of the testing is stored on disk (in the Scandisk log file in the C:\ folder) and, if it is, whether it replaces or is appended (added) to the existing file.
- *Cross-linked files* are files that, according to the disk's file allocation table, share the same disk space. If you try to read a cross-linked file, you may be denied access or see "garbage" displayed

on the screen. Although cross-linked files can rarely be fixed without losing some data, ScanDisk gives you several options for dealing with them. *Delete* erases the cross-linked files; *Make copies* copies each cross-linked file to a new location (the "safe" alternative), and *Ignore* leaves the problem unfixed. (The last option is actually the best one *if* you have other, more advanced disk-repair software with which to attack this problem.)

- *Lost file fragments* (or *lost clusters*) are parts of the disk that, according to the disk's file allocation table, contain data which does not belong to any file. The *Free* option deletes these files; the *Convert to files* option is almost always the better choice — you can then try to view the resulting files (which are named File0000, File0001, etc.) to see if they contain useful information.

**Choosing the Options button**

The Options button in the ScanDisk window provides options for thorough testing only. Choosing this command button displays the dialog box shown in Figure 13.

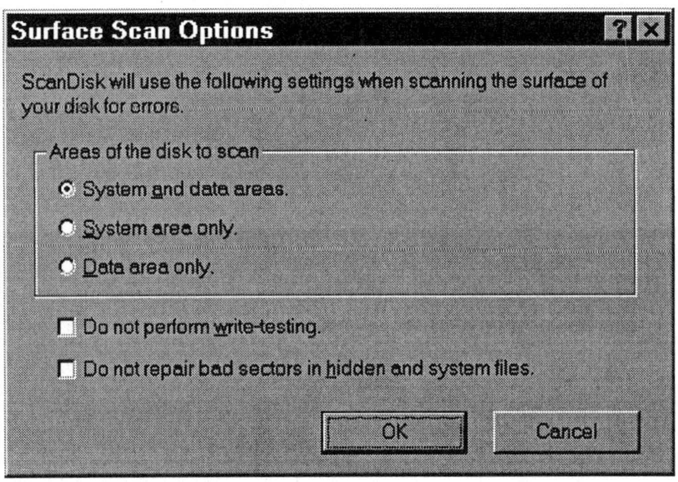


**Figure 13** Options for Thorough Testing

Here's a description of these options. (The defaults are set for the most thorough, and most time-consuming, disk testing.)

- *Areas of the disk to scan:* In this context, the disk is divided into two parts — the system area (consisting of operating system files that control startup, file allocation, and the like) and the data area (everything else). Be aware that disk surface errors in the system area can rarely be fixed (at least by ScanDisk).

- By default, ScanDisk tests the surface of a disk by both reading from and writing to every disk location. If you want to speed up the testing process, using a less rigorous test, select the *Do not perform write-testing* check box.
- Hidden and system files are usually used for special purposes. Although it may be possible to move such a file to a new location if the disk area in which it is stored has become damaged, the file may not work in the new location. So, unless you observe problems in running Windows or an application that seem to be related to the file in question, it may be best to select the *Do not repair bad sectors in hidden and system files* check box.

## *Disk Defragmenter*

When a file is stored on disk, Windows writes it to the first available location. If that area is not big enough to hold the entire file, the file becomes *fragmented* — parts of it are stored in noncontiguous locations. This occurs often and isn't as bad as it sounds. You won't have any trouble accessing the file (the operating system keeps track of where the various parts are stored); it may just take slightly longer to read the file into RAM.

However, if a disk has become highly fragmented, its performance may suffer. The **Disk Defragmenter** accessory tells you the degree to which a disk has become fragmented and, if you wish, you can use this utility to *defragment* the disk — rearrange its files so that each is stored as a single contiguous unit.

**Running Disk Defragmenter** To start the defragmenting process:

1. Click on the Start button to display the Start menu.
2. Point at Programs, then at Accessories, and finally at System Tools on each resulting submenu.
3. Click on the Disk Defragmenter item on the System Tools submenu. This action starts the utility and displays the small window shown in Figure 14, on the next page.
4. Select the drive to be analyzed for fragmentation (and possibly, to be defragmented) from the drop-down list and choose the OK command button.
5. Disk Defragmenter will determine the degree of fragmentation of the selected drive and display it (as a percentage) in another

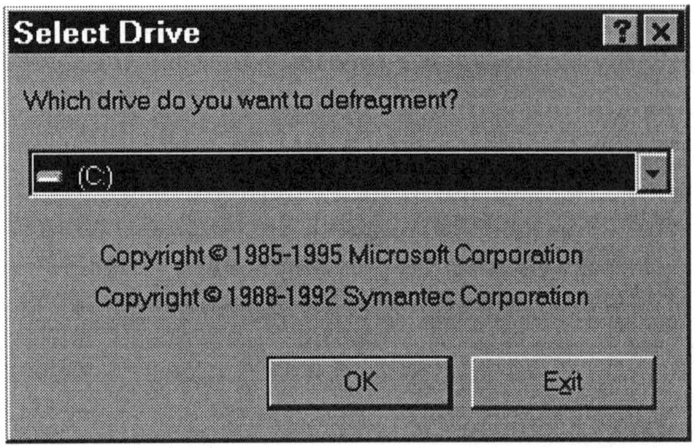


**Figure 14** Initial Disk Defragmenter Window

window (Figure 15). It also makes a recommendation concerning whether or not defragmentation is desirable.

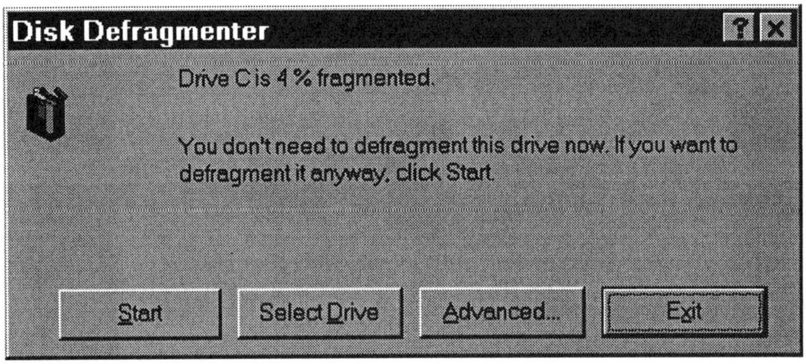


**Figure 15** Assessing the Amount of Fragmentation

6. You now have four choices, as provided by the command buttons:
   - To close the Disk Defragmenter utility, chose *Exit*.
   - To select another drive for analysis and possible defragmentation, choose *Select Drive*. You will be returned to the dialog box of Figure 14.
   - To select certain defragmentation options, choose *Advanced*. We will discuss these options later in this section.
   - To begin the defragmentation process, choose *Start*. The following dialog box, which shows the progress of the defrag-

mentation, will be displayed:

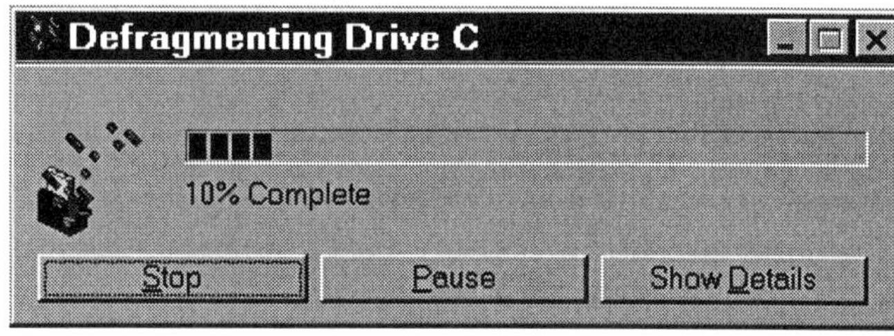


To halt the process at any time, chose the Stop button; to halt it temporarily, choose the Pause button. (The Show Details command button opens another dialog box that provides a graphical display of the defragmentation process.)

**Disk Defragmenter Options** Prior to beginning the defragmentation process, you can select options by choosing the Advanced command button (see Figure 15), which opens the dialog box shown in Figure 16. The default settings (which are shown in Figure 16) provide the most thorough (and most lengthy) defragmentation. Here is a rundown of the available options:

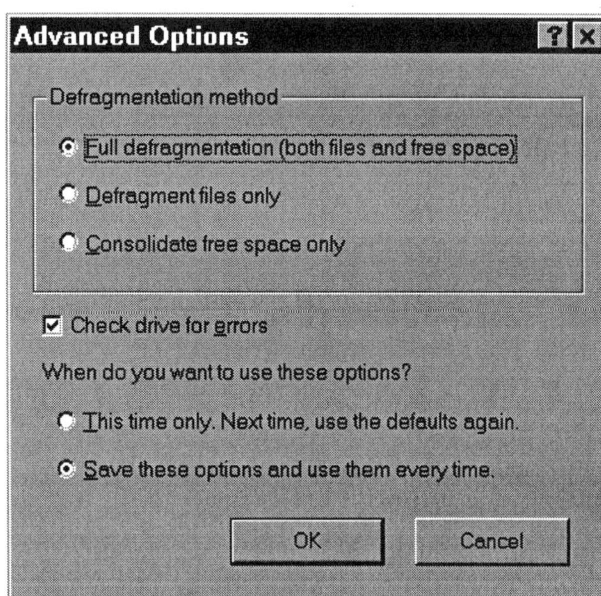


**Figure 16** Defragmentation Options

- The first set of option buttons in the Advanced Options dialog box determines the extent of the defragmentation to be undertaken (and the amount of time it will take to complete the process). The top option does the most thorough job; *Defragment files only* consolidates each fragmented file into a single contiguous unit, but leaves existing free disk space spread across the disk; *Consolidate free space only* makes a single contiguous unit of your disk's free space but does not defragment files.
- Selecting the *Check drive for errors* box is equivalent to running ScanDisk's "Standard" test option prior to defragmentation. It takes extra time, but is a good idea unless you have just run ScanDisk.
- The last pair of option buttons determine whether or not the current settings will be used for just this run of Disk Defragmenter (the upper button) or will become the new default settings for future runs (the lower button).

## *DriveSpace*

Modern hard disks have seemingly limitless capacities, at least when they're new. However, if you use audio, video, or complex graphics files, even the largest of disks will eventually fill up. At this point, you could buy a larger hard disk, but it's easier to increase the storage capacity of the existing one by *compressing* it — encoding the files on the disk in such a way that they take up much less space.

The **DriveSpace** accessory compresses and "uncompresses" both hard and floppy disks. It does this by creating a single large file on the disk to hold all the compressed files. The original disk that contains this *compressed volume* is called the *host drive.* When a file is written to a compressed disk, it is automatically compressed; when a file is read from a compressed volume, it is automatically decompressed. To the user performing a read or write operation, a compressed disk is indistinguishable from an uncompressed one.

**WARNING**

It takes a long time — often several hours — to compress a disk, especially if it already contains a lot of files. First, DriveSpace checks the disk for errors and defragments it (the compressed volume must occupy a single unbroken unit of disk apace). Then, an empty compressed volume is created. Finally, DriveSpace copies each file to this area, compressing it in the process and erasing it from its original location.

The compression process usually goes through without a hitch.

Nevertheless, with an operation of this scope and complexity, something may go wrong. To avoid the potential loss of valuable data, it's a very good idea to back up the entire disk (see Section 9.3) before proceeding.

**Running DriveSpace** To use DriveSpace to compress a disk:

1. Click on the Start button to display the Start menu.
2. Point at Programs, then at Accessories, and finally at System Tools on each resulting submenu.
3. Click on the DriveSpace item on the System Tools submenu. This action starts the utility and displays the window shown in Figure 17.

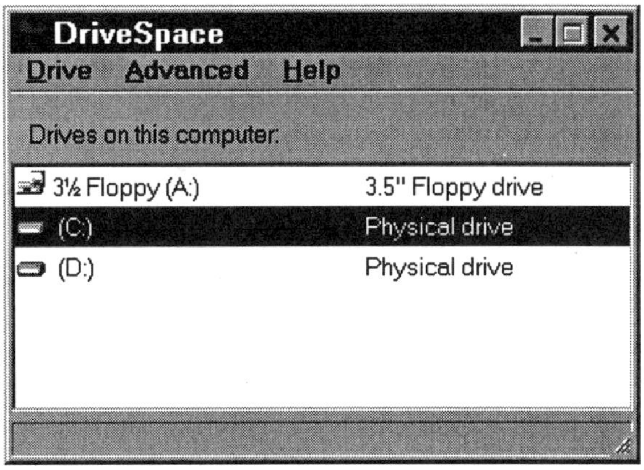


**Figure 17** The DriveSpace Window

4. Select the drive to be compressed.
5. Choose the Compress command on the Drive menu. The Compress a Drive dialog box shown in Figure 18 (on the next page) will open.
6. Choose the Start command button. A dialog box will appear giving you the opportunity to back up your files. If you have not yet backed them up, do so now!
7. Chose the Compress Now command button to begin the compression process. A dialog box will open, showing the progress of the this procedure.

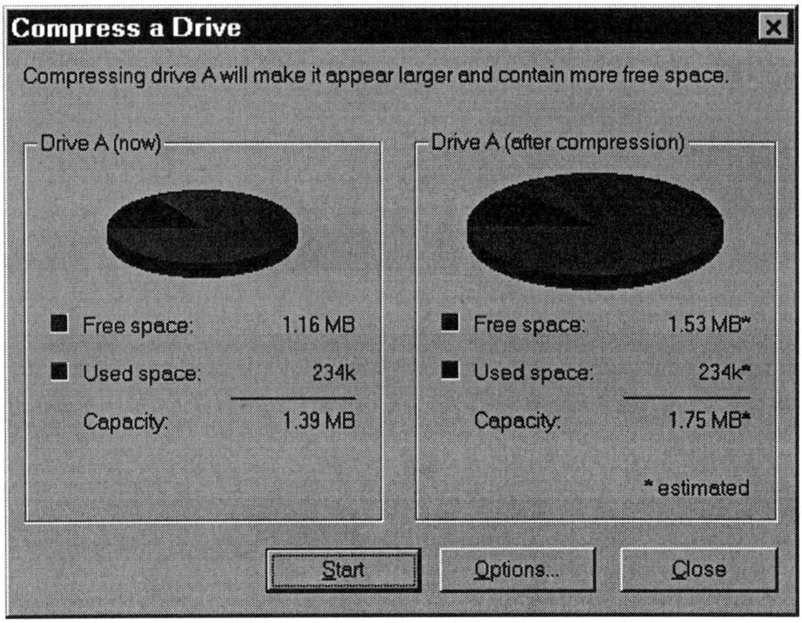


**Figure 18** Compressing a Drive Begins Here

8. At the completion of the process, you may be prompted to restart Windows or you may have to close the Compress a Drive dialog box and the DriveSpace window.

NOTE

The compressed volume takes on the drive letter of the original drive and the host drive is assigned a new letter, such as H. By default, the entire disk is compressed, so that no "free" (uncompressed) space remains on the host drive. However, it is sometimes desirable to leave free space on a hard disk to store, for example, important disk utilities should something go wrong with that disk.

Prior to compression, you can specify the amount of "free" space on the compressed drive by choosing the Options command button in the Compress a Drive dialog box. After compression, you can accomplish this by selecting the drive in the DriveSpace window and choosing the Adjust Free Space command from the Drive menu.

**Uncompressing a Disk** If you want to, you can *uncompress* a compressed drive — decompress all files on it and delete the compressed volume. To do so:

1. Start DriveSpace, as described earlier. The DriveSpace window

(Figure 17) will be displayed.

2. Choose the Uncompress command from the Drive menu. The Uncompress a Drive dialog box (which is similar to the one in Figure 18) will open.
3. Choose the Start command button. The resulting dialog box will give you the opportunity to back up your files. If you have not done this already, do it now!
4. Choose the Uncompress Now command button to begin the process. Another dialog box will appear, showing the progress of the operation.
5. When the operation is complete, close the Uncompress a Drive dialog box and the DriveSpace window.

**9.4 TUTORIAL**

Try the following exercise on your own.

1. Insert the Lab Exercises disk in its drive.
2. Check the floppy disk for errors:
   - Start the ScanDisk utility from the System Tools submenu of the Start button's Accessories menu.
   - Select the relevant floppy drive in the ScanDisk window.
   - Select the Standard option button (which checks the disk for file and folder errors, but not for physical flaws). Leave all options (available from the Advanced command button) at their defaults.
   - Choose the Start command button.
   - When testing is complete, close the Summary window and the ScanDisk window.
3. Defragment the floppy disk:
   - Start the Disk Defragmenter utility from the System Tools submenu of the Start button's Accessories menu.
   - Select the relevant floppy drive from the Select Drive drop-down list and choose the OK command button.
   - In the Disk Defragmenter window, choose the Advanced (options) command button; then, select the *Full defragmentation* option button, deselect the *Check drive for errors* check box (because you have just used ScanDisk to do this), select the *This time only* option button, and choose the OK command button.
   - In the Disk Defragmenter window, choose the Start button.
   - When the defragmentation starts, choose the Show Details command button and then the Legend button to obtain a

graphical view of what is going on.
- When defragmentation is complete, choose the Yes command button in the message box to close Disk Defragmenter.

4. Compress the files on the floppy disk:
   - Start the DriveSpace utility from the System Tools submenu of the Start button's Accessories menu.
   - Select the relevant floppy drive in the DriveSpace window.
   - Choose the Compress command from the Drive menu.
   - Choose the Start command button in the Compress a Drive dialog box and then the Compress Now button in the resulting dialog box.
   - When the process is complete, close the Compress a Drive dialog box.
5. Uncompress the floppy disk:
   - Select the relevant floppy drive in the DriveSpace window.
   - Choose the Uncompress command from the Drive menu.
   - Choose the Start command button in the Uncompress a Drive dialog box and then the Uncompress Now button in the resulting dialog box. (If the Remove Compression dialog box appears, choose the Yes button.)
   - When the process is complete, close the Uncompress a Drive dialog box and the DriveSpace window.
6. Remove the diskette from its drive.

# *9.5 Additional Accessories*

In this section, we will briefly discuss a few other Windows accessories: Character Map, and some multimedia and communications utilities.

## *Character Map*

**Character Map** lets you insert special symbols into a document open in another Windows application. To use Character Map:

1. Click on the Start button, point at Programs, then at Accessories, and choose the Character Map item from the resulting submenu. The window shown in Figure 19 will open.

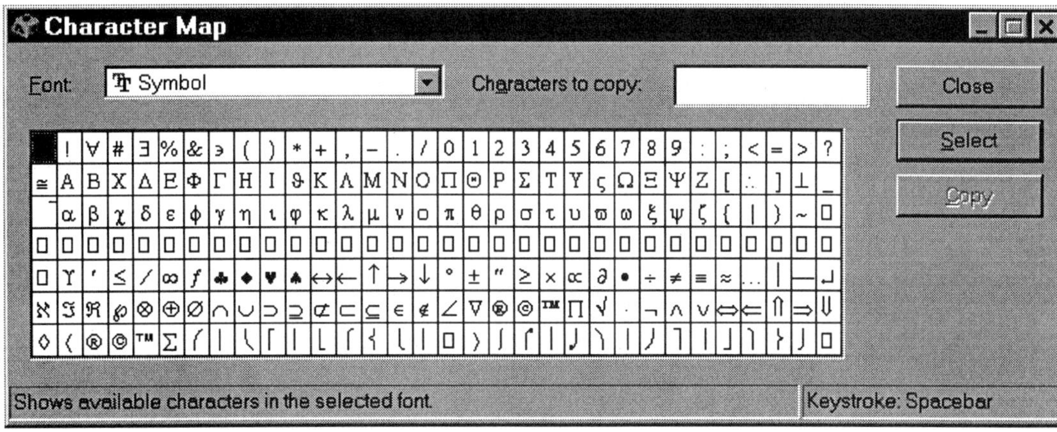


**Figure 19** The Character Map Window

2. Select a typeface from the Font drop-down list. The *character set* for the selected font will be displayed in the window.
3. Select a character from those displayed by double-clicking on it (or by clicking on it and choosing the Select command button). The selected character will appear in the Characters to copy box.
4. If you want, repeat step 2 to select additional characters.
5. Choose the Copy command button to copy the selected characters to the Clipboard.
6. Switch to the application and document in which you want to insert the characters.
7. In this document, position the insertion point where you want the characters to be inserted, select the same typeface as the one used in Character Map, and choose the Paste command from the Edit menu.

## *Multimedia Accessories*

**Multimedia** is a catch-all term that refers to the creation, recording, display, or playback of documents that contain sophisticated sound, graphics, and/or video components. If your computer is equipped with multimedia devices (such as a sound board or CD-ROM drive), the Multimedia item on the Accessories submenu provides access to programs that manipulate these devices. The particular multimedia accessories available to you depend on how your system is configured. They may include:

- **CD Player** allows you to play audio compact discs on your CD-ROM drive. Its interface resembles the control panel of the compact disc player connected to your stereo system. The music is transmitted by the computer's sound board and played through its speakers.
- **Media Player** allows you to play multimedia files of various kinds and control a variety of multimedia devices, including CD-ROM drives, sound boards, and MIDI (Musical Instrument Digital Interface) keyboards. Each available Media Player "device" corresponds to a separate set of files and controls. For example, if you choose the Sound command from the Device menu, a collection of sound files will be displayed. Double clicking on one of them "plays" the content of the file through the sound board and speakers.
- **Sound Recorder** allows you to record sound (input via a microphone or a line-in cable to the sound board), edit it, and store the result as a file on your hard disk. The Sound Recorder's interface resembles the controls on an audio tape player.
- **Volume Control** lets you adjust the volume, balance, and tone of the various sound devices connected to your computer system.

## *Communications Accessories*

If your computer is equipped with a **modem**, a device that translates computer-generated data into signals that can be sent (usually over phone lines) to another computer, you can access information on other computer systems. Using computer-to-computer communication:

- You can access the vast quantities of data supplied by an **online information service**, such as CompuServe, America Online, or the Microsoft Network. With such a service, you will be able to receive *e-mail* (electronic mail), use encyclopedias, obtain stock market quotes, make airline reservations, and even "chat" with other subscribers.
- You can post messages on electronic *bulletin boards* and read messages posted there by others.
- You can make use of the **Internet** — a worldwide system of computer networks — to browse through the information posted by hundreds of thousands of organizations and individuals on the *World Wide Web.*
- You can connect to your campus computer network and access the software and data on it that have been authorized for public use.

- If your modem contains fax capabilities (as virtually all modems do, nowadays), you can send computer-generated faxes and receive any fax transmitted by others.

To take advantage of these communication possibilities, you not only need a modem and phone line, but also *communications software*. For this purpose, Windows supplies two key accessories:

- **HyperTerminal** is a communications software package that allows you to configure, dial, and pass commands to the modem from your keyboard. It ensures, with your input, that the signals sent by your computer, through its modem and the telephone lines, will be understandable to the hardware setup on the remote system.
- **Microsoft Fax** is a fax communications program; it helps you to send and receive faxes through your computer's fax modem. In order to use Microsoft Fax, the Microsoft Exchange software (also supplied with Windows) must be installed on your computer, as well. **Microsoft Exchange** acts as a clearinghouse for all electronically transmitted documents received by your computer, regardless of their source.

## Review Exercises

**Section 9.1**

1. In the Calculator accessory, you can display a standard or scientific calculator by choosing the corresponding item from the ___________ menu.
2. To clear Calculator's memory, click on the ___________ button.
3. In Scientific mode, to have Calculator find the mean and standard deviation of a collection of numbers, begin by clicking on the ___________ button.
4. True or false: Clicking on Calculator's Back button deletes the last digit entered into the display.
5. True or false: It is not possible to copy the number in Calculator's display to the Clipboard.
6. True or false: To calculate the sine of an angle using Calculator's Scientific mode, you must enter the angle in radian measure.
7. If you want to multiply 3.14 by the number in Calculator's memory, enter 3.14 into the display, click on the multiply symbol (*), and then

a. Click on the MC button.
b. Click on the MR button.
c. Click on the MS button.
d. Click on the M+ button.

8. The default number system used by Calculator when in Scientific mode is:

   a. Binary
   b. Octal
   c. Decimal
   d. Hexadecimal

**Section 9.2**

9. Notepad is a simple word processor that has no text formatting capabilities and is thus known as a ___________.

10. By default, ___________ is turned off in Notepad, so the text you type remains on the same line until you press the Enter key.

11. A ___________ for a document is text that is automatically placed at the top of every page.

12. True or false: Although Notepad can search a document for a specified word, it cannot automatically replace it with another word of your choice.

13. True or false: To read a page that is printed in portrait orientation, hold it so that the long side is vertical.

14. True or false: In Notepad, you can specify the number of copies to be printed before the printing process begins.

15. Which of the following operations can be performed by Notepad?

    a. Aligning text with the right margin.
    b. Setting top, bottom, right, and left margins.
    c. Changing the font displayed on the screen.
    d. Indenting the text in a given paragraph.

16. Which of the following sequences of symbols is used to create a Notepad footer that displays the current page number at the left margin and the current date at the right margin?

    a. &p &d
    b. &l &p &d
    c. &l &p &d &r
    d. &l &p &r &d

**Section 9.3**

17. The Backup utility is found on the ___________ submenu of the Start button's Accessories menu.

18. To ___________ a backed up file means to copy it from the backup medium to its original location.

19. True or false: In Backup, a shaded, checked box next to a folder icon in the *Select the files to back up* window means that some, but not all, of the files in that folder have been selected.

20. True or false: You can place a shortcut on the Desktop which, when double-clicked, not only starts the Backup utility, but also makes predefined selections and starts the backup process.

21. The Backup utility cannot back up a file on the hard disk to:

    a. A tape cartridge, even if your computer is equipped with a tape drive.
    b. A floppy disk.
    c. Another location on the hard disk.
    d. None of the above is correct.

22. The Backup utility cannot be used to:

    a. Back up files and folders from the hard disk to a floppy.
    b. Restore backed up files from a floppy to the hard disk.
    c. Move (copy and delete) files from the hard disk to a floppy.
    d. Compare a backed up file to the original.

**Section 9.4**

23. If you want to locate and delete lost file fragments, use the Windows ____________ utility.

24. A disk file is said to be ____________ if it is stored in two or more nonadjacent locations on disk.

25. When DriveSpace ____________ a file, the file takes up less space on disk than it did formerly.

26. True or false: The ScanDisk utility can be set up to detect errors without fixing them.

27. True or false: Disk Defragmenter tells you the degree to which the selected disk is fragmented before starting the defragmentation process.

28. True or false: DriveSpace can uncompress disks that it had previously compressed.

29. To use the ScanDisk utility to check for physical flaws on the surface of a disk:

    a. Choose the Advanced command button.
    b. Select the Standard option button.
    c. Select the Thorough option button.
    d. ScanDisk cannot perform this test.

30. When Disk Defragmenter does a full (complete) defragmentation:

    a. It defragments files, but does not consolidate free space.
    b. It consolidates free space, but does not defragment files.

c. It defragments files and consolidates free space.
d. It neither defragments files nor consolidates free space.

**Section 9.5**

31. The Windows ____________ accessory enables you to insert special symbols into documents open in another Windows application.
32. The term ____________ refers to applications that contain sophisticated graphics, sound, and video components.
33. True or false: To copy a character from the Character Map accessory to the Clipboard, choose the Copy command on the Edit menu.
34. True or false: To use ordinary telephone lines to access an online information service, your computer needs to be equipped with a modem.
35. Which of the following is not a multimedia device?
    a. A sound card
    b. A CD-ROM drive
    c. A modem
    d. A MIDI keyboard
36. Which of the following applications does not deal with computer-to-computer communications.
    a. Media Player
    b. HyperTerminal
    c. Microsoft Fax
    d. Microsoft Exchange

## *Lab Exercises*

Work each of the following exercises at your computer. Begin by turning the machine on (if necessary) to start Windows 95 and closing any open windows.

**Lab Exercise 1 (Section 9.1)**

a. Start Windows Calculator and display the Standard calculator. Can you maximize the Calculator window?

b. What value would you expect for the expression 4 + 5 * 6, 34 or 54? Why? Use Calculator to find its value. What did you get?

c. Enter the number 13 into memory. Which memory key did you use? Did an "M" appear in the box above the memory keys?

d. Add 22 to the number in memory? What memory key did you use?

e. Now, find 6% of the current number in memory. What did you get?

f. Clear both memory and the current calculation. What two keys did you use to accomplish this?

g. Find $1/\sqrt{11}$ and $\sqrt{1/11}$. Did you get the same answer for both expressions?

h. Close Calculator.

**Lab Exercise 2 (Section 9.2)**

a. Start Notepad and maximize its window.

b. Type your name and class on separate lines, and skip a line (by pressing the Enter key twice).

c. Type the sentence: This is a test of the copy and paste operations. Then, press the Enter key.

d. Select this sentence. Describe how you accomplished this.

e. Copy the selected text to the Clipboard. What menu command or mouse actions did you use?

f. Paste the text from the Clipboard onto the end of the document. What menu command or mouse actions did you use?

g. Repeat step *f* four times. Try pasting the text without reselecting and recopying it. Did this work?

h. Print the document.

i. Save the document (see Section 2.2) if you wish and exit Notepad.

**Lab Exercise 3 (Section 9.2)**

a. Start Notepad and maximize its window.

b. Insert the Lab Exercises disk in its drive and open the History2 document (see Section 2.2, if necessary).

c. In the Page Setup dialog box:

- Set the orientation to *portrait* and all margins to one inch.
- Create a header that contains your name (left-aligned) and your class (right-aligned).
- Create a footer that displays the date, centered on the line.

d. Open the Find dialog box and enter the word *large* in the *Find what* box. Now, use this utility to determine the number of times the word *large* occurs in the document.

e. At the end of the document, type complete sentences stating the number of times the word *large* occurs and the number of times words containing *large* occur in the document.

f. Print the revised document.

g. Save the document if you wish, exit Notepad, and remove the diskette from its drive.

**Lab Exercise 4 (Section 9.3)**

a. Start the Backup utility and insert the Lab Exercises disk in its drive (we will assume this drive is A:).

b. Perform a partial backup of the Lab Exercises disk:

- In the left window, select the A: drive.
- In the right window, select the Paint folder and the Testfile and Memo files to be backed up. Does a check mark appear in the box next to the A: drive icon in the left window?
- Try to select A: as the destination for the backup. What message is displayed?
- Select the root folder of the C: drive (C:\) as the destination for the backup.
- Use Backup Test as the label for the backup set and start the backup. How long did it take?

c. Compare some of the backed up files with the originals:

- In the *Compare from* window, select the C: drive.
- For *Files to compare*, select the Testfile and Memo files "From drive A:".

How long did the comparison take?

d. Restore some of the backed up files:

- Restore from the C: drive and the Backup Test set.
- Select as the "Files to restore": Testfile and Memo "From drive A:".

Was an error message displayed? If so, what caused the error?

e. Start Explorer and locate the Backup Test file in the C:\ folder. What size is it? Delete the Backup Test file.

f. Close Explorer and Backup and remove the diskette from its drive.

**Lab Exercise 5 (Section 9.4)**

a. Start the ScanDisk utility.

b. Insert the Lab Exercises disk in its drive and select this drive in the ScanDisk window.

c. Select the Thorough test mode, but elect not to perform write-testing or repair bad sectors in hidden or system files. In which dialog box are the last two options found?

d. Elect not to print a "log file" but do check files for invalid dates and times. Also, make sure that a summary is displayed whether or not there are errors. In which dialog box did you select these options?

e. Start the ScanDisk tests. Were any errors found? If so, what are they?

f. Use the summary to answer the following questions:

What is the total disk space for this disk?
How many bytes of space are there in bad sectors?
How many files are there are on this disk?

g. Close ScanDisk and remove the Lab Exercises disk from its drive.

**Lab Exercise 6 (Section 9.4)**

a. Start the Disk Defragmenter utility.

b. Insert the Lab Exercises disk in its drive, select this drive from the drop-down list, and choose the OK button. What is its degree of fragmentation (as a percentage)?

c. Elect to perform a full fragmentation, but not to check the disk for errors. In which dialog box did you select these options?

d. Start the defragmentation process and choose the Show Details button, then the Legend button. Use the Defrag Legend window to answer the following questions. (You can choose the Pause button to give yourself more time to find the answers.)

What color is used to represent free disk space?
Are any parts of the disk marked as "bad (damaged) area"?
What does each box in the display represent?

e. Resume the defragmentation, if necessary. When defragmentation is complete, close Disk Defragmenter and remove the diskette from its drive.

**Lab Exercise 7 (Section 9.5)**

a. Start Notepad, WordPad, and the Character Map accessory.

b. In Character Map, choose the Symbol font from the drop-down list.

c. Position the mouse pointer over a character and hold down the mouse button. What happened?

d. Select several characters (of your choice), displaying them in the

*Characters to copy* box.

e. Choose the Copy command button. What does this action accomplish?

f. Switch to WordPad and display the Format Bar, if necessary. What is the current font (as indicated on the Format Bar)?

g. Choose the Paste command from the Edit menu. Are the same characters displayed in the WordPad document window as were copied from Character Map? What is the current font now?

h. Switch to Notepad and choose the Paste command from the Edit menu. Are the same characters displayed in the Notepad window as were copied from Character Map?

i. Close Notepad, WordPad, and Character Map (responding No to the "save changes?" messages).

APPENDIX A

# General Shortcut Keys

As befits software running under a graphical user interface, Windows and its applications make extensive use of the mouse. Nevertheless, some operations can be performed more quickly using keystrokes (or keystroke combinations), which Windows refers to as *shortcut keys*. In this appendix, we will list some important shortcut keys and their functions. Other shortcut keys (for example, those for WordPad) are described at the appropriate place in the text.

## On the Desktop

| | |
|---|---|
| **Alt+Enter** | Displays the properties sheet for the selected item. |
| **Alt+Esc** | Cycles through the Taskbar buttons. |
| **Alt+Print Screen** | Copies the active window to the Clipboard (anywhere in Windows). |
| **Arrow keys** | Selects the closest icon to the selected one in the specified direction. |
| **Ctrl+Esc** | Displays the Start menu. |
| **Del** | Sends the selected item to the Recycle Bin. |
| **Enter** | Opens the selected item. |
| **F1** | Starts Windows Help. |

| | |
|---|---|
| **F2** | Prepares the selected item for renaming. |
| **F3** | Opens the Find dialog box. |
| **Print Screen** | Copies the entire screen to the Clipboard (anywhere in Windows). |
| **Shift+Del** | Deletes the selected item without sending it to the Recycle Bin. |
| **Shift+F10** | Opens the selected item's right-click menu. |
| **Tab** | Moves the focus to the Start button. |

## In a Dialog Box

| | |
|---|---|
| **Alt+Down Arrow** | Opens a drop-down list (if it has the focus). |
| **Alt+F4** | Closes the dialog box, putting all changes into effect. |
| **Alt+Spacebar** | Opens the Control menu. |
| **Arrow keys** | Cycles through a group of option buttons (if one of them has the focus). |
| **Ctrl+Tab** | Cycles forward through the dialog box tabs. |
| **Ctrl+Shift+Tab** | Cycles backward through the dialog box tabs. |
| **Escape** | Closes the dialog box, canceling all changes. |
| **Tab** | Moves the selection cursor (focus) from item to item. |
| **Shift+Tab** | Moves the selection cursor from item to item in the reverse direction. |
| **Spacebar** | Selects or deselects a check box (if it has the focus). |

## In Most Windows Applications

| | |
|---|---|
| **Alt** | Activates the application's menu bar. (Or, closes all open menus and deactivates the menu bar.) |
| **Alt+*underlined letter*** | Opens the corresponding menu. |
| **Alt+F4** | Closes the application. |
| **Alt+Spacebar** | Opens the Control menu. |

| | |
|---|---|
| **Alt+Tab** | Switches among the running applications. |
| **Ctrl+C** | Copies the selected data to the Clipboard. |
| **Ctrl+V** | Pastes the contents of the Clipboard. |
| **Ctrl+X** | Cuts the selected data to the Clipboard. |
| **Escape** | Closes an open menu or dialog box. |
| **F1** | Starts Help for the application. |
| **F10** | Activates the application's menu bar. (Or, closes all open menus and deactivates the menu bar.) |
| **Shift+F10** | Opens the selected item's right-click menu. |

## In Explorer and My Computer

| | |
|---|---|
| **Alt+Enter** | Displays the properties sheet for the selected object. |
| **Backspace** | Opens the parent folder. |
| **Ctrl+A** | Selects all objects. |
| **Ctrl+Z** | Undoes the last action. |
| **Del** | Sends the selected objects to the Recycle Bin. |
| **Right/Left Arrow** | Expands/collapses the selected folder (Explorer only). |
| **Plus/Minus** (on numeric keypad) | Expands/collapses the selected folder (Explorer only). |
| **Asterisk** (on numeric keypad) | Expands all folders (Explorer only). |
| **F2** | Prepares the selected object for renaming. |
| **F3** | Opens the Find dialog box. |
| **F4** | Displays the Go To drop-down list. |
| **F5** | Refreshes the display. |
| **F6** | Switches between the left and right panes (Explorer only). |
| **Shift+Del** | Deletes the selected objects without sending them to the Recycle Bin. |
| **Shift+F10** | Opens the right-click menu for the selected object. |

**When Starting Up** The following keys apply when the message "Starting Windows 95 ..." appears on the screen.

| | |
|---|---|
| **F4** | Starts the previously installed version of DOS (if possible). |
| **F5** | Starts Windows 95 in safe mode (a very basic configuration). |
| **F6** | Starts Windows 95 in safe mode, with network support. |
| **F8** | Displays a menu of startup options. |

**For "Windows 95 Keyboards"** The following shortcut keys only apply to keyboards (such as the Microsoft *Natural Keyboard*) that contain a "Windows key", which we designate by Win.

| | |
|---|---|
| **Win+E** | Starts Explorer. |
| **Win+F** | Opens the Find dialog box to search for files. |
| **Win+Ctrl+F** | Opens the Find dialog box to search for computers. |
| **Win+F1** | Starts Windows Help. |
| **Win+M** | Minimizes all open windows. |
| **Win+Shift+M** | Undoes the Minimize All command. |
| **Win+R** | Opens the Run dialog box. |
| **Win+Tab** | Cycles through the Taskbar buttons. |

APPENDIX B

# *Running DOS Applications*

A program that was designed to run under the DOS operating system, but not under Windows, is known as a *DOS application*. Although Windows-based software has many advantages over DOS applications (see the Introduction), the latter often run faster and make more efficient use of computer resources. For this reason, some contemporary graphics-intensive computer games are designed as DOS applications.

DOS applications are normally started in the same ways as Windows programs (see Section 2.1). You can run several DOS and Windows programs at the same time and switch among them using the techniques described in Section 2.3. In addition, Windows 95 provides special features for DOS applications that make them easier to use. We will discuss these features in this appendix.

## *Running DOS Applications under Windows*

Unlike Windows applications, which always run inside a window on the Desktop, DOS programs can be run in a window or *full-screen*, in which case the application occupies the entire Desktop, as shown in Figure 1 on the next page.

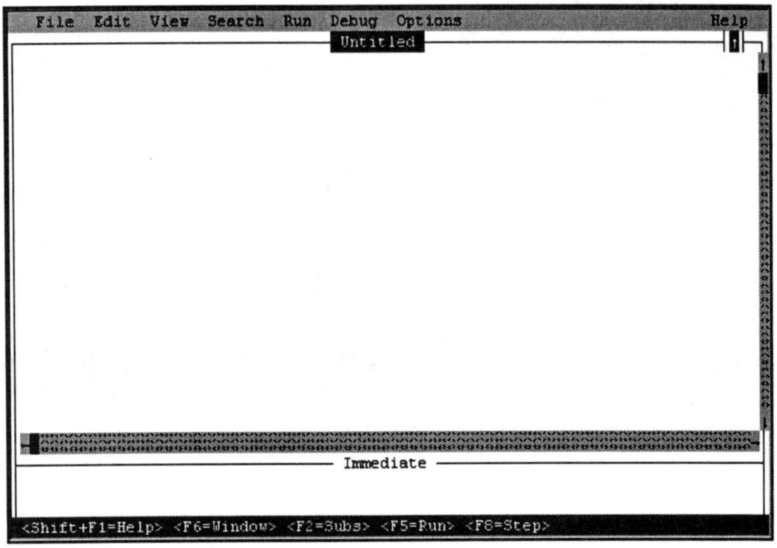


**Figure 1** A DOS Application Running Full-screen

**Switching screen modes**

To switch from one mode to the other, press the Alt+Enter keystroke combination. When the application of Figure 1 is switched to window mode, the result is shown in Figure 2. Notice that the application window contains a title bar (complete with minimize, maximize, and close buttons) and a Toolbar. (The Toolbar can be toggled on and off by clicking on the Control icon, which opens the Control menu, and then choosing the Toolbar command.) We will only consider window mode in the remainder of this section because the special features described below cannot be accessed in full-screen mode.

**Mark, Copy, and Paste** Text in a DOS window can be selected and copied to the Windows Clipboard, and information on the Clipboard can be pasted into the current document. (See Section 2.3 for general information about these operations.)

**Selecting text**

To select (or *mark*) text in the document in a DOS window:

1. Click on the Toolbar's Mark button (see the figure at the right).
   *or*
   Click on the Control icon (or right-click on the title bar) to display the Control menu, point at the Edit item, and choose the Mark command on the resulting submenu.

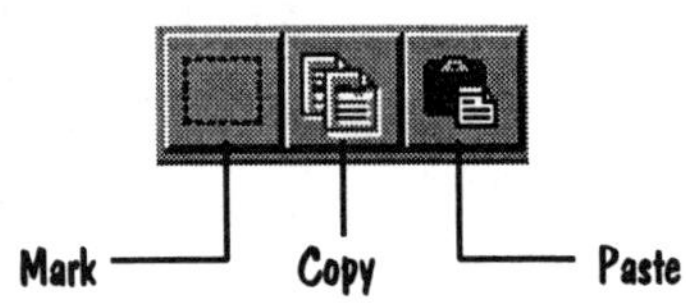

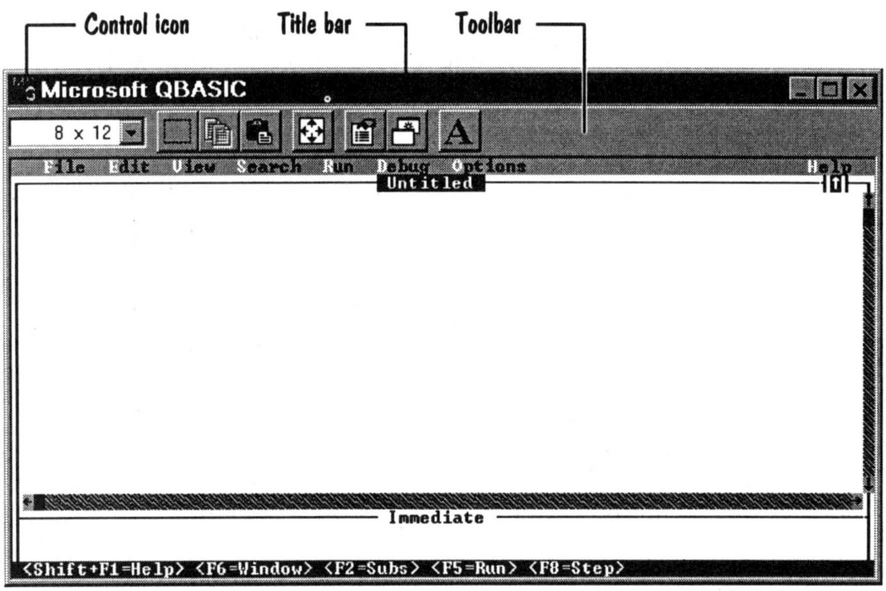


**Figure 2** A DOS Application Running in a Window

2. Use the mouse or keyboard to position the cursor at the beginning of the block of text to be selected and either mouse-drag the cursor to the end of the block, or hold down the Shift key and move the cursor to the end of the block.

The selected block of text will become highlighted.

**Copying text** To copy a selected block of text to the Clipboard, take any of the following actions:

- Press the Enter key.
- Click on the Toolbar's Copy button.
- Click on the Control icon (or right-click on the title bar) to display the Control menu, point at Edit, and choose the Copy command from the resulting submenu.

**Pasting text** To paste text from the Clipboard into a document:

1. Position the cursor where you want to paste the text.
2. Click on the Toolbar's Paste button.
   *or*
   Click on the Control icon (or right-click on the title bar) to display the Control menu, point at Edit, and choose the Paste command from the resulting submenu.

**Selecting a Font** You can change the size of the font used to display the text in a DOS window by:

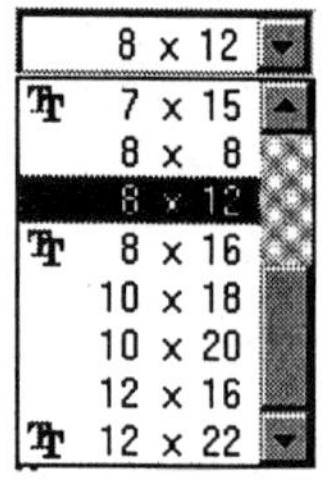


1. Opening the drop-down list on the Toolbar (the result is shown at the right).
2. Selecting (clicking on) one of the listed sizes.

The various font sizes are given in *pixels*; for example, the current font in Figure 2 is 8 pixels wide and 12 pixels high. Be aware that:

- Selecting a larger font size means that the text will be easier to read, but less text will fit in a given window. Selecting a smaller font has the opposite effect.
- Selecting the Auto item from the top of the list sizes the text so that a full DOS "screen" automatically fits the current window. If you resize the window, the font will resize accordingly.

NOTE

You can also change the size of the display font by clicking on the Toolbar's Font button (shown at the right). Doing so opens the Font page of the Properties dialog box. The same font choices are available here as on the Toolbar drop-down list, but when you select a font in this dialog box, its preview windows show the resulting window size and font size.

**Other Toolbar Buttons** Three other buttons reside on the Toolbar (Figure 3). Here are their functions:

Figure 3 Other Toolbar Buttons

- Clicking on the Full Screen button switches the DOS application from the current window mode to full-screen mode.
- Clicking on the Properties button displays the application's Properties dialog box*. This dialog box allows you to fine-tune the way the application runs under Windows. Most of these settings are fairly sophisticated, and we will not discuss them further here.

*You can also open a DOS program's Properties dialog box (or "properties sheet") by right-clicking on the application's shortcut icon in Explorer or My Computer and choosing Properties from the pop-up menu. In Windows 3.1, the function of the Properties dialog box was carried out by the PIF Editor utility.

- The Background button determines whether or not the DOS program will continue to process data when you switch to another application. If the button appears to be "depressed" (indented), background processing will take place.

## *Running a DOS Session*

If you are familiar with the DOS operating system, you may want to issue commands or run programs within DOS from time to time. You can do this — run a *DOS session* — without shutting down Windows 95 by starting the MS-DOS Prompt utility. *MS-DOS Prompt* gives you access to the DOS prompt, so that you can view directories, copy files, start programs, and so on, just as if you were actually running DOS.

**Starting MS-DOS Prompt**

To start MS-DOS Prompt:

1. Click on the Start button to display the Start menu.
2. Point at the Programs option to open its submenu.
3. Click on the MS-DOS Prompt item on this submenu. The window shown in Figure 4, sometimes referred to as a *DOS box*, will open.

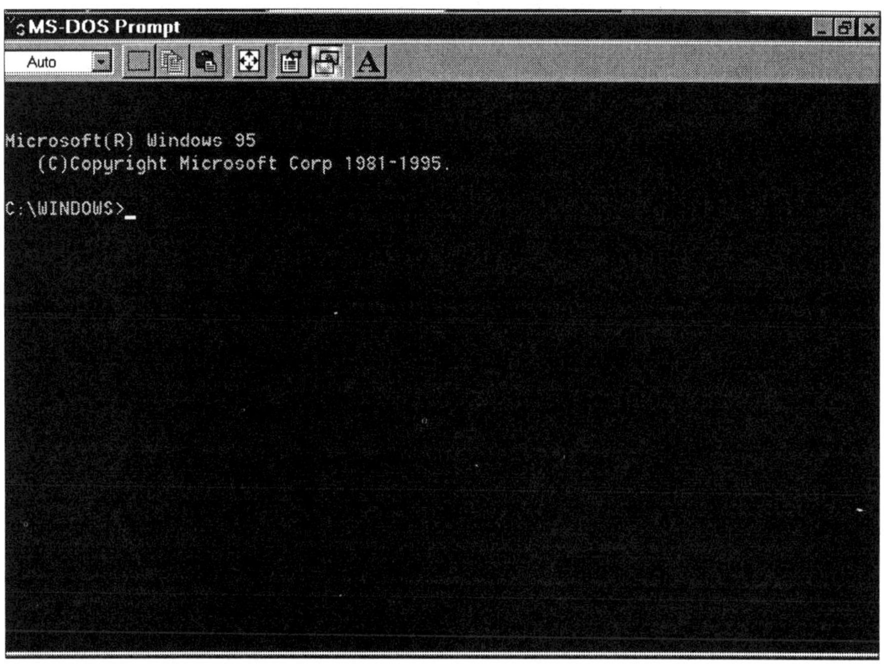


**Figure 4** The MS-DOS Prompt Window

The DOS box provides all the features (described in the first part of this appendix) afforded to any DOS program running in a window. Using the Toolbar or Control menu, you can mark, copy, and paste text within the window, change the display font, switch between window and full-screen mode, and change certain properties. Moreover, from the DOS prompt, which is `C:\WINDOWS>` in Figure 4, you can issue any available DOS command.

### Exiting MS-DOS Prompt

To exit MS-DOS Prompt, close the program that's running (if any), and then take any of the following actions:

- Type `exit` at the DOS prompt and press the Enter key.
- Click on the close button.
- Double-click on the Control icon.
- Click on the Control icon to open the Control menu and choose the Close command.

**NOTE**

There are two basic ways to run DOS by itself, outside of Windows 95 — before startup and after shut down.

- To run DOS before Windows starts up, turn on your computer and press the F8 function key when you see the message "Starting Windows 95". Now, select the menu item entitled "Safe mode command prompt only" and press the Enter key. A version of DOS packaged with Windows 95 will start, but you may not have access to certain hardware devices and software enhancements. This technique should only be used in special cases; for example, if Windows 95 refuses to load and you would like to use diagnostic software that runs under DOS.
- To run DOS after Windows shuts down, while in Windows, choose the Shut Down command from the Start menu. Then, select the *Restart the computer in MS-DOS mode?* option button in the resulting dialog box, and choose the Yes command button. DOS will start after the computer reboots. This technique for running DOS may be useful if one of your DOS applications will not run under Windows; it may run after Windows has been shut down.

APPENDIX C

# Answers to Odd-Numbered Review Exercises

## *Introduction*

1. hardware
3. eight
5. tape *or* CD-ROM
7. true
9. false
11. false
13. false
15. d
17. a
19. operating system
21. graphical user interface
23. false
25. true
27. c
29. ENIAC
31. 1975
33. Apple Macintosh
35. false
37. false
39. d

## *Chapter 1*

1. icon
3. false
5. left mouse button
7. dialog box
9. false
11. c
13. title bar
15. right border / left border
17. true
19. a
21. A: Control icon B: Title bar
    C: Minimize button D: Maximize button
23. OK *or* Close

25. check box
27. true
29. c
31. Start
33. true
35. c

## Chapter 2

1. Ctrl+Esc
3. Close (*or* Exit)
5. true
7. c
9. Accessories
11. open
13. true
15. true
17. a
19. Taskbar
21. Clipboard
23. true
25. c
27. Start
29. book
31. true
33. true
35. c

## Chapter 3

1. file
3. true
5. b
7. contents (*or* right)
9. Details
11. true
13. d
15. Ctrl (Control)
17. Send To
19. true
21. a
23. Recycle Bin (*or* Recycled)
25. box
27. false
29. d
31. double-click
33. true
35. d
37. right-clicking
39. true
41. b

## Chapter 4

1. Settings
3. true
5. b
7. Display
9. screen saver
11. false
13. b
15. Appearance
17. true
19. d
21. Keyboard
23. false
25. d
27. Date/Time
29. Add/Remove Programs
31. true
33. d

## Chapter 5

1. spool
3. queue
5. true
7. false
9. a
11. plug-and-play
13. true
15. a
17. Sounds
19. multimedia
21. false
23. c
25. Accessibility Options
27. numeric keypad
29. false
31. c
33. modem
35. cache
37. true
39. c

## Chapter 6

1. top
3. tiled
5. true
7. d
9. shortcut
11. Start Menu Programs
13. false
15. d
17. Named
19. double-click
21. true
23. c
25. registered
27. false
29. d
31. sheet
33. true
35. a

## Chapter 7

1. Home
3. Ctrl+Z
5. false
7. c
9. 72
11. true
13. d
15. landscape
17. one-half
19. true
21. false
23. a
25. Object
27. true
29. c
31. Print Preview
33. false
35. true
37. d

## Chapter 8

1. left
3. false
5. a
7. Shift
9. foreground
11. false

13. false
15. a
17. c
19. red
21. true
23. d
25. Shift
27. Edit
29. true
31. b
33. Print Preview
35. false
37. c

## Chapter 9

1. View
3. Sta
5. false
7. b
9. text editor
11. header
13. true
15. b
17. System Tools
19. true
21. d
23. ScanDisk
25. compresses
27. true
29. c
31. Character Map
33. false
35. c

# Index

## A



## B

## E



## F

## G



## H

## N



## O

## P